Patterns of European Urbanisation since 1500

Edited by H. SCHMAL

CROOM HELM LONDON

©1981 H. Schmal
Croom Helm Ltd, 2-10 St John's Road, London SW11
ISBN 0-7099-0365-0

Printed and bound in Great Britain by
Redwood Burn Limited
Trowbridge and Esher

Library of Davidson College

PATTERNS OF EUROPEAN URBANISATION SINCE 1500

Contents

Preface

The contributors

Foreword: Patterns of urban growth since 1500, mainly in
Western Europe *H.A. Diederiks*   1

1. Urbanization. What's in a name? *P. Kooij*   31
2. Urbanisation and economic development in the
   western world: some provisional conclusions of an
   empirical study *P. Bairoch*   61
3. Patterns of urbanization in pre-industrial Europe,
   1500-1800 *J. de Vries*   77
4. The impact of functional differentiation within systems
   of industrialised cities *B.T. Robson*   111
5. Some examples of analyzing the process of urbanization:
   Northern Italy (eighteenth to twentieth century)
   A. Caracciolo   131
6. The influence of industrialization on urban growth in
   Prussia (1815-1914) *H. Matzerath*   143
7. Urbanisation in Sweden, 1840-1920 *B. Öhngren*   181
8. The rise of the 'Randstad', 1815-1930
   R. van Engelsdorp Gastelaars and M. Wagenaar   229
9. The population growth of the urban municipalities in
   the Netherlands between 1849 and 1970, with particular
   reference to the period 1899-1930 *M.C. Deurloo and
   G.A. Hoekveld*   247
10. Epilogue: one subject, many views *H. Schmal*   285

Preface

This volume contains the proceedings of the International Conference on Urbanisation* and Functional Differentiation, which took place from Thursday, October 25 to Saturday, October 27, 1979, at the University of Amsterdam and the Free University in Amsterdam.

The conference was organised by the Dutch Urban History Group, an inter-university and inter-disciplinary study group involved with the history of cities and with urbanisation in the widest sense of the word. The study group was founded in the spring of 1974 on the initiative of the late Prof. de Jonge and Prof. Wieringa (who has been chairman ever since 1975). On an international level, there has been contact with the Urban History Group in England, the Institut für vergleichende Städtegeschichte in Münster, the Freie Universität in Berlin and the Maison des Sciences de l'Homme in Paris.

The initial initiative for a conference of this name was taken by H.A. Diederiks and M. Wagenaar. The central questions were focused on the comparative aspects of the process of urbanisation in the past few centuries in various countries, the ways in which the phenomenon of urbanisation is studied in various countries, what the most important factors are in determining the rate and direction of the urbanisation pattern etc.

These questions were dealt with at the conference.

In this book, in the papers (chapters 1-9) as well as the introduction and epilogue, urbanisation is approached from the various angles of the different disciplines and countries.

A number of organisations and individuals helped to make this international conference possible, and I am extremely grateful to them for their co-operation. In the first place, I would

---

*Some of the authors used American spelling and others used British spelling, so that the reader is immediately struck by the different spelling of the key word urbani(s)(z)ation. In this international anthology, no attempt was made to introduce conformity in spelling; the papers were left as they were.

like to thank the Ministry of Education and Science, whose contribution was so essential to the international aspect of the conference. I would like to express my gratitude to the University of Amsterdam and the Free University in Amsterdam for the facilities which they made available to the conference.

A large number of staff members of the Institute of Geography and Planning at the Free University in Amsterdam worked to make publication of this book possible. I would like to thank Mr. Ter Haar, whose steady hand is evident in so many of the figures. In organising the conference and correcting the papers I received a great deal of help from various student-assistants. In particular, Guda Wildeboer and Ronald Kleine Rammelkamp did a large amount of work. Hanneke Hummeling was extremely helpful in typing the papers. I am very grateful to her, as I am to Miss Hilgeman and Miss Smelt for their work on the tapes and the texts themselves.

H. Schmal

The Contributors

P. Bairoch	: Professor of Economic and Social Science, University of Geneva, Switzerland
A. Caracciolo	: Full Professor of Modern History, University of Perugia, Italy
M.C. Deurloo	: Lexturer in Geography, Free University, Amsterdam, Netherlands
H.A. Diederiks	: Lecturer in Social History, State University, Leiden, Holland
R. van Engelsdorp Gastelaars	: Lecturer in Geography, University of Amsterdam, Netherlands
G.A. Hoekveld	: Professor of Geography, Free University, Amsterdam, Netherlands
P. Kooy	: Lecturer in Economic and Social History, State University, Groningen, Netherlands
H. Matzerath	: Assistant Professor of Economic and Social History, Freie Universität Berlin, Germany
B. Öhngren	: Assistant Professor of History, University of Uppsala, Sweden
B.T. Robson	: Professor of Geography, University of Manchester, England
H. Schmal	: Lecturer in Geography, Free University, Amsterdam, Netherlands
J. de Vries	: Professor of History, University of California, Berkeley, United States
M.F. Wagenaar	: Lecturer in Geography, University of Amsterdam, Netherlands

Foreword: Patterns of urban growth since 1500, mainly in Western Europe
H.A. Diederiks

1. Introduction	3
2. The concept of urbanization	4
3. Stages in the process of urbanization	8
4. Urban functions and urban growth	10
5. Urban systems	15
6. Urban systems in the history of Europe	17
7. Concluding remarks	24
References	26

Foreword: Patterns of urban growth since 1500, mainly in Western Europe
H.A. Diederiks

1. Introduction

During the seventh international economic history congress in 1978 in Edinburgh (U.K.) two sessions were devoted to the theme 'Urbanization and Social Change'. David Herlihy had the task to present a survey on recent work on this subject. He expresses his embarassment in his report (Herlihy 1978 : 55). As one can imagine it is not easy to find criteria to include or exclude studies, articles, and so on, concerning such a large subject. The discussions during the sessions made clear that often a confusion of tongues impeded any accumulation of knowledge in this field of 'urban history'. Subsequent discussions within the Dutch Urban History Group led to the conclusion that the theme of urbanization deserved another treatment. One of the starting points was that the planned conference and the contributions should have an international and comparative character.

Upon further consideration the conference theme was formulated as: functional and territorial specialization and the process of urbanization, Europe 1500 till present. In the letter of invitation the organizers gave a more precise description of their ideas. Urbanization, they wrote, is primarily a phenomenon of spatial concentration: concentration of people and their artefacts in comparatively large settlements. Analysis and comparison of these phenomenons in different countries will create a need, first of all, to standardize the units which are to be compared. The next question is: what societal, historical processes are to be held responsible for urbanization in the period since 1500. Of course, considerable differences in both speed and scale of urbanization in the various countries may create problems for the comparison. Nevertheless, most of the European nations experienced the fundamental and transforming power of industrialization, of modernising trade and agriculture, and saw the rise of services, like banking and insurance. How did this work out on the existing urban network? What sorts of urban specialization, flows of migration and resultant urban growth did it cause? The role and structure of central cities (capitals), regional political administrative centres, of seaports, of monofunctional mining, textile or metallurgical towns etc. might be dealt with.

The papers submitted cover urban development in Europe from 1500 till 1800 (Jan de Vries), general aspects of the process of urbanization in the Western world from 1700 till the present (Paul Bairoch) and for the nineteenth century: Italy (Alberto Caracciolo), Sweden (Bo Öhngren), Prussia (Horst Matzerath), United Kingdom (Brian Robson) and the Netherlands (Gerard Hoekveld/Rinus Deurloo, Rob van Engelsdorp Gastelaars/Michiel Wagenaar, and Pim Kooij). The evaluation of these contributions and also of the discussions during the conference is handled from the point of view of a geographer by Henk Schmal, and forms the epilogue. In this introduction I will try as an 'urban historian' to sketch some problems and to offer some solutions on the basis of historical evidence available in books, articles or conference papers.

2. The concept of urbanization

2.1. Although one might expect an historian to start with empirical findings, with the 'facts', I would like to put forward some thoughts about concepts first. The concept of urbanization was more or less defined in the letter of invitation for the conference. In that definition the spatial aspect was emphasized, the spatial arrangement of people and artefacts in relatively large settlements. If Manuel Castells proposes to replace the current definitions by 'the social production of spatial forms', he is weakening the concept by leaving out the positive or negative value (Castells 1970 : 1162). The additional condition: "in relatively large settlements", is in this context rather determining. For, it is precisely the intensive use of land by concentrations of people that constitutes one of the key variables of the formation of cities and the urbanization process. We can deal with 'urbanization' on an aggregated level, e.g. the level of a nation state, without going into the aspects of the distribution of cities over a certain territory. One of the important questions in the present volume concerns the factors determining of influencing this distribution. But, first the problem rises of a description of the distribution and that leads to the concept of 'urban systems'. Changes in those systems bring us on the topic of factors of urban growth. How far can this be generalized, and how far are national, regional or historical peculiarities present?

2.2. Urbanization

Three concepts of urbanization have currency in the social

sciences: the behavioral, the structural and the demographic. The first one refers to the way of life. The second one is economic and relates urbanization to the movement of people out of agricultural communities into other and generally larger non-agricultural communities. The third meaning refers to demographic developments. There is a preference for 'ecological' above 'demographic', for 'demographic' carries different inferences. In the last meaning 'urbanization' is seen as the "organizational component of a population's achieved capacity for adaptation. It is a way of ordering a population to attain a certain level of subsistence and security in a given environment" (Carter 1976 : 32). Lampard argues that the fundamental distribution of populations in their environments is ecological and not economic. The patterning of cities and their systems is intimately bound up with technologies of transport and communications. Change may originate with any of the four ecological variables (population, technology, organization and environment), but their effects will always be registered in organization (Lampard 1965 : 549). Leonard Reissman applies his ideas to the industrial city only, thereby excluding all earlier cities - the medieval city, the city of antiquity, the sumerian city - because the industrial city was a radical break from earlier urban history. Reissman puts four variables forward as parts of his theory of urbanization: urban growth, industrialization, the restructuring of power relations and the rise of nationalism (Carter 1976 : 30). Charles Tilly sees urbanization as a collective term for a set of changes which generally occur with the appearance and expansion of larger scale coordinated activities in a society. These activities may consist of the operation of a centralized state, or the control of water for irrigation, or the conduct of a religion with a professional priesthood or the production of goods in a factory system. Tilly thinks that the contrasts between preindustrial and industrial urbanization are not so great and that both have a number of important elements in common. Urbanization brought with it a differentiation of social positions, standardization of forms of organization, change in the quality of social relationships tending to become more instrumental, and concentration of population at points of coordination (Tilly 1976 : 16).

Reissman, Tilly and others try to explain 'the whole society' and processes embracing the entire humanity. As such this approach looses comprehensiveness and means of operationalization. If Reissman, e.g. tries to measure the amount of nationalism on the basis of the literacy among the population over the age of fifteen, one may wrinkle the eyebrows.

2.3. Urbanization in history handbooks

We may wonder how writers of textbooks of economic and social history deal with problems related to the development of the city in history and its role in the general societal process. What elements are brought forward? Elias Tuma deals with this subject as follows:

> As centers of exchange and trading, towns must be accessible. Therefore, they are usually built in economically strategic areas. They may be on rivers and seacoasts where water transportation is available, or in locations to which roads can be built, or close to sources of raw material. However, a town's location must be strategic for its ideal administrative purposes. On the other hand, the town should be easy to defend militarily. The problem becomes more complex when a town is expected to serve all three functions. In such cases there may be a division of labor between towns. The center of power and political administration may not be the economic center, in which case it remains relatively small. In contrast, the economic center tends to grow, especially if it is serving other functions. The structural aspects described above should be considered relative to the conditions prevailing at the time. Although the functions may remain the same, the means by which they are fulfilled may vary. For example, a change in technology could easily change a town's defense requirements or render its means of transportation obsolete. It might also reduce, the dependence on natural conditions. Under these circumstances, the growth of particular towns may be checked or advanced, depending on their new comparative advantage (Tuma 197 : 73, 74).

Tuma mentions a number of valuable factors to be discussed later. The location, the role as administrative or economic centre, the technological aspect play a role in his approach to the city in history. His approach is not especially tied to a certain period and although he speaks about functional differentiation, he does not use the term urbanization.

Another vision is reflected in Peter Stearns' much used textbook on European social history since 1750. Stearns presumably shares the point of view of Reissman. Both link urbanization up to industrialization although Stearns also recognizes other elements, like political and commercial factors, as important. His firm statement that urbanization was the natural result of population growth and industrialization, has been weakened by his additional remarks. He mentions:

> The peak rate of urban expansion corresponds to the rise of the factories, usually two or three decades after the industrial revolution began - 1820-1840 in England, 1850-1870 in France, 1870-1890 in Austria and so on. Other types of cities grew in the nineteenth century, without necessarily developing an elaborate factory

> system. Trade, banking and government encouraged the
> growth of traditional political centres such as London,
> Paris and Amsterdam, and newer ones such as Berlin,
> more than industry did. So urbanization and factory in-
> dustry should not be too closely linked. City growth
> slowed down in most countries after the first decades
> of industrialization, though there was still substantial
> increase   (Stearns 1975 : 109).

His argument seems to be neither fish nor flesh.

2.4. Urbanization and modernization

The general concepts of urbanization and industrialization are often matched in vagueness with that of 'modernization'. The three have been mentioned in one breath as complementary and sometimes overlapping concepts. There are voices contesting this overleap. Wrigley wrote: "in contrast to the pattern of city growth of London, the large urban sprawls which unrolled across the industrial north and midlands from the end of the eighteenth century might almost be described as industrial but not modern" (Wrigley 1972 : 258). Tilly also uses the two concepts of urbanization and modernization more or less as synonymous. On the question "what do we mean by backward?" he answers that an examination of urbanization in western France provides some of the elements (Tilly 1976 : 16). Urbanization as a behavioural concept is also related to the concept of modernization. In some of the theories of modernization developed in the 1950s and 1960s assumptions about the role of the city are implicitly or explicitly present. With the continuing rapid growth of cities in Asia, Africa and Latin America, social scientists have expected a clear shift of political power from rural to urban-based groups. The usual assumption is that this shift would stem from the process of urban economic growth which would lead to political centralization and political integration, both centred in the city (Migdal 1977 : 328-350). Kiernan has pointed to the consequences of the separation of industrial power and the industrial proletariat from the centre of state power. In England the capital lacked modern industry and a strong working-class movement, whilst movements in the industrial north because of their distance from the capital lacked a 'hegemonic impulse'. In England the old towns appear at the head of the hierarchy as spectators in the process of industrialization (Kiernan 1972 : 73-90). The meaning of the concept 'modernization' is very loose, as loose as that of 'capitalism'. Fernand Braudel argues that capitalism and the towns were basically the same thing in the west (Braudel 1973 : 400). When we speak of capitalism the idea of economic growth is quite near. One might situate into the discussion the role of cities in respect of economic growth. Daunton and Wrigley came to different conclusions concerning this role. Within the economic process the towns would specialize and take a specific function. Daunton concluded that "certainly, the towns of the eighteenth century merit study - but perhaps not as useful analytical tools in explaining economic growth" (Daunton 1978 : 277). Wrigley, however, thinks that "urban history, taken in the wider sense to connote the study of the function of the town within the economy as a whole, is therefore a strategic point to entry into the larger question of what stimulated or inhibited growth and improvement in the past" (Wrigley 1978 : 309). Daunton keeps it for probably that rural industry increased relative to urban industry and that the process of industrialization proceeded ahead of urbanization in eighteenth century England. "There are good reasons to deny the towns any role - or rather any positive role - in the build-up to the industrial revolution". But the proponents of towns as key agents for modernization or the development of capitalism can put up a reasonable case as the locus of a new attitude to life (Daunton 1978 : 250). And here we are back on the behavioral concept of urbanization. This approach is finally based on a positive answer on the question in how far is behavior determined by the size of the settlement in which the individual lives.

It is not yet the moment to draw general conclusions about the usefulness of special meanings of the concept of urbanization. First chronology in urban history, factors in urban growth, urban systems and urban developments in some regions and countries must be dealt with.

3. Stages in the process of urbanization

On the basis of different criteria different stages have been formulated in respect of the development of cities. The sociologist Geoffrey Hurd distinguishes three stages of urbanization. The first was the longest: from the first emergence of cities until the eighteenth century. The second stage was brief but of great importance; it was the very rapid growth of cities that accompanied early industrialization. Next to an enormous increase in population, an ever increasing proportion of the people were living in towns. The third stage has been called: metropolization. The latter process is the urban concentration that accompanies the centralization of industry and the economy. The larger cities take on an increasing importance, both in terms of their population and in terms of the functions they serve in the society as a whole. All the countries that are currently highly industrialized can be said to have passed through these three stages of urbanization (Hurd 1978 : 45-46).

Lampard distinguishes four stages of urbanization: primordial, definitive, classic and industrial urbanization. The term 'classic' means pre- or non-industrial. In the definitive phase a uniform urbanization did not take place.

Where urban centres have emerged, they have not conformed to any one spatial or structural pattern. The great variety of urbanizing experiences underlines the fact that population concentration is everywhere an adaptive process. They form an additional and alternative form of collective adaptation, an innovation in ways of living. In the definitive phase urbanization involves increasingly vertical stratification, closely tied to controls over land use and raw material supplies. Definitive urbanization was the organization and appropriation of an agricultural surplus. Before the industrial revolution of the eighteenth century the most ubiquitous form of specialization for a city was at all times in its historically definitive role as a general central place. 'Classic' components exhibit comparatively stable relationships of interdependence in ascending order of nodality: hamlets, villages, towns, metropolis or capital. The notably 'static' order of classic urban systems was rooted in the constraints of a largely undifferentiated agrarian base. Industrial urbanization has revealed itself to be a cumulative process with rising incidence and more differentiated structures during its rapid unfolding since the introduction of fuel burning machines (Lampard 1965 : 539-545).

Rozman identified seven distinct stages of urban networks according to the number and pattern of levels of central places present. The first four are distinguished from the subsequent stages of premodern urban history. The principal force behind the maturation of the urban network in these early stages was administrative centralization. Commerce remained a secondary factor. While in the first stages the hierarchy was essentially administratively based, the three last stages had a commercial hierarchy even though many of the major commercial nexuses were found in cities which also had administrative functions. Changing urban networks should be reflected in: demographic rates, patterns of settlement, organizational contents, redistribution processes and aspects of personal relationships (Rozman 1978 : 65-91).

Transport and transport technology are important factors in the phasing of the urban process. Sam Bass Warner Jr.'s periodization concerning some stages in American urban history is based on these criteria. The periods 1820-1870, 1870-1920 and from 1920 till present correspond to the impact of transportation and technological innovation upon the system of American cities. The reason is that from a particular technological climate and a particular configuration of transportation the form of cities, the business institutions, etc. etc. inevitably takes shape. The first period was characterized by handtools, water- and horsepower, canals, steamboats and railways. The second one by mechanized production techniques, electricity, a national system of railways, cheap mass transit and the introduction of the motor-truck and auto. While the modern period is distinguished by sophisticated advances in all forms of technology, especially communications and the introduction of atomic energy, a national system of highways, the emergence of the trucking industry and intensive use of the auto, airplanes and pipelines (Hershberg 1978 : 11; Warner 1972 : 60-62). In general the distinction of the urban development into a certain number of stages only can be considered as an instrument, and as such the stages don't have an explanatory value. The operational value will increase as the general characteristics of each stage correspond to the 'real' facts.

4. Urban functions and urban growth

The functions of cities and urban growth are two interdependent variables. The process of growth is due to the development of certain functions or of one function.

Herlihy mentioned in his report as causes for the growth of cities and as urban functions <u>ceremonial functions</u>. These called cities into life in the five regions of the world where they first spontaneously appear. In the ancient city the peasant was an integral element, but not in the medieval; the guild was an integral element in the medieval city, but not in the ancient; Finley put the Athenian agora next to the Grande Place in Brussels to show the difference between the ancient city and medieval cities and later ones (Finley 1977 : 322). One may compare the features of the ancient city with the large cities in the third world.

Next to the 'ceremonial' factor <u>state centralization</u> and <u>market expansion</u> are city building forces which leave their marks not only on the size but also on the character of a society's urban centres (Tilly 1976 : 18). Political and economic causes of urban growth have received ample attention from geographers, economists and historians. How the balance was kept between the two is a matter judged in various ways. Jane Jacobs seems clearly to choose for the economic factors.

> The great capitals of modern Europe did not become great cities because they were the capitals. Cause and effects ran the other way. Paris was at first no more the seat of the French kings than were the sites of half a dozen other royal residences. Paris bacame the genuine capital only after it had already become the largest and economically the most diversified commercial and industrial city of the kingdom. The same was the case with Berlin and London (Jacobs 1972 : 138, 139).

Discussing the problem of how cities start growing, Jane Jacobs mentions three factors necessary for growth: local goods and services, that remain local, export, starting with the initial exports, local goods and services that become exports (Jacobs 1972 : 133). The very specialized 'company towns' didn't witness growth because they lacked one of these factors. They seem to have a lot of reasons for growth: they are specialized and have a high productivity. But they created no additional economic reasons for their existence, as do even little cities that grow only briefly (Jacobs 1972 : 125).

We have already mentioned discussions about the role of <u>industrialization</u> for the urban growth. In England e.g. industrialization occurred before urbanization started in the same regions. The old cities were spectators of the coming of the industrial ages. More or less the same picture emerges in respect of a country at some distance of the Atlantic world: Russia. The most spectacular feature of economic development in the post-reform period there was the rapid growth of industry, particularly the emergence of large scale factory industry. Urban and industrial development, however, were not spatially coincident. In 1902 still 61 per cent of the total employment in factory industry were located outside the cities. The Russian cities did not become the organizational centres of industry (Fedor 1975 : 175).

The lack of urban growth under the impact of industrialization can be considered in view of the city as a <u>labor market</u>. Some factors restrict free migration, other factors determine the character of the migration which can not be seen as a uniform phenomenon. The Russian example may serve as a picture of the restraints of the former. The formation of a permanent and reliable labor force in the Russian cities was greatly impeded by a web of legal, social, economic and personal links which more or less effectively tied the urban worker of peasant origins to the countryside.

On the other hand, the gentry generally encouraged peasant involvement in trade and industry and so stimulated industry in the countryside. Although the cities grew, the level of urbanization remained low. The demographic revolution in Russia brought not a significant redistribution of the population. There was a slight in-migration into the cities, but the numbers of these migrants were more the expression of the freedom to move after the emancipation of the serfs in 1861 and the Stolypin reforms of 1905-1906 than the result of a pull of economicly expanding cities (Fedor 1975 : 177, 178). The growth of the industrial labor force does not always lead to an increase of the urbanization. In this respect the circular migration has been mentioned. This sort of migration is caused by a pull of an industrializing town, but the settlement of the migrant is only temporary. The industrial worker returns to his village during the summer or winter, when his labor is needed on the farm. Four categories can be distinguished: peasant visitors, migrant laborers, temporarely urbanized and permanently urbanized and this classification depends on the time spent in the city and the permanence of ties to the village of origins (Van de Muijzenberg 1973 : 449). These observations have been made in respect of countries of the third world and to nineteenth century France as well (Weber 1977 : 278-292).

One may also wonder whether, given the fact that the relationship urbanization-industrialization is not a simple one, the city has contributed something to industry. The road toward a modern city only was made possible by the industry, creating work and providing financial support by tax paying. But what did the city do for the industry? Did it create an infrastructure favorable to the industry? The social question arisen in the industrial cities made these problems into urban problems. At the end of the nineteenth century the city governments recognized their task in this respect and education, housing and health care were drawn into the worksphere of the cities. This created an infrastructure for the industrial laborers (Marschalck 1978 : 61).

Another factor already introduced in general terms concerns transportation and more specific the railways. The latter had various effects on the urban process. They strengthened in some regions the position of the central city. Railways effectively created e.g. in Lancashire, even within two decades a system of cities which was dominated operationally by Manchester. The case of Manchester could be asserted to have wide and general application to the cities of Birmingham, Liverpool, Glasgow and London (Kellett 1979 : 172). In other regions - e.g. in Great Britain - a number of important urban communities or townships were virtually created by the railways. Some of these were of course created by the railways primarily for their own use. New Swindon and Crewe became great centres of rolling stock construction. The rise of Middlesborough and Barrow as industrial towns can be attributed almost solely to the influence of the railways. The Taff Vale Railway between Cardiff and Merthyr Tyfdil, had been conceived by Brunel primarily as an outlet for iron, but two branch lines were quickly added to the scheme before it opened in 1841 so as to make pit development possible and it was the coal traffic which was soon providing the bulk of this highly profitable line's revenue and turning Cardiff into the chief coal-port of the region (Dyos & Aldcroft 1974 : 193, 194). In Russia the construction of railroads, promoted the concentration of economic activities. Under the impact of the regional specialization and the expansion of the railroad network the volume of domestic trade grew rapidly (Fedor 1975 : 174).

The slackening of the process of urbanization can be mentioned as a third sort of result. For instance, in Belgium there was cheap transport by railway after 1869. In the early twentieth century, the operation of this system was the subject of prolonged inquiry. The conclusion reached in the inquiry of 1910 was that the existence of 'abonnements' had served to delay the loss of population from the countryside, while facilitating the transition from agricultural to industrial employment, and correspondingly to retard the growth of the major urban centres. It is noteworthy that between 1890 and

1910 the class of commune which claimed the largest share of
the national increase was that of 5,000 to 25,000 inhabitants
(Vollans 1970 : 179, 180).

The process of deconcentration has been connected to other
developments of transportation. The introduction of the streetcar should have stimulated suburbanization.
Jackson has shown that in the U.S.A. the streetcar only involved a quantitative change and not a qualitative one. The
process of deconcentration was already under way. Jackson
uses five definitions of urban deconcentration and these five
concepts provide five indications. They are: higher peripheral
rates of growth, leveling of densities, absolute loss of population at the centre, movement of the upper and middle classes
to the periphery and the lengthening of the average journey to
work. They were all present in the largest American cities before the introduction of the electric streetcar in the 1890's
(Jackson 1975 : 140).

The development of the means of transport influenced the
patterns of settlement. 'New areas' differed from old industrial ones. Whereas railway transport had tended to encourage
the development of factories grouped around nuclear points
with radial distribution of goods from the centre, motortransport, with its greater flexibility and ease of movement,
made possible the building of factories along arterial roads
with no specific focal point (Dyos & Aldcroft 1974 : 373).

Four more factors will be briefly discussed. The cities seen as
the expression of capital formation, as investment, the role of
the entrepreneurs, the influence of demand and planning.

We can see cities as investment: streets, houses, public
buildings are capital formation. The take-off into selfsustained economic (industrial) growth is in principle connected to
capital formation. The process of urbanization can also be
analysed from this point of view. The construction of cities
is an investment. Robson mentions in his contribution to this
volume the surplus value circulating, but once invested in
buildings or harbor equipment or streets and so on, the circulation is almost finished. The evidence on the levels of
capital formation for the eighteenth century is far from conclusive. Indeed, for the first four or five decades it is difficult to find anything to justify the view that the level had
risen apart from a steady increase in the rate of urbanization
and an expansion in overseas trade in the 1740's. In the middle
of the century, however, there is unmistakeable evidence of a
rising rate of capital accumulation in roads, canals, buildings
and agricultural enclosures. The pace of urbanization in
Britain accelerated (Dean and Cole 1969 : 261). Urbanization
and capital formation haven't been the subject of many historical studies. The only research touching the topic is Brinley
Thomas' book about Migration and Urban Development. For the
later part of the nineteenth century Thomas makes the following

observation: "Residential building was the most important element in the upswing in domestic capital formation in the 1890's. The composition and geographical distrubution of the investment were determined partly by changes in the pattern of consumer's expenditure, which favoured the growth of seaside towns, and by the location of government expenditure on the armed forces" (Thomas 1972 : 183).

Two other factors can be derived from this statement: the function of consumers, the <u>demand factor</u>, and that of <u>entrepreneurs</u> or investors. Both can be considered as complementary. The spread of gasworks, electricity and other utilities may originate from initiatives of entrepreneurs acting on the basis of a demand or expected demand. The details of the spatial patterns can only be interpreted in terms of the particular factor endowments and historical events which underlaid the growth of certain towns and the decay of others. "The diffusion of entrepreneurial innovations through a set of nineteenth-century cities may well be characterized by a simultaneous process of hierarchical space-jumping from larger to smaller cities and of localized spread outwards from the regional centres" (Robson 1973 : 186). Robson has analysed the process of innovations in Britain and stressed the role of entrepreneurs. Alan Pred's study can be seen as complementary. He investigated the circulation of information to compare it to the existing urban system and the possibility to communicate as an urban growth factor (Pred 1975 : 51-74). Innovations are more initiated in large cities than in smaller ones. Robert Higgs has shown that in large cities during the period 1870-1920 in the U.S.A. proportionally more inventors registered patents than in small towns. The inventiveness was linked to urbanization (Higgs 1975 : 247-259). Information and inventiveness can be considered as two aspects of the same thing: inventive activity is nothing more than the process of creating new information (Higgs 1975 : 248).

The last factor of urban growth concerns planning. Urban systems and urban functions are not just the results of forces working on a free market. Not only is the market not free, the forces can also be directly by other than economic reasons. When regional planning got an impact, the outcome in terms of city hierarchies and urban systems came under the influence of politicians, ecologists, next to entrepreneurs. Although planning started as urban planning, it developed after the Second World War into regional planning. Even planning on a national scale or European level may have left some traces. In respect to the Netherlands there are the two reports on Physical Planning in the Netherlands (Hall 1975 : 234). On the development of residential and industrial centres this planning has had considerable impact. Hall pointed to great changes during the 1960's in respect to the content of the plans themselves. A new emphasis was placed on broad-based plans stressing basic policies rather than on detailed landuse allocations, the importance of transportation planning as perhaps the central element of physical planning at this scale, the link between city-region planning and economic planning. New features were the stress on environmental quality, the growing concern with social planning and a new emphasis on economic rationale in planning (Hall 1975 : 185, 186). Together with the British new towns, the Stockholm suburbs represent one of the most admired planning achievements of the mid-twentieth century (Hall 1975 : 232).

The factors mentioned above might be complemented by less structural ones giving the historical process a glimpse of its traditional uniqueness. The elite building houses, parks, plants and so on during a period without much intervention of public authorities and giving shape individually to the urban environment might not been overlooked.

We have made a broad 'tour d'horizon' of factors influencing urban functions and urban growth. The ceremonial and consumption functions have been touched as well as the role of state centralization and the expansion of domestic and foreign trade.

We discussed the role of industrialization in general and the place of specialized 'company towns'. There is not a one way relationship between urbanization and industrialization. The other functions of a city concern among others the labormarket. This aspect involves in-migration and the restraint on it. The development of means of transport also influenced strongly the function and growth of cities. During the nineteenth century the railroad and streetcar and during the twentieth century the motorway gave shape to cities and their relationships. Investment and capital formation might seem a neglected subject as far as the process of functional differentiation of cities is concerned.

Consumer demand, supply and ways of entrepreneurial innovation are also topics that must be dealt with. As a final point the influence of planning was introduced.

5. Urban systems

One of the classic topics in urban geography is the urban system or the city hierarchy. In this introduction a few remarks will be enough. In the contributions in this volume of Robson, Matzerath, Öhngren, Jan de Vries and Caracciolo elements of urban systems are more or less elaboratedly treated and in the epilogue they will be evaluated. Urban systems are mostly conceived as to consist of hierarchies of villages, towns and cities including all sorts of relationships between cities and their hinterlands, between cities and cities and so on. In historiography the relation of towns to their direct hinterland has been dealt with extensively, especially for the period since the rebirth of the city in the middle ages (Hoekveld 1975 : 1-47; De Boer 1975 : 48-72).

Towns sought to obtain not only legal rights to tax market operations but also the right to regulate the trading operation (who should trade, when it should take place, what should be traded). Furthermore, they sought to restrict the possibilities of the countryside engaging in trade other than via their town. The result was a sort of urban colonialism (Wallerstein 1974 : 120; Dobb 1946 : 95). The concept of urban colonialism brings us to another aspect of city systems: the relationships between colonial settlements or colonial towns and the homeland.

> Expanding mercantile empires, each centered in a dynamic metropolis - Madrid, Lisbon, Amsterdam, Paris, London - were establishing rival colonial outposts in North and South Asia as well, in the sixteenth and seventeenth centuries. Each of these outposts represented an advanced stage in the urbanization of its mother country, and each had provincial ties with its metropolitan progenitor. The new urban centres, like the old cities in Europe, were all preindustrial, but the contrasts with the provincial towns at home were almost as striking as those among the mercantile outposts themselves. These latter differences sprang in part from varied geographic settings, but chiefly from divergent cultural traditions and the urban functions they fostered (McKelvey 1973 : 3).

To measure functions and central place 'tasks' a number of indicators or variables can be used. To analyse the urban system in Westfalen during the eighteenth century Blotevogel (1975 : 148) uses the following factors:
a. administrative, juridical and religious central functions;
b. economic functions: the number of people employed in some occupations, market function, artisans, commercial people;
c. cultural functions: universities and institutions for the training of priests, gymnasia, printing companies and booksellers, newspapers, theater, music, cultural societies like the freemasons;
d. health services: medical doctors, chemists, hospitals;
e. traffic function: since the beginning of the nineteenth century the construction of high roads was as important as fifty years later the construction of the railroad;
f. postal traffic, post offices;
g. migration streams.

This checklist can be brought into a model, that means that the elements are situated in a weighed relation to each other; e.g. the economic function can be deduced from the administrative function, health services from the traffic function, and so on. It depends on the questions to be answered, what kind of interrelationships are put into the model.

In the next part of this introduction some specific historical situations will be briefly discussed and some ideas concerning specific models may emerge.

6. Urban systems in the history of Europe

6.1. The European economy in the seventeenth century can be understood as a collection of regions, with cities as their focal points. In the course of the seventeenth century the demographic fortunes of cities varied enormously with their social and economic functions. And while overall urbanization made no gains, the size distribution of European cities was radically transformed. Jan de Vries (1976 : 148-154) distinguishes: princely residences and centres of absolutist administration, the Atlantic ports, naval stations like Portsmouth and Plymouth in England and Brest and Toulon in France, towns in America. The trading interests of Europeans did export the European city itself. While the four categories of cities mentioned before experienced growth, the cathedral towns, centres of provincial administration, inland commercial centres and industrial cities all experience checks to their development. Two significant changes occurred: first, by the late seventeenth century urban population was shifting to selected centres in north western Europe and along the Atlantic coast; second, the larger cities were gaining at the expense of the smaller. Trade, finance and government were increasingly attracted to a relative handful of the hundreds of cities with which medieval society endowed Europe. There arose a considerable disparity among regions in their ability to respond to trade opportunities. By the eighteenth century a clear distinction could be made between the Dutch Republic and the Atlantic Ports of France and Germany on the one hand and the interior regions of Europe on the other. In the first regions mundane investments in roads, canals and coastal vessels achieved significant increase in the speed of passenger travel and reductions in the cost of freight carriage, although no spectacular transport innovations appeared. Among these favored regions, England stood out because of its ability to integrate its industrial sector most fully into the Atlantic trading system (De Vries 1976 : 175).

J.E. Vance introduced the so called 'maritime' model: the maritime navigation and the rise of commercial capitalism were the main factors of differentiation. Jean-Claude Boyer introduced another model that he coined the 'continental' one. He derives the main features from the ideas of Etienne Juillard. Juillard emphasizes the relationship of consumption and the availability of goods as important; in respect to the last factor the accessibility of the cities for goods is determining. In preindustrial periods the region is about two hours traveling around an urban centre; in the middle ages between

8 and 11 km. and till 1830 about 8 till 24 km. Juillard has put
question marks in respect of these factors: first, is it legitimate to base an urban system on the exchange of consumer goods?
Secondly, the increase in quality of means of transport only
had an impact on a small group of urban people; most urban
(and rural) inhabitants did travel. Thirdly, he objected because this model did not suit very large cities and did not
offer an explanation for these concentrations. In respect of
the maritime and continental models of city systems, Boyer
suggests that both models may occur in successive stages of
development (Boyer 1977). The 'maritime' model suits the 'selected' centres in north western Europe and along the Atlantic
coasts and the 'continental' one the 'interior' regions of
Europe mentioned by Jan de Vries.

Till the industrial revolution the share of people living
in cities could not surpass 20-25 per cent because of the agrarian surplus necessary to sustain them. Although there are exceptions like the Dutch Republic, with around 45 per cent of
its population in the western provinces living in the cities,
this can be accepted as a general level. The whole of the
Dutch Republic only constituted 2-3 percent of the European
population during the seventeenth century and if one takes
into account the people outside Europe involved in the exchange of goods with the Dutch, they will be less than one
per cent. Two periods show a very rapid urbanization: between
1830-40 and 1900 and between 1946 and 1974. The first phase
witnessed an annual growth of the urban population of 1.9 per
cent. During the second phase the percentage accounted to 1.6
per cent. Paul Bairoch has calculated the annual growth rate
and expressed it as the percentage of the population in cities
in respect of the total population. The differences in growth
rate between the European countries reflect around 1800 on the
one hand the first impact of the industrialization, and the
influences of the commercial expansion during the preceding
centuries on the other. The highest rates experienced the industrializing countries, England and Belgium, and the old
commercial nations as Denmark, Spain, Portugal and the Netherlands. But, after 1800 England and Belgium and also France and
Switzerland witnessed an increase of the growth rate while the
second group showed a stagnation and even a decline of the
rate. This process lead to a great diversification of the
growth rates in the European countries (Bairoch 1976 : 311).

6.2. Great-Britain

When we consider specific countries specific features may come
to the fore. The two main questions concerning England after
the industrial revolution may be, first, the role of London
and, secondly, the 'new' industrial towns. For the period before the Industrial Revolution Clark and Slack suggested a definition of urbanism under four headings: a specialist economic
function, a peculiar concentration of population, a sophisti-

cated political superstructure and a more than logical role in the economy and society of the day. The English towns could be grouped into three major tiers: an upper tier including London and the major provincial capitals, a middle tier of incorporated towns as well as developing market towns and industrial centres (Clark & Slack 1972). The rankorder concerning 1600 may more or less reflect this division into three categories. The situation in 1750 exemplifies the impact of the commercial development while the industrial city made its presence felt in 1801.

On the basis of the changing urban hierarchy in the years 1600, 1750 and 1801 Daunton argues that the old cities with London in the lead were spectators of the growth of towns containing the modern industry. There was a direct relationship between the new towns and industrialization, and maybe an indirect one between the develpoment of industry and the growth of London (Daunton 1978:247). What about the role of London? In his article 'London as an engine of economic growth' F.J. Fisher says: " we may easely speak of textile centres, of mining centres, of commercial centres. But it is with less confidence that one can speak of a centre to the economy as a whole, and especially when the economy is largely agricultural for agriculture, is essentially a dispersed activity that defies centralization". A growth in population will increase the demand for basic necessities and, by enlarging the markets for them, stimulate both investment and the division of labor. A growth in non-local trade will not only widen markets, and thereby stimulate investment an specialization, but will provide an additional stimulus to effort by widening the range of goods available. Both these factors were at work in Tudor and Stuart England, and it was with respect to them that the role of London changed in such a way as to justify the concept of the capital as the centre of the economy (Fisher 1976: 205-207).

As a good example of the fate of a minor 'metropolis' Bristol may serve. Bristol's importance had been founded on foreign trade. But additional functions also played a role: Bristol was the main market for the agricultural produce of the area. The second category of goods for which Bristol was a market was industrial raw materials. Bristol also had a function in the life of its hinterland as a source of capital. Bristol capital was invested in enterprises in its hinterland, not in already developed, mature textile industries but in the growing mining and industries. It found its major outlet in South Wales. Towards the end of the eighteenth century the position of Bristol began to decline; this continued in the nineteenth century. As a metropolis Bristol derived its importance from a network of predominantly water communications. The construction of canals elsewhere shifted the outlet of goods away from Bristol. Also the basis of Bristol's importance, the foreign trade decreased. The American Revolution and the decline of the textile industry in Bristol's hinterland were the causes. By 1850 Bristol was no longer the 'Welsh metropolis'. In successive directions regional isolation was broken down and the coming of the railway made the influence of London all pervasive. The improvement of communications and the growth of institutions and methods of organization appropriate to expanding industrialism were responsible for the decline in Bristol's position (Minchinton 1976: 297-308). Although the pattern of urbanization in Britain had a great number of constant features during the nineteenth century already present around 1800, the end of the century witnessed a shift of the centre of gravity from the industrial cities in the north to the south (Thomas 1972: 184).

6.3. France

For France three sorts of networks ('armatures') of cities may be distinguished in the beginning of the seventeenth century. The traditional administrative network, the religious network (episcopal cities and the convents of the mendicant order) and the market towns. Since the seventeenth century a number of changes influenced these networks. The creation of the office of the 'intendant' (the provincial governor) gave some cities more dominance than others. Also other royal institutions had an urbanizing impact.
The new religious orders (Jesuits, Capucins, Ursulins) founded their convents in towns, which increased culturally and also economically by this settlement. The establishment of 'colleges' (institutions for education) and 'hopitaux generaux' (combination of work- and poorhouse and prison) stimulated urban functions (Favier: 1977). Although even at the end of the century the population in cities of any size at all was no more than 15 percent of the French total, it was in growing metropolises like Lyon, Marseille, Bordeaux, Nantes and, of course, Paris, that we could see a new society being shaped. Four percent of the French population at the time of the Revolution lived in cities of 50,000 or more, about 7.5 per cent in cities of 20,000 or more. A large share of France's urban population was concentrated in one great metropolis, Paris. This is a condition which in the twentieth century is often associated with instability. Overurbanization commonly implies not only the presence of an unusually dominant city, but also forced 'idle,impoverished and rootless masses' in the cities, and acute discontent. These conditions favor political instability (Tilly 1976: 22-24). Tilly uses the concept of urbanization to approach the counterrevolution in the Vendée during the French Revolution. The general conceptions of urbanization and of its relationship to community organization, helped to identify economically and accurately the significant differences among the areas and groups of southern Anjou which varied in their response to the Revolution. The most urbanized sectors of the west gave the most uniform support to the Revolution (Tilly 1976: 340).

In respect to France after the Revolution Bergeron and Roncayolo propose three modifications of the urban network: the Revolution had brought a new administrative frame and this should have implied a new urban hierarchy; the railway construction has changed the speed goods, information and people traveled, the distances decreased relatively and as a third point the spread of commercial banks in France is mentioned. The studies of Jean Labasse (1955) and of Jean Bouvrier (1961) might reveal this point. These studies concern regional banking systems and there is no systematic study up to now on the national scale. (Bergeron & Roncayolo 1974, 22,23).

6.4. Germany

The comparison of the maps of 1500 and of 1800 in respect of Germany might reveal that the centre of gravity concerning urban concentrations has been moving eastward. While in 1500 Vienna, Berlin and Prague are almost nonexistent, in 1800 they are very important cities. In 1500 five of the six largest cities were commercial settlements and four of them were free Imperial towns (freie Reichsstädte). At the end of the eighteenth century the situation has been changed drastically. Five of the nine cities with more than 40,000 inhabitants were court cities. In general, the growth of the court cities during the period 1500-1800 amounted to the ninefold, while the free imperial cities only witnessed an increase (Francois 1977). On the basis of commercial contacts before the take-off into industrialization a distinction is made into three economic regions with three important central places: Cologne-Elberfeld and Bremen in Germany and Amsterdam in the Dutch Republic whose influence also reached parts of Germany. That was the situation during the second half of the eighteenth century (Blotevogel 1975: 97-104). Cologne was the most important centre and central place in the region of Westfalen. Already during the Middle Ages Cologne was important as Hanseatic trading town with also an extensive ecclesiastical function. Although some functions disappeared other took a more prominent place and prevented a decline and promoted even the importance of the city. Cologne could keep a central position concerning the distribution of goods within the regional trade system among others by defending with success its staple until 1831 (Blotevogel 1975: 197-199).

In respect to the classification of nineteenth century cities some scholars make a classification into five types of cities: the old maritime ports, textile towns expanding rapidly between 1750 and 1850, nine cities in the Ruhr and Saar owing their initial growth to their favorable location in relation to natural resources, eleven inland commercial cities and nine court cities; the naval port Kiel and Ludwigshafen growing around a great chemical enterprise defy convenient categorization. Except for the cities that grew on natural resources, all other towns are 'old cities'. Three quarters of the German cities in 1915 were already leading urban centres a century previously. The most important influence on this pattern of urbanization appears to be the manner in which the railway came to Germany. The railways helped transform the court cities from parasitic into generative types. As far as migration is concerned Germany witnessed an enormous shift. Half the population were classified as internal migrants in the occupational census of 1907. Despite the spectacular east Elbian influx into the Ruhr after 1895 the migration was a local affaire (Lee 1978: 279-293).

Although the role of industry in the process of urbanization and in the shift of functions of cities was always present, industrialization as such was located in its first phase on the countryside. Henning has calculated the role of the rural domistic labour force in Germany for the period 1800-1900. During the 'Gründerzeit', the period of rapid industrialization about 40 percent of the industrial workers are employed outside the urban factories (Henning 1975: 151).

The problem of factors of urban growth in Germany may be exemplified by the development of the towns of Rheindahlen and Rheydt in the western part of Prussia. In the period 1798 till 1910 Rheindahlen witnessed a population growth from 3,645 to 8,484 and Rheydt from 2,625 to 43,999. The first town was the most promising at the end of the eighteenth century. Both were situated in the same economic and cultural region at only five kilometers distance from each other. The only difference was that Rheindahlen was catholic and Rheidt protestant. What factors determined the uneven development? Matzerath concludes that factors of innovative initiatives of the entrepreneurs of Rheydt were very important. These initiatives didn't have a change in the agrarian social structure of Rheindahlen, determined by the catholic petty bourgeois groups with a conservative outlook. There was also a spatial element. Rheydt had a more urban landscape in the beginning of the nineteenth century because it was built within a more limited area (Matzerath 1978: 77-79).

Between 1870 and 1910 in Germany the growth of towns dominated by mining, heavy industry or machinery manufacture was above the average; e.g. Duisburg, Dortmund, Essen, Düsseldorf, Mannheim, Saarbrücken, Nürnberg, Augsburg. In most cases the population increased 3.5 to 5 times its former size, but the mining town of Gelsenkirchen held the record with a ten fold increase over its population in 1870. Most textile towns which had been in the lead in the early phase of the industrialization now lagged, noticably behind in population growth; e.g. Elberfeld, Barmen, Krefeld. In 1871 the German Empire had only 8 cities over 100,000 inhabitants, by 1900 there had been a sharp increase to 33 and by 1910 there were 48 (Reulecke 1971: 27). The move eastward of the concentrations of population during the period 1500-1800 turned during the nineteenth century again into a move westwards.

6.5. U.S.A.

Although this volume is devoted to developments of urban systems in Europe a comparison of a region outside the old world may be useful. The urbanization process in North America was different from the European experience in two respects: the absence of old cities and the relative great speed. The colonial experience also showed varieties within the whole of the American continent.
The differences between the British and Spanish colonial cities in America have been pointed out. In Latin America they were the products of an early stage of mercantilism and they were the precursors of the 'parasitic' cities established by later intruders in South East Asia. The growth of these places tended to check rather than stimulate the economic development of their hinterlands; the Spanish and also the Portuguese colonists stayed in the coastal settlements; in contrast with the urban beginnings in south and central America, the mainland ports to the north were at the start bridgeheads through which adventurous British and other migrants passed enroute to their nearby village or rural settlements (McKelvey 1973: 4-5). Specialized production and the efficiency it achieved were the key features of the new urban system. In Europe this development was usually tied closely to the technological innovations achieved in each city. In America, on the other hand, industrial specialization was more frequently based on the natural resources and expanding needs of the area. Although the origin of British industrial cities was also tied to the natural resources, the differences with the U.S.A. were the larger regional setting in the New World. (McKelvey 1973, 145). By 1900 nine tenths of industrial production occurred in urban factories located within America's twenty-five principal cities or in immediately adjecent industrial satellite cities within their metropolitan districts. Then the sorting out and clustering of specialty manufacturing in specific cities was largely completed and each specialty was increasingly located at its best site and from this single base or cluster of bases sold its products throughout the nation. Clearly industry outstripped commerce as the chief source of urban growth in the major cities between 1870 and 1900 (Klebanow, Jonas, Leonard 1977: 157; Bass Warner 1972: 71).

As an exemple of a town with a diverse pattern of economic activities turning at the end into a very specialized city, Detroit may serve. Young Detroit began its growth in the 1820s and 1830s, its chief export was flour. For the people in the settlement, for the garrison at the fort and for the nearby farmers, the workshops produced some everyday necessities. Along the waterfront were small shipyards where passengerships and ships for the flour trade were built to cross the lakes. Detroit shipyards were among the first in the world to build steamships. By the 1860s marine engines themselves were a major Detroit export. While the engine business was growing, it was supporting a growing collection of its own suppliers refineries and smelters that supplied copper alloys. The refineries became so succesful that between about 1860 and 1880 copper was Detroit's largest export. About 1880 the local ores ran out. The refineries closed and the proprietors built company towns outside Detroit. There was a diversity that took over within the city. This was the diversifying economy from which the automobile industry emerged two decades later. This automobile industry turned Detroit into a company town (Jacobs 1972 : 120).

In respect to the process of urbanization in the U.S.A. Jean Gottmann has introduced the concept of Megalopolis. In this belt of cities located along the east coast there was an emphasis and in its New England and New York parts in particular, on the lighter products, more finished and ready for mass consumption (medicines, footwear, household furniture and electrical machinery). For all four of these products megalopolis had the greatest concentration in the U.S.A. in 1956 (Gottmann 1961 : 466). There was a moving of manufacture southward within Megalopolis itself and also a gradual shifting of Megalopolitan specializations toward the more complicated and 'upper stages' of production or of the manufacturing process as exemplified by rapid growth in the fields of printing and publishing, instruments, electrical machinery and petroleum research. Centrifugal forces fostered the dispersal of manufacturing: the search for more not too expensive space, the preference for cheaper less organized and abundant labor the flight from local and state taxes. But there were enough forces retaining industry within Megalopolis: size of the regional market, favourable transportation facilities, independence of (labor) costs because of automation. The ordinary function of modern manufacturing - the mass production of stadardized goods - still goes on in Megalopolis but it plays a declining role in the region. This region retains a very great concentration of manufactures of the kinds in which it is especially difficult to replace human labor by machinery (Gottmann 1961 : 473, 490-499).

7. Concluding remarks

In this introduction the concept of urbanization, factors of urban growth, various urban systems and historical processes concerning urbanization in a selected number of areas have been discussed. As far as the term 'urbanization' is concerned a preference should be made for a neutral definition: concentration of people in relatively large settlements. The behavioral approach to urbanization darkens a number of social phenomena. Specific relationships between the size of the settlements and the way of life, e.g. is not a given fact, but something to be demonstrated. If we already bring the 'explanandum' and the 'explanans' in our definition, there remains nothing to explain.

A checklist of factors of urban growth has been offered: from the modern process of industrialization, the railways etc. to planning. Only in respect to a specific region or country these factors ca be put into a model, that means that they get a specific value. This value has to have a dynamic character, e.g. the railroad can be responsible for the way urban centres grew in a period under the impact of specific circumstances. Timeless generalizations, like urbanization and industrialization are always interlinked, hence are useless. In this respect the brief discussion on a number of historical stages may have been illuminating. Urban systems are supposed to have existed in the history of Europe and do still exist, but in different forms. While during the Old Regime the nation-state did not play an important role as creator of city-systems, the rapid development during the nineteenth century made the nation-state into one of the agents, not of the growth of cities as such, but of their network. In the samples introduced, like that concerning the U.S.A., the economic processes may have come more to the fore, but the state-building forces in some European countries certainly also gave an impetus to specific urban developments, like in France and Germany. The comparison made to recent urbanization in the Third World may have exemplified the fragility of the assumptions of the linear process of urbanization in combination to industrialization. A last remark may point out things to come in this present volume. The choice of the theme of functional, urban differentiation and the results presented in the subsequent contributions will hope fully clarify the importance of a clear use of concepts, and of a comparitive, historical approach of such an important and much embracing social phenomenon: the city.

REFERENCES

Bairoch, P. 'Population urbaine et taille des villes en Europe de 1600 à 1970, Présentation de série statistique', Revue d'histoire economique-sociale, 3 (1976) pp. 304-335.

Bergeron, L. and M. Roncayolo, l'Historiographie urbaine en France (XVIIIe - XIXe siècles) report presented at a seminar Della citta preindustriale alla citta industriale (Naples, 1973).

Blotevogel, H.H. Zentrale Orte und Raumbeziehungen in Westfalen vor der Industrialisierung (1780-1850) (Münster, 1975).

Boer, D.E.H. de, 'De verhouding Leiden-Rijnland, 1365-1414. Veranderingen in een relatie', Economisch en sociaalhistorisch Jaarboek. (Den Haag, 1975) pp. 48-73.

Bouvier, J., Le Crédit Lyonnais de 1863 à 1882 (Paris, 1961).

Boyer, J.C., Transports et échelles de l'organisation urbaine paper presented at a seminar of the Internation Urban History Group in the Maison des Sciences de L'Homme (Paris, 1977).

Braudel, F., Capitalism and material life, 1400-1800 (New York etc., 1973).

Carter, H., The study of urban geography (London, 1976).

Castells, M., 'Structures sociales er processus d'urbanisation analyse comparative intersociétale', Annales, Economies, Sociétés, Civilisations (1970) pp. 1155-1199.

Clark, P. and P. Slack, Crisis and Order in English towns, 1500-1700 essays in urban history (London, 1972).

Daunton, M.L., 'Towns and economic growth in eighteenth century England' in Ph. Abrams and E.H. Wrigley (eds) Towns in Societies, Essays in Economic History and Historical Sociology (Cambridge, 1979) pp. 245-278.

Dean, Ph. and W.A. Cole British economic growth 1688-1959 (Cambridge, 1962).

Dobb, M. Studies in the development of capitalism (London, 1946).

Dyos, H.J. and D.H. Aldcroft British Transport, An economic survey from the seventeenth century to the twentieth (Harmondsworth, 1974).

Favier, R. Elements de définition fonstionelle d'un reseau urbain au XVIIe siècle paper presented at a seminar of the International Urban History Group in the Maison des Sciences de l'homme (Paris, 1977).

Fedor, T.S. Patterns of Urban growth in the Russian Empire during the nineteenth century (Chicago, 1975).

Finley, M.I. 'The ancient city: from Fustel de Coulanges to Max Weber and beyond', Comp. Studies in Society and History 19,3 (1977) pp. 305-328.

Fisher, F.J. 'London as an engine of economic growth' in P. Clark (ed) The early modern town (London, 1976).

Francois, E. Des republiques marchandes aux capitales politiques, remarques sur les armatures urbaines du Saint-Empire à l'époque moderne paper presented at a seminar of the International Urban History Group in the Maison des Sciences de l'homme (Paris, 1977).
Gottmann, J. Megalopolis, the urbanized northeastern seaboard of the United States (New York, 1961).
Hall, P. Urban and Regional Planning (Harmondsworth, 1974).
Henning, F.W. 'Industrialisierung und dörfliche Einkommensmöglichkeiten' in H. Kellenbenz (ed.) Agrarisches Nebengewerbe und Formen der Reagrarisierung im Spätmittelalter und 19.20, Jahrhundert (Stuttgart, 1975) pp. 155-176.
Herlihy, D. 'Urbanization and social change' in Proceedings of the seventh international economic history congress (Edinburgh, 1978).
Hershberg, Th. 'The new urban history, toward an interdisciplinary history of the city', Journal of urban history vol. 5, 1 (1978) pp. 3-40.
Higgs, R. 'Urbanization and Inventiveness in the United States, 1870-1920' in L.F. Schnore (ed.) The New Urban History, Quantitative Explorations by American Historians (Princeton, 1975) pp. 247-259.
Hoekveld, G.A. 'Theoretische aanzetten ten behoeve van het samenstellen van maatschappijhistorische modellen van de verhouding van stad en platteland in de nieuwe geschiedenis van Noord-West-Europa', Economisch en sociaalhistorisch Jaarboek (Den Haag, 1975) pp. 1-48.
Hurd, G. Human Societies, an introduction to sociology (London, 1973).
Jackson, K.T. 'Urban deconcentration in the Nineteenth century a statistical inquiry' in L.F. Schnore (ed.) The New urban History, Quantitative Explorations by American Historians, (Princeton, 1975) pp. 110-145.
Jacobs, J. The economy of cities (Harmondsworth, 1972).
Juillard, E. La 'région', contribution à une géographie générale des éspaces regionaux (no place, 1974).
Kellett, J.R. Railways and Victorian Cities (London, 1969).
Klebanow, D.F., L. Jonas and M. Leonard Urban legacy, the story of America's cities (New York, 1977).
Kiernan, V. 'Victorian London: unending purgatory', New Left Review, LXXVI (1972) pp. 73-90.
Labasse, J. Les capitaux et la région essai sur le commerce et la circulation des capitaux dans la région lyonnaise (Paris, 1955).
Lampard, E.E. 'Historical aspects of urbanization' in Ph.M. Hauser and L.F. Schnore (eds.) The study of urbanization (New York, 1965) pp. 519-554.
Lee, J.J. 'Aspects of Urbanisation in Germany 1815-1914' in Ph. Abrams and E.A. Wrigley (eds.) Towns in Societies, Essays in Economic History and Historical Sociology (Cambridge, 1978) pp. 279-293.

Marschalck, P. 'Zur Rolle der Stadt für den Industrialisierungsprozess in Deutschland in der 2. Hälfte des 19. Jahrhunderts' in J. Reulecke (ed.) Die Deutsche Stadt im Industriezeitalter, Beiträge zur moderne deutschen Stadtgeschichte (Wuppertal, 1978) pp. 57-66.
Matzerath, H. 'Industrialisierung, Mobilität und sozialen Wandel am Beispiel der Städte Rheydt und Rheindahlen' in H. Kaelble a.o. Probleme der Modernisierung in Deutschland, Sozialhistorische Studien zum 19. und 20. Jahrhundert (Opladen, 1978) pp. 13-80.
McKelvey, B. American Urbanization, a comparative history (Glenview/Brighton, 1973).
Migdal, J.S. 'Urbanization and political change: the impact of foreigh rule', Comp.Studies in Society and History 19,3 (1977) pp. 328-350.
Minchinton, W.E. 'Bristol -metropolis of the west in the eighteenth century' in P. Clark The early modern town (London, 1976).
Muijzenberg, O.D. van den, Horizontale mobiliteit in Centraal Luzon, kenmerken en achtergronden (Amsterdam, 1973).
Pred, A.R. 'Large-City interdependence and the pre-electronic diffusion of innovations in the United States' in L.F. Schnore (ed.) The New Urban History, Quantitative Explorations by American Historians (Princeton, 1975) pp. 51-74.
Reulecke, J. 'Population growth and urbanization in Germany in the 19th century', Urbanism, Past and Present (1971) pp. 21-32.
Robson, B.T. Urban growth, an approach (London, 1973).
Rozman, G. 'Urban networks and historical stages' Journal of Interdisciplinary History IX,1 (1978) pp. 65-91.
Stearns, P.N. European Society in upheaval, social history since 1750 (New York, London, 1975).
Thomas, B. Migration and Urban development, a reappraisal of British and American long cycles (London, 1972).
Tilly, C. The Vendée, 1964.
Tuma, E.H. European Economic History (New York etc., 1971).
Vollans, E.C. 'Urban development in Belgium since 1830' in R.P. Beckinsale, J.M. Houston (eds.) Urbanization and its problems essays in honour of E.W. Gilbert (Oxford, 1970) pp. 171-199.
Vries, J. Economy of Europe in an age of crisis, 1600-1750 (Cambridge, 1976).
Wallerstein, I. The modern world-system, capitalist agriculture and the origins of european world economy in the sixteenth century (New York, 1974).
Warner jr., S.B. The urban wilderness (New York, 1972).
Weber, E. From peasants into Frenchmen, the modernization of rural France, 1870-1914 (London, 1977).

Wrigley, E.A. 'The process of Modernization and the Industrial Revolution in England', Journal of Interdisciplinary History (1972) pp. 225-259.

Wrigley, E.A. 'Parasite or Stimulus: The Town in a Pre-Industrial Economy' in Ph. Abrams, E.A. Wrigley (eds.) Towns in Societies, Essays in Economic History and Historical Sociology (Cambridge, 1978) pp. 295-309.

1. Urbanization. What's in a name
P. Kooij

1.1.	Introduction	33
1.2.	Urbanization. A demographic concept	33
1.3.	Urbanization. A macro concept which cannot be brought down to size	35
1.4.	The national past. No town in sight	37
1.5.	The ecological complex. A framework that is too large	38
1.6.	Town systems. A spatial form of urbanization	40
1.7.	Geographic concepts. A too rigid regularity	42
1.8.	The formation of networks. A primarily economic happening	46
1.9.	A town system for the Netherlands. A glimpse	47
1.10.	Concentration numbers	49
	References	57

1. Urbanization. What's in a name *
P. Kooij

1.1. Introduction

Urbanization is a term which is frequently used in urban history, yet it is seldom defined. More often than not, its meaning has to be deduced from the context. Since it concerns an important basic concept in urban history, to which many theories have been attached, it initially seemed to me of use to assemble the definitions as applied in the urban historiography. An evaluation of the material would then produce the most appropriate definition which could, in turn, be propagated for further use. However, it soon became evident that most authors meant the same by this term, i.e. the numerical growth of towns and/or the related growth of urban population in general. Although there were some interesting varieties within that definition, they were too few in number to justify a continuation of the projected approach.

What did become obvious, however, was that the current definition of orbanization is not fit for use within urban history. I shall now attempt to demonstrate why one cannot apply that definition in urban history.
Naturally, I shall then try to offer a workable alternative, followed by an investigation into whether, and how, this new concept of urbanization can be put to use.

1.2. Urbanization. A demographic concept

Since the appearance of the first major studies about urbanisation in the second half of the nineteenth century, of which the most important, as well as the most influential study is that of Adna F. Weber (1899), the term urbanization has primarily been associated with numbers of people. One wrote about the migration of people from the countryside to the towns, about the rise of metropoles, that is to say, towns with a large population, about the differences in the growth of population in the towns, and in the countryside, and so forth. This concept has

---

* translated by Dineke Prince-van Wijnen

become so common, that an explicit definition is usually no longer given. More recent works are also guilty of this. In the cases where a definition is not omitted, one usually refers to the one applied by Hope Tisdale Eldridge in 1942; 'Urbanization is a process of population concentration. It proceeds in two ways: the multiplications of points of concentration and the increase in size of individual concentrations'.
In this concept, towns are the result of urbanization, causing Ms Eldridge to renounce rather vehemently the definitions in which that was excluded.

There are two classes of definition which are deemed unacceptable. The first regards urbanization as a process of radiation whereby ideas and practices spread out from the urban center into surrounding areas. This is an objectionable definition because it makes the city the cause of urbanisation rather than the result or the product of urbanisation .... The second class of definition is more objectionable than the first, and more peculiar. It defines urbanization as the increase in intensity of problems or traits or characteristics that are essentially urban. Again we have the confusion of cause and effect .... (1942 : 338).

Although this article does not refer to any source, nor to other works, it is clear that the first attack is aimed at the "Schlesinger-approach", and the second at a somewhat sociological approach of which L. Wirth (1938) was the principal proponent. Schlesinger (1933), and others with him, regarded the towns in the U.S.A. as the hearths of creativity and innovation containing a vast radiating power. Well-known in this connection, is R.E. Turner's theory (1940), that the pioneers of innovation and progress were primarily to be found in the urban 'melting-pots' and not, as his namesake presumed, on 'the frontier'. W. Diamond (1941) was the first of quite a number of historians who criticised this approach, and little by little, the concept of urbanisation that had evolved from it, disappeared from (urban) history.

According to Louis Wirth, a distinct way of living developed in towns, and was characterized by a stronger interaction and frequency of social contacts, which as a result were rather superficial, than had been the case before. People no longer saw each other during the whole day, but came into contact with only a partial aspect of the other person, namely, as postman, as neighbour, etc. The resulting segmentation of social restraint produced, on the one hand, more freedom for the individual, but on the other hand, symptoms such as lawlessness. Wirth labelled this way of life in towns 'urbanism' and wished it to be interpreted solely in the specifically sociological sense. Some of the characteristics attributed by Wirth to 'urbanism' were subsequently dismissed as being irrelevant, or just not accurate, for instance by, among others, Gans (1962). That does not alter the fact that, research into the urban way of life and its diffusion, still occupies, especially in the field of sociology, an important place. At times, though, the term urbanization is used instead of urbanism, which leads to confusion, and that ought to be avoided.

Eldridge, it must be admitted, did go to a lot of trouble to produce a definition so extensive that, so to speak, research can begin at zero-point, that is, in periods and in places characterized by a lack of towns. The aim, obviously, was to generalize, and to make it possible to go back in time to the cradle of mankind. As a result, the definition became somewhat vague, and that is not what we want. Fortunately, this misty veil has been lifted in the course of time. Thus, in 1965, Philip Hauser adopted the above-mentioned definition but added to it, "As a result the proportion of the population living in urban places increases" (1965 : 9).
Although this then creates the problem of how to define precisely the word 'urban' - and Hauser devotes several pages to this - the introduction of the proportional relationship urban-rural population clarifies the situation and makes it more concrete. What are involved here, are facts that can be measured. Such a definition can be found either implicitly or explicitly among almost all the later authors. Quite recently, Bo Öhngren even suggested to label as urbanization only those changes in the distribution of population that were to the benefit of towns. The real growth of towns, according to Öhngren, can better be qualified as 'urban growth' (1978 : 75).

In fact, these are really only variations of the same theme. More and more, urbanization came to be regarded as a demographic process, and it has been defined as such almost exclusively in the last years.

1.3. Urbanization. A macro concept which cannot be brought down to size

The demographic concept of urbanization appeared to be quite usable in economic history, such as in dividing the upward trend of population into rural and urban growth, and in measuring the shifts within them. This process could then be functionally matched to other developments. Thus, links have been made between urbanization and economic growth, and between urbanization and industrialization. Research into this usually involved the use of models and of statistics on a national level. Thus, figures concerning the distribution of population were related to figures concerning the growth of production or the growth of labor force in the secondary sector. Most interesting facts have come to light as a result of such an approach. At the Economic-Historical Conference held in Edinburgh, H. van Dijk stated that, in the Netherlands, the relative growth of urban population preceded industrialization (1978 : 101).

When such a relation between urbanization and industrialization is established with the aid of aggregated facts on a national level, then the spatial element no longer plays a part in the analysis. The division into urban and rural population is numerical and not spatial. The absence of this spatial element is, in my opinion, a compelling and sufficient reason to place these studies among the 'normal' economic history, and not to consider them as urban history. I am, of course, quite aware of the fact that there is no consensus at all as to what urban history as a distinctive subdiscipline of economic and social history entails, or ought to entail, but, urban history without space seems to me urban history without towns. That is, unless one declares a town to be a state of mind or something like it; unfortunately, that does happen sometimes, as has been pointed out, for instance, in evaluations of the theory and practice of the urban history by Dyos (1968) and Kooij (1975).

At that same conference in Edinburgh, David Herlihy attempted to make a connection between urbanization and industrialization in separate towns. His conclusion was, that some towns, such as Naples in the 18th and Athens in the 19th century, underwent an extremely large increase in population without any form of industrialization taking place (1978 : 59). Thus when pertaining to individual towns, such studies seem to have to be considered as 'urban history'. However, the concept urbanization suddenly seems to be inapplicable. For, industrialization can be examined at a local level, but urbanization, by definition, cannot. The applied definition, which is based on a proportional distribution of the population, prevents this, so that the phenomena cannot be compared.

The current definition of urbanization in social history is also quite suited for application, and that is not surprising considering the fact that historical demography constitutes an important subdiscipline of social history. Even then, though, some immense problems arise. These manifest themselves once they leave the macro-level. Urbanization can in no way functionally be connected to local social phenomena, neither can it be applied to research concerning small groups. As soon as the micro-sphere is given a central position, it becomes apparent that urbanization forms a neutral category which can only function in the sense of: society urbanized, so something must also have happened in the individual towns.

The above-mentioned provides an explanation for the, in my opinion, somewhat disappointing course of the session about the relation between 'urbanization and social change' at the conference in Edinburgh. The papers there were primarily concerned with social change in towns, with the result that urbanization more or less was forced into the role of a peg on which to hang one's theory as it suited, but from which no interpretation whatever could be derived.

The papers did include some elements, nevertheless, which can be regarded as positive ones within the framework of this theme. Bo Öhngren produced, as has already been referred to, an explicit definition of the concept urbanization, while Henk van Dijk emphasised the phenomenon migration. The concept migration

seems to me to be a good one within which it is possible to
show a relation between urbanization and social change. After
the facts concerning the relative growth of towns have been
subdivided into figures about groups of people who settle
somewhere, who leave, or perhaps sojourn somewhere, a picture
of the movement of people evolves, which can, so to speak, be
drawn on a map. As a result, the macro-concept of urbanization
not only obtains a pronounced spatial elaboration, but can,
moreover, be related to social phenomena at a local level.

It seems to me, that this is the only way in which the
demographic concept urbanization can be fitted usefully into
urban history. That is, of course, only in a very restricted
sense. It has, moreover, proven to be extremely difficult to
analyse social phenomena in the micro-sphere in such a way that
the town is an active element, and not just the background
scenery for a play. It is not without reason that the 'new
urban history', an epithet given by Thernstrom (1971) to the
more social and quantitative urban history, has been repeatedly stigmatized as social history within an urban framework.

Urbanism, as defined by Wirth, quite obviously included
spatial characteristics, since it was linked to density and
separation in local settlement-patterns. This is not surprising,
as the Chicago-school regarded the interaction between man and
environment as the principal element in its research. However,
it is not desirable that the micro-concepts are adjusted to the
limited range of macro-concepts, with the result that, in the
future, only the relation between urbanization and urbanism
will be examined. That would be putting the clock back, the
'new urban history' is currently undergoing a stormy development and pretends to want to enlarge her field rather extensively, particularly into the economic sphere. The volume "The
New Urban History" (Schnore, 1975), contains important promises
to that extend, and they continue to be made good in, for instance, articles in the Journal of Urban History. The spatial
element is now receiving more attention in quantitative studies
about the patterns of settlement such as have been presented in
Peter Knights' (1971) work on Boston. Such a wide range of
urban developments needs a large macro-framework, and to that
end, the concept urbanization now in force is not suited at
all.

1.4. The national past. No town in sight

A conception such as urbanization which is insufficiently applicable, naturally ought to stimulate the search for an
alternative macro-framework for urban history. Unfortunately,
this does not seem to exist in urban historiography. The researcher has more often than not shut himself up in his own
town and looked no further than the top of the town wall.
When an exception is made, it is usually an attempt to compare
local developments to those on a national level. An example of

this, for instance, is the connection made between the economic development of Manchester and that of England. Similarly, a study concerning the rise of socialism in the Hague was placed next to a study concerning the rise of socialism in the Netherlands. In such instance, problems occur that are identical to the ones mentioned in the preceding paragraphs. It appears to be impossible to connect national and local developments in such a way that an interaction can be traced. A parallel in the descriptions is the nearest that has been achieved.

The primary reason for this is, that the current picture of the social-economic past of a country is hardly regionally differentiated. There are facts about, and studies have been made of, economic growth, the growth of production, of population, of trade unions, and of the development of transport, and so forth. In these studies, especially when they are of a quantitative nature, the nation as a whole represents a statistical rather than a spatial unity. One can only then determine the contribution of the individual towns to these macro-processes if these towns are regarded as statistic entities. Even then, it will be of partial success. The statistics are often only available on a national, and not on a local level. In the Netherlands, for instance, it is impossible to determine the G.D.P. of a town for the 19th century, and also later. One is able to measure the contribution of individual towns to the increase in the national population, but it is impossible to subdivide the economic growth of a nation into urban growth.

Apart from the limited availability of source material, there is another fundamental difficulty. The attempt to adjust micro-studies to those existing on macro-level would result in a minimalizing of the spatial element. This would mean a complete loss of identity for urban history. It is, of course, necessary to study those elements, but urban history deserves a more spatial approach. The rather hybrid nature of the subject, within whose framework the national past serves as a neutral reference, ought really to disappear. For, it leads, at the most, to studies in the sense of "There was an industrial revolution in England, so something probably also happened in London". Research titled, for instance, as, Middletown and the Industrial Revolution, ought by now to be substituted by studies named Middletown in the Industrial Revolution. It is not the micro-framework that needs to be adjusted, but the macro-framework. Progress within urban history will be stimulated in particular by a picture of the national past which is spatially constructed. The answer, in my opinion, is to re-examine the current concept of urbanization.

1.5. The ecological complex. A framework that is too large

Upon examining the publications on urban history, one discovers that, since many years there is a slight dissatisfaction with regard to the concept urbanization. Particularly in the 1960's,

several studies appeared in whose title one frequently finds
the term 'urbanization'. Their observations purport many similarities. One could call it an ecological-complex approach.
The most important proponants of this approach within urban
history were Eric Lampard and Leo Schnore. Characteristic is
the following passage:

> At stake in a broader view of urban history is the possibility of making the societal process of urbanization
> central to the study of social change. Efforts should be
> made to conceptualize urbanization in ways that actually
> represent social change. For this purpose urbanization
> may be regarded as a process of population concentration
> that results in an increase in the number and size of
> cities (points of concentration) and social change as an
> incremental or arhythmic alteration in the routines and
> sequences of everyday life in human communities. The
> method will be to explore possible interrelationships
> between the phenomenon of population concentration and
> certain apparent trends in social organization, structure,
> and behavior (Lampard, 1963 : 233).

At first glimpse, it seems as if the well-known Eldridge definition has been quoted, but Lampard claims to be able to
isolate urbanization from the too limited demographic context
by relating it to environment, technology and 'social organization'. This quartet together forms the ecological complex
(Lampard, 1965).
It roughly entails that increasing populations adjust themselves to the circumstances, specifically speaking, to environment, by way of technology and social organization. The
establishment of towns is one of these adjustments. At times
it seems that Lampard labels as urbanization this very process
of adjustment, that is, the origin of towns and their growth
in the widest sense. In the end, he adheres to a demographic
concept.

> The demographic concept of urbanization, in short, is not
> as constricting as it first might have appeared; its
> scope allows inquiry into many facets of social change,
> and its root in population preserves a vital interest in
> the attributes and conditions of human beings living in
> organized communities (1965 : 522).

However, it was that very relating to other matters that was
more difficult than presumed. One is here concerned with
gigantic variables which are barely manageable and difficult
to quantify. The element population appears to be the easiest
to quantify with the result that it is the most frequent object of research. An absolute highlight was obtained in the
shape of Lampard's article "The Urbanizing World" (1973), in

which all the aspects of population development, which fit into the framework of the ecological complex, have been rubricated in a useful and well-considered manner, and brought into relation to each other. Nevertheless, even then, it only foreshadows the connection to other variables in the ecological complex. A real relation has not been brought about. Even if this should ever succeed, the circumstance that the different elements are so comprehensive, probably results at the most in a sort of history of society in which room is also made for towns, and that is not what urban history is waiting for.

Leo Schnore still has great expectations of the ecological complex, particularly in the micro-sphere (1975). Perhaps he is right; for, after all, it contains the element space. Several important studies have been made concerning the spatial distribution of the urban population. The question remains, however, whether they ought to be made within the framework of the ecological complex. Environment is rather deterministic, and that is no longer easy to prove in modern times. Studies such as by Knights and Warner (1962) have, in any case, proven that these things ought to be examined more pragmatically.

1.6. Town systems. A spatial form of urbanization

It must be admitted, though, that the ecological complex does contain, apart from much unnecessary ballast, material fit for a new concept of urbanization. It is to Eric Lampard's merit that he produced these elements and introduced them emphatically in urban history (1954/55). For it was he, who identified the concentration of a large number of functions in a central area such as towns, as one of the characteristics of the rational adjustment of man to his environment. These towns became a centre of production, of transport, of services, of politics and of culture, etc. They fulfilled this central rôle not only for the inhabitants, but also to the surrounding, mostly agricultural, areas. Moreover, the towns became more and more interwoven in all kinds of ways, because, for instance, there was an exchange of goods, or perhaps, because a flow of migration evolved. A whole network, or system of towns, evolved, which primarily could be determined horizontally. Besides that, however, there was the phenomenon that some towns acquired more, and sometimes more important, central functions than others. That lead to hierarchical characteristics within the system of towns. Lampard c.s. assembled these into a type of pyramid structure, but it is also possible to present them horizontally, which I hope to do further on.

A similar view was also evident, quite early on, in the work of Oscar Handlin. In the article, "The modern city as a field of historical study" (1963), he states that the modern town has developed from an organism into an organ. From an independent entity, often even quite tangibly divided - either due to water or to walls - from her surroundings, the town de-

veloped in the course of time more and more as a part of a
larger entity. What one ought to envision by that was not exactly described; Handlin primarily touched on the mutual political and economic dependence of towns, but even then the description remains an stimulating one. The transformation from
organism to organ was accomplished by three developments, according to Handlin: the rise of centralized national states,
the transformation of the economy from a traditional household,
to a capital-using basis and the "technological destruction of
distance". Although this has not been elaborated on further,
one may make two important conclusions about this theory.
Firstly, that the contributing forces belong to different
spheres - in this case, the economic and the political - and,
secondly, that the creation and development of town systems
must be brought back to the pre-industrial era. In a subsequent
paragraph it will be demonstrated that the first forms an obstruction to the shaping of a new concept of urbanization, while
the second seems to be confirmed by practical research.

Whilst Handlin's view on town systems remains somewhat
vague, that of Lampard is embedded with great difficulty in that
burdensome ecological complex. Nevertheless, the introduction
of the concept of town networks within urban history proved to
be a very important development. Thus, it became possible to
remove towns from their isolation and to examine them within a
useful framework. The realization, that the town constitutes a
part of a larger framework, and that it is attached to it in
all sorts of ways, should prevent the urban historian from pronouncing his own town as the pivot of the world commanding an
eternal myopic fascination.

Theoretical concepts such as nodality, centrality and
hierarchy, are suited for use within urban history. For the
first time, a framework is within reach that includes a spatial
dimension and, since urban history always primarily regarded
the individual towns as spatial units, it is, at last, possible
to study the micro- and macro-level with regard to their mutual
interaction.

Such an important framework deserves an important name. It
seems to me desirable that the concept urbanization receives a
broader definition, which also contains the above-mentioned
processes. This can be done simply by defining urbanization not
only as the concentration of people at central points, and their
distribution throughout the nation, but also as <u>the concentration
of activities at central points and their distribution throughout the nation</u>.

In this sense, towns need to be seen as multifunctional central
points, as a point where people, goods, services, power and impetus are concentrated. As for the concentration of activities,
they include not only those of an economic and social nature,
but also the political and the cultural. The dosage of the various activities over the towns in a nation produces absolute,
as well as relatively large, differences which increase the more

the towns become independent. This is expressed by the differences
in the central functions, and the shifts within these functions.
This mutual dependence can, for the most part, quite manifestly
be spatially determined, even in the past. Thus, one could determine quite early on the flow of goods from one town to another,
the migration of people, and the exchange of correspondence,
whilst that same mutual dependence was given an added emphasis
by (water)ways, railways, and, later on, by high tension masts
and telephone cables.

By introducing a definition of urbanization which is based
on the presence of central functions and the development of de-
pendency-relations, urban history benefits more than when one
clings to a sterile, and solely demographic concept of urbanization. The concentration of people and of activities are a logical
extension of each other; there is a quite obvious interaction.
In research that has been done up until now, one can observe repeatedly, that the consolidation of activities in a central point
always occurred in interrelation to the numeric growth of towns.
This cannot be contradicted by the assertion that, in some towns
a large increase in population preceded industrialization. In
those cases, the central functions were to be found in other
spheres, varying from the political function as national capital,
to the cultural function as a "magical centre". Moreover, the
definition I suggested, bypasses the difficulty encountered by
Hope Tisdale Eldridge, and which prevented her from producing
a wider concept of urbanization, that is to say, that in that
event, one could distinguish towns before urbanization had
actually taken place.

Of course objections can be made to the new definition.
The most important one, it seems to me, could be that, it is
still difficult to provide a precisely outlined content for the
concepts activities and central functions. By activities is
meant in the first place, of course, production, consumption,
and services. However, it also includes activities such as ex-
erting political power, creating new standards and values, and
accepting innovations. Practical research should throw more
light on this; but, obviously, this research into the way in
which, and to what extent, towns form a part of a larger entity,
is only possible after introducing a new concept of urbanization.
As for the concepts centrality and hierarchy, it must be noted
that they have already been well-tested and deemed applicable
in another, pre-eminently spatial, discipline, namely, geography.

1.7. Geographic concepts. A too rigid regularity

One will not find the stone of wisdom in the field of geography,
either. There are no theories on town systems at hand that can
be applied directly to urban history. The only concept which up
until now has somewhat found its way into urban history is that
of Walter Christaller. In 1933, he created the concept central
place. In the course of time, certain towns have acquired a central

service function with regard to the smaller towns and villages. In a spatial dimension, these small nuclei are situated at an equal distance from the service-centres so that they form corners, so to speak, of a hexagon of which that central town is the pivot. This same pivot can, in turn, be regarded as a corner of a hexagon around a more important service-centre, thus creating a hierarchy of central points in a horizontal pattern.

Naturally, such a pronounced theory resulted into much discussion among geographers. Although Christaller's theory is, in general, no longer accepted, the concepts centrality and hierarchy have not really been meddled with; in fact, they are still often applied. Of the various criticisms of this theory, the following aspects in particular are relevant to urban history,

a) Empirical research has never really produced regular hexagons. The regularity-aspect in particular has turned the theory into a sort of Procrustean bed into which reality will only then fit after having undergone far-reaching mutilation. Also to be mentioned in this context, is Jefferson's "law of the primate city". Jefferson (1939) stated that, in each country, a capital city evolves, which attracts so many central functions that, with regard to growth and inhabitants, it by far outdoes the nearest ranking towns. I need not to travel far to find evidence to the contrary. In the Netherlands, the three towns Amsterdam, the Hague and Rotterdam have been much the same in size since the 19th century, and this can also be said of the Belgian towns of Antwerp and Brussels. Not very convincing is Jefferson's argument that the three Dutch towns are situated so near to each other that they are to be regarded as one large town, nor that Antwerp and Brussels must be seen as exponents of, respectively, Flemish and Wallonian Belgium; this is especially unconvincing when one looks back into history. In any case, regularity is something which a historian will never accept in advance; if he does, it will only be after thorough research.

b) Christaller employed an institutional method of regulation. He began with institutions such as schools, markets, hospitals, and so forth, and on the strength of that, produced a honeycomb structure of primary towns. This approach meant that emphasis was laid on the services, and that industry was neglected. In this way, a new industrial town, which fabricated products for a national and an international market, and, therefore, made an important contribution to the gross national product, could obtain a very low score. This result was then accentuated even more by the fact that such industrial towns were very often situated near each other, so that they had to share the various central functions.

The emphasis on regularity disappeared from subsequent theories, and an attempt was made, often with success, to shift the accent from services to industry. An evaluation of these

theories on town systems is not necessary at this point; let me
suffice by referring to such competent studies as those by Berry
(1973), Buursink (1971), Hoekveld (1975), Pred (1966) and Robson
(1973). Research in the field of geography, however, has progressed so far now, that today's USA and most West European
countries have been subdivided into regional service-centres
which sometimes, but not always, display hierarchical characteristics. These classifications are based on the number of inhabitants of the towns and the functions these towns occupy in the
economic sphere whereby an important criterion was usually the
presence of institutions in the services sector.
This is quite easy to measure, but attempts have also been made
to weigh other economic activities (e.g. Alexandersson, 1956).
These classifications of towns are made with the aid of refined
techniques and are possible thanks to the enormous amount of
data which is available for the present.

Such an approach cannot be applied just like that to the
past. Much data which is available concerning the present will
be searched for in vain with regard to the past; similarly,
data concerning the past cannot always be applied to the present.
Moreover, it is quite the question whether one ought to apply
this method to the past without making some adjustments to it.
One of the primary criteria is the range of the service capacity
of a town. This quite obviously depends on the available transportation and communication facilities, and these varied for
each historical period. Similarly, the factors determining the
establishment of industry differed as time passed.

When one looks into town systems, its extension, and the
changes within them - and that is, in my opinion, that with which
urban history should primarily be concerned with at a macro-
level - then, the current divisions and criteria can be applied
only in part. That is why I am not so certain that urban history
benefits from an approach as was recently presented by Sam Bass
Warner and Sylvia Fleisch (1977). They advocate the introduction
in historical research of an accounting system drafted by the
Bureau of Economic Analysis in co-operation with geographers.
This system divides the U.S. towns into Standard Metropolitan
Statistical Areas (SMSA). These SMSA's correlate to the service
sectors around primary towns and have been shaped with the aid
of statistics compiled from the census of 1960. Since this division uses as its point of departure the county of which long
series of figures are available, Warner and Fleisch consider
its application to the past of use, because, by retaining the
same divisions throughout time, all sorts of quantitative comparisons become possible. However, maintaining this very SMSA
throughout time will produce a distorted picture. It just is
not possible to deduce the past linea recta from the present.
Moreover, the present is sometimes completely different from
what the past seemed to lead to. In any case, urban historians
cannot accept a priori that the network of towns in 1960 corresponded to that of a century earlier, even though it may seem

to be so. In point of fact, the authors recognize this, but as
far as studying problems within the range of social history is
concerned, they see the objection as something that can be overcome. Moreover, they point to the fact that research into town
systems in the past still has to commence, so, there is no alternative method.

There are, indeed, hardly any extensive studies about town
networks in the past, and of the few that exist, most concern
the pre-industrial period and/or specific countries such as
Russia and China. As far as the industrialized society is concerned, it was Eric Lampard once more who emerged as the pioneer.
In the article "The evolving system of cities in the United
States" (1968), the period after 1800 was thoroughly examined.
In it, by the way, he adhered to the demographic definition of
urbanization, and that proved to be, as he himself admits in his
concluding sentence, an obstacle to a further examination of
the material. Important relevant passages can also be found in
Pred's work, which is more concerned with the general spatial
aspects of urban-industrial growth in the U.S.A. in the period
1800-1914. After that, research at a national level was hardly
pursued. There is, however, the important study of Michael
Conzen (1975) about the role of transportation in the town
network.

Further important research has been done into the spatial
diffusion of innovations. These, as well, have been initiated
by geographers, of which the pioneer was Hägerstrand (1953).
Due to their nature, these studies could not become anything
but historical studies, since the acceptance of innovations
has to involve time. Not only did they look into the diffusion
of artefacts such as the steam engine, the automobile and the
telephone, but also of matters in a more institutional sphere.
Thus, Hägerstrand examined the diffusion of the Rotary, and
Pred (1975) that of information. These studies showed that innovations often tend to diffuse in a hierarchical way, and that,
at the same time, the factor distance was of crucial importance.
Not only did diffusion occur towards central points at a lower
level, but also to the immediate surrounding area. A representative study in this connection, is that of Brian Robson (1973)
into the diffusion of gasfactories, telephone and building societies. It was there obviously a matter of ranking order
(number of inhabitants) and at the same time of the distance
between primary towns and dependent towns. With this, this
study indicates that knowledge concerning the diffusion-pattern
of innovation can be an important aid in reconstructing town
systems.

Although expressions such as central points or hierarchy
are not at all employed in F.J. Fisher's article "London as an
engine of economic growth" (1971), this work deserves to be
mentioned, as it sketches rather evokingly how London acquired
an indisputable position in the 18th century at the top of the
English town pyramid, with the result that there was a strong

numeric increase in population. Another interesting aspect of this article is that it also includes the element political power, as exerted by London in order to get its own way. This political aspect can also be found in the pleasant study made by Johan de Vries (1965) about the economic rivalry between Amsterdam and Rotterdam where, in some sense, the top of the Dutch town-hierarchy was at issue. That, then, is the only Dutch historical study concerning this subject, that exists of recent times. An important article not to be omitted was written some thirty years ago by the geographer H.J. Keuning (1948) about the town-hierarchy between the two World Wars.

1.8. The formation of networks. A primarily economic happening

If we regard urbanization as not only the concentration of activities in the socio-economic sphere, but also in the political and cultural spheres, complications arise. Since it is impossible to measure the importance of these spheres with respect to each other, more town systems ought to be constructed. Apart from an economic hierarchy, it is also possible to construct a political one, and they need in no way coincide.* The Netherlands itself provides a clear example of that, as political power has of old been exercised from the Hague. Under that come the capitals of the eleven provinces; the Hague occupies a double function, national as well as provincial capital. The two largest, and economically most important cities, Amsterdam and Rotterdam, do not appear at the top of the political network, being neither national nor provincial capitals.

As to the cultural sphere - and here I primarily think of patterns of standards and values, and the changes within them - one encounters matters that are often hardly to be measured. However, there are possibilities of measuring the spatial diffusion of cultural innovations, but then in a roundabout way, such as by analysing the contents of local newspapers or comparing police regulations. It is not unlikely that what will then become evident is that the frequency of cultural activities can be related functionally to the size of the town. (That is where we see Wirth's urbanism reappearing.) Such a conclusion is less probable in the political sphere as it is characterized by a hierarchy of rigid, venerable and often age-old institutions.

It is, of course, not very inspiring to have to work continually with several hierarchies which only partly overlap each

---

* Even within the economical sphere, it is possible to create different systems, according to the criteria used for classification. These are, however, easy to bring into one line, as has been shown clearly by Brian Robson elsewhere in this volume.

other. For that reason, macro-research within urban history can best devote itself primarily to socio-economic activities that are concentrated in central points. This concentration of activities was the major driving force behind the increase in the labor market, which in turn largely caused the numeric growth of towns. Political activities can also be included, in so far as they can be translated into the number of jobs involved. Even a more outdated or materialistic interpretation of culture can be translated into the labor market and into artefacts, but that seems to me to be less desirable.

In any case, there do exist theories within the field of geography, which can function as a guide for research into the spatial diffusion of social and economic activities in the past. A pragmatical approach, in which the outlines of the spatial system have not been determined in advance, is possible only if an ample amount of sources of sufficient quality is avialable. In my opinion and considering the results that have been achieved, there are enough possibilities to reconstruct the spatial diffusion of people, goods, services and information with the aid of archives. Some of these possibilities will be mentioned in the next paragraph. In doing that, I shall not again cross boundaries, but, in order to achieve a reasonable unity of time and place, I shall limit myself to the Netherlands, and to the turn of this century, the period within which the industrial revolution began. In doing this, I shall elaborate on an example which was not entirely an arbitrary choice.

1.9. A town system for the Netherlands. A glimpse

The most manifest characteristic of town systems comes in the shape of the communications between them. Most useful observations about the presence and the development of town systems were recorded by Jan de Vries (1978) in his study concerning the development of a network of (tow-)barges in the pre-industrial period. This can also be done with regard to the industrial period. Railroads, overland routes and waterways were the channels along which goods were transported from one town to another. The quantity and the nature of these goods are, alas, usually no longer to be traced, even though there are sources available. For instance, the Staats Spoorwegen (National Railways), for many years published in their annual report the volume of goods that was transported from one town to another. However, this was not subdivided into the nature of the goods. The figures available concerning tolls and clearances of goods are usually not very reliable. Nevertheless the course of the connecting routes, the frequency of various types of regular and carrier services, information about the number of passengers carried, and such, do present us with operational indications concerning the nature of the system.

The nature and the volume of the flow of people between towns can be reconstructed with precision. A hypothesis worth putting to the test, is, that these flows of people moved particularly in the direction of those centres where the flow of the most goods originated. This migration can be measured with the aid of registrations concerning settlement and departure, which were made by each town. After comparing this information with the town registers, one can classify these migrants according to age, profession, place of origin, size of family, etc. Unfortunately, this type of research has only been done for a few towns, so that there is no prospect at all yet of a national picture subdivided into towns (Hille de Vries, 1971; Van Dijk, 1976).

The spatial diffusion of innovations with regard to the Netherlands, has barely been subject of investigation. A first attempt was the research into, among other things, the diffusion of bicycles and electric services (Baudet et al., 1974). The diffusion of the first (electric) power stations, though, offers a picture which is somewhat difficult to interpret (Table 1.1).

Table 1.1 : The establishment of electric power stations in the Netherlands 1886-1910.

	Private	Municipal
1886	Kinderdijk	Nijmegen
1889	Den Haag	
1892	Amsterdam	
1895	Borne	Rotterdam
1898	Elst, Baarn, Terborg, Beek-Ubbergen	
1899	Boxtel, Hilversum, Naarden, Bloemendaal, Abcoude, Maarssen	
1900	Driebergen, Hengelo, Valkenburg, Watergraafsmeer	
1901	IJmuiden, Rijswijk, Terneuzen, Enschede, Veendam, Haaksbergen, Almelo	
1902	Rhenen	Groningen, Haarlem, Heerlen
1903	Voorburg	Soest
1904	Ginneken, Scheveningen	Amsterdam
1905		Utrecht
1906	De Bilt, Blaricum, Helpman (Groningen)	Den Haag
1907	Monster, Nunspeet, Wassenaar	Arnhem, Leiden, Naaldwijk
1908	Raamsdonk	Delfzijl, Nijmegen
1909	Aalsmeer, Ulft	
1910	Breskens, Cuyk, Eindhoven, Helmond, Kimswerd, Middelstum, Oosterwolde, Vlissingen	Delft, Dordrecht, Gouda

If one tries, one can discover the hierarchical aspect (though Bloemendaal, for instance, preceded Haarlem), but less that of proximity. Political motives were often at stake. In large towns, the local authorities often checked private initiative whilst they themselves wished to establish a power station at a later date. In small towns, the rich inhabitants, or the large industries, frequently forced the town council to approve the establishment of a private owned power plant. It is, furthermore, of interest that the diffusion of this innovation not so much emanated from the top of the town hierarchy, but more from the towns that were comparable either as to the number of inhabitants, or as to their social or political structure. For instance, when the debate concerning the introduction of electricity began in Groningen, one turned to Den Haag and Nijmegen for advice, not to Rotterdam and Amsterdam. As Pred (1975) indicated, this possibility of a horizontal diffusion is missing in most diffusion models. The top of the pyramid of towns is usually the only link between regional subsystems. Horizontal diffusion occurred in more areas. Thus, the twentieth century saw the development of chains of department stores – also an innovation –, which were confined to comparable towns such as Groningen-Arnhem-Nijmegen; although the locations Groningen-Amsterdam also accurred.

1.10. Concentration numbers

Much of the research done by geographers concerning the present, can, without much difficulty also be done for the past. The relatively easiest approach is the much-applied method of institutional regularity, based on the presence of institutions of the third sector.

There are, however, other approaches in existence as well which concentrate more on industry. These then seem more dynamic and indicate more rapidly the changes that occur within the system. One of these is the rather old, but still applied method of concentration numbers (Van Vuuren, 1938). A concentration number is:

$$\frac{\text{The proportion of the national labor force per category living in a town}}{\text{The proportion of the total population living in a town}} \times 100$$

High concentration numbers, therefore, show that a certain category is overrepresented, while low ones refer to an underrepresentation. One need not in this case regard the number 100 as an absolute turning-point, since some economic activities without doubt take place primarily in towns, and others in rural areas.

The concentration numbers indicate, in the first place,

regional specialization. They show to what extent, and for which goods and services a town depends on other towns, and to what extent some towns in turn supply others. Moreover, the height of the concentration numbers give some indication of the volume of the flow of goods from, and to, certain towns. That, then, introduces the hierarchical element into the picture, especially when the nominal figures are taken into consideration. The direction of the flow of goods can, theoretically, also be determined with the aid of the concentration numbers if one assumes that the goods flow from towns with high scores to those with low ones in a certain category, whereby an attempt is made to limit the distance as much as possible. This, of course, should be examined with the aid of more concrete data; at the same time, attention should be paid also to the double role of the large ports, for they also provide connections with other national systems.

The concentration numbers have been calculated for those 20 Dutch towns which, according to the census of 1889 had the most inhabitants, and also for the top 20 of 1909. The source of information is the census of the labor force held in 1889 and 1909 (see for the national totals Table 1.2).

The division into categories in the census of 1889 showed some disparity with that of 1909. This difference has been wiped out by joining together three categories of trade, and by dividing the category illumination into chemical production and the fabrication of gas. The numbering of the categories corresponds to that of 1909. It must be noted, though, that the figures are only partially comparable since in 1889 the profession was that one was concerned with, while in 1909, it was the place where one worked. According to the calculations made by J.A. de Jonge (1968 : 457), 8,16 and 22,23 in particular cannot be compared. As far as 16 is concerned, this has been set right.

For most of the above-mentioned categories, the concentration numbers have been determined.* Some have been omitted, either because there were too few laborers concerned, or because they included professions that were too dissimilar. Furthermore the diamond-cutting profession occurred, apart from in Amsterdam, only in Hilversum, so that it seemed of little use to include it in the comparison (see Table 1.3a and 1.3b).

A further complication is the fact that the results for 1909 include the complete information pertaining to only the 10 largest towns. For the other towns, only the most important professions were mentioned. Consequently, the concentration numbers

---

* Theun Dankert's expertise in determining the concentration numbers was of great assistance to me, while Piet Pellenbarg offered useful advice as to how I could apply them. I am grateful to them both for this.

for Dordrecht, Maastricht etc. are relatively too low and sometimes are not even mentioned. A comparison between the complete and the incomplete figures for the 10 largest towns revealed that there are rather large discrepancies in 5, 6, 16, 17, 28 and 29-32. Either none, or practically no discrepancies were found in 11-13, 18-19, 27.

Table 1.2: The Dutch labor force, divided into catogories, 1839 and 1909

Category	1889	1909
1. Pottery, glass, lime, stone	18,080	27,907
2. Diamond cutting etc.	10,447	9,709
3. Printing	12,105	17,955
4. Building activities	120,975	174,877
5. Chemical products, candles, oil, wax	3,751	11,558
6. Wood-, cork-, straw-industries	37,387	48,529
7. Clothing, laundry	75,645	105,839
8. Arts and crafts	1,598	2,377
9. Leather, oil-cloth, caoutchouc	37,422	36,939
10. Bog-ore, coal, peat	15,371	22,174
11. Metal-industries	41,633	47,677
12. Steam- and other machines	6,456	58,176
13. Shipping, coach-works	13,516	26,006
14. Paper-mills	2,923	10,075
15. Textiles	44,455	57,054
16. Gas, electricity works	2,490	4,771
17. Food and luxuries	84,327	120,759
18. Agriculture	524,624	616,395
19. Fisheries, chase	16,650	23,182
20. Trade	135,669	185,357
21. Transport	131,255	216,603
22. Banking	708	3,506
23. Insurance	1,098	4,104
24. Professions such as doctors, artists, authors, accountants	30,015	65,221
25. Private education	9,655	19,199
26. Nursing, caring for the poor etc.	3,782	14,969
27. Domestic service	166,495	222,562
28. Free labour	25,164	22,744
29. Civil service	34,436	36,747
30. Provincial civil service	886	494
31. Local service	25,299	36,529
32. Polder-board	2,604	1,545
33. Church officials	12,208	10,088
Total labor force (1-33)	1,652,729	2,261,590

Table 1.3a: Concentration numbers of the largest dutch towns, 1889

Town	inh.	1. Pott	3. Prin	4. Buil	5. Chem	6. Wood	7. Clot	9. Leat	11-13 Metal	14. Pape	15. Text	16. Gas	17. Food	18-19 Agric	20. Trad	21. Tran	22-23 Bank	27. Dom	28. Free	29-32 Civil
1.Amsterdam	408061	35	249	127	123	101	163	86	138	45	16	94	117	1	185	183	279	165	162	110
2.Rotterdam	201858	41	198	130	85	133	216	92	150	89	28	204	142	2	189	221	208	138	194	90
3.Den Haag	156809	39	283	165	54	127	171	100	121	25	15	269	86	13	132	97	213	203	67	222
4.Utrecht	84346	88	255	147	135	96	178	102	183	16	14	256	130	11	137	123	234	150	301	199
5.Groningen	56038	60	298	122	116	144	155	94	97	22	49	262	132	8	185	152	205	165	235	126
6.Haarlem	50500	43	426	166	143	63	166	101	227	12	52	187	105	12	152	100	203	173	248	127
7.Arnhem	49727	115	234	157	49	102	186	119	105	99	40	281	101	18	133	117	226	193	67	202
8.Leiden	43379	55	336	124	123	135	200	126	130	14	405	200	122	6	142	123	150	147	91	202
9.Tilburg	33905	21	77	108	42	72	176	199	190	23	1415	75	103	28	74	77	192	75	29	21
10.Dordrecht	32622	89	187	141	205	178	156	107	256	47	21	222	159	6	158	191	337	153	51	112
11.Nijmegen	32101	105	248	136	115	104	121	113	84	87	7	316	119	35	105	104	265	151	77	162
12.Maastricht	32078	2376	115	51	75	157	181	162	173	1944	33	68	152	7	115	90	148	129	31	182
13.Leeuwarden	30433	92	252	118	163	107	199	104	132	669	23	167	108	16	199	125	246	177	240	248
14.Delft	28458	92	102	127	74	126	150	140	271	38	9	191	170	10	144	103	105	109	200	153
15.Den Bosch	27138	86	457	104	52	104	191	241	331	41	53	280	216	7	146	127	166	146	0	233
16.Zwolle	26384	30	230	134	256	200	141	111	289	41	27	254	107	20	145	172	256	153	10	117
17.Schiedam	25533	99	163	116	760	228	102	80	109	0	240	177	479	8	97	142	147	85	1	57
18.Deventer	22914	138	218	158	161	158	135	102	200	67	26	221	176	20	119	96	196	135	15	246
19.Den Helder	22221	3	81	112	36	42	59	94	166	7	49	114	63	19	111	143	22	72	64	804
20.Breda	22176	41	208	112	603	101	186	157	189	70	49	172	145	8	118	111	270	166	12	410
Apeldoorn	19275	18	66	103	54	107	110	61	62	2570	12	47	74	115	52	61	104	117	4	54
Enschede	15229	10	78	117	40	23	100	75	102	111	2286	131	6	9	87	66	180	66	67	56
Hilversum	12470	6	60	128	30	28	88	68	96	0	815	116	76	24	127	106	200	154	270	50

Table 1.3b: Concentration numbers of the largest dutch towns, 1909

Town	inh.	1. Pott	3. Prin	4. Buil	5. Chem	6. Wood	7. Clot	9. Leat	11-13 Metal	14. Pape	15. Text	16. Gas	17. Food	18-19 Agric	20. Trad	21. Tran	22-23 Bank	27. Dom	28. Free	29-3 Civil
1.Amsterdam	533131	19	267	109	152	104	190	85	101	160	103	522	140	2	225	140	979	142	183	116
2.Rotterdam	417989	19	172	103	127	122	149	74	113	66	32	290	133	4	192	254	382	106	3	101
3.Den Haag	271280	27	248	154	101	125	199	76	64	105	15	505	84	16	165	87	560	188	45	218
4.Utrecht	119006	71	225	133	288	75	174	84	112	121	8	498	126	9	168	134	347	136	103	188
5.Groningen	74613	21	261	113	170	146	207	78	70	156	61	362	152	9	218	142	364	146	304	124
6.Haarlem	69410	14	424	168	215	85	182	93	122	94	52	180	106	9	214	118	583	155	276	155
7.Arnhem	64019	45	232	149	107	113	174	92	102	103	49	393	114	17	175	95	545	169	263	193
8.Leiden	58253	67	313	124	187	100	171	92	92	110	528	365	150	9	183	66	164	119	281	169
9.Nijmegen	54803	56	263	148	230	55	141	111	78	139	10	338	109	24	122	91	233	143	182	151
10.Tilburg	50405	52	103	88	48	75	124	370	91	57	1157	234	95	24	115	119	174	62	75	30
11.Dordrecht	46355	35	118	79	127	55	21	86	266	40	..	..	43	5	121	83	..	115	269	..
12.Maastricht	37483	3376	..	46	72	24	59	178	41	455	..	..	137	..	95	12	..	114	10	..
13.Leeuwarden	36522	..	166	99	64	47	121	9	56	283	..	208	107	12	190	67	..	151	310	21
14.Apeldoorn	35626	12	62	117	111	127	121	66	54	878	107	..	10	74	72	37	..	103	80	..
15.Den Bosch	34928	..	229	60	..	..	46	339	101	123	46	206	..	2	121	56	..	113	9	..
16.Enschede	34201	36	83	114	233	35	91	65	103	134	2115	..	117	4	97	25	160	55	23	11
17.Delft	34191	264	122	65	629	59	35	98	141	..	..	..	..	9	123	22	..	104	167	..
18.Zwolle	34055	..	171	105	202	142	104	117	136	90	27	..	51	19	163	117	362	115	244	19
19.Schiedam	32055	472	123	47	377	161	6	49	169	145	..	139	..	4	73	41	..	72	302	..
20.Hilversum	31458	..	125	142	60	59	14	85	63	83	229	70	..	13	123	37	..	193	36	..
21.Den Helder	27159	..	78	58	..	236	41	69	149	..	..	..	..	28	105	24	..	66	237	1026
22.Deventer	27787	63	176	137	126	100	90	88	143	82	213	99	..	13	128	41	103	113	55	92
23.Breda	27389	..	117	62	..	166	51	167	110	..	39	..	35	4	109	31	..	128	73	..

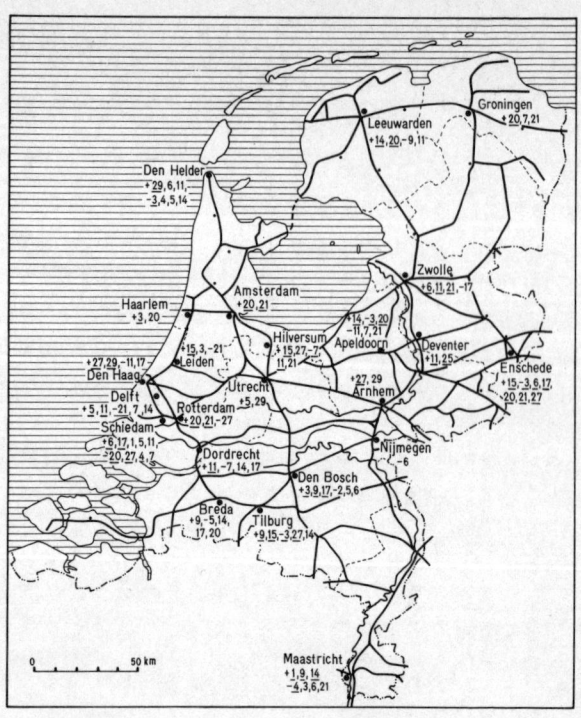

Figure 1.1: The largest towns in the Netherlands, 1909 and labor force catgories in which they are strongly over- and underrepresented *

* These figures following the name of a town that are preceded by a + sign refer to the categories that are strongly overrepresented in that town. The strongly underrepresented categories are indicated by the - sign. The situation refers to 1909, as it gives a clearer picture than that of 1889. If a certain categorie already showed a high or low concentration number in 1889, this is indicated by underlining the figure. One of the things that emerges, is, that towns which had specialized themselves in a certain sector and, therefore, showed a high concentration number in a certain categorie and relatively low in many others (for instance Schiedam, Den Helder, Apeldoorn, Enschede and Hilversum) had more chance to rise of fall in rank than towns which showed a more balanced pattern. This picture confirms the observations made by Brian Robson elsewhere in this volume.

Unmistakeably high concentration numbers are naturally not very revealing when they concern a small labor force. Thus, the impression is given that Leeuwarden was an important centre of the paper-manufacturing industry, and Schiedam of the chemical industry (see Figure 1.1). In reality, there was, respectively, one strawboard factory, and one candle factory. Similarly, the high concentration number for the banking business in Amsterdam is of no significance.

It's quite another thing when large categories such as the textile industry and trade are at issue. The high concentration numbers for Tilburg and Enschede confirm that these towns, followed at some distance by Leiden, supplied the greater part of the national production of textiles. Moreover, Tilburg and Enschede are both prime examples of new industrial towns, as reflected in the relatively low-scoring services category, and, as can be expected with factory-workers, few domestic services. These types of towns exported, as well as imported, many goods.

Other towns show a more stable build-up. This was, for instance, notable in the case of Amsterdam and Rotterdam. That trade was the primary function of these towns is, indeed, reflected in the concentration numbers. This is also the case with Groningen and Leeuwarden. Quite remarkable is the low figure noted for Schiedam; the proximity of Rotterdam is guilty to that. Then, especially if one takes into account that figures concerning the third category are incomplete, there is an unmistakeable rise in the services-function of Apeldoorn.

As far as Amsterdam and Rotterdam are concerned the concentration numbers do show that the industrialization in the Netherlands is to be attributed largely to the balanced growth of the industrial sector in these towns. The figures also reflect the transformation of the old trading centre, Dordrecht, and the agricultural centre, Delft, into industrial centres.

It is, by the way, not easy to distinguish, with the help of these concentration numbers, the peculiarly residential towns. Den Haag and Arnhem, which to us are known, thanks to other source-material, as offering attractive living-surroundings for the upper social classes, both had high concentrations of domestic services. This can also be said of Hilversum, where, in this period, many well-to-do citizens of Amsterdam took up residence, but not of the rapidly growing residential town of Apeldoorn.

The numbers seem to me of particular use when we examine the highest and lowest concentrations within a specific category. They give an indication as to the goods that left the towns and those that entered the towns. That also goes for the rendering or receiving of services. The high standard deviation in the category pottery confirms that production was primarily restricted to Maastricht. A comparison of the standards per category throughout time, may reveal that the concentrations dropped only to increase in other towns. This indicates a regional specialization. In the period 1889-1909, this is evident of, for instance, category 9, the shoe-industry, which was transferred to some towns in Brabant. Similarly, the rise of Groningen as a national clothing-centre, became apparent very gradually in the same period. The divisions in category 29-32 reveal less in this connection, since most of the labor force here represents the military.

The longer the series of concentration numbers become, the more conclusions can be made. Unfortunately, the few labor censuses that were held before 1889 are not very reliable. Perhaps of good use are the figures concerning license fees that have been preserved by many towns. Information about professions can also be found in nineteenth century registries.

Such series constitute only one brick in the reconstruction of a town system. In this case, they represent merely an example, and hopefully, can be related to facts and approaches which have been produced elsewhere. Combined together, it ought to yield, in the end, a picture of urbanization in which not only people, but also towns occupy a central place.

REFERENCES

Alexandersson, G. The industrial structure of American cities (Stockholm, 1956).
Baudet, H., J.W. Drukker, P. Kooij, H. van der Meulen, S. de Vries, W.G. Whitney, Innovation and consumer demand (Groningen 1974).
Berry, B.J.L. and A.R. Pred Central place studies, a bibliography of theory and application (Philadelphia, 1961).
Berry, B.J.L. Growth centers in the American urban system (Cambridge, 1973).
Buursink, J. Centraliteit en hiërarchie (Assen, 1971).
Christaller, W. Die zentralen Orte in Süddeutschland (Jena, 1933).
Conzen, M.P. 'A transportation interpretation of the growth of urban regions', Journal of historical geography (1975) pp. 361-382.
Diamond, W. 'On the danger of an urban interpretation of history' in E.F. Goldman (ed.) Historiography and urbanization (Baltimore, 1941).
Dijk, H. van, Rotterdam 1810-1880 (Rotterdam, 1976).
Dijk, H. van, 'Urbanization and social change in the Netherlands during the nineteenth century' in Proceedings of the seventh international economic history congress (Edinburgh, 1978) pp. 101-107.
Dyos, H.J. 'Agenda for urban historians' in H.J. Dyos (ed.) The study of urban history (London, 1968).
Eldridge, H.T. 'The process of urbanization' in 'Social forces' (1942) repr. in J.J. Spengler and O.D. Duncan (eds.) Demographic analysis (Glencoe Ill. 1956) pp. 338-343.
Fisher, F.J. 'London as an engine of economic growth' in J.S. Bromley and E.H. Kossmann (eds.) Britain and the Netherlands, vol. IV (The Hague, 1971) pp. 3-17.
Gans, H. 'Urbanism and suburbanism as ways of life' in A. Rose (ed.) Human behavior and social processes (Boston, 1942).
Hägerstrand, T. Innovation diffusion as a spatial process (Chicago, 1967).
Handlin, O. 'The modern city as a field of historical study' in O. Handlin and J. Burchard (eds.) The historian and the city (Cambridge Mass., 1963), pp. 1-26.
Hauser, Ph. 'Urbanization: an overview' in Ph.M. Hauser and L.F. Schnore (eds.) The study of urbanization (New York, 1965) pp. 1-47.
Herlihy, D. 'Urbanization and social change' in Proceedings of the seventh international economic history congress (Edinburgh, 1978) pp. 55-74.
Hoekveld, G. 'Theoretische aanzetten ten behoeve van het samenstellen van maatschappijhistorische modellen van de verhouding van stad en platteland in de nieuwe geschiedenis van Noordwest-Europa', Economisch en sociaalhistorisch Jaarboek (Den Haag, 1975) pp. 1-48.

Jefferson, M. 'The law of the primate city', Geographical review (1939) pp. 226-233.
Jonge, J.A. de, De industrialisatie in Nederland tussen 1850 en 1914 (Amsterdam, 1968).
Keuning, H.J. 'Proeve van een economische hiërarchie van de Nederlandse steden', Tijdschrift voor Economische en Sociale Geografie (1948) pp. 566-582.
Knights, P.R., The plain people of Boston 1830-1860 (New York, 1971).
Kooij, P. 'Stadsgeschiedenis en de verhouding stad-platteland' in Economisch en sociaalhistorisch jaarboek (Den Haag, 1975) pp. 134-141.
Lampard, E. 'The history of cities in the economically advanced areas' in Economic development and cultural change (1954/55) pp. 81-137.
Lampard, E. 'Urbanization and social change' in O. Handlin and J. Burchard (eds.) The historian and the city (Cambridge Mass., 1963) pp. 225-248.
Lampard, E. 'Historical aspects of urbanization' in Ph.M. Hauser and L.F. Schnore (eds.) The study of urbanization (New York, London, Sydney, 1965) pp. 519-554.
Lampard, E. 'The evolving system of cities in the United States' in H.S. Perloff and L. Wingo (eds.) Issues in urban economics (Baltimore, 1968) pp. 81-139.
Lampard, E. 'The urbanizing world' in H.J. Dyos and M. Wolff (eds.) The victorian city (London, 1973) pp. 3-58.
Öhngren, B. 'Urbanization and social change' in Proceedings of the seventh international economic history congress (Edinburgh, 1978) pp. 75-82.
Pred. A.R. The spatial dynamics of U.S. urban-industrial growth' 1800-1914 (Cambridge Mass., 1966).
Pred, A.R. 'Large city interdependence and the pre-electronic diffusion of innovations in the United States' in L.F. Schnore (ed.) The new urban history (Princeton, 1975) pp. 51-75.
Robson, B.T. Urban growth, an approach (London, 1973).
Schlesinger, A.M. The rise of the city (New York, 1933).
Schnore, L.F. (ed.) The new urban history (Princeton, 1975).
Schnore, L.F. 'Urban history and the social sciences: An uneasy marriage', Journal of urban history (1975) pp. 395-409.
Thernstrom, S. 'Reflections on the new urban history', Daedalus (1971) pp. 359-375.
Turner, R.E. 'The industrial city and cultural change' in C.F. Ware (ed.) The cultural approach to history (New York, 1940) pp. 228-242.
Vries, H. de, Landbouw en bevolking in Friesland tijdens de agrarische depressie (Wageningen, 1971)
Vries, Jan de, 'Barges and capitalism, Passenger transportation in the Dutch economy 1632-1839', A.A.G. Bijdragen no. 21 (Wageningen, 1978) pp. 33-398.

Vries, Joh. de, <u>Amsterdam - Rotterdam, Rivaliteit in economisch-historisch perspectief</u> (Bussum, 1965).

Vuuren, L. van, <u>Rapport betreffende een onderzoek naar de sociaal-economische structuur van een gebied in de provincie Utrecht</u> (Utrecht, 1938).

Warner jr., S.B. <u>Streetcar suburbs, The process of growth in Boston, 1870-1900</u> (Cambridge Mass., 1962).

Warner jr., S.B., S. Fleisch, <u>Measurements for social history</u> (London, 1977).

Weber, A.F. <u>The growth of cities in the nineteenth century</u> (New York, 1899).

Wirth, L. 'Urbanism as a way of life', <u>The American journal of sociology</u> (1938) pp. 1-24.

2. Urbanisation and economic development in the western world: some provisional conclusions of an empirical study
P. Bairoch

2.1. Introduction	63
2.2. Levels of urbanisation and the beginning of the industrial revolution	64
2.3. Economic development and urbanisation: strong and evident links	65
2.4. Urbanisation and economic development in the 19th and the 20th century: some certitudes but also a number of uncertainties	68

2. Urbanisation and economic development in the western world: some provisional conclusions of an empirical study
P. Bairoch

2.1. Introduction

Since this text is largely based on a chapter from a broader study, it is proper to first discuss the latter. The starting point was a course, given for three years at the University of Geneva between 1974 and 1978 under the title "Urbanisation and Economic Development". Enlarged by a large amount of complementary empirical research, it has been transformed into a book to appear in 1980 (Bairoch, P.: "La ville et le développement économique dans l'histoire. De l'origine des cités à l'explosion urbaine du Tiers-Monde"). The special character of the book leads it to be something between a research study and a general survey of the problem. Furthermore, since there are virtually no available general histories of urbanisation, this was also incorporated.

When I had to decide on contribution to this congress, I was faced with a dilemma: either to present a specific aspect of the above-mentioned book which would have been too narrow, or to discuss a broader issue, which, in many views, should be considered as provisory. I chose the latter. So this paper presents the conclusion of part three of the book which is devoted to the relationship between urbanisation and economic development of the Western world. The other parts of the study deal with the origins of the urbanisation processes; the evolution of Europe between the 5th and 18th century, and the Third World before, during and after colonisation.

But even limited to the Western world and the period from 1700 to 1980, this text has to tackle a very broad range of subjects. This also means that I will not be able to provide here all the underlying arguments which were presented in the 8 chapters that make up the part whose conclusions are here presented. Furthermore, some aspects of the research are still to be completed. To simplify, I have chosen chronological order.
I will begin with the role of urbanisation in the industrial revolution, then on to the relation between development and urbanisation, and, finally, to the more delicate problem of the impact of urbanisation on development.

2.2. Levels of urbanisation and the beginning of the industrial revolution

Two key questions can be asked here. What has been the role of urbanisation on the starting of the English industrial revolution? What has been the role of urbanisation in the process of international transmission of this industrial revolution? Let us start with question one, and with an important fact.

In the period which preceded the numerous upheavals and transformations linked to the industrial revolution, England, the "cradle" country, was not the most urbanised among the advanced European countries. On the contrary, it can be estimated that around 1700 the level of English urbanisation was lower than that of the Netherlands, Portugal, Italy and probably Spain. It was on the same level as France. London shared with Paris the rank of being the largest European city. But, the share of London in the total English population was below that of Lisbon in Portugal and Amsterdam in the Netherlands. This is already a strong indication that urbanisation was not the major element in the onset of the industrial revolution.

This conclusion is reinforced by the analysis of urbanisation trends. It is not the traditional network of cities which was the basis of the new industrialisation process. The opposite is true, this process was essentially located in very small towns or villages, which obviously later became big cities. Between 1700 and 1800, London's annual growth rate was only 0.6 per cent, and this rate was the same for the combined population of the six other biggest cities whose individual size in 1700 ranged from 12 to 30 thousand inhabitants. But, if we follow the six villages or small cities which became the main industrial cities during the industrial revolution, we see that their growth rate was of 2.0 per cent. Furthermore, a summary of the literature on the causes of the English industrial revolution, show an almost complete absence of any emphasis on the urban factor.

It is interesting to note that the same absence of the traditional urban network can be traced in the process of development of the other Western countries. Things become even more interesting if we realise that almost all the countries that had an early take-off (England, France, Belgium, Switzerland, the United States) had rather low levels of urbanisation. Where among the late comers, we find a majority of highly urbanised countries (Spain, Italy, Netherlands and Portugal). Furthermore, among the countries which stood between those and who achieved the highest level of industrialisation, we find countries which began this process with very low urbanisation levels (Germany and Sweden).

From this can we deduce that the industrial revolution owns nothing to the urban world? Such an extreme position could indeed be reinforced by the fact that this industrial revolution first started in agriculture. Let us remember that in England

the agricultural revolution preceded the industrial upheaval
by 40 - 50 years. Much of this upheaval was initiated by the
agricultural revolution. But such a position is certainly too
extreme. Urbanisation as a socio-economic phenomena has certainly contributed to the eclosion of the industrial revolution, and to its international diffusion. Technical innovations
have arisen and were diffused more often in urban than rural
settings. This is a proven fact. More subtle, however, is the
question of the urban contribution to agricultural progress.
The Dutch and other examples where urban population pressure
did not lead to a real agricultural revolution, strongly reduces the probability that this kind of pressure was a sufficient
element or the major cause of the agricultural revolution.
The English case reinforces the arguments of a rather limited
role for the city. However, it would be not only excessive but
also totally aberrant to rule out any contribution of urbanisation to the agricultural revolution.

But if, as I said, the city leads to innovation (and to
its diffusion) how can the negative impact of urbanisation on
the period of take-off and on the levels of industrialisation
be explained? Obviously, a lot of problems remain to be solved
before a somewhat final answer can be given to the question.
The probable answer to this paradox lies in the levels of urbanisation. In those cases, we probably have to draw upon the
modern notions of hyperurbanisation or overurbanisation. Spain,
Portugal, Italy and the Netherlands had, during the 18th and
the first half of the 19th century, levels of urbanisation
(and also the presence of large cities) which no longer corresponded to the original economic function of urbanisation.
Those cases are in many ways similar to those of the Third
World during the last 2 - 3 decades. But if the causes of their
overurbanisation are not similar (even if they are close in
certain aspects), the consequences are roughly the same. It is
obvious that such high levels of urbanisation have limited the
possibilities of productive investment, especially in the new
sectors. Consumption demand from cities or even construction
needs have absorbed a too large share of resources. High levels
of urbanisation also imply urban under-employment, and therefore lower productivity on the whole economy. This under-employment also leads to a too large tertiary sector, and therefore to rigidity in the offer and mobility of the labour force.

2.3. Economic development and urbanisation: strong and evident links

The linkage between the huge progress achieved by agricultural
productivity since the industrial revolution and the jump in
the level of urbanisation, is an evident one. Despite all the
successive advances made by ancient civilisations and by those
of Europe and Asia, the most advanced agricultural techniques
in the 18th century still had to mobilise some 70 - 75 per

cent of the labour force, just to produce food and agricultural raw material (mainly textiles). Or, said in other words, the proportion of labour population that was able to perform other activities could not exceed 20 - 30 per cent. This implies that in the absence of massive food imports (which was the rule in big entities) the urbanisation level could not be higher than some 20 per cent. This is based on a definition of urbanisation for settlements of over 2000 inhabitants. Otherwise 15 per cent would be the limit if the level was 5000 as is used (arbitrarily in some cases) in this study for the period after the industrial revolution.

I said above that the rule for big entities (in this context for countries of over 4 - 5 million inhabitants) was self-sufficiency in food. In fact, I should have spoken of an impossibility of a different situation, since in view of the general level of agricultural productivity, there were no large amounts of food available anywhere for exports. Only small countries with exceptional resources could, by mobilizing low food surpluses of large regions, import large shares of their food consumption. This was especially the case of the Netherlands in the 17th century, where urban population represented some 40 per cent of total population. But, in order to achieve such a level of urbanisation, this country had to import huge quantities of cereals. By using the data of professor De Vries (who is attending the conference) one can conclude that those imports were sufficient to feed some 50 per cent of the total population - and those cereals came from regions whose population (and even more so in terms of area) was 20 - 30 times greater than the Netherlands. Netherlands had then some 1.9 million inhabitants or 1.4 per cent of that of Europe including Russia. Thanks to such imports, some 55 - 70 per cent of the Dutch labor force could be employed in non-agricultural sectors.

In the other European countries which had no exceptional commercial orientations as well as in the advanced countries of traditional Asia, the proportion of non agricultural labour force had never exceeded, before the industrial revolution, 20 - 30 per cent. The proportion of urban population was never greater than 12 - 15 per cent. On the macro-regional levels, i.e. such as Europe and the large countries of Asia, the proportion of the non-agricultural labour force had never exceeded 15 - 20 per cent, and the proportion of city dwellers 10 - 13 per cent.

In England as early as 1820, and without any sizable imports of food product, non-agricultural labour accounted for some 70 per cent, and the level of urbanisation was in the order of 30 per cent (32 - 33 per cent if the 2000 criterium is used). In what was in 1913 the developed world, i.e. Western Europe and the countries of European settlement, already half of the population was in cities, and this without any external food import (for this region as a whole, the deficit of Europe being compensated by the excess of the rest of the developed world).

Statistical analysis confirms for the 19th century the exceptionally close links between levels of economic development and levels of urbanisation. This relationship can be better established than before because I have elaborated new series both on real per capita GNP and on urbanisation levels. The coefficient of linear correlation between those two variables provides very high and significant figures, and this for all periods for which such calculations could be performed (thus for the 19th century: 1800, 1850, 1880 and 1910).

If this calculation is restricted to the 14 European countries for which the estimates of urbanisation levels are fairly good, the result lies between a minimum of 0.68 for 1800 and a maximum of 0.89 for 1900, with an average of 0.83 for the other 3 periods. If the other developed countries are included (including the non European ones), the relation becomes less strict, but remains highly significative. For 22 countries, the coefficient of regression varies from a minimum of 0.46 for 1850 to a maximum of 0.67 for 1880; average for the other 3 periods: 0.65. Thus, it appears that inside Europe and from the 1850's, already differences in the level of economic development can explain some 60 - 70 per cent of the differences in urbanisation levels. The remaining 30 - 40 per cent being due to a large set of factors ranging from the levels of industrialisation to the size of the country, from the topography to the form of government, from the volume of foreign trade to its composition, etc., etc.

As one can expect, the relation between economic development and urbanisation in terms of evolution, whether based on a country or on a larger region is even much stronger. To illustrate this, here are the coefficients of regression for the developed countries. For the five periods, if Portugal is excepted, the average for the 22 countries is 0.97 (with a very limited dispersion: a coefficient of variation of only 2.6 per cent).

After 1930, and even more so after 1960, the relation between economic development and urbanisation becomes less strong, but remains significant. For 28 countries, the coefficient of correlation is 0.67 for 1930, 0.57 for 1950 and of 0.53 for 1970. Such an evolution can be expected expecially in view of the existence of an absolute limit for the urbanisation level and the absence of such limit as far as development is concerned. Already around 1950, a certain number of countries had reached a level of urbanisation which, although not very close to the absolute limit of 100 per cent, constitute a kind of real threshold limit, especially if we take into account new attitudes of the population toward urban life.

2.4. Urbanisation and economic development in the 19th and 20th century: some certetudes but also a number of uncertainties

2.4.1. Technical innovations and the city

From the impact of economic development on urbanisation, let us go over to the impact of urbanisation on development. A first and important certitude: the urban contribution to technical innovations. The city is without any doubt a factor of innovation, and this both from creative and diffusion aspects. The modalities and the causes of this innovative function of urban life are numerous and well known. Let us give a short summary of them. Higher population density facilitates contacts, and therefore leads to accelerated flows of information. The heterogeneity of urban activities leads to attempts to adopt or apply to one sector (or to a specific problem) solutions already used in another sector. The city has always concentrated the educational activities and institutions which have always combined education, if not with research in its modern expression, at least with reflections. The urban milieu is a natural shelter for original individuals who fit badly in rural societies where conformism is as a rule stricter. Last but not least, the city is the place of contact above all with other cities, through trade or migration of artisans, workers and managers, inter-rural migrations are much lesser frequent.

And since professor Robson is among us, let us recall that his findings for England fully confirm the previously available studies which have shown that the size of the city (together with proximity) plays a very important role in the spatial diffusion of innovation. In our department, a study was carried out which yielded to similar conclusions. Its object was to compare the structure of the sizes of the settlements where the most important innovators were born, and where they lived at the moment of their most important invention to the average size structure of cities. This was done for the 19th century for Great Britain, France and Germany.

All this and other more minor elements, lead to a unchallengeable conclusion: the city leads to more innovation, and especially to more technical innovation. The city favors the spread of those innovations. And, since the positive impact of innovations on economic development can be hardly questioned, the city is, through this channel, a factor of economic development.

2.4.2. Urban technical innovations and agricultural development

After this very certain aspect of urbanisation, let us go over to an area where there subsists a lot of uncertainties. It brings us in the heart of a very crucial problem, i.e. the effects of urbanisation on agriculture. Agriculture has certainly benefited from numerous technical innovations whose origins were urban. On one hand, we have those general technical changes which found obvious applications in agriculture. On the other hand, there are specifically agriculturally oriented innovations, but which have been developed in urban settings. Let us look at a few examples of each of these.

The story of general urban devised techniques with rural fall out is a very old one. It can be said that it begins at the very first stages of urbanisation with, among other, writing and metallurgy. But let us skip the traditional societies to stick with the beginning of the industrial revolution. Already, the two major innovations of this period had major fall out on agriculture. The most important is the production of iron with coal instead of wood. This leads to a very sharp decrease of iron's price, and moreover brought a sizeable improvement in the terms of trade of agricultural product versus iron manufactures. As an example of this, one can compare the wholesale price of wheat to that of iron. In France, around 1790, a kilo of wheat could buy 0.6 kg of iron, in 1850 the figures had already increased to 0.9 kg, and in 1914 it stood at 1.4 kg.

The price decline stemming from this and other technical innovations allowed a wider use of iron in traditional agricultural implements, as well as the development of entirely new implements. This led without any doubt, to an increase in the productivity of agriculture, even if other factors such as continuous crop rotation and seed selections had wider impacts. The impact on agriculture of the mechanization of spinning is less obvious, and therefore retains some unknown elements. When back in 1963 I tried to define the mechanism which accompanied the industrial revolution without having any specific interest in the problem dealt with here, I came to the conclusion that this mechanization had wide repercussions on agriculture. To simplify matters, it worked the following way: mechanization of spinning lead to the disappearance of rural textile activities. This disappearance had different consequences according to the characteristics of the "farms" where hand-spinning was done. In the farms which were on marginal lands with low productivity, this led in many cases to a total withdrawal from agricultural activities. On the contrary, on farms where the land was richer, most of the time previously devoted to textiles was transferred to agriculture. The obvious outcome of such a shift is an increase in average agricultural productivity.

Before passing to the so called "second" agricultural revolution, we have also to wonder whether the other very important innovations that took place in agriculture during the "first" agricultural revolution were connected to urban setting. Here there remains a lot of uncertainties as to which extent the methods used in seed and animal selection did not benefit largely or even derive exclusively from the general scientific movement of the 16th and the 17th centuries in which the city played a big role. The same question holds for the improvements in crop rotation. All this seems very probable but not certain, since history of technology shows us empirical groping has played, here as in industry, a key role.

With the technical innovations of the second agricultural revolution, one can be more affirmative. Let us recall that this revolution starts around 1840 - 1870, and that its main component was the introduction of real agricultural machinery and of artificial fertilizers. Let us see each of those.

And let us begin with fertilizers where the urban contribution was determinant. However, one should not neglect even in this case the empirical component which was essentially rural. Let us recall as an example the very ancient practice of marling (incorporation of clay in sandy lands). Despite such reservations there is no doubt that artificial fertilizers which began to be used in the second half of the 19th century, and which have played a key role in the European increase of yields, stem directly from progress in chemistry. Practically all names linked to this development are from the scientific world (in general University professors) and were strongly integrated in urban settings. This holds true for those who paved the way (Lavoisier, Cavendish, Hermbstadt and Thaer and not forgetting Palissy), as well for those scientists who have more directly taken part in the development of chemical fertilizers (Boussingault, Lawes, Liebig and Ville).

For the first phases of agricultural mechanization, the urban contribution is less overwhelming. The machines involved implied at least till the end of the 19th century, not enough complex principles to be beyond the reach of empirical inventors. Therefore, rural inventors could play a more important part. As an example, let us quote the case of McCormick who had been brought up in a farm where his father tried (and often succeeded) to develop various farm machinery among which the famous reaping-machine which McCormick junior improved and made really operational. Other such examples can be quoted. However, at a very early stage, production and further improvement of equipment became an urban activity. And, furthermore, without previous progress in metal production techniques and metal working procedures, those agricultural innovations would have encountered more problems, and this would have without any doubt retarded them.

The influence of chemistry on agriculture brings us directly to the 20th century, and even more so to the second half of this century. It is without doubt that the unprecedented rate of growth of yields and of productivity which agriculture experienced these last 30 - 40 years, is largely due to pecticides and herbicides (and obviously also to fertilizers), and that those products stem directly from research and even from fundamental research. Also of urban origin is the motivation and development of the petrol engine which have largely benefited agricultural machinery. Tractors owe much of their reliability and flexibility to the prodigious spread of the private car.

And even if the car was in the beginning and especially in the United States more widely used in rural areas, its development is inconceivable outside urban life. Besides, if we take the names of the innovators associated with the automobile, we see a predominance of the city. Although Ford did not leave his native farm till he was 16 to go to work as a mechanic apprentice, mechanics had been his passion (and we should not forget that vanadium steel was a very important element in the model T). And, with very few exceptions, the other automobile pioneers were all townsmen.

The car should not make us forget another transportation innovation which had a positive impact on agriculture: the railway. Even if it is obvious that for some regions the railway brought more problems than benefits to agriculture, the overall balance sheet was a positive one. First, there was (as it was the case with the impact of textile mechanization) a concentration effect: production tended to concentrate in areas best fitted. This was a global as well as a product shift process. Global: the major thing here was a transfer of a large share of European food agriculture and cattle breeding to the vast areas of temperate America and Oceania. Products: it was a process of regional concentration in production, each region getting more specialised, which brought increases in yields and productivity, but also in many cases social problems. Furthermore, on a more general basis, railways allowed more easy access to urban markets, and also larger possibilities of bringing machinery and especially fertilizers and other chemical goods to the farms. If we take the case of France, a moderate consumer of these chemical products, we see that agriculture used yearly around 1913 some 2.8 million tons of these products. This would have represented, if we suppose an average transportation distance of 300 km, a mobilisation during the entire year of some 300,000 horses and 150,000 men (this based on a rather high parameter: 300 kg and 30 km per day per horse, or 2,800 ton/kilometers per year).

To finish this section, let's deal with what is considered as an important contribution of urbanisation to agriculture in the first stages of the industrial revolution: the demand factor. There is no doubt that urban demand had a positive impact on the flow of agricultural goods. However, one should not overestimate this. The first element to be considered is the fact that there is not much difference in demand increases occurring from a larger urban population size than from a same larger rural population (the per capita consumption being more or less equal). Furthermore, till the beginning of the XXth century, city life was leading to smaller demographic growth through higher mortality and lower fertility. On the other hand, the spread of very liberal commercial politics as far as import of food is concerned, in the years beginning with the 1860's were diverting a large part of the demand accruing from European urban population to the wide land areas of overseas. This led to a decrease in grain prices which in some cases may have been an incentive to further progress. But judging from the changes in rate of growth of yield figures, this was far from being the general response. The progress in the average yields was greater after the reintroduction (around the first half of the 1890's) of more protective practices than during the free trade period. But, from a more general view, urbanisation in the 19th century and expecially in the second half of the 19th century, led to an increase in food demand without an increase of active population on the land, and this can be an important positive factor for progress in agricultural productivity. So, if on the demand side, urbanisation did not probably play, in the first phases of development as important a role as generally assumed, it does not mean that its effect on agriculture was nil or overall negative. It is very probable that the general outcome of the various aspects of urbanisation was positive for agriculture.

To a certain extent, one can assume that urban demand effect had been much more important after 1910 - 1920 than before. Beginning with those years, the rapid increase of average income (especially after World War II) combined with the already high share of urban population, resulted in a strong increase in demand of more elaborated agricultural products: milk, meat, vegetables, fruits, etc.. This was certainly a leading factor in the mutation of agriculture in the developed countries. But at this point of the economic evolution, agriculture is only one sector among others of those developed societies: in 1930 already agriculture occupies only 30 per cent of the total employment of Western Europe and only 23 per cent of North America.

2.4.3. The city and money

To the extent to which one considers that monetisation of the economy favors economic development, the city has without any doubt played a positive role. The rural world is above all a place where auto-consumption and barter exchange prevails. The urban world is a market world, and therefore a system where money is used widely. Besides, here industrialisation was as important as urbanisation. Indeed as long as industry was in the artisanal stage, three series of elements reduced the extent of the monetary system. The first is linked to the limited importance of manufactured goods in total consumption. Two: a substantial proportion of manufactured production was carried out by people whose main occupation was agriculture, and whose product was to a large extent intended for self-consumption. Finally, urban artisans also channeled part of their output through barter exchanges. It is obvious that with industrialisation the situation changed radically. The whole structure of the market underwent profound transformations leading among other things to almost total disappearance of rural industries, and of barter exchange.

2.4.4. The city and social mobility

To the ancient European proverb "City's air makes one free", one could add another one as valid especially for post-industrial period: "City's air favors social upward mobility". Without any doubt, the urban world is more favorable than the rural one to social mobility, whether horizontal or vertical.

Horizontal mobility: the mere fact of emigration to the city implied ipso facto a change in the occupational area. But the essential element is elsewhere. It resides in the possibilities offered by moving from one sector to another of the various urban occupational categories not only in industry but also in services. It also became possible to move within various firms of the same sector. Such mobility is much harder to achieve in agriculture both for the independant peasant and the wage earner.

Vertical mobility: this also is wide ranging. Inside a particular sector and inside a firm, the scope of promotions is much larger than in rural settings. The passage from blue collar to white collar, even inside the same sector, can also be considered as a substantial promotion, even if this is often more subjective than real. The educational world has a dual role: social promotion thanks to the education received, and social promotion also thanks to the rapid increase of jobs in this sector. Very often social promotion preceded migration. Becoming a schoolteacher for a peasant girl or boy meant often the necessity of emigration to the city.

Social mobility not counting its own virtue, is favourable to economic development since it leads on the average to better adequation between offer and demand of the qualified labour force. These positive aspects should not forget the other side of the coin which was really negative especially during the first phases of industrialisation. These phases combined limited overall progress compared to traditional societies and the absence of social laws. This was more or less the case until 1860 - 1880. During these phases, the shift from rural to urban life meant in most of the cases a loss of individual freedom since many emigrants became low skilled factory workers. It also implied longer working hours (on a yearly basis) and less favourable housing conditions. All this explains largely why urban mortality was so much higher than rural. Emigration to a city usually meant reducing by some 50 per cent the life expectancy of babies and by some 25 per cent that of the 15 - 20 age group.

2.4.5. The city and the market size for industrials goods

The general accepted view is that by concentrating more population, cities became progressively during the XIXth century, important markets. The rise of very big cities may lead us to infer such an evolution. As early as 1850, the 5 cities of over

500 thousand inhabitants that existed in Europe had a combined population higher than the total population around 1700 of the actual four Scandinavian countries plus Portugal and Switzerland. And, in 1900, the 9 cities of over a million inhabitants of the developed world had a population exceeding the abovementioned countries plus Belgium, Holland, England, Scotland, Ireland and the 5 Balkanic countries. Thus 9 cities in 1900 having a bigger population than 16 countries in 1700.

Let us recall that during the urban expansion of the 16 th and 17th centuries, the increase in the size of the cities had stimulated division of labour inside the cities, since they became by themselves a sufficiently large market for a wide variety of manufactured products and especially luxury goods. But, can we estimate that the same pattern took place during the 19 th century? I am not convinced of that since an important element is omitted which leads to increase the size of needed market of each individual industry. In fact, during the 16 th and 17 th centuries, there was an increase in the size of urban market without any fundamental change of technology, whereas in the 19 th century technology developed more substantially than the size of urban markets. As an example, let us take the iron industry. In the beginning of the 18th century, an average plant had a production capacity which represented the average consumption of some 100 - 200 thousand persons. Despite the fact that between this period and the end of the 19th century, per capita consumption of iron in Europe had been multiplied by 40 or 50, an average plant of the end of the 19th century did cover the needs of some 600 - 800 thousand people, thus five times more than in the beginning of the 18th century. Now, meanwhile, the average size of European cities has been at most multiplied by 3, if the 2 thousand inhabitants limit is used, or by 2.8 if the 5 thousands limit is used. The iron industry may not be representative of the average of the other industrial sectors. But, since there is a lack of knowledge about them, it is difficult to know which extent things were really different in the other sectors.

An interesting indirect approach can be provided by analyzing optimal sizes of industrial plants. For contemporary periods (in developed countries), if we except a few sectors such as the automobile industry, and steel production, this optimum level is not as high as generally assumed, but it is however much higher than in the pre-industrial period. According to data which we have assembled for another study, the dominant optimal size is around a working force of 600 - 800 persons (and average optimal size for the 50 per cent of the sectors where this is the highest: some 800 - 1000 persons). If account is taken of a full set of parameters, it can be estimated that a city of some 50 - 70 thousand inhabitants could provide enough labour force for an adequate number e.i. ten plants of near optimum size. From another angle, the outlet provided by the city's consumers is a much higher figure. For average manufactured goods, consumption representing 35 per cent of the total, a city of some 150 - 200 thousand is needed as an outlet for a dozen plants. For obvious reasons (such as the impossibility to limit the consumer's choice), it is totally irrational to consider that a city will remain a closed system. But as a working hypothesis, it is meaningful to compare the situation at two different historical periods.

Knowing the difficulties of assessing optimal sizes for the actual situation, one can easily see the quasi impossibility of repeating such estimates for traditional societies. However, if we use as a proxi the dominant sizes, there can be no doubt that the optimal size was below the 20 - 30 persons mark. But even taking a figure close to the above, and by assuming a 10 - 12 per cent manufactured goods share of consumption, and returning the same other parameters, ten "plants" of a size close to optimum are needed as an outlet for a city of some 10 - 15 thousand inhabitants. Thus ten times less than around 1970, where meanwhile the average city size has only been multiplied by three. However, even more meaningful is the fact that the share of urban European population living in cities above 15 thousand and around 1700 and those living in cities above 200 thousand in 1970, is the same (in fact the calculation yielded in each case exactly 66 per cent).

So, through this approach, as for the case of the iron industry, a rather paradoxical outcome is reached: technological evolution led probably to sharper increase in size of the market needed by industries than the increase in average city size, and close to the increase in the dominant size of cities. So, if we except the upper share of cities - let us say those of more than 500 thousand in the 19th century, and those above the million in the 20th century - it appears very unlikely that the city became - more than was the case before, through its concentration of population - a better outlet for industries, and by this became a more important factor of development. The contrary is even possible, if not probable, especially since I have overestimated the optimal size of plants in traditional societies. So, finally, the growth of city size has not been an important factor for the outlet of the industrial sector. However, if such an increase had not taken place, production rationalisation and the introduction of new technologies would have been harder. But, the urban component was not the leading element.

Let us now try to provide a concise general conclusion on the links of urbanisation and economic development in the first phases of the industrial revolution. These have been clearly positive ones. Urbanisation has helped the process of Western development, even if empirical analysis leads us to nuance some of the previous generalisations. However, there exists a large number of "unknowns": work for generations of historians on the complex urban process.

3. Patterns of urbanization in pre—industrial Europe, 1500—1800
J. de Vries

3.1. Introduction	79
3.2. The data and their transformation	79
3.3. The contours of European urbanization	81
3.4. City size distribution over time	89
3.5. An analysis of the patterns of urbanization	96
3.6. Comparative perspectives	105
3.7. Conclusions	108
References	109

3. Patterns of urbanization in pre—industrial Europe, 1500—1800
J. de Vries

3.1. Introduction

This paper is the first report on a project seeking to describe and analyse the pre-modern urbanization of Europe between 1500 and 1800. In the literature of economic, urban, and demographic history frequent reference is made to the broad contours of Europe's urban population. But the available information tends to be specific to particular cities, or, at most, single countries. No general statistical description of European urbanization exists.* This paper presents the data base on which the larger study of Europe's urban growth rests, identifies the broad contours of European urbanization, and concludes with several analytical and interpretive observations about the factors influencing European growth.

3.2. The data and their transformation

The project's first and most time-consuming task was to assemble a data base of population estimates for all cities of at least 10,000 inhabitants at 50-year intervals from 1500 to 1800.

---

* What I have in mind is the sort of analysis presented for European urbanization after 1800 by the classic work of Adna Ferrin Weber, The Growth of Cities in the Nineteenth Century. A Study in Statistics (New York, 1899; reprinted Ithaca, New York, 1965). For earlier periods one can turn to Rogier Mols, Introduction à la Démographie historique des villes d'Europe du 14e au 18e siècle, 3 vols. (Louvain, 1955). This work, while compendious, is not systematic. Another compendious, but unsystematic and often uncritial work is Tertius Chandler and Gerald Fox, 3000 Years of Urban Growth (New York, 1974). Paul Bairoch, Taille des villes, conditions de vie et développement économique (Paris, 1977), presents a systematic, but highly aggregative, overview of European urbanization.

The population estimates for each 50-year interval refer to a year within ten years of the date in question. Thus, figures for 1650 are drawn from evidence relating to the period 1640-1660. When such evidence is not available, but other estimates (say, for 1625 and 1680) exist, I interpolated to derive an estimate. If neither sort of evidence exists, the space was left blank.

In order to identify all the cities with at least 10,000 inhabitants, the national censuses held by most countries around 1800 served as a benchmark. Three hundred sixty-three cities then met the minimum criterion for inclusion. Cities which had once had 10,000 inhabitants in the period since 1500, but no longer did so in 1800 also belong in the data set. I have succeeded in identifying fifteen such cities, but it is easily possible that some have been missed. As a consequence, the information presented here may be biased to slightly overestimate the rate of urban growth over the time period.

Altogether, then, the date base consists of the 378 cities which contained at least 10,000 inhabitants at some point in the period 1500-1800 and are located in that portion of Europe that might best be described as Latin Christendom. Hungary, which should be included in such a Europe, is excluded because of the difficulty of gaining information for the sixteenth and seventeenth centuries. The Baltic states are also excluded. Much of the analysis is based on a still more restrictive definition of Europe, in which Poland and the Austrian lands are also excluded. This more restrictive Europe is, in turn, divided into three zones: "North and West" (Benelux, the British Isles, and Scandinavia), "Central" (France, Germany, and Switzerland), and "Mediterranean" (Italy and Iberia).

To be complete, the data base should include 2646 observations (378 cities x 7 observations). This ideal has not been attained; altogether 445 spaces, 17 percent of the total, had to be left blank. Unfortunately, these lacunae are not distributed evenly across space and time. Table 3.1 displays the distribution of unknowns by country and year. It shows that the unknowns are concentrated in the earlier years, as one would expect, and in two countries: France and Spain.

The next step was to divide the data base into size categories (see Table 3.2 for definitions) and to assign the unknown cases to their most likely categories. For example, a city whose population in 1500 was 11,000 and in 1650 was 18,000, but whose population in the intervening years is unknown, would be assigned to category 1 (10-19 thousand) as long as the city's history offered no reason to believe otherwise. Not all cases were as straightforward as this example, but following these procedures the 445 unknowns were each assigned to a category. The distribution of assignments is displayed in Table 3.3 There it is apparent that the great majority of unknown cases involved the smaller cities. (The higher categories are populated exclusively by the elusive Andalusian cities of Granada and Cordoba.) Consequently, errors in assignment may affect the

Table 3.1: Number of unknown Cities by Country and Year

Code	Country	Number of Cases	1500	1550	1600	1650	1700	1750	1800
1	Scandinavia	6	0	0	1	1	1	0	0
2	England	44	0	0	2	2	0	2	0
3	Scotland	8	1	1	0	2	1	0	0
4	Ireland	8	0	0	0	0	0	2	0
5	The Netherlands	21	0	0	0	0	0	0	0
6	Belgium	20	1	1	5	2	2	0	0
7	Germany	55	3	8	8	7	7	11	0
8	France	77	28	34	32	35	0	3	0
9	Switzerland	4	0	0	0	1	0	1	0
10	North Italy	36	12	4	2	10	12	3	1
11	Central Italy	11	3	1	1	0	0	0	0
12	Southern Italy	29	9	5	3	4	6	6	1
13	Spain	43	33	20	0	19	19	24	0
14	Portugal	5	3	3	3	0	3	1	2
15	Austria	8	3	4	4	3	3	3	0
16	Poland	3	0	0	0	0	1	1	0

Regions

1-6	North and West	107	2	2	8	7	4	4	0
7-9	Central	136	31	42	40	43	7	15	0
10-14	Mediterranean	124	60	33	9	33	40	34	4
15-16	East	11	3	4	4	3	4	4	0
1-16	Europe	378	96	81	65	87	55	57	4

number of cities in category 1, but are unlikely to greatly alter estimates of the total urban population. To demonstrate the implications of this fact, consider the data for 1650. While 27 percent of all cities with 10,000 or more inhabitants were assigned for that year, their small average size had the consequence that only 15 percent of the aggregate urban population was accounted for by cities for which no specific information is available.

Once the assignments were made each of the 378 cities could be identified by size category (0 through 6) for each 50-year interval from 1500 to 1800. Table 3.2 displays this information. (A table displaying the underlying population estimates and a list of the many hundreds of sources on which it is based could not be presented here. These data will be presented in a forthcoming book, tentatively titled Europe's Pre-Modern Urbanization.) Frequency distributions of the size of Europe's cities are displayed in Table 3.4.

3.3. The contours of European urbanization

Of the several thousand settlements in Europe vested with city rights or otherwise acknowledged as urban places in 1500, only 156 were inhabited by 10,000 or more people, and only four contained over 100,000. Italy alone claimed 28 percent of these cities (and three of the four cities with over 100,000).

Table 3.2: Size Categories of European Cities, 1500-1800

Country and Region Codes

Code	Country or Areas	Code	Region
1	Scandinavia	1-6	North and West
2	England and Wales	7-9	Central
3	Scotland	10-14	Mediterranean
4	Ireland	15-16	East
5	The Netherlands		
6	Belgium	1-9* + 15 and 16	Northern
7	Germany	10-14 **	Southern
8	France	1-16	Europe
9	Switzerland		
10	Northern Italy		
11	Central Italy		
12	Southern Italy		
13	Spain		
14	Portugal		
15	Austria and Bohemia		
16	Poland		

* minus Provence and Languedoc in France
** plus Provence and Languedoc in France

Size Categories (all numbers in thousands)

1	10 - 19.9
2	20 - 29.9
3	30 - 39.9
4	40 - 49.9
5	50 - 99.9
6	100 and over
0	Cities under 10,000 inhabitants that at some other time in the period 1500-1800 rise to at least 10,000.

Size categories of European Cities

	city	code	1500	1550	1600	1650	1700	1750	1800
0	Bergen	1	0	0	0	0	0	1	1
1	Copenhagen	1	1	1	1	2	5	5	6
2	Goteburg	1	0	0	0	0	0	0	1
3	Karlskrona	1	0	0	0	0	0	0	1
4	Oslo	1	0	0	0	0	0	0	1
5	Stockholm	1	0	0	1	4	4	5	5
6	Bath	2	0	0	0	0	0	0	3
7	Birmingham	2	0	0	0	0	2	5	
8	Blackburn	2	0	0	0	0	0	0	1
9	Bolton	2	0	0	0	0	0	0	1
10	Bristol	2	1	1	1	2	2	4	5
11	Cambridge	2	0	0	0	0	0	0	1
12	Carlisle	2	0	0	0	0	0	0	1
13	Chatham	2	0	0	0	0	0	0	1
14	Chester	2	0	0	0	0	1	1	1
15	Colchester	2	0	0	0	1	1	0	1
16	Coventry	2	0	0	0	0	0	1	1
17	Derby	2	0	0	0	0	0	0	1
18	Exeter	2	1	0	1	1	1	1	1
19	Greenwich	2	0	0	0	0	0	0	1
20	Hull	2	0	0	0	0	0	0	2
21	Hundersfield	2	0	0	0	0	0	0	1
22	Ipswich	2	0	0	0	0	0	1	1
23	Kings Lynn	2	0	0	0	0	0	0	1
24	Leeds	2	0	0	0	0	0	1	3
25	Leicester	2	0	0	0	0	0	0	1
26	Liverpool	2	0	0	0	0	2	5	
27	London	2	4	5	6	6	6	6	6
28	Manchester	2	0	0	0	0	1	5	
29	Newcastle	2	1	1	1	1	1	2	2
30	Norwich	2	1	1	1	2	2	3	3
31	Nottingham	2	0	0	0	0	1	2	
32	Oldham	2	0	0	0	0	0	0	1
33	Oxford	2	0	0	0	0	0	0	1
34	Plymouth	2	0	0	0	0	0	1	4
35	Portsmouth	2	0	0	0	0	0	1	3
36	Preston	2	0	0	0	0	0	0	1
37	Reading	2	0	0	0	0	0	0	1
38	Salford	2	0	0	0	0	0	0	1
39	Sheffield	2	0	0	0	0	1	1	3
40	Shrewsbury	2	0	0	0	0	1	1	1
41	Stockport	2	0	0	0	0	0	0	1
42	Sunderland	2	0	0	0	0	0	1	2
43	Warrington	2	0	0	0	0	0	0	1
44	Wenlock	2	0	0	0	0	0	0	1
45	Wigan	2	0	0	0	0	0	0	1
46	Wolverhampton	2	0	0	0	0	0	0	1
47	Worcester	2	0	0	0	0	0	1	1
48	Yarmouth	2	0	0	0	1	1	1	1
49	York	2	0	0	1	1	1	1	1
50	Aberdeen	3	0	0	0	0	0	1	2
51	Dundee	3	0	0	0	0	0	1	2
52	Edinburgh	3	1	1	3	3	4	5	5
53	Glasgow	3	0	0	0	0	1	2	5
54	Greenock	3	0	0	0	0	0	0	1
55	Inverness	3	0	0	0	0	0	1	1
56	Paisley	3	0	0	0	0	0	0	1
57	Perth	3	0	0	0	0	0	0	1
58	Belfast	4	0	0	0	0	0	0	2
59	Cork	4	0	0	0	0	2	5	5
60	Dublin	4	0	0	0	1	5	5	6
61	Galway	4	0	0	0	0	0	0	1
62	Limerick	4	0	0	0	0	1	1	3
63	Kilkenny	4	0	0	0	0	0	0	1
64	Newry	4	0	0	0	0	0	0	1
65	Waterford	4	0	0	0	0	0	0	2
66	Alkmaar	5	0	0	1	1	1	0	0
67	Amsterdam	5	1	3	5	6	6	6	6

Table 3.2, page 2

	city	code	1500	1550	1600	1650	1700	1750	1800		city	code	1500	1550	1600	1650	1700	1750	1800
68	Arnhem	5	0	0	0	0	0	0	1	135	Hamburg	7	1	2	4	5	5	5	6
69	Delft	5	1	1	2	2	1	1	1	136	Hannover	7	0	0	0	0	1	1	1
70	Dordrecht	5	1	1	1	2	2	1	1	137	Heidelberg	7	0	0	0	0	0	1	0
71	Enkhuizen	5	0	0	1	2	1	0	0	138	Hildesheim	7	1	0	0	0	0	0	1
72	Gouda	5	1	1	1	1	1	1	1	139	Kassel	7	0	0	0	0	0	0	1
73	Groningen	5	1	1	1	2	2	2	2	140	Koblenz	7	0	0	0	0	0	0	1
74	Haarlem	5	1	1	3	3	3	2	2	141	Koln	7	3	3	4	4	4	4	4
75	The Hague	5	0	0	1	1	3	3	3	142	Koningsburg	7	0	1	2	2	3	5	5
76	'sHertogenbosch	5	1	2	1	1	1	1	1	143	Leipzig	7	1	1	1	1	2	3	3
77	Hoorn	5	0	0	1	1	1	1	1	144	Lubeck	7	2	2	2	3	2	2	2
78	Leeuwarden	5	0	0	1	1	1	1	1	145	Luneburg	7	0	0	0	0	0	0	1
79	Leiden	5	1	1	2	5	5	3	3	146	Magdeburg	7	1	4	4	0	1	1	3
80	Maastricht	5	1	1	1	1	2	1	1	147	Mainz	7	0	0	1	1	2	2	2
81	Middelburg	5	0	0	2	3	2	2	2	148	Mannheim	7	1	1	1	1	1	2	2
82	Nijmegen	5	1	1	1	1	1	1	1	149	Munchen	7	1	1	2	1	2	3	3
83	Rotterdam	5	0	0	1	3	4	4	5	150	Munster	7	0	0	0	0	0	0	1
84	Utrecht	5	2	2	2	3	3	2	3	151	Nurnberg	7	3	4	4	2	4	3	2
85	Zaandam	5	0	1	1	2	2	2	2	152	Potsdam	7	0	0	0	0	0	1	2
86	Zwolle	5	0	0	0	0	1	1	1	153	Quedlinburg	7	0	0	0	0	0	0	1
87	Aalst	6	0	0	0	0	0	0	1	154	Regensburg	7	1	1	1	1	1	1	2
88	Antwerp	6	4	5	4	5	5	4	5	155	Rostock	7	0	0	0	0	0	0	1
89	Brugge	6	3	3	2	3	3	2	3	156	Stralsund	7	0	0	0	0	0	0	1
90	Brussels	6	3	4	5	5	5	5	5	157	Soest	7	1	1	1	0	0	0	0
91	Dunkirk	6	0	0	1	1	1	1	2	158	Stettin	7	0	1	1	0	0	1	2
92	Ghent	6	4	5	3	4	5	4	5	159	Stuttgart	7	0	1	0	0	1	1	2
93	IJper	6	1	1	1	1	1	1	1	160	Ulm	7	1	1	2	1	1	1	1
94	Kortrijk	6	0	0	0	0	1	1	1	161	Wurzburg	7	1	0	1	1	1	1	1
95	Liege	6	2	2	3	3	4	5	5	162	Abbeville	8	0	0	1	1	1	1	1
96	Lier	6	0	0	0	0	0	0	1	163	Agen	8	0	0	0	0	1	1	1
97	Lille	6	2	2	3	4	5	5	5	164	Aix en Provence	8	1	2	2	2	2	2	1
98	Lokeren	6	0	0	0	0	0	0	1	165	Albi	8	0	0	0	1	1	0	1
99	Louvain	6	1	1	0	1	1	1	2	166	Alencon	8	0	0	1	1	1	1	1
100	Mechelen	6	2	2	1	2	2	1	2	167	Amiens	8	2	2	2	2	3	3	3
101	Mons	6	1	1	1	1	1	1	1	168	Angers	8	2	2	2	3	2	2	2
102	Namur	6	0	0	0	1	1	1	1	169	Angouleme	8	0	0	0	0	0	0	1
103	Oostende	6	0	0	0	0	0	0	1	170	Arles	8	1	1	1	2	2	2	2
104	Sint Niklaas	6	0	0	0	0	0	0	1	171	Arras	8	1	1	1	1	1	1	1
105	Tournai	6	2	2	2	2	2	2	2	172	Auxerre	8	0	0	0	0	0	0	1
106	Valenciennes	6	1	1	1	1	1	1	1	173	Avignon	8	2	2	2	2	2	2	2
107	Aachen	7	1	1	1	1	1	1	2	174	Bayeux	8	0	0	0	0	0	0	1
108	Altona	7	0	0	0	0	1	1	2	175	Bayonne	8	0	0	0	0	0	0	1
109	Ansbach	7	0	0	0	0	0	0	1	176	Beauvais	8	1	1	1	1	1	1	1
110	Augsburg	7	2	4	4	2	2	2	2	177	Besancon	8	0	1	1	1	1	2	2
111	Bamberg	7	0	0	0	0	1	1	1	179	Beziers	8	1	1	1	1	1	1	1
112	Barmen	7	0	0	0	0	0	0	1	180	Blois	8	1	1	1	1	1	1	1
113	Bautzen	7	0	0	0	0	0	0	1	181	Bordeaux	8	2	2	4	4	5	5	5
114	Berlin	7	1	1	2	1	5	5	6	182	Boulogne	8	2	0	0	0	0	1	1
115	Brandenburg	7	0	0	0	0	0	0	1	183	Bourges	8	0	0	1	1	1	2	1
116	Braunschweig	7	1	1	1	1	1	2	2	184	Brest	8	0	0	0	0	0	2	2
117	Bremen	7	1	1	2	2	2	2	3	185	Caen	8	2	2	3	3	3	3	3
118	Breslau	7	2	3	3	3	3	5	5	186	Cahors	8	0	0	0	0	0	0	1
119	Chemnitz	7	0	0	0	0	0	1	1	187	Cambrai	8	1	1	1	1	1	1	1
120	Danzig	7	2	2	5	5	5	4	4	188	Carcassonne	8	0	0	0	1	1	1	1
121	Dresden	7	0	0	1	0	1	4	5	189	Castres	8	0	0	0	0	0	0	1
122	Dusseldorf	7	0	0	0	0	0	1	2	190	Chalons-s.Marne	8	0	0	0	0	1	1	1
123	Elberfeld	7	0	0	0	0	0	0	1	191	Chalons.Saône	8	0	0	0	0	0	0	1
124	Elbing	7	1	1	1	1	1	1	1	192	Chartres	8	0	0	1	1	1	1	1
125	Emden	7	0	1	1	1	0	1	1	193	Cherbourg	8	0	0	0	0	0	0	1
126	Erfurt	7	1	1	1	1	1	1	1	194	Clermont-Ferr.	8	0	0	0	0	0	2	3
127	Flensburg	7	0	0	0	0	0	0	1	195	Colmar	8	0	0	0	0	0	1	1
128	Frankfort a.M.	7	1	1	1	1	2	3	3	196	Dieppe	8	0	0	1	1	1	1	1
129	Frankfort a.D.	7	1	1	1	0	0	0	1	197	Dijon	8	1	1	2	2	2	2	2
130	Freiburg	7	0	0	1	0	0	0	0	198	Douai	8	1	1	1	1	1	2	1
131	Furth	7	0	0	0	0	0	0	1	199	Falaise	8	0	0	0	0	0	0	1
132	Gotha	7	0	0	0	0	0	0	1	200	Grenoble	8	1	1	1	2	2	2	2
133	Halberstadt	7	0	0	0	0	0	0	1	201	La Rochelle	8	1	1	2	1	1	1	1
134	Halle	7	0	0	0	0	0	0	1	202	Le Havre	8	0	0	0	0	0	1	1

Table 3.2, page 3

	city	code	1500	1550	1600	1650	1700	1750	1800		city	code	1500	1550	1600	1650	1700	1750	1800
203	Le Mans	8	0	0	1	1	1	1	1	269	Reggio	10	1	1	1	1	1	1	1
204	Le Puy	8	0	0	0	0	1	1	1	270	Savigliano	10	0	0	1	0	0	1	1
205	Limoges	8	1	1	1	1	1	1	1	271	Trevisio	10	1	1	1	0	0	1	1
206	Lisieux	8	0	0	0	0	0	0	1	272	Trieste	10	0	0	0	0	0	1	2
207	Laval	8	0	0	0	0	1	1	1	273	Turin	10	0	1	2	3	4	5	5
208	Lorient	8	0	0	0	0	0	0	1	274	Udine	10	1	1	1	1	1	1	1
209	Lyon	8	5	5	4	5	5	6	6	275	Verona	10	3	5	4	3	4	4	4
210	Macon	8	0	0	0	0	0	0	1	276	Venice	10	6	6	6	6	6	6	6
211	Marseilles	8	3	3	4	5	5	5	5	277	Vercelli	10	0	0	1	0	0	0	1
212	Metz	8	1	1	1	1	2	2	3	278	Vicenza	10	1	2	3	2	2	2	2
213	Montauban	8	1	1	1	1	1	1	1	279	Vigevano	10	0	0	0	0	0	0	1
214	Montpellier	8	0	1	2	2	2	3	3	280	Ancona	11	0	0	0	1	0	1	1
215	Moulins	8	0	0	0	0	1	1	1	281	Bologna	11	5	5	5	5	5	5	5
216	Nancy	8	0	0	0	0	1	2	2	282	Ferrara	11	3	4	3	2	2	3	3
217	Nantes	8	1	1	2	3	4	5	5	283	Firenze	11	5	5	5	5	5	5	5
218	Nevers	8	0	0	0	0	0	0	1	284	Livorno	11	0	0	0	1	1	3	5
219	Nimes	8	0	0	1	1	1	3	4	285	Lucca	11	2	2	2	2	2	2	1
220	Niort	8	0	0	0	0	0	0	1	286	Perugia	11	1	2	2	1	1	1	1
221	Orleans	8	2	2	3	3	3	3	4	287	Pisa	11	1	1	1	1	1	1	1
222	Paris	8	6	6	6	6	6	6	6	288	Rome	11	5	4	6	6	6	6	6
223	Perpignan	8	0	0	0	0	0	0	1	289	Siena	11	1	1	1	1	1	1	1
224	Poitiers	8	1	1	1	1	1	1	2	290	Viterbo	11	1	1	1	1	1	1	1
225	Rennes	8	1	1	1	1	1	2	2	291	Acireale	12	0	0	1	0	1	1	1
226	Reims	8	1	1	2	2	2	2	3	292	Altamura	12	0	0	0	0	0	0	1
227	Riom	8	0	0	0	0	0	0	1	293	Bari	12	0	0	1	1	1	1	1
228	Rochefort	8	0	0	0	0	1	0	1	294	Caglia	12	0	0	1	1	1	1	1
229	Rouen	8	4	5	5	5	5	5	5	295	Caltagirone	12	0	1	1	1	1	1	2
230	St. Etienne	8	0	0	0	0	0	0	1	296	Caltanisseta	12	0	0	1	1	1	1	1
231	Saint Omer	8	1	0	0	0	1	1	2	297	Castelvetrano	12	0	0	1	1	1	0	1
232	Saint Quentin	8	0	0	0	0	0	0	1	298	Castrogiovanni	12	1	1	1	1	0	1	1
233	Strasbourg	8	2	2	2	2	3	4	4	299	Catania	12	1	2	2	1	1	2	4
234	Toulon	8	0	0	1	2	2	2	3	300	Foggia	12	0	0	0	0	0	0	1
235	Toulouse	8	3	3	3	4	3	4	4	301	Girgenti	12	1	1	1	0	1	1	1
236	Tours	8	1	1	2	2	3	2	2	302	Lecce	12	1	2	3	1	1	1	2
237	Troyes	8	1	1	1	1	2	1	2	303	Marsala	12	0	0	0	1	1	1	2
238	Versailles	8	0	0	0	0	0	1	2	304	Mascali	12	0	0	0	0	0	1	1
239	Vienne	8	0	0	0	0	0	0	1	305	Mazzarino	12	0	0	0	0	0	1	1
240	Basel	9	0	0	1	1	1	1	1	306	Messina	12	2	3	5	5	4	3	4
241	Bern	9	0	0	0	0	0	1	1	307	Modica	12	1	1	1	1	1	2	2
242	Geneva	9	1	1	1	1	1	1	2	308	Monopoli	12	0	0	0	0	0	0	1
243	Zurich	9	0	0	0	0	1	1	1	309	Naples	12	6	6	6	6	6	6	6
244	Alessandria	10	0	0	1	0	0	1	1	310	Noto	12	0	0	0	1	0	1	1
245	Asti	10	0	0	1	0	1	1	1	311	Palermo	12	5	5	6	6	6	6	6
246	Bergamo	10	1	1	2	1	2	2	2	312	Piazza	12	1	1	2	1	0	1	1
247	Brescia	10	4	4	4	2	3	2	2	313	Ragusa	12	0	0	0	0	0	1	1
248	Chioggia	10	0	0	0	0	1	1	1	314	Reggio in Calab.	12	0	0	0	0	0	1	1
249	Como	10	1	1	1	0	1	1	1	315	Sassari	12	1	1	1	1	1	1	1
250	Crema	10	1	1	1	0	0	0	0	316	Siracusa	12	1	1	1	1	1	1	1
251	Cremona	10	4	3	3	1	2	2	2	317	Taranto	12	1	2	1	1	1	1	1
252	Cuneo	10	0	0	1	0	0	1	1	318	Termini	12	0	0	1	0	0	1	1
253	Fossano	10	0	0	1	0	0	1	1	319	Trapani	12	1	1	1	1	1	1	2
254	Genoa	10	5	5	5	5	5	5	5	320	Alcala	13	0	0	1	0	0	0	1
255	La Valetta	10	0	0	0	2	0	1	1	321	Alcazar	13	1	2	1	0	0	0	1
256	Lodi	10	0	0	1	1	1	1	1	322	Alicante	13	0	0	0	0	0	0	1
257	Mantua	10	2	3	3	1	2	2	2	323	Andujar	13	0	0	1	0	0	0	1
258	Milan	10	6	5	6	6	6	6	6	324	Antegnera	13	0	1	1	1	1	1	1
259	Modena	10	1	1	2	1	1	1	2	325	Aracena	13	0	0	1	0	0	0	1
260	Mondovi	10	0	0	1	0	0	0	1	326	Avila	13	1	1	1	0	0	0	0
261	Monza	10	1	1	1	0	0	1	1	327	Badajoz	13	0	0	1	0	0	0	1
262	Nice	10	1	1	1	1	1	1	1	328	Baeza	13	0	1	2	1	1	1	1
263	Nicosia	10	1	1	2	1	1	1	1	329	Barcelona	13	2	3	4	4	4	5	6
264	Novara	10	0	0	0	0	0	0	1	330	Bilbao	13	0	0	0	0	0	0	1
265	Padua	10	2	3	3	2	3	3	3	331	Burgos	13	0	2	1	0	0	0	0
266	Parma	10	1	2	3	1	3	3	3	332	Cadiz	13	0	0	0	2	5	5	
267	Pavia	10	1	1	1	2	2	2		333	Cartagenea	13	0	0	0	1	2	3	
268	Piacenza	10	2	2	3	2	3	2		334	Cordoba	13	3	3	3	3	2	3	4

84

Table 3.2, page 4

	city	code	1500	1550	1600	1650	1700	1750	1800		city	code	1500	1550	1600	1650	1700	1750	1800
335	Cuenca	13	0	1	1	0	0	0	0	357	Toledo	13	2	3	5	2	2	2	2
336	Ecija	13	1	1	2	1	1	1	2	358	Ubeda	13	0	1	1	1	1	1	1
337	Granada	13	5	5	5	5	5	5	5	359	Utrera	13	0	0	1	0	0	0	0
338	Jaen	13	1	2	2	1	2	2	2	360	Valencia	13	3	3	4	5	5	5	5
339	Jerez de la Fr.	13	1	2	2	2	2	2	3	361	Valladolid	13	3	4	4	1	1	1	2
340	Lucena	13	1	1	1	1	1	1	1	362	Zaragoza	13	1	1	2	2	2	3	4
341	Madrid	13	0	3	4	6	6	6	6	363	Coimbra	14	0	0	1	1	1	1	1
342	Malaga	13	0	1	1	1	2	3	3	364	Elvas	14	0	1	1	1	1	1	1
343	Medino del Ca.	13	1	1	1	0	0	0	0	365	Evora	14	0	1	1	1	1	1	1
344	Medino de Riose	13	1	1	1	0	0	0	0	366	Lisbon	14	3	5	6	6	6	6	6
345	Moron de la Fr.	13	0	0	0	0	0	0	1	367	Oporto	14	0	1	1	2	2	2	3
346	Murcia	13	1	1	1	2	2	3	4	368	Brunn	15	0	0	0	0	1	1	2
347	Ocana	13	0	0	1	0	0	0	0	369	Graz	15	0	0	0	0	0	1	3
348	Orihuela	13	0	0	1	0	0	1	1	370	Innsbruck	15	0	0	0	0	0	0	1
349	Osuna	13	0	0	1	0	0	0	1	371	Klagenfurt	15	0	0	0	0	0	0	1
350	Palencia	13	0	0	1	0	0	0	1	372	Linz	15	0	0	0	0	0	0	1
351	Palma	13	1	1	2	2	2	2	2	373	Prague	15	2	2	3	2	3	5	5
352	Ronda	13	0	0	0	0	0	0	1	374	Salzburg	15	1	1	1	1	1	1	1
353	Salamanca	13	1	1	2	1	0	1	0	375	Vienna	15	2	3	4	5	6	6	6
354	Santiago	13	0	0	0	1	1	1	2	376	Krakau	16	0	0	0	0	0	1	2
355	Segovia	13	2	2	2	1	0	0	0	377	Posen	16	0	0	0	0	0	0	1
356	Sevilla	13	2	5	5	5	5	5	5	378	Warsaw	16	0	1	1	2	1	2	5

Table 3.3: The Assignment of Unknowns

Code		1500	1550	1600	1650	1700	1750	1800
0	under 10	30	27	18	37	27	23	0
1	10-19	50	40	32	37	20	22	4
2	20-29	12	10	9	10	6	6	0
3	30-39	6	4	5	4	1	2	0
4	40-49	0	1	0	0	0	0	0
5	50-99	0	0	1	1	2	2	0
6	100 +	0	0	0	0	0	0	0
Σ	1 - 6	68	55	47	52	29	32	4
Estimated population (000's)		1108	933	860	933	572	647	54
Unknowns as % of number of cities 10,000 and over		44	32	22	27	13	13	1.1
Estimated population as % of total urban population		32	21	15	15	8	7	0.4

rough, estimates of total population for each region* generate the urban percentages presented in Table 3.6. The percentage of Europe's population living in cities of at least 10,000 inhabitants displays a relentless upward pressure, climbing from 5.3 percent in 1500 to 9.4 percent in 1800, and rising in every 50-year interval without exception.

Table 3.6: The Urbanization of Europe, 1300-1890

	1300	1500	1550	1600	1650	1700	1750	1800	1850	1890
	Population in Cities of 10,000 and Above									
North and West	4.4	6.0	6.7	8.1	10.7	13.0	13.8	14.7	25.1	45.3
Central	3.6	3.8	4.1	4.8	6.6^1	6.7	7.1	7.1	18.2	27.8
Mediterranean	8.7	9.7	11.3	13.2	12.5	11.7	11.7	12.9	18.0	20.7
Total E 1-14	5.5	6.1	6.8	8.0	9.3	9.5	9.9	10.6	20.1	31.0
Europe (incl. East)	--	5.3	--	7.0	8.0	8.2	8.7	9.4	--	--
	Estimated Population in Cities of 5,000 and Above									
Europe		8.6	--	9.9	10.6	--	11.0	12.1		
	Population in Cities of 40,000 and Above									
North and West	0.1	1.3	2.5	3.0	5.9	8.7	9.0	8.9		
Central	0.7	0.7	1.2	1.9	3.0^1	3.2	3.6	3.2		
Mediterranean	4.5	4.5	5.7	7.0	7.2	7.0	6.5	7.7		
Europe Σ1-14	2.2	2.0	2.9	3.8	5.0	5.7	5.9	6.2		

* The estimates of total population used in this study are presented in summary form in Jan de Vries, Economy of Europe in an Age of Crisis (Cambridge, 1976) p. 5. They are based on the following sources: Andre Armendaud, Marcel Reinhard, and Jacques Dupâquier, Histoire générale de la population mondiale (Paris, 1968); Charles Wilson and Geoffrey Parker, An Introduction to the Sources of European Economic History, 1500-1800 (Ithaca, New York, 1977); J.A. Faber, et al., "Population changes and economic development in the Netherlands: a historical survey", A.A.G. Bijdragen 12 (1965)pp.47-110; Rogier Mols, "Der Bevölkerungsgeschichte Belgiens im Lichte des heutigen Forschung", Vierteljahrschrift für Sozial- und Wirtschaftsgeschichte 46 (1959)pp.491-511; H. Aubin and W. Zorn, Handbuch der deutschen Wirtschafts- und Sozialgeschichte, vol. 1 (Stuttgart, 1971); W. Bickel, Bevölkerungsgeschichte und Bevölkerungspolitik der Schweiz (Zürich, 1947); K.J. Beloch, Bevölkerungsgeschichte Italiens, 3 vols. (Berlin, 1937-61); J. Nadal, La población espanola, sieglo XVI a XX (Barcelona, 1966); Jose-Gentil Da Silva, "Au Portugal: Structure demographique et développement economique", Studi in onore de Amintore Fanfani, vol. 2, pp. 490-510.

The setbacks of the early seventeenth century, while affecting the number of cities, apparently had much less effect on the size of the urban population. Once again, we face a situation where a large-scale demographic contraction apparently had much less effect on the urban population than it had on the size of the rural population. As a consequence, the urban percentage continued to climb, even though many individual cities undeniably encountered grave problems.

To put this another way, these calculations raise the possibility that urbanization persisted in the face of a seventeenth-century contraction of the "urban network". This raises the question of concentration of urban population. Did the cities of Europe follow Gibrat's law of proportionate effect, or did scale systematically affect city growth? Since we are dealing here with three centuries of urbanization temporal changes in the trends of urban concentration also deserve attention.

3.4. City size distribution over time

The phenomenon of urban concentration and related issues concerning the structure of the urban system can best be introduced with the help of rank-size distributions. Geographers have long observed that the distribution of settlements by size shows a regularity that is found in a remarkable variety of other aspects of human life (such as wealth-holding and the number of publications of university professors). This regularity, the rank-size rule, can be expressed as

$$p_i = p_1/i,$$

where p_i is the population of the city in the series 1, 2, 3, ... n where all cities in a region are arranged in descending order of population, and p_1 is the population of the largest city. In other words, in large systems of cities, the second largest city is likely to be half the size of the largest, the third largest city one-third as large, etc. When this formula is vast in logarithmic form

$$\log p_i = \log a - b(\log i),$$

the regularity is expressed by a straight line relating rank and population of cities with an intercept (a) and a slope (b). The intercept is the population of the largest city; the slope is expected to be -1, although this should be regarded as an empirical finding rather than a logical necessity.*

---

* For further information see G.K. Zipf, Human Behavior and the Principle of Least Effort (Cambridge Mass. 1949); B.J.L. Berry, "City Size Distribution and Economic Development", Economic Development and Economic Change 9 (1961) pp. 573-588; B.J.L. Berry and F. E. Horton, Geographic Perspectives on Urban Systems, (Englewood Cliffs, New Jersey, 1970), Chapter 3 and literature cited here.

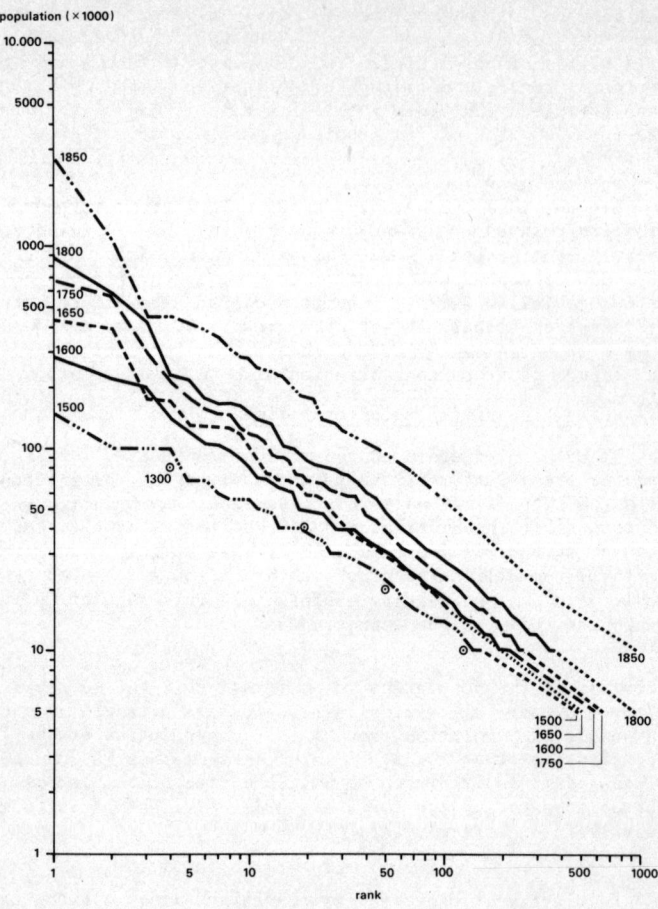

Figure 3.1: Rank-size distributions : Europe, 1300-1850

It follows from this that proportionate growth throughout the relevant range of city sizes will generate a series of rank-size distributions over time that preserve the same overall slope. To achieve this constancy there must exist a long-term balance between the growth of the component cities (the cause of vertical shifts) and the growth of the urban system as a whole, i.e. the introduction of new cities (the cause of horizontal shifts). The persistence of rank-size regularity is often interpreted to reflect the existence of a stable equilibrium in a system where city growth is part of a stochastic process.

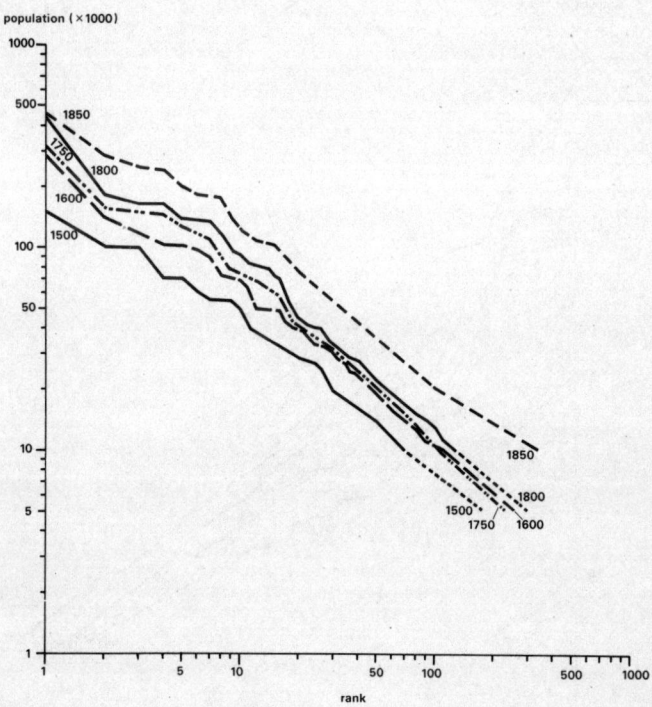

Figure 3.2: Rank-size distributions : Southern Europe, 1500-1850

Without going further into the possible explanations of
these regularities, we can simply reiterate that parallelism
among the distributions is a demonstration of proportionate
(or allometric) growth. Is this observed in the urbanization
of Europe between 1500 and 1800?

Figure 3.1 displays the rank-size distributions for
Europe as a whole, while Figures 3.2 and 3.3 do so for northern and southern Europe, respectively (for definitions see the
code to Tabel 3.2). Each line plots the cities, ranked by
size, for a given date. The unknown are dispersed proportionately among the other cities of their size category. For com-

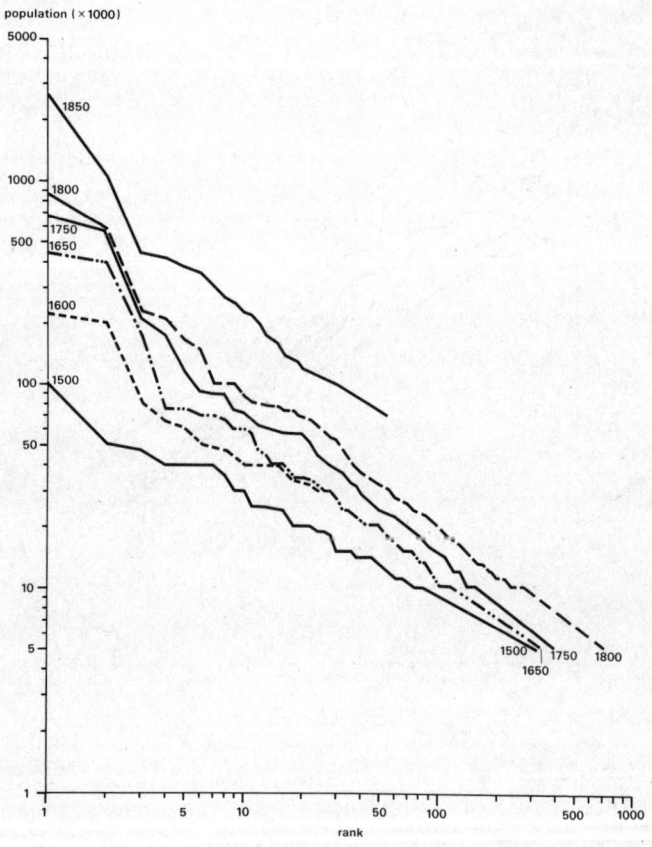

Figure 3.3: Rank-size distributions : Northern Europe, 1500-1800

parative purposes the rank-size distributions for Europe around 1300 and for 1850 are also included. Finally, the slope of each distribution (for as great a portion of the distribution as seemed reasonable) was extended downward in order to estimate the number of cities in the 5 to 9.9 thousand population category (Table 3.7 displays these estimates).

Table 3.7: Estimated Number of Cities in 5-9.9 Thousand Population Category

Year	Range of Estimated Number of Cities	Estimated Population (in millions)	Percentage of Population in Cities 10,000 +
1500	325 - 345	2.1 - 2.2	62%
1600	375 - 390	2.4 - 2.5	41
1650	315 - 330	2.0 - 2.1	33
1750	360 - 375	2.3 - 2.4	26
1800	535 - 600	3.5 - 3.9	26 - 32

What do these distributions tell us about the process of urban growth in Europe? To begin with, they do not display proportionate growth: the lines are not parallel nor does their slopes at any time come close to -1. The slopes are without exception less.

In 1500, just as two centuries earlier, the distribution shows a small slope coefficient with a "flat" top. That is, the largest ten cities are smaller than "predicted", and the size of the four largest cities are not at all consistent with the rank-size rule. The same basic pattern is apparent in the southern and northern distributions but is extreme in the latter case, where apart from the largest city (Paris) cities down to the seventh rank are all in the same general size range. Following Harris one is inclined to interpret these distributions as evidence for a lack of integrations of the various regions of Europe (Harris, 1970). The summation of many small, relatively autarkic urban systems - which seems to be a good description of medieval urbanism - is likely to generate a flat-topped curve with a shallow slope. (The stepped character of the distribution, which Harris also argues, on theoretical grounds, to be indicative of unintegrated regions, is here simply the consequence of bunching in the population estimates. Just as in age-distributions of population in pre-literate societies, certain, usually round, numbers are more likely to be picked than others.)

By 1600 the slope of all three curves has increased. Moreover, the European curve is remarkably regular (only the largest city is smaller than predicted) suggesting that Europe, despite its division into many polities, has progressed substantially in the direction of an economic integration of its regions and an associated development of an hierarchy in the system of cities. Still, a clear distinction can be made between the Mediterranean and northern Europe. In southern Europe the slope in the upper range is distinctly flatter than the lower tail - just as it was a century earlier. In the north the upper range is erratic, but shifting unmistakably toward a situation where the largest cities are more populous than the rest of the distribution would predict. By 1650 this new structure is achieved; then London, Paris, and Amsterdam are "dominant" cities, while the rest of the distribution is quite regular, and much steeper in slope than any earlier distribution. The same tendencies persist, although in a more muted form, to 1750.

The process of urban growth in Europe as a whole as well as in the two great zones treated here can be summarized by a rank-size curve which, step-by-step from 1500 to 1750, straightens out (loses its flat top) and rotates to achieve a gradually steeper slope from the pivot of an almost stable number of small cities. This is an abstract way of saying that urban growth in this long period was heavily concentrated in the large cities (and cities that became large) and was not characterized by the "birth" of numerous new cities.

After 1750 the process of urbanization as reflected in the rank-size distributions changes fundamentally. It is now the smaller cities which grow disproportionately. This together with numerous city "births" reduces the slope of the lower tail of the distribution. Until 1800 this is essentially a characteristic of northern Europe (with Great Britain, of course, playing an important role); in the first half of the nineteenth century southern Europe joins in.

After 1750 the largest ten or so cities of Europe are conspicuous for their lethargic growth relative to the rest of the cities. Table 3.8 and Figure 3.4 provide data illustrating the strong tendency toward urban concentration that was at work throughout the period up to 1750. It must be remembered that the population figures for the size category 5 - 9.9 thousand are not based on the data set assembled for this study. They are estimates derived from the rank-size distributions and their validity hinges on the stability of the calculated slope in this (unobserved) tail of the distribution.

The total number of cities of 5,000 and over grows from

Table 3.8: Concentration of Urban Population, 1500-1800

	Cities of 5-39,000			Cities of 40,000 +			All Cities
	No.	Population (in millions)	% of Total	No.	Population (in millions)	% of Total	% of Total
1500	470	4.5	6.9	17	1.1	1.7	8.6
1600	560	5.5	6.6	35	2.7	3.3	9.9
1750	580	6.1	6.0	48	5.0	5.0	11.0
1800	840	8.9	6.9	62	6.8	5.2	12.1

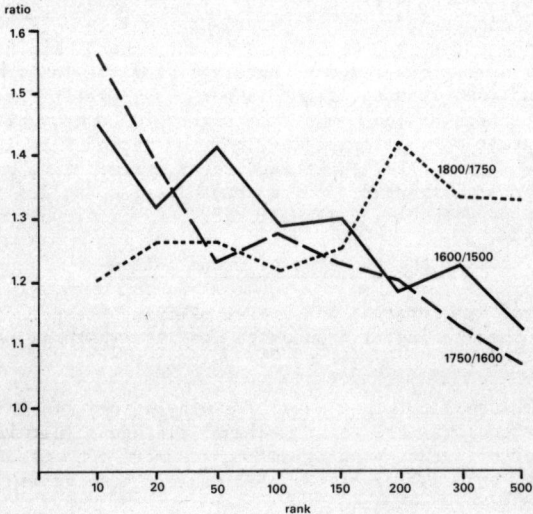

Figure 3.4: Population Growth Ratios at successive City-size Ranks

something under 500 in 1500 to about 600 in 1600 and to very little more than that - perhaps 630 - in 1750. In the following half century the number climbs quickly to at least 900, and continues to climb in the nineteenth century in an environment of rapid overall population growth. While the number of cities with at least 5,000 inhabitants grew between 1500 and 1750 by only a quarter, the total population of these cities doubled. But the population in cities of 5 - 9.9 thousand grew by less than 10 percent while that of cities with from 10 to 39 thousand inhabitants was barely able to exceed the growth rate of the overall population. In other words, very nearly the entire increment to European urbanization in this period (from 8.6 to 11.0 percent) is attributable to the 48 cities which by 1750 had populations of at least 40,000 inhabitants. (Note: these were not necessarily the largest cities in 1500. The origins of these cities will be examined in greater detail below.)

Figure 3.4 demonstrates this process of concentration more systematically. Each point connected by a curve shows the increase in the size of cities of a given rank in the European rank-size distributions. Thus, if the tenth largest city in Europe had 60,000 inhabitants in 1600, but only 30,000 in 1500, the value of rank ten for the interval 1500-1600 is 60/30 = 2.0. The higher the ratio, the more rapid is the growth of cities at that rank during the relevant interval. For the intervals 1500-1600 and 1600-1750 the figure shows a systematic diminution of the ratios as one moves from higher to lower ranks, i.e. from larger to smaller cities. For the period 1750-1800 the opposite is the case. The structure of urbanization had been dramatically reversed, and, presumably, the sources of urban growth were fundamentally altered.

3.5. An analysis of the patterns of urbanization

At the risk of exaggerating and oversimplifying the process of pre-modern urbanization, I propose to distinguish three periods (see Figure 3.5) and to discuss the characteristics of each in turn.

I. 1500-1600/1650. The long sixteenth century. In this period distributions lose their medieval flat tops (particularly in the north); urban population becomes more concentrated in large cities, but smaller cities also exhibit some growth. Europe becomes more urban.

II. 1600/1650-1750. The age of the rural proletariat. Very few new cities are "born", and there is an overall stagnation of smaller cities. Meanwhile the size of the big cities continues to burgeon. There is less net urbanization than in period I but a great deal of redistribution of the urban population among cities and regions.

III. 1750-1800/50. The new urbanization. The processes at work in periods I and II are reversed. The growth of most large cities is retarded while a rash of city "births" and the rapid growth of smaller cities extends the lower tail of the rank-size distribution and lowers its slope.

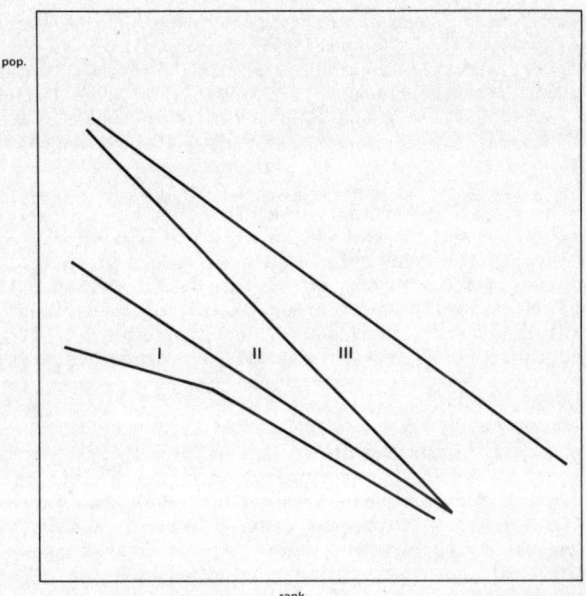

Figure 3.5: Three Periods of pre-modern Urbanization in Europe

I.

A major achievement of medieval society had been the creation of a distinctive urban civilization. Through the revival from near extinction of decayed Roman settlements and the creation of wholly new urban foundations, Europe became endowed with hundreds of highly autonomous municipalities. But from the thirteenth century until the end of the eighteenth century new foundations were rare in the extreme. A handful of planned towns (Göteburg, Cette, Lorient, for example) and another handful of existing settlements infused with new, urban functions (examples are Cadiz, Versailles, Brest) are the only additions to the stock of cities inherited from the Middle Ages. Adding to the sense of stability is the fact that the overall size distribution, geographical spread, and percentage of the total population of European cities differed little between 1300 and 1500, despite the disruptive demographic events that intervened.

The economic and demographic expansion of the "long sixteenth century", which by itself was bound to cause a certain measure of urban growth, was paired with state-building efforts (in England, France, and Spain, most notably) that had the effect of undermining the independence and autonomy of many cities and subordinating their economic interests to those of the Renaissance Monarchies. This plus the Reformation's impact on Cathedral towns in newly Protestant lands had the cumulative impact of undermining the viability of many cities at the same time that certain cities gained enormously in growth potential as the administrative centers of the new monarchies (Madrid, London, Paris, and, in a sense, post-Trentine Rome) or as the economic handmaidens of imperial ambition (Genoa, Augsburg, Antwerp).

An old urban world was under attack, but the evidence for this in our data base is partially hidden by the overall economic and demographic vigor of the age. The economic vigor is associated with the connection with each other of Europe's trading areas and the growth in volume of interregional trade. This together with the first steps toward the achievement of bureaucratic government endowed the urban system - if it can be called that in 1500 - with a novel element of hierarchy.

II.

No single date can be assigned to divide the first from the second period, for the shift is associated with the slowing or reversal of sixteenth-century population growth. This occurred earlier in the Mediterranean area (about 1600) than in central Europe (Thirty Years' War), and central Europe, in turn, was hit before the north and west, where population growth was slowed, but on the whole not reversed in the second half of the seventeenth century.

From these varied dates until approximately the mid-eighteenth century urban growth was influenced by a unique combination of forces whose net effect was to bring about a sharper differentiation among the component parts of Europe's urban world.

This second period is shaped by the cessation of both the rapid growth of total population and the expansion of the non-European areas of trade and colonization that had been so important in the preceding period. In this new environment, with seemingly fewer impulses stimulating urban growth, a series of organizational innovations affected state and society to the benefit of a selective group of cities, permitting them to assume new functions in the urban system. At the same time a larger group were being undermined sufficiently that they declined in relative standing and, often, in absolute population.

Despite the modest total population growth over the period 1600-1750 (about 20 percent, most of which was concentrated in the last 50 years) the total urban population grew by over three million (53 percent), raising the urban percentage from about 8 to 10 percent. In this period the relative position of the three regions, which had been stable from 1300 to 1600, and would change relatively little in the century after 1750, was drastically altered. The well-known seventeenth-century decline of Mediterranean urban populations, which caused the region's percentage of total urban population to fall from half to nearly one-third, stands behind this transformation, and means that the entire net growth was concentrated in northern Europe, and particularly in the north and west European region. However, a notable characteristic of all three regions in this period is the wide dispersion around the mean registered by the individual cities. Thus, even in the Mediterranean area there are rapidly growing cities, while in the north there are several big losers.

This is also the period of the most intense concentration of urban population into big cities. Fully 80 percent of the total growth of all cities over 5,000 inhabitants in this period is attributable to less than 50 cities of over 40,000 inhabitants. In order to be more specific about the sources of urban growth in this period, I have identified with the use of transformation matrices the most rapidly growing and most rapidly declining cities. The matrices single out 16 cities that grew by at least 3 size categories between 1600 and 1750. To them must be added three other rapidly growing cities that were already in or near the largest size category and, hence, could not be identified by this procedure. To this group I have added those cities that were small in 1600 (less than 20,000) and rose to at least the next size category (and added at least 8,000 inhabitants) by 1750. In this way 22 cities whose absolute growth was not enormous, but whose rate of growth was high are added to the 19 cities that became very large.

The 19 large cities alone account for 62 percent of the total urban growth of the period; when the 22 smaller cities are added 78 percent of the growth is accounted for. What sorts of cities are these? The large cities are listed at the top of Table 3.9 , grouped by primary function. Despite the fact that several cities have more than one primary function, all but one of these cities fit comfortably under the two headings of national capital and port. Only Lyon is neither of these, but rather a predominantly industrial city.

When we broaden our gaze to the smaller cities listed below on Table 3.9 the ports (including naval ports) and capitals continue to predominate. Among the remaining twelve cities several English industrial towns make an appearance as harbingers of bigger things to come. But, otherwise, only Zaandam (actually a collection of villages rather than a conventional city) can be described as a predominantly industrial city. Among the cities that declined markedly between 1600 (or 1650) and 1750, it is striking that none are capitals, only one, Messina is a port (its decline is the result of an earthquake) and most of the remainder possessed substantial industrial activities (Toledo, Augsburg, Brescia, Segovia, and Leiden).

The exercise of identifying the major gainers and losers is based on a large number of transformation matrices. Space limits me here to mentioning only the most summary findings of their analysis. But those findings are striking. In contrast to both the preceding and succeeding periods, the years from 1600 to 1750 witness several cities that move swiftly up (and

Capitals	Ports	Capitals and Ports
Berlin	Amsterdam	Copenhagen
Dublin	Bristol	Stockholm
Dresden	Cadiz	London
Madrid	Cork	
Paris	Koningsburg	
Turin	Livorno	Industrial
Vienna	Nantes	Lyon
	Rotterdam	

London, Paris and Amsterdam grow by 976,000.

The remaining 16 cities grow by 901,000.

In addition, 28 cities initially in category 0 or 1 grew to the next category - and by at least 8,000 inhabitants by 1750. These cities that grew rapidly, but from a small base, are:

Capitals/Courts	Ports	Other
The Hague	Altona	Arles
Hannover	Cartagenia	Birmingham
Potsdam	Chioggia	Besancon
Stuttgart	Glasgow	Frankfurt a.M.
	Le Havre	Leipzig
Naval Ports	Liverpool	Manchester
	Malaga	Metz
Brest	Newcastle	Murcia
Plymouth	Santiago	Nancy
Toulon		Nimes
		Norwich
		Zaandam

Their combined growth amounted to about 440,000. In addition, the 17 of these cities that rose from category 0 transferred into figures an existing population of about 50,000.

The total net growth of urban population in cities above 10,000 inhabitants: 3,042,000

Growth of 3 large cities	976,000 (32%)
Growth of 16 rapidly growing cities	901,000 (30%)
Growth and transfer of 28 small cities that grew rapidly	490,000 (16%)
Total of 47 cities	2,367,000 (78%)

Table 3.9: Most rapidly growing Cities in Europe, 1600-1750

down) the scale of size categorie: Dublin, Cork, Livorno, and Rotterdam, for example, all come to fulfill functions, on an international scale, that were wholly foreign to them in the early seventeenth century.

It will not come as a surprise to most students of European society that capitals and ports were conspicuous among the rapidly growing cities, but our exercise shows them to have very nearly monopolized the considerable urbanization of the era. In absolutist and constitutional states alike, in big states and small, administration, the military, and the legal apparatus provided a major expansion of employment. These cities were, of course, not devoid of industrial activity. But, in contrast to the classic medieval industrial town, whose output was exported to rural and foreign markets, the artificers of the capitals depended primarily on the markets within their own cities.

The ports were, with only a few exceptions, engaged in the Atlantic trade. Among the exceptions are the Mediterranean ports that grew as outposts of the northwest European merchant interests at the expense of "indigenous" ports.

To summarize, the urbanization of the period 1600-1750 marked a parting of the ways of the southern and northern regions, and it was marked by a high degree of volatility in the positions of many cities in the urban hierarchy. Urban growth was accounted for - in the aggregate - exclusively by cities that, by 1750, exceeded 40,000 population; it was the result, specifically, of the rapid growth of less than 50 cities, overwhelmingly capitals and ports. The obverse of these statements is no less important to an understanding of Europe's pre-modern urbanism: the population of the 600 or so remaining cities with at least 5,000 inhabitants, not to mention the thousands of smaller cities, stagnated or declined. There was a net de-urbanization of cities under 40,000 population, which again makes period II unique in the three centuries under analysis here. The great bulk of inland trading centers, seats of ecclesiastical administration, and, particularly, industrial towns, suffered at least relative loss of standing between the early seventeenth and the mid-eighteenth centuries. Many lost their political autonomy at the hands of absolutist policies. As a group, Europe's cities saw their distinctive municipal culture dismissed by rightthinking servitors of the modern state as a medieval relic. More concretely, powerful economic forces were speeding the abandonment of cities as locations for many of the most labor-absorbing industries. The spread through the countryside of the putting-out system, or proto-industrialization, is a subject that cannot be discussed in detail here. While the phenomenon was by no means unique to the seventeenth and eighteenth centuries, it seems to have spread then with particular vigor, stimulated by changes in relative prices, the character of colonial markets, demographic trends, and even the policies of cities.

It is fascinating to observe the parallel between this period of urban industrial decline in Europe and that experienced by Japan in the eighteenth and early nineteenth centuries. Thomas C. Smith (1973) called attention to the de-urbanization of Japan in this era of spreading rural industry and sought to account for it with factors he held to be unique to Japan (particularly, the absence of foreign trade and population growth). He argues that pre-modern growth in Japan, accompanied by de-urbanization, affected social class relations and culture as well as economic structure in ways that contributed significantly to what he regards as the major difference between the processes of economic development of Japan and Europe.

He contrasts the stagnation and decline of many Japanese

cities to the situation in Europe where, following the conclusion of Roger Mols, he observes that "The major cities of Europe as a whole grew in number and size in every century from 1300 to 1800" (with the possible exception of the period 1350-1450). In the seventeenth and eighteenth centuries he concludes "the growth of urban population in western Europe is not in doubt (Smith 1973 : 147). Indeed, the data presented here confirm the truth of this last statement; but we have also seen that this growth issued from an exceedingly narrow range of specific stimuli. The smaller cities of Europe as a whole, and vast regions of Europe (particularly inland regions) experienced the same general fate as Smith observes for Japan.

Not only did most cities stagnate or decline in both areas, but they did so for much the same set of reasons: a transfer of industrial production to the countryside, and the rise of numerous villages and local market towns as nuclei of the putting-out system. In this way, just as Smith notes of Japan, an industrial labor force could be recruited without withdrawing it totally from the agricultural sector. At the same time, the heavy burden of capital investment associated with urban growth could also be avoided. In the absence of major technical innovations and rapid population growth, pre-modern industry achieved a growth of output and a reduction of production costs by effecting organizational changes - a primary consequence of which were to cut short the flow of migrants and investment to the cities.

Except for the handful of cities that could attract these flows through the opportunities of foreign trade or could compel them through the growth of the public sector, urban Europe faced grave problems. Between the political challenge of the sixteenth century and the economic crisis of the seventeenth and early eighteenth centuries, most cities had, by about 1750, lost much of the pride and vigor typically associated with medieval European urbanism.

III.

Beginning around the mid-eighteenth century the basic factors underlying European urban growth and the nature of the urban hierarchy changed fundamentally. Rapid population growth, technical innovation, and changed relative prices that brought a new prosperity to the agricultural sector all combined to reverse a centuries-long process of urban population concentration in the largest cities. This "new urbanization" (which becomes fully apparent in the Mediterranean area only after 1800) had the effect of shifting the rank-size distribution sharply to the right, but the shift was much more forceful in the lower tail of the distribution than in the highest ranks. Because total population rose rapidly, most cities grew substantially; but the net urbanization of the period 1750-1800 was, in fact, not usually large (an incremental urbanization of 1.1 percent) and was disproprtionately the result of the growth of smaller cities and the addition of new cities to the "system". Table 3.8 shows cities of 40,000 and more to have increased their percentage of the total population by only 0.2 percent while cities of 5 to 39,000 increased their share by over four times as much.

The reduction of large city growth to approximate proportionality with total population growth for the first time in at least 250 years stems in part from the fact that the objective of state centralization had in large part been achieved in most states by 1750. The stimuli to urban growth provided by foreign and, particularly, intercontinental trade after 1750 remains in need of further study. The conventional wisdom has it that early industrialization moved forward on the strong back of colonial trade. However, it is not impossible that historians have exaggerated the importance of long-distance trade in this period.

The "new urbanization" was an urban growth from below. Consequently, our task is to identify the new forces nurturing the "grass roots" of Europe's urban system. An obvious factor was simply the rate of overall population growth. To the extent that the demographic variables acting upon the rate of natural increase did so in settlements of all sizes, many small cities were bound to find themselves in higher categories. But there were two basic additional factors at work that acted to expand the base of the urban system.

As is well known, the early stages of the Industrial Revolution tended to be played out in relatively small cities and in rural locations. Both institutional and technological factors encouraged this. As a consequence, many small cities with resource-based industries such as metallurgy grew as a consequence of technological innovation, and many rural places that had grown thick with people as proto-industrial textile production spread in the preceding era broke through to become industrial cities as technological change encouraged factory organization. This is the primary cause of the first concentrated wave of new city formation since the thirteenth century.

The Industrial Revolution of the eighteenth century was primarily a British phenomenon, yet the growth of small cities was much more widespread. The rapid growth of these cities on the continent is often observed to begin somewhat later than in Britain; in the Mediterranean region it is, in fact, most pronounced in the period 1800-1850. The surprising universality of small-city growth can in large part be accounted for by a second stimulus: the increase in agricultural incomes and the expansion of farm production. Regional marketing and administrative centers expand their employment bases as the volume of marketed farm output grew, and the retailing and services sectors grew with the increase in landlords' rental incomes.

All these forces combined added some 200 cities to the category of 5 - 9.9 thousand and over 100 cities to the 10 - 19 thousand category. The process of urban growth from below seems to have continued into the nineteenth century, although systematic research still remains to be done on this. In Britain, where the process was vigorous in the eighteenth century, the research of Brian Robson (1973) found concentration in larger cities to be evident from the first decade of the nineteenth century (although the trend is weak until the third decade). On the other hand, the data presented by Weber (1889/1965) shows urban growth in Italy and Spain to have been from below until at least the mid-nineteenth century.

Ever since the pioneer analysis of Adna Weber it has been abundantly clear that modern urbanization is characterised by urban population concentration in large cities. It now appears that this modern urbanization was preceded by an interval – my third phase of pre-modern urbanization – in which the opposite was the case and in which Europe received, for the first time since the Middle Ages, a sizeable infusion of new cities. However, more research is needed to specify the dimensions and identify the temporal limits of this phase. For now, Figure 3.6., which divides the urban population of Europe by size category of residence, must suffice to illustrate the broad trends and point out the uniqueness of the "new urbanization".

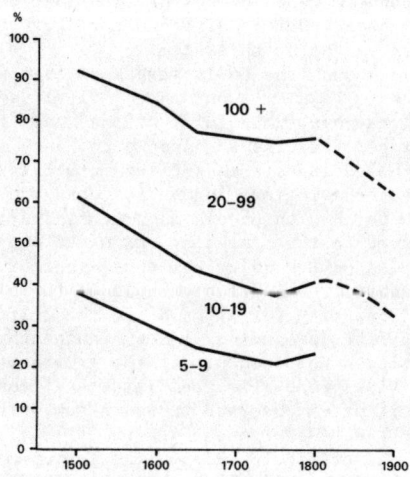

Figure 3.6: Percentage Distribution of European Urban Population by size of City, 1500-1900

3.6. Comparative perspectives

If we now step back to view the entire three-century epoch of European urbanization in a broader temporal and spatial framework, several additional characteristics will become evident.

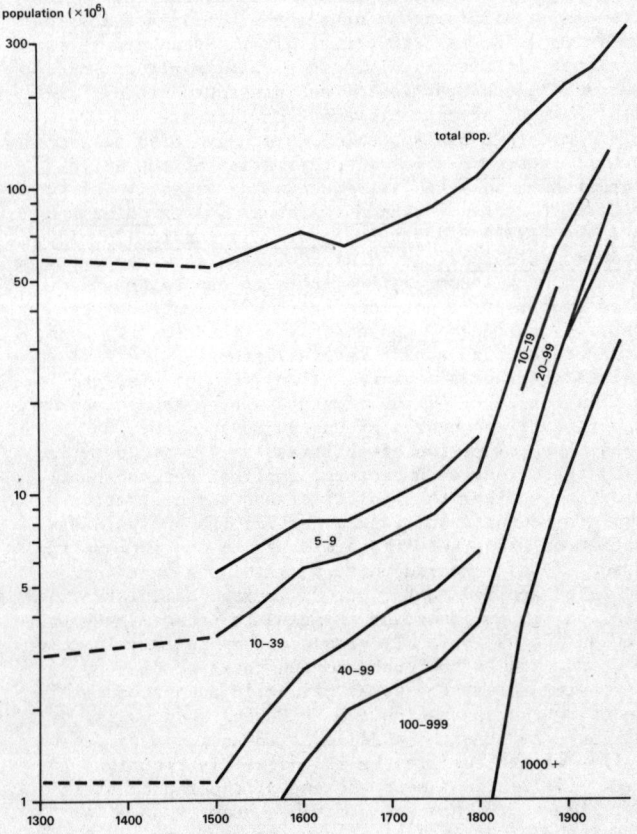

Figure 3.7: Population of Europe by Size of Settlement, 1300-1970

Figure 3.7 brings together the available information on Europe's total population and that of its urban population by size of city from the early fourteenth century to the present day. The intermediary, or preparatory position of the era of pre-modern urbanization stands out clearly. When compared to the small, stable, but unintegrated urban world of the Middle Ages and the dynamic urbanization of European society beginning in the early nineteenth century, the era of pre-modern growth shows up as being distinctive. In it urban growth is substantial but without dissolving the rural world in which it is placed. The construction of an integrated urban hierarchy also shows up as an achievement of this era.

The pre-modern urban system of Europe can also be compared with its contemporaries in other areas of the world. Such a comparative analysis is, indeed, the objective of two books by Gilbert Rozman, Urban Networks in Ch'ing China and Kokugawa Japan (1973) and Urban Networks in Russia 1750-1800 and Premodern Periodization (1976). While no detailed critique or application of his comparative approach can be provided here, it is important to note one basic difference between the urban system of Europe and those analyzed in detail by Rozman. While China, Japan, and Russia were all states (albeit of varying sizes and levels of integration), Europe was, and is, a designation for a collection of states which themselves vary enormously in size and degree of unity. To speak of "an" urban system in such a collection of polities, as I feel justified in doing by the seventeenth century, implies that the basis of integration is other than political and administrative. Since Rozman's concepts and categories for the analysis and periodization of urban networks are based on the administrative needs of a well-ordered unitary state, one must wonder how they can be applied to Europe. Of course, administrative centralization was an important stimulus to urban growth in many European states, but only France offers an example that can bear comparison to the non-European cases studied by Rozman. The urban hierarchy based primarily upon economic integration is, one suspects, unique to Europe, and calls for different concepts than those deployed in Rozman's studies.

Finally, we can compare the rank-size distributions for major world civilizations near the end of their pre-modern histories. Figure 3.8 presents Rozman's summary data for late eighteenth- or early nineteenth-century Japan and Russia, and Skinner's detailed data for China in 1843, together with the European rank-size distribution for 1800 (Skinner, 1977). The Chinese and European distributions (to which, for reasons of space limitation, this discussion will be confined) show these two great arenas of world civilization to have endowed with approximately the same number of cities of at least 20,000 population and with largest cities of about the same size (circa 900,000). Their total urban populations in cities above 5,000 population were also similar, with the significant

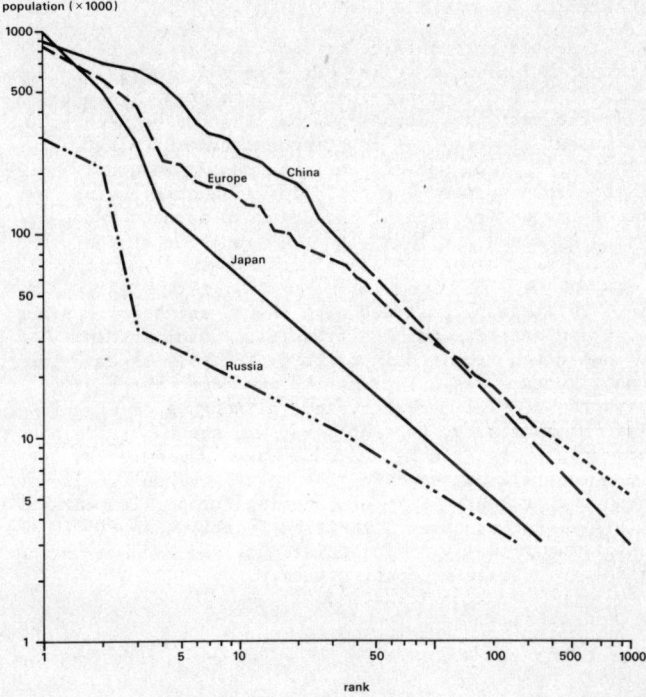

Figure 3.8: Rank-size distribution of four pre-modern
Societies:
Russia and Japan, circa 1800;
China, 1843;
Europe, 1800.

difference that the Chinese urban population was concentrated in large cities while in Europe the more numerous small cities weighed more heavily in the total. This pattern (summarized by the difference in slope of the two distributions) is a direct indication of the higher level of local market organization and commercialization attained by Europe. A second, even more striking, indicator of the same difference is that the European rural population that supported an urban structure of approximately the same population and with a similar number of cities as that of China was only one-third the size of the Chinese rural population.

107

3.7. Conclusions

The data presented here suffice to confirm that Europe's premodern urbanization was anything but a random process of city growth or the uniform, proportionate growth of a stable urban system. On the contrary, Europe's urban history between 1500 and 1800 has at its core the changing relationships between cities and the rest of society and the changing internal structure of the urban system. One could describe this process as consituting the destruction of an old urban structure and its replacement by a new one, but with the proviso that the constituent cities of these two structures remained the same. As a consequence, the histories of individual cities during these three centuries are largely concerned with their search for a place in a new urban environment. The transition involved many hazards, and often resulted in failure precisely because the new urban structure was not primarily an administrative hierarchy or a central market system (although elements of both were, of necessity, present), but was shaped by the needs of a commercializing economy and came to be dominated by competitive mercantile centers. In this setting urban development did not so much take the form of endowing Europe with sets of cities fulfilling essentially the same functions as it did the creation of functionally differentiated cities capable of finding a niche in a large economic system.

REFERENCES

Harris, C.D. *Cities of the Soviet Union: Studies in their functions, size, density and growth* (Chicago, 1970).
Robson, B.T. *Urban growth, an approach* (London, 1973).
Rozman, G. *Urban Networks in Ch'ing China and Tokugawa Japan* (Princeton, 1973).
Rozman, G. *Urban Networks in Russia 1750-1800 and Premodern Periodization* (Princeton, 1976).
Russell, J.C. *Medieval Regions and their Cities* (Newton Abbot, 1972).
Skinner, G.W. 'Regional Urbanization in Nineteenth Century China' in G. William Skinner (ed.) *The City in Late Imperial China* (Stanford, 1977) pp. 211-249.
Smith, C.Th. 'Pre-modern Economic Growth: Japan and the West', *Past and Present* 60 (1973) pp. 127-160.
Weber, A.F. *The growth of cities in the nineteenth century* (New York, 1899; reprinted Ithaca, New York, 1965).

4. The impact of functional differentiation within systems of industrialised cities
B.T. Robson

4.1. Introduction	113
4.2. The urban economic base	114
4.3. Urban functions	117
4.4. Specialisation and growth	120
4.5. The British example	123
References	129

4. The impact of functional differentiation within systems of industrialised cities
B.T. Robson

4.1. Introduction

The three essential elements of a system are interdependence, closure and differentiation. In studies of systems of cities, these three elements have been paid very different amounts of attention. The great bulk of interest has focussed on interdependence, on the extent to which cities 'behave' as a set in terms of such characteristics as their rates of population growth or in terms of the regularity or irregularity of their size distributions. Interdependence between the component of a system has been measured by inter-urban flows of various kinds: streams of migration, flows of information or the diffusion of innovations between cities. Such work has given us a considerable knowledge of the links between cities and of the overt mechanisms which go some way to explaining the regularities in urban growth and size distributions. Less interest has been shown in closure since most studies make the heroic assumption that national sets of cities can be thought of as relatively closed - and indeed that the individual cities themselves can be regarded as valid entities within such a closed system. Assumptions of closure are, of course, a mere working device. The interdependent nature of national economies has become progressively greater over time, but even in the nineteenth century it is clear that, at the very least, an 'Atlantic economy' existed which makes it difficult to consider sets of cities in the then developed world as separate selfcontained systems (Thomas, 1954). However, it is the third attribute, differentiation, which has been most ignored by studies of city systems. To a large extent the only characteristic by which systems writing has differentiated cities has been their population size; this apart, cities have been considered as an undifferentiated homogeneous set. The closest such studies have come to considering functional differentiation has been the use of central-place hierarchies to distinguish categories such as hamlets, villages, regional and national metropolises, each with its characteristic bundle of service activitites. In so far as such hierarchical types are closely related to population size and in as much as the central place arguments

ignore anything other than service functions, this does not
represent a marked improvement over simple differentiation
by size alone. It is significant, for example, that of the
39 essays in a recent text on urban systems only one
(Crowley, 1978) directly addresses the question of functional
specialisation; the others either consider it implicitly - as
in classification, central place structure and the study of
flows - or ignore it completely.

4.2. The urban economic base

This neglect of the concept of urban differentiation in studies
of city systems seems both curious and unfortunate. It is
curious in that we are all very ready to give appellations to
towns - to talk of 'mining' or 'textile' or 'seaside' or
'university' towns - and also in that a vast amount of work
was concerned with urban classification, especially in the
1960s. Perhaps it is less curious when one looks at the product
of all that work on classification since most of it is based
simply on purely statistical descriptions of employment percentages, with cut-off points selected either informally, as
in the earliest work (Harris, 1943), or more formally in the
later and statistically more sophisticated work (Nelson, 1955;
Smith, 1965) and in the large number of classifications based
on multivariate methods and grouping procedures (Berry, 1972;
Moser and Scott, 1961; Hadden and Borgatta, 1965; King, 1966;
Ahmad, 1965). The closest that one comes to classifications
which draw on any body of theory are those which derive from
economic base theory with its slippery dichotomy between
'city-forming' and 'city-serving' activities and the associated
concept of the 'basic/non-basic' split. It is from this concept
that the various indices of 'surplus workers' or of 'diversity'
in city employment have derived (Alexandersson, 1956; Mattila
and Thompson, 1955; Ullman and Dacey, 1962). Useful as such
classifications are, in the absence of more robustly derived
typologies, they suffer from all of the limitations of the
economic base concept itself: from the conceptual and practical
problems of its dependence on the definition of basic activities
and basic employment, and from the sensitivity of this
definition to the spatial boundaries of the urban units which
are used.

The neglect of functional differentiation seems also
unfortunate, both from the point of view of the systems studies
and from that of research which looks at individual towns. For
the latter, it would help greatly to be able to put in context
any discussion about the attributes of an individual town and
this is possible only if one draws on the wider concepts of
sets of towns and the part that particular towns play within
the broader economic system of a set of cities. One can only
understand the predominance of white-collar employment in the
towns of Kent or Sussex, for example, within the context of the

manufacturing base of the towns of northern England; equally one can appreciate the functional role of a resort town such as Blackpool only in the context of the wider background of the nearby industrial towns of Lancashire. While studies of individual towns may recognise the importance of differentiation, if they ignore the interdependence of sets of towns they can only take the role which any one town plays as an externally generated 'given'. Contrariwise, from the point of view of systems studies, the neglect of urban functions is equally unfortunate. Is it difficult to think of any substantive topic of interest or any dependent variable which will not be affected by the functional role that a town plays within a system of cities: political, demographic, economic and social topics can all be shown to be influenced by urban differentiation. A number of examples can reinforce the point. Foster (1968) for example, has shown the way in which class relations in the nineteenth century were strongly related to the social roles of employer and employee and that these were strongly conditioned by the nature and organisation of the dominant industrial employment of the towns concerned. Mid nineteenth century Oldham had two-thirds of its employment in cotton, coal and engineering; Northampton had almost one half in the shoe industry; South Shields had one half employed in activities connected with the coal trade to London. Whereas the textile industry of Oldham was associated with a resident bourgeoisie, the industries of the other two towns were not, and it is this factor which Foster argues as being critical in the development of strong labour solidarity in Oldham. A different example is provided by Pinard (1963), who, drawing on the American water fluoridation programmes of the 1960s, shows the inverse relationship between the proportion of managers and professionals in a town and the success of fluoridation schemes. Again one can argue from this, and the many similar 'ecological' studies, that a town's economic base is a vital ingredient to a whole host of social and political aspects of urban 'performance'. There are obvious implications in this for system-based models of diffusion based on flows of inter-urban contacts. Models based on gravity analogies or entropy maximisation may provide satisfactory statistical description of such flows, but must necessarily throw little substantive light on processes such as those Pinard considers which are influenced by the varying economic base of the towns which form a functioning system.

Without unduly labouring the point, let me further illustrate the importance of the economic base of towns from the research design of some current work on which I am engaged concerning ethnic minorities in British towns. It is clear from various studies (Peach, 1968) that initial black migration into Britain was highly selective of particular types of town, specifically that disproportionate numbers of migrants moved to and settled in large declining towns with a manufacturing base. The streams of migration have been not only to the very largest towns such as London, Birmingham and Liverpool, but to such textile towns as Bradford and Huddersfield and manufacturing towns like Wolverhampton. Not only has there been differential selection of places for settlement; there has equally been a degree of selection of different migrants in terms of the predominant economic base within each of the towns concerned. Thus, for example, the Asian immigrants to Manchester, a town with a higher proportion of servicing activities than of textile manufacturing, have been of a higher status and more involved in entrepreneurial enterprise than the Asian immigrants to Huddersfield where more are involved as semi-skilled and unskilled workers within the textile industry itself. In designing a research strategy to look at the degree to which Muslim Punjabi girls either retain or reject the traditional culture and mores of their 'indigenous' Pakistani society, a comparison between the Asian communities in Manchester and Huddersfield has to start with the economic base of each town since it is this which acts as the appropriate context, not only as a determinant of the type and number of Asian immigrants but also as a determinant of their industrial and social composition (Figure 4.1). These factors help to determine the degree of segregation and of integration of the minority ethnic group, which in turn affect the strength of parental and community control of young girls and the ethnic mix of the schools they attend. In addition, the absolute and relative size of an ethnic minority will serve to reinforce or to weaken the effects of segregation. These factors all combine to govern the retention or rejection of traditional values. This, of course, is not a one-way process since the retention of traditional values may serve to further influence the social and industrial composition of the minority group. Population size by itself is not necessarily a surrogate for the effects of such differentiation. The springboard from which one starts is the economic base which, taken in conjunction with the way in which productive relations are organised, provides an entree to the social formation of the towns concerned.

It is not simply social topics such as these which are affected by the differentiation of towns. So, too, are the demographic fortunes of sets of towns - the very topic on which the bulk of

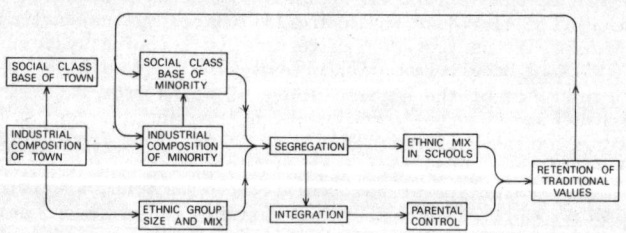

Figure 4.1: Research design - ethnic assimilation

systems work has been based. It may be possible to characterise a set of towns differentiated only by their size and to trace out the patterns of growth and population change within them. However, the typical model which is used in this subsumes the fluctuating fortunes of towns simply as a form of random noise in which the growth of one place is cancelled by the decline of another so as to maintain overall system-wide stability. Such models throw little other than statistical light on nature of the urban system under consideration. The dramatic growth of Middlesborough, the stagnation of Bewdley, which lost its potential role as an inland entrepot port to the rival town of Stourport, or the failure of Ironbridge to capitalise on its early start as a centre of the iron industry; all of such examples may be random noise to the formal models of systems theory, but they must be of substantive interest to any evolving theory of the genesis of urban growth and change.

4.3. Urban functions

In criticising such urban modelling, I am aware that it is a style of work that I have myself adopted, and I am conscious of the fact that in that work (Robson, 1973) my approach to urban growth was precisely to regard cities as largely undifferentiated units in a system in which size together with location could be taken as the explicanda of change and development in the system. What I want to explore here is the extent to which some rather primitive notions of urban differentiation can be fed in to such systems analyses to throw some further light on the nature of towns within a national city system. Specifically I want to pose the question of the extent to which functionally specialised towns can be shown to grow in ways different from less specialised places.

For this, two preliminaries seem essential; a concept of urban growth and a means of classifying cities. If we see cities as locations which embody the realisation of surplus value in an economy, then the overall system growth of a set of urban places will be controlled by the surplus which is generated. Periods such as the industrial revolution, in which increments to surplus are generated by new technologies and the application of new innovations, represent times at which major growth impulses and major readjustments to the ranking of cities might be expected (Carter, 1969). Yet, while there are periods of unusually high flux as measured by the changes in the rank order of towns, differential growth occurs continuously within city systems and is reflected in rank changes even amongst the largest and most stable of cities (Table 4.1). The relative rises and falls of cities can be seen as the product of the shifting from one location to another of the surplus value within the total economic system such that overall stability, the average change and growth within the system around which fluctuations occur, is conditioned by the total size of the surplus value and the

Table 4.1: Rank-order fluctuations in the largest 21 towns in England and Wales

A Long-term fluctuations

(a) Period	(b) No. of towns newly entering the 'top 21'	(c) Approximate no. of years	(d) 'Index' of fluctuation *
1334-1524	8	190	42
1524-1662	7	140	50
1662-1801	12	140	81
1801-1901	6	100	60

* Higher values signify greater fluctuation. The 'index' is $100(b \div c)$.

Sources: Rank orders of towns for 1334, 1524/5 and 1662 from Darby (1973); for 1801 and 1901 from Robson (1973). It hardly warrants noting that the earlier data are highly suspect.

B Short-term fluctuations

(a) Period	(b) Index of fluctuation in rank order *
1801-11	14
1811-21	8
1821-31	15
1831-41	14
1841-51	18
1851-61	7
1861-71	7
1871-81	8
1881-91	7
1891-1901	5
1901-11	4

* Higher values signify greater fluctuation. The 'index' is one-half of the sum of rank moves up or down the hierarchy of the largest 21 towns. Towns entering or leaving the top 21 are assumed to have moved from or to rank position 22.

Source: Rank positions of towns at each decade from (1973).

detailed fluctuations of individual cities tend to balance each other out as surplus is invested or reinvested in one set of places while disinvestment occurs elsewhere. Such an interpretation is consistent with the empirical findings that the relationship of city growth and city size is often regular, as in Figure 4.2, with a narrowing fluctuation around a national average as one moves to larger cities. The lower variance at larger size can be seen as a function of the fact that larger cities have a broader economic base and that new investment or disinvestment will therefore have a lesser impact on the variegated bundle of activities represented by a large city. The wider variance of smaller cities reflects the considerable im-

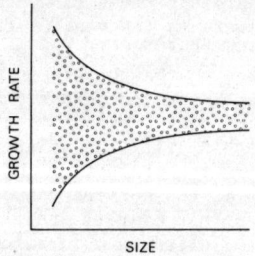

Figure 4.2: The relationship between size and growth rate

pact which such investment and disinvestment can have on the few activities of a small city.

We must, however, draw a distinction in the impact of this circulation of surplus as between 'basic' and 'non-basic' towns. The patterns of investment and disinvestment of surplus value will have a direct impact on 'basic' urban acitivities (however difficult this may be to define). The service activities, on the other hand, will be affected by new investment or the withdrawal of investment only at one degree removed since the existence of service activities is dependent on a local population and will not of itself be involved directly in the generation of value. This difference reinforces the value of using a simple dichotomy as a means of classifying urban functions; a dichotomy between production-based and central-place based towns or between a 'basic' and 'service' definition of towns. The types of classification which seem appropriate are therefore either those drawing on economic base theory or, more simply, typologies such as Bird's (Bird, 1973) or the Duncans' (Duncan et al., 1960). Bird suggests three axes of classification (Figure 4.3): one being the central place set of cities ranged along a hierarchical scale from hamlet to metropolis; a second being manufacturing cities with variations based on value added; and a third being 'port' or entrepot cities. The three axes converge to meet the national metropolitan centres which combine elements of all three.

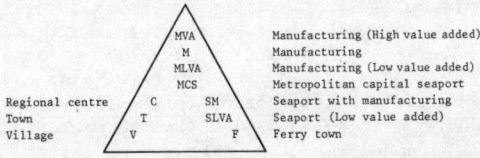

Figure 4.3: Bird's town classification (After Bird, 1973)

Bird's simple typology was conceived partly in relation to locational principles and it is clear that his model essentially embodies two different facets; first of central-place region-serving attributes of towns, and second their productive manufacturing and exchange attributes. This is similar to the typology suggested by Duncan et al., whose American-based classification was comprised equally of two separate concepts which produce two divergent branches which meet in the national metropolitan centres:

	National Metropolis	
	Diversified manufacturing with metropolitan functions	Regional metropolis
	Diversified manufacturing with few metropolitan functions	Regional capital, sub-metropolitan
Specialised manufacturing		

Again, the distinction between a central-place hierarchy and a set of manufacturing cities provides the substance of this classification.

4.4. Specialisation and growth

Given this basic dichotomy, which can loosely be related to the distinction between basic and non-basic urban activities, and can in turn be seen in the context of surplus value being invested in basic activities thereby producing urban change and growth, one can begin to develop some expectations about the relationships between functional types of city and their performance in a national system of cities. First, one can expect that there would be a two-stranded relationship between city size and the degree of specialisation within towns. The central place branch of our simple classification would show little specialisation whatever the population size range at which one looks; the manufacturing branch, on the other hand, would show increasing levels of specialisation at progressively smaller city sizes. At the one extreme of the large city, employment would consist of a variety of types of employment representing successive and continuing increments of investment in the sequences of different types of technology within the nation. To such multi-faceted investments of the surplus within large towns would be added the whole range of service activities which would be justified both in terms of the size of population of the place itself and the role that the town plays in consequence as a regional centre. The town which may start as a one-industry town lacking in service provision will, assuming its continuing ability to attract further investment and growth, inevitably begin to develop service functions of its own. At this extreme, such 'manufacturing' centres as Newcastle or Manchester develop as organising nodes for a regional system of manufacturing activity and, with this comes the development not only of the financial enterprises which lubricate the regional productive economy, but also retail, warehousing and commercial activities which are non-industry specific (Roberts, 1978). At the other extreme, the smallest manufacturing or industrial centres would be highly specialised, often consisting of only a single dominant firm or employer. The coal-mining villages of County Durham or the

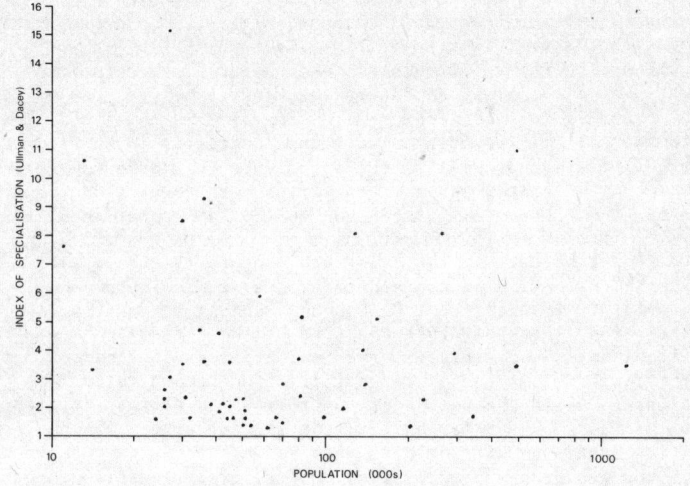

Figure 4.4: Size and specialisation. Data from Ullman and Dacey (1962)

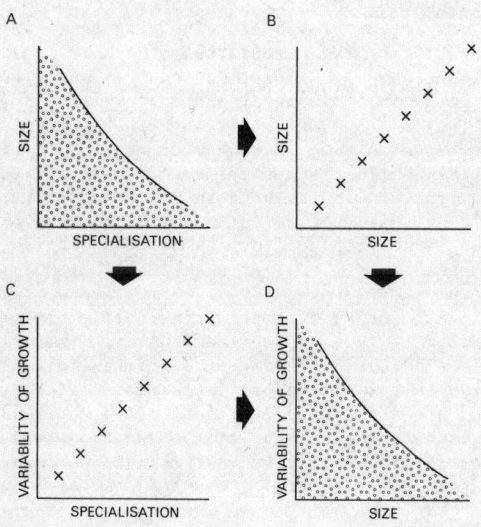

Figure 4.5: The relationship between size, specialisation and variability of growth

South Wales villages dominated by an iron firm are the classic cases. Only rarely would one expect, within the manufacturing towns themselves, that population size and specialisation would not be inversely related, even in the nineteenth century. Instances such as the domination of Consett by its iron works, for example, must be seen as exceptional. More usually, large size was clearly associated with some degree of industrial diversification as well as the appearance of a more complete range of associated service activities both to provide for the population of the town itself and that of neighbouring places.

We can see some confirmation of this expected relationship from American data in the twentieth century (Figure 4.4). With the exception of the special cases of Washington and Detroit, it is clear that Ullman and Dacey's index of diversification plotted against the size of the largest cities in the United States shows a scatter in which, at smaller population sizes, there is a range of specialisation from high to low, but at larger sizes the degree of specialisation narrows progressively. These data refer only to the largest cities of the United States and it would seem reasonable to suggest that the scatter would grow progressively wider, or at least would not narrow, at smaller and smaller population sizes.

Given this relationship between size and specialisation, we can suggest its connection with the sample two-fold classification of towns (Figure 4.5a). We can also readily suggest the expected relationship between these two attributes and the variability in the population growth of towns (Figure 4.5c and 4.5d). First, the concept of the circulation of surplus value between different locations with investment and disinvestment in different towns leads one to suggest a direct relationship between specialisation and the variability of growth (Figure 4.5c). The more specilised a town is, the more at risk it will find itself of suffering either very rapid growth, as new technology or new infrastructure is invested in it, or of relative stagnation or decline as existing investment is withdrawn or becomes obsolete and is not replaced by new. At the other extreme, the unspecialised town is either able to withstand the contraction of some part of its variety of activities or to compensate for disinvestment by a compensating ability to attract new investment if it is a productive town. Alternatively, if it is a service town, it will be divorced from the direct effects of productive investment and disinvestment decisions. This direct relationship between specialisation and variability of growth thus suggests that the shape of the relationship between size and variability should be as in Figure 4.5d, a shape which mirrors the relationship of size and specialisation.

4.5. The British example

To what extent to real-world data bear out this expected pattern? We can provide a somewhat coarse test by looking at the set of towns of over 2,500 population in England and Wales during the period 1801 to 1911. Of almost 1,000 towns which reached a population of 2,500 during that period, some 580 had ascertainable populations of this size or greater for six or more consecutive Census dates. It is these towns with five or more 'growth periods' that are shown in Figure 4.6. The X axis, size, shows the largest population attained by a town. The Y axis, variability, is somewhat more complex. It measures the size of the residual from the regression of standard deviation of growth rates on the average growth rate for each town. Standard deviations (SD) themselves cannot be used as a measure of variability since they are related to average growth (GR); the larger the growth the greater the deviation ($SD = 6.1 + 0.36\ GR$ with a standard error of 4.8). The residuals are shown in Figure 4.6 in terms of standard errors above or below the regression line. Positive residuals show greater growth variability than expected: negative residuals show greater stability of growth.

First, it is evident that the scatter of size and variability does conform to the expected shape. Large towns in general show a high degree of stability of growth over time, whereas smaller places cover the whole range of variability from highly stable to highly irregular. Second, however, can we show that the irregularly growing towns are specialised 'productive' places whose variability can be explained by shifts in the circulation of the surplus, whereas stable towns are service towns or less specialised productive towns? In practice, the first part of this question is easier to demonstrate than the second. If we look at the most extreme set of irregularly growing towns (those which lie above line AB in Figure 4.6) which are listed in Table 4.2, it is clear that they are indeed comprised of specialised towns which are largely, and in some cases overwhelmingly, dominated by a single or a small range of activities. They include ports and resort towns which are clearly subject to the whims of investment decisions; they include the textile towns of Yorkshire and Lancashire, some of the tin and copper mining and exporting towns of the South West, coal mining villages and towns of the North East. All of these are places directly dependent upon the patterns of investment and disinvestment of the surplus which can produce alternating periods of rapid and slow growth in town populations. Amongst them are some of the most dramatic instances of rapid urban growth, such as the iron manufacturing town of Middlesborough. Others had less dramatic, but just as variable growth. Macclesfield, for example, "is noted for the manufacturing of silk, which is carried on in all its branches to a considerable extent" (Lewis, 1844). Rawtenstall developed textiles and, at the end of the

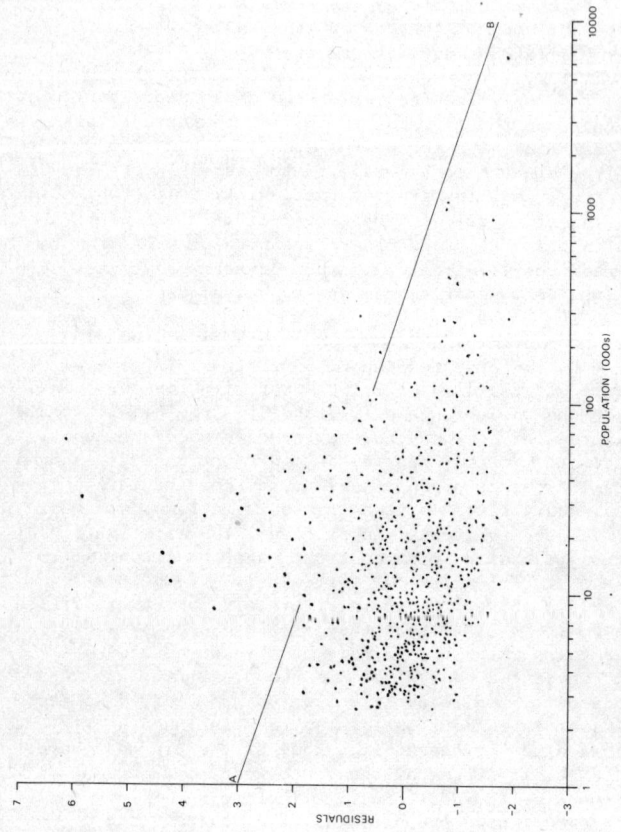

Figure 4.6: Size and variability of urban growth, 1801-1911. Towns lying above AB are shown in Tabel 4.2.

Table 4.2: Towns with the most highly irregular growth

	Town	County	Economic base
1. Textiles	Hyde	Cheshire	Cotton
	Macclesfield	Cheshire	Silk
	Ashton-u-Lyne	Lancs.	Cotton
	Bacup	"	Coal, wool, cotton
	Horwich	"	Cotton
	Pendlebury	"	Cotton
	Rawtenstall	"	Cotton, footwear
	Hacknall	Notts.	Hosiery
	Nuneaton	Warwicks.	Silk
	Bradford	Yorks.	Wool, worsted
	Brighouse	"	Worsted
	Halifax	"	Wool
	Keighley	"	Wool
	Shipley	"	Wool
2. Iron, Coal, Port	Crewe	Cheshire	Iron, railways
	Cleaton Moor	Cumberland	Iron
	Workington	"	Iron, port
	Crook	Durham	Coal
	Hetton-le-Hole	"	Coal
	Spennymoor	"	Coal
	Portland	Dorset	Stone, port
	Aberdare	Glamorgan	Coal, iron
	Folkestone	Kent	Port
	Barrow	Lancs.	Iron, port
	Grimsby	Lincs.	Port
	Tredegar	Monmouth	Iron, coal
	Tynemouth	Northumberland	Port, coal
	Middlesborough	Yorks.	Iron, port
3. Other industrial	Penzance	Cornwall	Tin, copper
	Truro	"	Tin, copper
	Tavistock	Devon	Tin, copper
	Widnes	Lancs.	Chemicals
	St. Helens	"	Glass
	Hanley	Staffs.	Pottery
	Burton-on-Trent	"	Brewing
	Newcastle-u-Lyme	"	Coal, pottery
4. Resort	Cheltenham	Gloucester	Resort
	Ryde	Hants.	Resort
	Newport	Isle of Wight	Resort
	Southport	Lancs.	Resort
	Brighton	Sussex	Resort
	Eastbourne	"	Resort
	Leamington Spa	Warwicks.	Resort

The list shows all towns lying above line AB in Figure 4.6.

century, "a felt slipper industry developed especially at a time of comparative depression in the cotton trade" such that no slipper factory was developed initially for that purpose" (Smith, 1953). Hyde "remained until a few years since a merely agricultural district, thinly inhabited, but is now become a rapidly improving place, by the establishment of the cotton manufacturing, for which there are some of the largest spinning and power-loom establishments in the kingdom" (Lewis, 1844). Specialisation, in all such cases, demonstrably carries with it both the prospect of rapid growth and of relative decline once investment or re-investment are discontinued.

On the other hand, by no means all of the specialised towns in this set of 580 places show high degrees of variability in their growth. If we select one category of town and look at its distribution, rather than at only the extreme cases, this can readily be seen. Figure 4.7 shows the resort towns - selected only because they are perhaps the easiest of any to define - and illustrates the way in which, even though some show highly

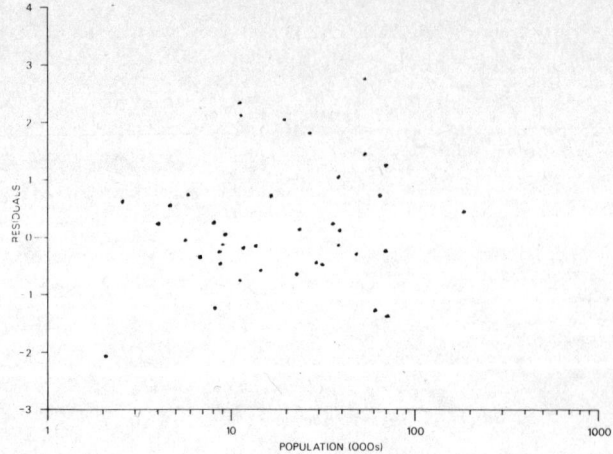

Figure 4.7: Size and variability of urban growth - resort towns, 1801-1911

Towns are : Cheltenham,Ryde,Newport,Leamington Spa,Eastbourne, Southport,Torquay,Hastings,Brighton,Lyme Regis, Ventnor,Tenby,Dawlish,St.Ives,Teignmouth, Sidmouth,Rhyll,Aberystwyth,Matlock,Ilfracombe Bognor,Bangor,Deal,Malvern,Exmouth,Cowes,Weston-super-Mare,Tunbridge Wells,Margate,Scarborough, Worthing,Ramsgate,Weymouth,Harrogate,Bath, Blackpool,Southend.

variable growth, many do not. For some, this is because the period 1801-1911 is inappropriate to capture the pattern of their rise and relative fall. Places such as Blackpool grew consistently throughout the period since 1861 when it first reached over 2,500, and it was only in the later part of this century that its surge of growth was to be reversed. Some places, too, never proved successful and the initial investment proved ill-timed or mistaken.

Aberystwyth, for example, began to be developed as a resort just at the turn of the century and, while still continuing as a modest resort town, was too late to benefit from the phenomenal growth that some of the earlier resort investments were to accrue. Its railway hotel was never completed and, taken over by its university, it stands as testament to the competition within an increasingly saturated market and hence to the possible penalties of the late-comer. Just as with such resort towns, so it is with the productive specialised manufacturing towns. The predominantly specialised Lancashire textile towns are represented amongst the highly variable growth rates, but most of its towns had relatively stable growth; some of the pottery towns have variable growth, but by no means all; and so one could continue.

Thus it is not the case that it is only the service towns which
are found to have more stable growth rates. Indeed, some of the
service towns show less stable growth than one might anticipate
because of their decline in population in the latter half of
the century, reflecting at one degree removed, the shift of
productive activity and hence of support population to the
manufacturing areas of the north and the midlands. In general,
however, the market towns and service centres show an expected
degree of stability, with negative residuals regardless of the
size of the town concerned.

In general, then, this measure of growth variability does provide some support for the extreme form of the hypothesis;
places which are most highly variable are indeed those which
are specialised, highly dependent upon a limited range of
activities, most highly functionally differentiated and therefore most critically dependent upon the circulation and shift
of the social surplus within the economy. The tendency towards
functional differentiation within a total economic system
carries with it the promise of higher overall growth, just as
Adam Smith's analysis of the division of labour suggested in
the case of individual enterprises or activities. Equally, as
the social surplus seeks new outlets for profit and capitalises
upon new innovations and inventions, so does functional differentiation of towns carry with it the risk of highly fluctuating fortunes no less than did specialisation in individual
skills like the hand-loom weaver.

The argument that has been developed here is that, by conceiving
of growth as a function of the circulation of the surplus, one
can go some way to combining the strengths of systems concepts
as applied to sets of cities with the concept of functionally
differentiated towns which systems analysis largely overlooks.
The rise and fall of particular places is a function of the
individual patterns of investment, disinvestment and reinvestment in given locations which can produce the simple rise and
fall of, say, a mining town such as Hetton-le-Hole in Durham
or an exporting port such as Penzance in Cornwall; it can give
rise to the more complex histories where reinvestment occurs
such as in Rawtenstall or as in Wallsend whose "ruins of an
ancient quay still further evince that this was anciently a
considerable trading colony of the Romans, who nearly sixteen
centuries since discharged their freight where now are numerous
staithes ..... at which vessels are continuously taking on immense quantities of the celebrated coal" (Lewis, 1844), or as
in south western towns such as Tavistock which had been an important centre for the manufacture of serge and coarse woollen
cloth, which later was to grow through its connection with tin
smelting and copper and lead mining and later still to fall
into relative obscurity as a market town. "The history of
particular cities can therefore be understood only in terms of
the circulation of surplus value at a moment of history within

a system of cities" (Harvey, 1973). While a more systematic demonstration of this concept would require a fuller and more precise definition of specialisation and of differentiation than is provided here, sufficient has been done at least to suggest the value of incorporating the concept of differentiation into our studies of systems of cities.

REFERENCES

Ahmad, Q. Indian cities: characteristics and correlates (Chicago, 1965) Dept. Geogr. Research Paper 102.
Alexandersson, G. The industrial structure of American cities (Lincoln, Nebraska, 1956).
Berry, B.J.L. 'Latent structure of the American urban system' in B.J.L. Berry (ed.) City classification handbook: methods and applications (London, 1972) pp. 11-60.
Bird, J.H. 'Of central places, cities and seaports', Geography, 58 (1973) pp. 105-18.
Crawley, R.W. 'Labor force growth and specialization in Canadian cities' in L.S. Bourne and J.W. Simmons (eds.) Systems of cities: readings on structure, growth and policy (London, 1978) pp. 207-19.
Darby, H.C. A new historical geography of England (Cambridge, 1973).
Duncan, O.D., W.R. Scott, S. Lieberson, B. Duncan and H. Winsborough Metropolis and region (Baltimore, 1960).
Foster, J. 'Nineteenth-century towns: a class dimension' in H.J. Dyos (ed.) The study of urban history (London, 1968) pp. 281-99.
Hadden, J.K. and E.F. Borgatta American cities: their social characteristics (Chicago, 1965).
Harris, C.D. 'A functional classification of cities in the United States', Geographical Review, 33 (1943) pp. 86-99.
Harvey, D.W. Social justice and the city (London, 1973).
King, L.J. 'Cross sectional analysis of Canadian urban dimensions, 1951 and 1961', Canadian Geographer, 10 (1966) pp. 205-24.
Lewis, S. A topographical dictionary of England (London, 1844), 5th edition.
Mattila, J.M. and W.R. Thompson 'The measurement of the economic base of the metropolitan area', Land Economics, 31 (1955).
Moser, C.A. and W. Scott British towns: a statistical study of their social and economic differences (London, 1961).
Nelson, H.J. 'A service classification of American cities', Economic Geography, 31 (1955) pp. 189-210.
Peach, C. West Indian migration to Britain: a social geography (London, 1968).
Pinard, M. 'Structural attachments and political support: the case of fluoridation referendums', American Journal of Sociology, 68 (1963) pp. 513-26.
Roberts, B.R. 'Agrarian organization and urban development' in J.D. Wirth and R.L. Jones (eds.) Manchester and Sao Paulo: problems of rapid urban growth (Stanford, 1978) pp. 77-105.
Robson, B.T. Urban growth: an approach (London, 1973).
Smith, R.H.T. 'Method and purpose in functional town classification', Annals, Association of American Geographers, 55 (1965) pp. 539-48.

Smith, W. *An economic geography of Great Britain* (London, 1953) 2nd edition.

Thomas, B. Migration and economic growth: *a study of Great Britain and the Atlantic economy* (Cambridge, 1954).

Ullman, E.L. and M.F. Dacey 'The minimum requirements approach to the urban economic base' in K. Norborg (ed.) *Proceedings of the IGU Symposium in Urban Geography, Lund 1960* (Lund, 1962) pp. 121-43.

5. Some examples of analyzing the process of urbanization: Northern Italy (eighteenth to twentieth century)
A. Caracciolo

5.1.	Some basic and long term elements	133
5.2.	Expansion of the big towns in aggregate terms	134
5.3.	The most important cases of urban densification	136
5.4.	Lines of urbanization in a research on the lower Po Valley after 1880	140

5. Some examples of analyzing the process of urbanization: Northern Italy (eighteenth to twentieth century)
A. Caracciolo

5.1. Some basic and long-term elements

In the period under consideration, opening towards the end of the 18th century and closing in the first decades of the 20th, urban and demographic facts are conditioned in Northern Italy by several important elements:
First, the survival of a century-old tradition of medium and small-sized urban centres dating back at least to the time of the medieval communes: these centres, which made it possible to speak of Italy as a country with "a hundred cities", were an integral and often dominant part of crowded rural provinces and were the home of the moneyed and landed classes.
Second, the existence of a plurality of sovereign States, so that this apparently homogeneous area was in fact devided between the Kingdom of Savoy, the Duchy of Milan, the Republics of Genoa, Lucca and Venice, the Duchies of Parma and Modena, the Grand Duchy of Tuscany, Papal Legations: even Italian political unity after the Risorgimento (1859-1866), the end result of a series of mergers of minor States, retained many elements of the old subdivision.
Third, the persistent economic subordination of all the territories of the Po Valley and Tuscany to Mid-Western Europe where mechanisms of capitalistic industrial development had been evolving since the 18th century: these territories acted principally as exporters of raw materials and semi-finished products and importers of capital and manufactured goods.
This is the general framework within which individual developments are diversely articulated and take place at varying speeds.
Let us take a rapid view of some statistical data, beginning by recalling the situation obtaining in the most recent years. Thus, half-way through the twentieth century in the North (including Tuscany) about 1,276,000 persons are registered as "resident" in Milan, 720,000 in Turin, 690,000 in Genoa, 375,000 in Florence, nearly 340,000 in Bologna, 317,000 in

Venice, 273,000 in Trïeste; another 10 cities number roughly
between 100 and 200,000 inhabitants, and on a total of nearly
33 million inhabitants registered in the Northern provinces
at that date, about 5,530,000 belong to towns with over 50,000
inhabitants, representing about 16-17% of the total population
of Northern Italy. This is a European level of development,
particularly noteworthy when compared with the slow rate of
urbanization in the eighteenth and early nineteenth century.

To remain in this more recent period, it should for example be remembered that as late as 1861 (in the first census
of the Kingdom of Italy) even Milan and Turin had respectively
about 192,000 and 172,000 inhabitants, considerably more than
Genoa (131,000), Venice (128,000), Bologna (113,000), Trïeste
(111,000), with both Florence and Livorno as low as 95,000 and
all the rest even further behind. It should also be observed
that the incidence of the "centralized population" (i.e. that
residing in centres of over 5,000 inhabitants) in 1861 reached
its maximum in Lombardy with 71.6% and Liguria with 63.5% and
its minimum in Emilia with 33.5%, but by 1911 a maximum of 79%
had been reached in Liguria and of 76.9% in Lombardy (40.7% in
Emilia) and by 1951 it was at 85.3% in Liguria and 82.7% in
Lombardy (54% in Emilia). It should finally be added that the
number of "centres" (as opposed to "scattered population") in
Northern Italy - within the 1860 borders - rose from 7,341 in
the 1861 census to 12,338 in 1951. In short, the entire range
of urbanization dimensions underwent radical changes in the
space of a century. I shall now examine various aspects of this
phenomenon, including brief references to the period preceding
1861 for which homogeneous statistics and precise territorial
divisions similar to those of the Kingdom of Italy are lacking.

5.2. Expansion of the big towns in aggregate terms

Pausing for a moment on the medium-large towns and on the
capitals or former capitals of the Italian States, it may be
noted that the urbanization process in Northern Italy follows
three different logical directions. From half-way through the
18th century up to the post-Napoleonic Restoration - around
the 1820s in other words - town population remains stationary,
below the total population increase, which, if anything, appears to be heavier in isolated houses (in sharecroppers
"poderi" or "cascine" and farms worked by wage-labourers and
day-labourers) or in medium-small centres. From the Restoration
to the early period of Italian Unification, on the other hand,
there is a stage of urban increase (with the exception of
Venice, which continued to decline) that is tendentially
superior or at least not inferior to the natural growth of the
population and to the increase that is taking place in the
country.

This stage eventually gives way, particularly after Unification, to a new phase registering a sharp acceleration in

the process of immigration towards urban centres and a more
evident divergence between the two sectors in their population
development (with a decreasing and ultimately even negative
natural balance in the towns). As to the succession of these
phases it is sufficient to remember that Turin, which had been
practically stable between 1720-30 and 1810, suddenly swings
upwards, doubling its population by 1848 (about 137,000), to
accelerate again, reaching 250,000 in 1881 and 415,000 in 1911.
Milan, in its turn, after oscillating between 130 - 140,000 for
a century, settles at over 200,000 in the middle of the 19th
century and leaps to 320,000 in 1881 and to 490,000 in 1901.
The port of Livorno rises from 36 - 40,000 to nearly double in
1850 and triple in 1860. More gradual, but also evident, are
the advances of Bologna and Florence in the central decades
of the 19th century while the decline of Venice has already
been mentioned.

This occurs in a period in which the total population in
almost every region is undergoing a sharp increase: in terms
of thousands of inhabitants, the mainland states of the Kingdom of Sardinia pass from 2,916 in 1821 to 3,536 in 1861 (+
620, i.e. an increase of over 21%), Lombardy-Venetia from
4,085 to 5,572 (+ 1,487, or over 36%), Tuscany from 1,383 to
1,826 (+ 443, or over 32%), etc. Average rates are thus for
the first time lower than rose attributed to Milan and Turin
but higher than Venice and similar to Genoa, Florence and
Bologna.

Concentrating mainly on the century following Unification,
we have the following distribution among towns in Northern
Italy:

Table 5.1: Number of towns by size category in Northern Italy,
1780-1951

Size category x 1000	1780 approx.	1840 approx.	1861	1881	1901	1921	1951
20 - 50	13	14	30	36	48	56	68
50 - 100	6	5	10	13	15	21	28
100 - 200	2	4	5	4	3	6	10
200 - 500	-	1	2	3	3	5	4
500 - 1000	-	-	-	-	1*	2**	3***

* Milan
** Milan and Genoa
*** Milan, Genoa and Turin

This discussion should now however be broken up into its various
parts, with an examination of the most important of the veri-
table urban networks that appear in Italy in the corse of more
recent history. Calculations - limited to the post-Unification
period - have been made as to the percentage of population in-

crease in the urban centres due to immigration from the country. Such increases prove to be absolutely decisive, as was to be expected in a period of rapid urbanization. Between 50 and 40% of the increase is to be found in the final decades of the last century, until - that is - the increase in size is to make similar rates impossible. On the other hand, the rate of natural increase in the towns is very modest, since the rise in the average life expectancy occurring in this period is balanced by a heavy contraction in the birth rate.

5.3. The most important cases of urban densification

In most of the 19th century the dislocation of urban centres appears to be determined by the narrow and static balance between farming and trade, represented, in its most typical form both on hill and plain, by the small lease-farm or freeholding, although this gradually tends to give way to larger and wealthier forms of farming enterprises, from the Lombard "cascina" to the Piedmontese and Venetian "fattorie" and the Tuscan "poderi". A first group of villages is thus the traditional one of villages immediately connected with agricultural production. But between the second half of the 18th and the 19th century a number of centres emerge on account of their strategic position in relation to more important commercial activities: towns like Lodi, for example, south of Milan, Imola south of Bologna and a group of small towns south and east of Turin. Other centres are being populated through the installation of industries such as a silk factory at Como, a woollen factory at Schio, metalworks at Savona, engineering concerns at Monza and so on.

On a higher level, there is a population, building and territorial expansion, in towns vested with an administrative function. Until the unification of Italy these are capitals of States, such as Turin, Milan, Florence or near-capitals like Bologna and Genoa. After this it is to be the turn of the capitals of the Kingdom of Italy, Turin from 1860-61 to 1864 and Florence from 1865-1871, until the government and Court finally settle in Rome. Not surprisingly, ill-content and serious disorders break out both in Turin and Florence when they lose the profitable title of capital. A certain degree of stimulation for urban development is also given to towns appointed (not always according to precise and uniform criteria) as "provincial capitals" in the new Kingdom, assuming administrative and public functions. As is evident, what could be called the "bureaucratic" component is as important in Northern Italy as in the South in attracting population from the country where phenomena of de-structuration together with the penetration of the European agrarian crisis are spreading pauperism and underemployment.

About a generation after the birth of Unified Italy further phenomena - such as the completion of the major railway net-

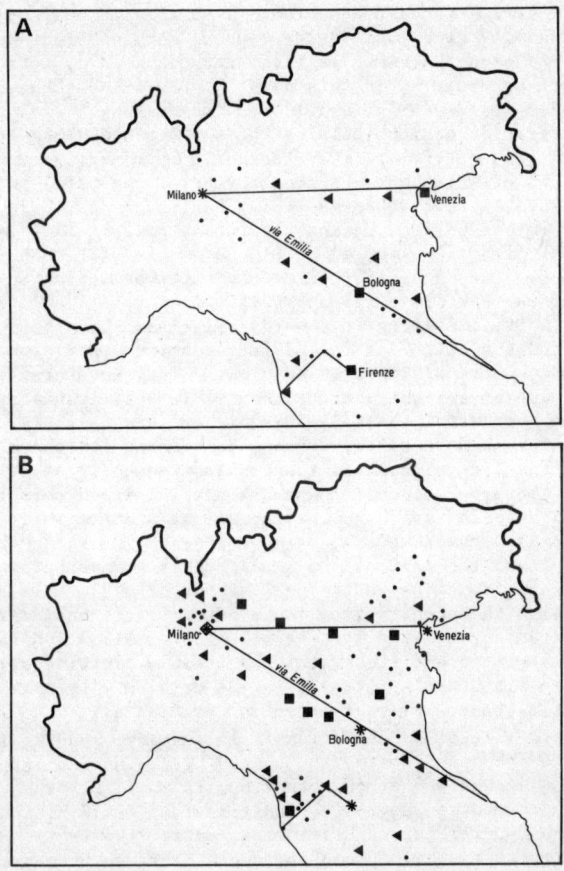

Figure 5.1: Distribution of towns in Northern Italy in 1861 (map A) and 1961 (map B)

- •   20,000 -   50,000 inhabitants
- ◀   50,000 -   100,000 inhabitants
- ■ 100,000 -   200,000 inhabitants
- ✳ 200,000 -   500,000 inhabitants
- ▦ 500,000 - 1.000,000 inhabitants

work and a strong tendency to create a single national market in the economy - come to maturity causing more coherent and precise settlement "systems". At least three main directions may in fact be detected at this point in the wake of the previous tendencies (see Figure 5.1).

The first direction includes the settlements along the Via Emilia through cities like Placenza, Parma, Modena, Reggio, Bologna (all of which have become provincial capitals) and then towards the coast through Imola, Forli, Faenza, Lugo, Ravenna, Rimini, Cervia, Cesena, as far as Pesaro. This is a traditional direction, where the old Roman consular road (later the railway and still later the motorway), pick up the traffic of the fertile rural and partly industrialized areas adjacent to it, conveying it towards Milan and the Alps on the one hand and the South and the Adriatic on the other. The influence of the transformation and growth of agricultural economy on these nuclei which are to become largely manufacturing as well as commercial around 1950-60 is evident over the whole of the century and up to the present day. Among its characteristics is the lack of a macro-town and consequently of a "metropolitan area" since Bologna has never assumed this role (partly because it never was the capital of a State while smaller towns such as Modena, Parma and nearby Ferrara were for a long time the capitals of small duchies). Another characteristic consists in the persistence of a close relationship with the country from the productive, financial and even human aspect: the activities of transformation and transit focusing on these cities retain an organic tie with agriculture and its social protagonists and develop within an area that is still basically restricted and provincial.

Another line of urbanization is in Tuscany, leading from Florence to the sea. Limited at one end by the ancient capital of the Grand Duchy and at the other by its port, Livorno, it also includes modern provincial capitals like Pistoia, Lucca and Pisa, a traditional manufacturing centre like Prato (which tends to create a single urban unit with Florence by way of Sesto Fiorentino and Rifredi) and other fairly important centres such as Montecatini, Pescia and Altopascio. This is a wealthy area, based on the sharecropping system, where industry has a more intense and at times more extensive development than in Emilia. Here too, in any case, an important element is the existence of an efficient road and railway network, which favour this route over the other more southern route (through Empoli) which also links Florence to the coast by way of the Arno valley. Here is also located the modern motorway which, after reaching Lucca and Pisa turns towards the crowded tourist area (Viareggio, Versilia) and the industrial area (Apuania, Liguria, Milan itself). Overpopulation of these centres, caused by the influx of inhabitants from the nearby Appenines or of persons driven away from sharecropping "poderi", already dense before Unification becomes particularly strong afterwards.

A third area worth mentioning, round which, indeed, towards the middle of the 20th century, urbanization has been so pronounced that it is possible to speak of a metropolitan area, is that of the pre-Alpine plain of Lombardy. It has been noted that in the course of the 19th century, before the Unification of Italy, the traditional nucleus of Milan had already been breaking through the circle of its Spanish walls and preparing to annex the populous suburban villages called the "Corpi Santi". The concentration all round the city of an extremely prosperous countryside, together with the establishment of a wide range of business and commercial activities over a fairly vast territory, gave rise from the very first phase of prosperity and maturity in Lombardy that began in 1830-1860, to a population growth that took place contemporaneously in the capital, the minor centres surrounding it, the isolated houses and the country villages proper: the result, in other words, as appears from what is by now very precise data, not only of a high natural balance but also of immigration from the mountains, the Venetia and later even from other regions. The process of "annexing" the new inhabited areas passes through a number of stages: the gradual absorption of the Corpi Santi as housing areas beginning in 1874; the incorporation of strips of other communes in the direction of the new big industry situated in Sesto Fiorentino and its so-called "port" in the first 20 years of the 20th century; the suppression of 11 adjacent communes in 1913: the population of the Commune of Milan after its first gradual increase from around 250,000 in 1861 to 600,000 in 1911 is soon to include within its new boundary about a million inhabitants (1931 census), making it possible to talk of a single "urban area" of Milan.

The favourable geographic position, connected on the one hand with the vast and fertile countryside of the Po Valley and on the other with Central Europe, make Milan a particularly dynamic pole of expansion in the age of rapid European development in the 19th century. South of Milan, as far as the districts of Lodi, Crema, Pavia, Brescia, Cremona, intensive and well-watered agriculture, with the considerable commercial, financial and manufacturing activities connected with it, are particularly well developed. North, especially round Como, there is a concentration of advanced silk spinning and throwing, the silk being then worked at Como itself and Milan, both on domestic looms and in a growing number of factories put up beside the cotton mills and destined to show an impressive upsurge towards the end of the century.

Between the 19th and 20th centuries the main heavy industry installations - from iron and steel to engineering - are made in this region. On the whole a scattering of population and economic activities is to be observed in a large number of middle and lower towns distributed in two kinds of concentric semicircles, one very close to the provincial capital (from Biusto Arsizio to Rescaldina and from Saronno to Monza and as far as the Adda) and another further away (Novara, Varese, Como, Lecco, Bergamo). By the first quarter of this century the urban network of Milan and the Milan area has already established the close enveloping structuring covering the residual rural areas that it will continue to develop up to the present day.

5.4. Lines of urbanization in a research on the lower Po Valley after 1880

Considerable importance in connection with the fairly rough indications given up to now is assumed by a research undertaken by a study group (conducted by C. Carocci, A. Mioni, R. Rozzi) on the basis of the elaboration of original archive and cartographic sources. The research examines a group of towns situated east of Milan in the direction of Venice and south east of Milan in the direction of Rimini. It is based on the hypothesis that an increase in the growth of urban size and population is not necessarily the effect of industrialization, but the consequence of a series of concomitant historical causes or even, rather, a favorable condition for modern industrialization.

The group thus began by verifying a number of more specific hypotheses that can be expressed as follows:
(a) The 'original' characteristics of an urban structure determine certain characteristics of its subsequent development even in the field of production;
(b) Recent urban growth depends in part of the size and nature of the pre-existent patrimony of real estate, services, facilities;
(c) The effectiveness of its size and nature is in its turn dependent on the degree of its 'convertibility' to modern needs.

A number of criteria were subsequently established for finding and reading the basic data. Among these criteria are those (a) of considering the population within an effectively urbanized area (to be defined) rather than within the communal administrative area; (b) of examining quantitative and qualitative aspects contextually (for example, the occupational distribution of the population); (c) of noting the variations in the relation between areas destined respectively to residential, service or productive use; (d) of analyzing the relationship between population and urbanized (or housing) area, establishing the utilization "intensity" of the urban areas. In this manner a cross between topographic (good military maps of Italy on a 1:25,000 scale have been available since 1880) and demographic data (census data subdivided into communes and fractions of communes exist for every decade since 1881) has been achieved, to be completed by the monographic studies on the individual towns that may in the meantime have been produced by administrators, technicians, population experts, economists and sociologists.

The research was carried out on 21 centres in a former and on another 31 in a later phase. In the early phase, judging from a publication produced by the group, one phenomenon is already evident: the population in centres located along the two main directions Milan-Venice (the present "Serenissima" motorway) and Milan-Rimini (Via Emilia), has gradually increased while the more decentralized urban nuclei inside this fan have been considerably 'alleviated' in their economic and demographic development. To explain this fact it is observed that the impetus that is typical in proximity of traffic routes must have counted considerably: the commercial 'position' had an important weight in development in this case as in several other cases of early industrialization. It must also be observed that all the centres that were to develop most in the course of time belonged, before the period under consideration, to a high 'grade' both from an administrative, cultural and military as well as mercantile aspect: they either possessed universities, for example (Milan, Pavia, Padua, Modena, Bologna, Ferrara), or were capitals of large or small pre-Unification States (Milan, Venice, Modena, Parma and, in the more distant past, even Ferrara, Bologna, etc.).

Among its provisional results, the research group has been able to establish the following points:

1) Since the early years of the 20th century, with an interval between 1935 and 1950 aproximately, the rate of urban physical growth has been on average definitely higher than the population increase (the 'intensity' of human settlement is falling, in other words).

2) While the relation between housing areas and other urban areas was 3:2 at the beginning of the period, it rises considerably at the end, ultimately reaching 2:1.

3) These phenomena condition the level of land revenue, which remains low in the first decades to speed up subsequently.

4) The urban structure of the various centres taken into consideration situated on its main lines of direction, tends to become more homogeneous as time passes.

In conclusion, this is an exemplary research, even if for the time being it only replies in an articulate fashion to a limited number of queries. At the end of its first stage of work the group was, above all, able to transform the initial question ("Why, and in what relation to industrialization, does a city grow?") into another, more exact, question ("With what modalities and diversifications in its physical structure can a town answer, in the course of time, the needs of the social classes that reside there?"). In any case, it has been confirmed that the traditional expression of the problem in terms of the influence of industrial development on urbanization is incongruous and needs to be reversed. If this is the case for the lower Valley of the Po, it also corresponds to a more general situation in the whole of Central-Northern Italy: it suggests, in short, a more correct way in general of putting the problem of the relation between modern urbanism and modern industrialization.

6. The influence of industrialization on urban growth in Prussia (1815–1914)
H. Matzerath

6.1. Introduction 145
6.2. The initial phase (1815-40) 149
6.3. Urban growth under the influence of the Industrial Revolution (1840-71) 155
6.4. Urban growth in the main industrialization period (1871-1914) 160
6.5. The structure of the overall development 166
Appendix 173
References 176

6. The influence of industrialization on urban growth in Prussia (1815–1914)
H. Matzerath

6.1. Introduction

Urbanization plays a central role in almost all theories of social change. In most concepts of modernization the urbanization-ratio is defined as the proportion of the population living in towns (Städte) of a certain size (2,000; 5,000; 20,000 inhabitants) to the total population. This represents, along with industrialization, education, franchise, mass-media, and formation of the nation state, a key variable with which to register secular changes in the development of various nations (Zapf 1969; Flora 1974; Wehler 1975 with a discussion of the main concepts of Lerner, Deutsch, Eisenstadt, Almond, and Rokkan). The connection between industrialization and urbanization is, moreover, a subject of relevant interest to the disciplines of Economic and Social History. Yet these concepts, however apt and fruitful they may be for a global analysis of general social change, initially raise more questions than they answer in the case of historical analysis. There is as yet little certainty as to the long-term demographic structure of the urbanization process, as has been demonstrated by the renewed interest in A.F. Weber's classical study (Weber 1899, reprint). There is even less clarity as to the link between urbanization and economic growth for which we lack a discussion as it has begun in the United States (Pred 1966; Williamson/Swanson 1966; Higgs 1970/71; Swanson/Williamson 1970/71).

Is urbanization simply an epiphenomenon of industrialization, or is it, though still closely linked with industrial development, an independent process? Is urbanization a universal structure in the development of modern society; can a recurring pattern of urbanization be observed in various industrial nations, or can similar structures be seen at least within Germany? And finally: can one observe components in the urbanization-process that are clearly divided into urban and rural, or is one confronted with a rural-urban continuum? (Sorokin/Zimmermann 1929; Dewey 1960/61).

The following discussion can make at best a very limited contribution to the debate of these questions. The limitations of this study lie not so much in the period of time under examination: in Germany 1815 is well before the beginning of the Industrial Revolution and 1914 coincides with the approximate end of the period of industrialization. As for the problem of development -disparities within Germany (Borchardt 1966; Hohorst 1974; Fremdling/Tilly 1979), here, too, it is not of major significance that the study is confined to Prussia in its various forms: not only did Prussia encompass, both before and after the First World War, more than 60% of the territory and population of the German Empire, it also embraced a large number of areas greatly differing in tradition and culture as well as in their social and economic structures.

More substantial limitations lie in the material used and the method of approach. The study is based, firstly, on the official Prussian and German Imperial statistics on the distribution of population between town and country and, secondly, on the evaluation of a set of data which contains the population statistics from almost every census. These latter statistics are for all legally recognized towns and after 1867 for all communities of over two thousand inhabitants whether these were recognized as towns or as land-communities (Landgemeinden). The study, which attempts to draw a connection between demographic and economic development, thus makes use of both the legal and statistical concepts of town.

Urbanization as a demographic process is defined here as the overproportional growth of the urban population in relation to the population as a whole, or, to put it another way, as the increase of the urban population's proportion to the total population (urbanization-ratio). Using this criterion it is possible to distinguish three phases of urban growth for the period of time up to 1910 (Figure 6.1).

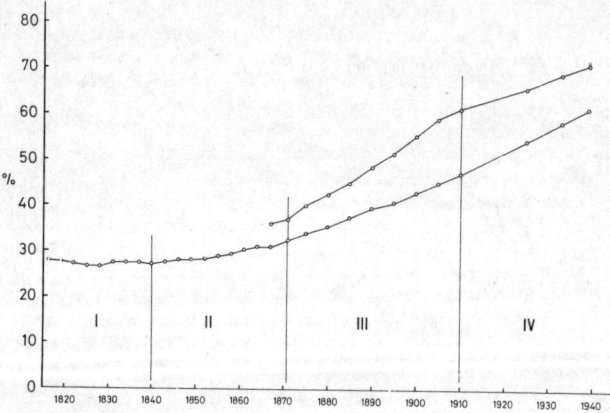

Figure 6.1: Phases of urbanization
% of living in towns (in the legal sense), 1816-1940 and in communities over 2,000 inhabitants 1867-1940

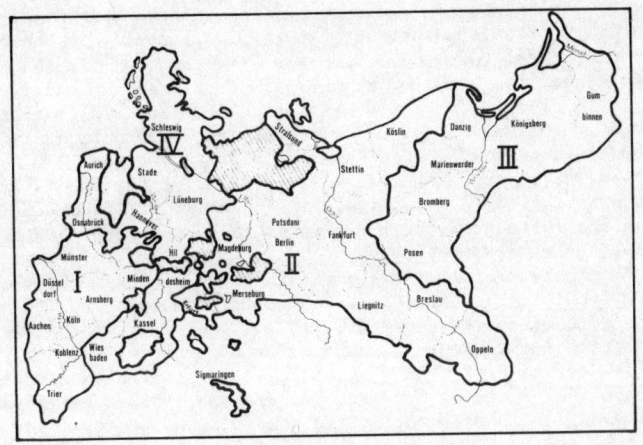

Prussia (1866–1918)

I Western provinces: Rhineland
                       Westphalia

II Middle provinces: Brandenburg
                       Saxony
                       Silesia
                       Pomerania

III Eastern provinces: East Prussia
                       West Prussia
                       Posen

IV New provinces: Hannover
                       Hessen-Nassau
                       Schleswig-Holstein

Figure 6.2:   Regions in Prussia

Despite certain waverings growth stagnates until about 1840; between then and 1867/71 the urbanization-ratio rises moderately, but steadily; not until after 1871 does the urban-rural relationship really begin to alter markedly - by 1910 less than half of the population was urbanized according to the categories of the legal town-concept, but two-thirds according to those of the statistical town-concept. There are also economic and political factors that support this division into phases: the beginning of the Industrial Revolution or industrialization-process in Germany is placed varyingly at the middle or end of the 30's (Mottek 1973 : 76; Henning 1973 : 112) or at 1850 (Rostow 1961; Borchardt 1972 : 22). Similarly, the foundation of the Empire, or alternatively the economic crisis of the seventies (Gründer-Krise), are taken to be the start of the main industrialization-phase.

Regional differentiation within Prussia causes far greater difficulties for analysis: the administrative units (and it is only for these that material is available) do not tally with the economic regions, and more importantly because "region" may be defined differently according to historical, cultural, political or economic factors, because the area of a region may change in the course of time and because the new type of region - taking the form of agglomeration-areas - only came into being during the period examined here. Thus I will restrict myself to very rough regional divisions like the ones used by Prussian statisticians of the time (figure 6.2): Firstly the little developed Prussian eastern Provinces (East and West Prussia, Posen), not a part of the German Reich before 1806; and then the Middle Provinces (Brandenburg, Pomerania, Saxony, Silesia), of which Pomerania displayed strong similarities with the eastern Provinces; the western Provinces (Rhineland, Westphalia) which were only integrated in this form into the Prussian state after 1815 as a result of the Vienna Congress: and finally the new Provinces (1864/66): Schleswig-Holstein, Hessen-Nassau, Hannover).

Until recently urbanization has been only to a limited extent the object of systematic study in German historiography (Thienel 1973, Jasper 1977), in addition to the early statistical ground-work of A.F. Weber and Werner Sombart (Sombart 1955 : 399; Ipsen 1956 : 786). German studies have been mainly critical of towns and have centered on the problem of "rural flight" (Landflucht). The latter set the tone of discussion in Germany until the early 30's (Pfeil 1972 : 27; Quante 1958; Haufe 1936). No new development was introduced here until the 60's with Croon's study on the Rhineland (1960) and with the works of Köllmann, which were mainly devoted to the development of the city between 1871 and 1914.

Here the attempt will be made to discuss the urbanization process according to phases and in relation to economic development, taking into consideration regional diversities, (6.2. - 6.4.) and finally, the structure of the development as a whole (6.5.).

6.2. The initial phase (1815-40)

The statement above - that in this first phase there was no urbanization in the sense of an overproportional growth of the urban population - provokes further questions. Can this period be viewed as having still been in a state of inactivity, as "pre-modern" and "pre-industrial", still marked by a sharp urban-rural contrast?

Discussion in recent years has increasingly emphasized that the urban-rural contrast was already lessening in the early Modern Age (Kellenbenz 1963; Van Houtte 1966) and that trades were already spreading from the towns to the open land. This expansion of trades into the countryside was, under the concept of "proto-industrialization", declared an independent form of economy - in the context of the rural family-economy (Mendels, Kriedtke, Medick, Schlumbohm 1977). On the other hand, Prussian General Common Law even as late as 1794 contains formulations that point to an irrefutable division of functions between town citizen (Bürger) and peasant, urban trade and artisanry and rural agricultural production.

The reorganization of the Prussian state in 1815 encountered differing conditions in its various territories: in certain parts of middle and eastern Prussia - most especially in Silesia - the old urban-rural division had already been broken down by earlier developments, in other parts it was still relatively intact. The Prussian reform-laws, with the liberation of the peasants, the free access to trade (Gewerbefreiheit), removal old compulsory guilds and the granting of urban self-administration, brought about increased mobilization, even though practical problems and local resistance hindered the execution of these reforms in many cases. The generally more advanced western areas, especially the Rhineland, insisted on retaining the French principles of law which had altogether abolished the old economic and social privileges - and thus the special status - of the towns.

The trade-census of 1822 (Table 6.1) gives an idea of the actual differential then in existence. Ignoring for the moment the rural skilled-workers (e.g. blacksmiths) and the locally-tied, early-industrial iron-works, a clear urban-rural contrast can be established in almost every dimension, much greater generally in the East than in the West. While various trade-functions were more strongly pronounced in the East (clearly concentrated in the towns), the bulk of skilled production lay definitely in the West. The disposition-functions of the entrepreneurs and bankers of that time ("merchants without open shops") can be counted among these. As there was a differential not only between the "large" towns (over 10,000 inh.) and the open land, but also between medium to small towns and the rural areas, it is possible to start from the premise of

Table 6.1: Economic urban-rural differential, 1822 (association-index)

	bakers	black-smiths	lock-smiths	specialised artisanry	weaver looms	textile finishing	hammer mills, foundries	merchants (without open shops)	merchants (with open shops)
	(1)	(2)	(3)	(4)	(5)	(6)	(7)	(8)	(9)
Prussia	1,00	1,00	1,00	1,00	1,00	1,00	1,00	1,00	1,00
towns	0,45	1,42	0,47	0,29	0,49	0,31	1,49	0,28	0,29
country	1,74	0,91	1,64	7,06	1,58	4,74	0,90	9,22	6,64
eastern provinces	1,57	0,89	2,55	1,86	6,43	1,53	11,45	1,27	1,03
middle provinces	1,01	1,02	1,53	0,91	1,03	0,99	2,07	1,63	0,96
western provinces	0,75	1,07	0,47	0,80	0,57	0,79	0,37	0,53	1,05
country east. prov.	7,46	0,80	24,93	37,92	30,49	11,82	9,01	45,50	91,00
country middle prov.	1,56	0,91	7,78	10,29	1,97	13,01	1,73	?	9,21
country west. prov.	1,20	1,03	0,53	3,18	0,74	1,84	0,35	2,30	2,90
towns eastern prov.	0,44	1,46	0,65	0,46	1,81	0,39	112,00	0,30	0,25
towns middle prov.	0,54	1,49	0,51	0,28	0,47	0,30	4,14	0,44 (?)	0,30
towns western prov.	0,34	1,25	0,40	0,23	0,32	0,27	0,45	0,15	0,34
towns 10000 inhab.	0,72	3,94	0,63	0,22	0,28	0,53	65,45	0,14	0,27
over: eastern prov.	0,70	3,86	0,73	0,28	5,38	0,87	28,00	0,10	0,21
middle prov.	0,98	4,29	0,69	0,21	0,30	0,61	80,40	0,22	0,29
western prov.	0,46	7,28	0,50	0,22	0,13	0,34	0,00	0,09	0,30
towns 10000 inhab.	0,40	1,14	0,43	0,33	0,72	0,27	1,08	0,47	0,30
with eastern prov.	0,39	1,21	0,63	0,59	1,48	0,33	0,00	1,08	0,26
less middle prov.	0,46	1,18	0,46	0,33	0,61	0,25	3,00	0,76	0,30
than: western prov.	0,30	1,00	0,30	0,24	0,67	0,27	0,33	0,20	0,35

Note: In the case of the artisans only masters and self-employed individuals are considered here.

1) These include: girdlers (col. 46), coppersmiths (col. 48), foundrymen (col. 50/52), plumbers (col. 54), mechanics (col. 56), watchmakers (col. 57), gold- and silversmiths (col. 59), gem cutters (col. 62), printers (col. 62), bookbinders (col. 64).
2) Professionally operated looms, including stocking and ribbon weaving (this category excludes looms which were used only to supplement another occupation). It is possible that in some cases workers within the rural "putting-out" system have been attributed to the towns.
3) Cloth finishing (Tuchscherer und Tuchbereiter, col. 95) as well as dyers and cloth printers (col. 97).
4) Either miscalculations or misprints in the original. The association index is computed as the ratio of percentage of population employed in each respective trade.
total population given area

Source: "Gewerbetabelle der Preuss. schen Monarchie für das Jahr 1822" and "Gewerbetabelle von sämtlichen Städten des Preussischen Staates ..... 822", Hauptstaatsarchiv Düsseldorf, Regierung Düsseldorf 2159.

an urban-rural contrast that was still plainly recognizable, though of uneven strength. Even the weaving and textile-industries and the cottage-iron industry, those branches of industry usually regarded as specifically "proto-industrial", were predominantly concentrated in the towns in certain parts of the country. All in all, it is already possible to deduce from this table a development in the West towards the industrial town. In the East, however, the town still functioned mainly as a regional center with commerce and specialized skilled-workers. The East-West differential visible here (and equally clearly in other dimensions - road-buildings, for example) was also not reduced significantly during the first phase.*

The question arises from this finding whether the extent of urbanization corresponded with the state of economic development. The urbanization-quota alone can hardly be taken as a measure, since there were considerable variations between the individual parts of the country - between, for instance, the province of Posen with numerous small towns, some with less than 500 inhabitants, the administrative-districts Danzig and Cologne with a small number of towns which were totally dominated by the largest one among them, Gumbinnen, with few and small towns, or Düsseldorf with numerous, relatively large towns. These different types of urban systems make it seem sensible to take several aspects of urbanization into account: number and population of the towns, size of the total population as well as the surface-area of a particular region. This creates further working categories in addition to that of the urbanization-ratio: the average size of population of a town, urban density, population density; in addition comes the

---

*Association-index 1837

	Bakers	Mechanics	Merchants without open shops
Town	0.50	0.44	0.31
Country	1.54	1.83	4.77
Eastern Provinces	1.73	2.87	1.94
Middle Provinces	0.1	1.53	1.46
Western Provinces	0.67	0.46	0.50

J.G. Hoffmann, Die Bevölkerung des Preussischen Staats, Berlin 1839, pp. 114 ff.

average annual growth rate.*

The individual dimensions of urbanization diverge considerably from one another in 1816 (Table 6.2): it is immediately noticeable that not even the regional pattern of the urbanization-ratio concurs with the picture gained above: the West, despite being the economically most advanced region, had by far the smallest urbanization-ratio.

The average town-size, however, points to a more efficient town-system in the western regions. The fact that the middle provinces are out in front in both dimensions is substantially due to Berlin. In the case of urban density and population density, though, a clear East-West differential is perceivable: in the West twice as many towns and two-and-a-half times as many people were concentrated on a similar area than in the eastern provinces. This means that extremely varied conditions prevailed during this initial period: a higher concentration of population in the towns in the East contrasted with greater urban diffusion in the framework of denser population in the West.

The development between 1816 and 1840 provides a few surprises: to begin with, the urban population rose by 41% (from 2.9 to 4.1 million inhabitants) within 24 years despite a slightly falling urbanization-ratio. The growth rates reveal a definite counter development regionally: the East registered the strongest total population-increase, however with the smallest growth of the urban population, whereas in the West the reverse process occurred; the middle provinces displayed roughly equal growth in the towns and in the rural areas. This development is also expressed in a rise in the urbanization-ratio in the West and in a corresponding fall in the East.

---

*The individual values are worked out by means of the following simple formulae:

urbanization-ratio: $\frac{\text{urban population}}{\text{total population}} \times 100$

average town size: $\frac{\text{urban population}}{\text{number of towns}}$

urban density: $\frac{\text{surface-area (square kilometers)}}{\text{number of towns}}$

population density: $\frac{\text{population}}{\text{surface area}}$

average annual growth-rate: population year

$$100 \left(\sqrt[n]{\frac{\text{population year } t_2}{\text{population year } t_1}} - 1 \right)$$

Simultaneously a rationalization of the town-system was carried out: in the West the number of towns was reduced by 34 from 256 to 222, which especially affected small communities with indistinct urban status and ineffectual urban functions, mainly in the Düsseldorf administration district. While urban density remained stable in the Middle Provinces, it deteriorated slightly in the eastern region. For Prussia as a whole, this signified that the differences in town density were reduced. The removal of small, weakly functioning towns and the overall increase in urban population caused a noticeable rise in the average town-size, which suggests a more efficient town-system.

If the various modes of urbanization are taken together, a clear tendency towards polarization between East and West becomes apparent, except in urban density. An intensification of the differences can be established most distinctly in the development of population density.

How, though, did this undeniable urban growth throughout Prussia take place during this period? Before we can answer this question we must note another, similarly unexpected piece of information: the smaller the town, the higher the growth-rates.* Another surprising fact is that the towns in the middle and eastern provinces recorded on average more vigorous growth

Table 6.2: Dimensions of urbanization, 1816-40

	Urbanization ratio		Average town-size		Urban density		Population density		growth-rates 1816-40	
									total pop.	urban pop.
	1816	1840	1816	1840	1816	1840	1816	1840		
East	26.9	22.9	2248	3046	344	355	24	38	1.86	1.16
Middle	30.3	30.4	3146	4599	282	282	37	54	1.56	1.59
West	24.6	25.2	2825	4515	174	212	59	84	1.27	1.37
Prussia	27.9	27.2	2678	4103	271	282	37	53	1.55	1.45

Sources: Das Anwachsen der Bevölkerung im Preussischen Staate seit 1816, in: Zeitschrift des Königlichen Preussischen Statistischen Bureaus, vol 1 (1861), pp. 10 ff.; (Hoffmann), Beiträge zur Statistik des preussischen Staats, Berlin 1821, p. 22 f.; 1840: Tabellen und amtliche Nachrichten über den preussischen Staat für das Jahr 1849, vol. 1, Berlin 1851, p. 398.

---

* (Pearson's) correlation-coefficient r for the connection between town size and population growth = 0.189 (N = 919, s = 0.001). Cf. also appendix tab. C.

than those in the western provinces (Table 6.3). This apparent contradiction is partially explained by the fact that in the East towns, especially the very small towns with less than a thousand inhabitants, expanded the most.

In the West the larger towns tended to display above-average growth, especially in those administration districts with an early industrial development such as Düsseldorf, Cologne and Aachen. At the same time a tendency is apparent here, for example in the economically weaker districts Münster, Minden and Koblenz, towards below-average growth in the smaller towns, an indicator that urban growth conditioned by early industrialization led to a differentiation of the growth-structures.

This picture becomes clearer if one analyzes the centers that experienced extreme growth (more than 2.4% average* annual increase) during this period. In the East, except where this was caused by territorial alterations or the transfer of military units, the places in question were small agricultural towns (Ackerbürgerstädte) with limited commercial functions. The Middle provinces, in contrast, offered a far more complex

Table 6.3: Regional urban growth, 1816-40 (average annual growth-rates)

	East		Middle		West		Prussia	
	towns	%	towns	%	towns	%	towns	%
population decline (below 0.00)	7	2.7	8	1.7	4	2.8	19	2.1
moderate growth (0.0-0.6%)	24	9.1	29	6.1	28	15.9	82	8.9
(0.6-1.2%)	58	22.0	114	23.8	57	32.4	229	24.9
vigorous growth (1.2-1.8%)	92	34.8	178	37.2	48	27.3	318	34.6
(1.8-2.4%)	50	18.9	96	20.0	23	13.1	169	18.4
extreme growth (over 2.4%)	33	12.5	54	11.3	15	8.5	102	11.1
total	264	100.0	479	100.0	176	100.0	919	100.0

picture: here, it was mainly the medium-sized towns with minor centrality-functions, artisanry and agriculture that displayed above average growth; there were, nevertheless, no signs of industry in this group - with the exception of Gleiwitz in Upper Silesia. In the West, however, (with the exception of Düsseldorf, Koblenz and Trier, which were places with highly developed centralist functions) it was predominantly early

---

* i.e. a 77% increase in 24 years.

industrial manufacturing plants of the textile and metal industries, mainly on the Lower Rhine, in the Bergisch Land and in the Sauerland, places which were not elevated to the status of town until this time, but which, to a significant extent, lay in these early industrial growth-zones.

From this follows the theory of a split development: if the conditions of growth in eastern Prussia were substantially of an agricultural nature, in the West they lay mainly in industrial factors. Since no figures are available for the number of workers involved in agricultural production, it is not possible to gauge the exact causes of the strong population increase. It cannot be exclusively reduced to the boost in agricultural productivity, which was at a higher level in the West at the outset and which continued to climb there during this period (von Finkenstein 1960 : 313). The causes are more likely to be found in the area of legal reforms, the innovations within the agricultural production, and the extended cultivation of the land (Landesausbau) that these reforms set in motion, thereby causing a leap in development for the agricultural East.

Demographically, the greater population growth in the East was determined by two factors: firstly, the birth and marriage rates were higher there than in the West (Köllmann 1974 : 64; Lee 1979 : 222), and, secondly, a migration surplus is also detectable for the greater part of this period. It is impossible to deduce from this to what extent migration from West to East occurred. At any rate there are signs pointing to an influx of immigrants from outside Prussia at this time (Obermann 1972 ; Thümmler 1977 : 59).

Early industrialization and agricultural reform thus stand side by side as the conditions for differing forms of urbanization. Nevertheless the most important characteristic of the total Prussian development during this phase is the fact of population growth in the agricultural East, with its more rapid increase of the rural population.

6.3. Urban growth under the influence of the Industrial Revolution (1840-71)

How did the above mentioned limited rise in the urbanization ratio in the second phase of development come about? What led up to it, and what was the nature of its relation to the incipient industrialization process?

First it must be stated that the relatively minimal rise in the urbanization ratio conceals rather than reveals the extent of change. Taking the actual urban population growth in Prussia, drawn from the territorial situation in 1840, one arrives at an increase of 65%. More important, however, are the structural alterations that can be gleaned from Table 6.4. Evidently, the growth tempo of the Prussian population as a whole had lessened, but urban growth had become vigorous and was now distinctly above the growth of the total population. In contrast to the previous phase, the amount of growth was almost identical in all three regions. However, in the eastern areas it only lay a little above that of the total population, whereas in the West it was almost twice as strong. The West-East differential perceivable here is repeated in the cases of population density and urban density, while in the other two dimensions the figures in the West were becoming increasingly assimilated to those of the Middle Provinces. Thus the growth differential was now reversed and the gap between the East and the other provinces had grown ever wider.

Table 6.4:   Dimensions of urbanization, 1840-71

	Urbanization ratio		Average town size		Urban density		Population density		Growth-rates 1840-71	
									total pop.	urban pop.
	1840	1871	1840	1871	1840	1871	1840	1871		
East	22,9	24,2	3046	4337	355	348	38	52	0,93	1,11
Middle	30,4	37,0	4599	7607	282	276	54	75	1,01	1,64
West *	25,2	34,2	4515	7594	212	198	84	112	1,01	2,00
Prussia	27,2	33,2	4103	6623	282	271	53	74	0,99	1,64

* Incl. Hohenzollern

Sources: 1840: see table 2. 1871: R. Jannasch, Das Wachsthum und die Concentration des preussischen Staates, in: Zeitschrift des Kgl. Preussischen Statistischen Bureaus, vol. 18 (1878), p. 278; Preussische Statistik, 39ᴵ, p.2.

The alteration in the growth structures also expresses itself in another way: a positive correlation was now beginning to develop between town size and rate of growth.* This means that there was a high percentage of shrinking or weakly growing small towns, that growth was roughly equally distributed in the middle groups, and that the large towns were growing at an above average rate (Appendix Table D).

The regional differences are clearer still (Table 6.5). Whereas the eastern and middle provinces displayed similar distributions which signified, in the East especially, a relatively distinct normal distribution, the development in the West was strongly divergent; not only were the towns with extreme growth overproportionally represented, so too were those with diminishing populations. A process of differentia-

---

* (Pearson's) correlation-coefficient for the connection between size of population and growth rates came out at 0.0919 (s = 0.002) using 951 pairs.

tion is becoming evident here, a process that had previously only been discernable in isolated instances in the western provinces.

Table 6.5: Regional urban growth, 1840-71
(average annual growth-rates)

population decline	East		Middle		West		Prussia	
	towns	%	towns	%	towns	%	towns	%
(below 0.0%)	19	7.3	30	6.3	33	15.1	82	8.6
moderate growth (0.0-0.6%)	68	26.2	143	29.9	53	24.2	264	27.6
(0.6-1.2%)	86	33.1	171	35.8	51	23.3	304	31.8
vigorous growth (1.2-1.8%)	63	24.2	83	17.4	32	14.6	177	18.5
(1.8-2.4%)	16	6.2	30	6.3	11	5.5	56	5.9
extreme growth (over 2.4%)	8	3.1	21	4.4	39	17.8	68	7.1
total	260	100.0	478	100.0	219	100.0	957	100.0

Which are the towns here with diminishing population and extreme growth respectively, and to what extent are the causes of growth and stagnation reflected in them? Among the cases with annual rates of growth of more than 2.4%, those whose growth was primarily, or exclusively, the outcome of territorial alterations must be treated separately. Included here in some cases is a series of new towns from the Lower Rhine textile area (e.g. Viersen, Rheydt, Mönchengladbach, Odenkirchen, Süchteln) and from the area of the Bergisch Land cottage-iron industry (Cronenberg, Lüttringhausen, Velbert, Radevormwald, Wülfrath). To these were added, as a result of the Rhine Municipal Corporation Act of 1856, the outer-burgermasteries ("Aussenbürgermeisterei") which also recorded considerable growth in their own right during this period.

Apart from such places as these, this group was now headed by mining and metal industry towns, mainly in the Ruhr area: Essen, Dortmund, Hoerde, Bochum, Witten, Duisburg. To these must also be added Beuthen in Upper Silesia. Only then come towns from the Bergisch Land that led the growth tables in the previous period, for example Hagen, Elberfeld, Barmen, Wipperfürth, and Solingen. Another group with extreme growth is a series of textile industrial towns in the Lausitz (Luckenwalde, Spremberg, Cottbus, Forst), while in the same region Wittenberge grew more as a result of the machine industry. The two moderately large towns in the Aachen area, Eschweiler and Stolberg, developed particularly favourably during this period, primarily because of the metal industry. And finally there was a new type of town emerging, one with especially vigorous growth: towns with the function of suburbs. This development took place very early in the case of towns with a restricted surface area: Berlin (Spandau, Charlottenburg) and Cologne (Deutz, Mülheim).

Among the towns that suffered a decrease in population, certain definitive characteristics can similarly be made out. They were either towns that lay very much on the border or outside the main-streams, such as in the Saarland (St. Wendel, Saarburg, Saarlautern), in the Münsterland (Vreden, Anholt, Tecklenburg), the Province of Posen (Bnin, Mieschkow, Witkowo), or Silesia (Rothenburg/Oder, Freystadt). Or else they were towns in the German Middle Mountains ("Mittelgebirge"): in the Eifel (Monschau, Prüm), the Hunsrück (Sobernheim, Simmern), the Sauerland (Winterberg, Berleburg), the Harz (Stolberg), or in the Silesian Giant Mountains ("Riesengebirge") (Kupferberg). This change in growth structures can be traced back to altered conditions of location. To begin with, railway construction played a decisive rôle during this period, both as an economic factor and as a means of transport. Towns with an early rail link grew on the average more rapidly than other towns, because both their production and trade functions were substantially strengthened by the more favourable transport facilities. However, one must not overlook the fact that it was, in the first instance, towns with economic interests and of economic significance that were initially included in the emerging railway system.

Then a new independence in energy had now been brought about by the advent of the steam engine which allowed metal working in particular to lose its dependence on water energy. But steam power was also increasingly finding its way into textile production, first into spinning, then weaving and finally textile processing. The modern style of mining and metallurgy was dependent on these new sources of energy from the outset. Taking the progress of horse power figures as an indicator for industrialization, one is again confronted with the familiar West-East differential. However, the impact of machines on the urbanization process was not unilateral (Table 6.6).

The impact depended upon both the area and industry in question: generally the towns had the bulk of mechanical power for general production, in the East steam engines were used mainly for the running of mills. The mining and metallurgy industries were predominantly concentrated in rural areas. Of course, some of these rural installations, especially in the metal industry, must be attributed to the urban economy, since the new, large installations tended to locate in the proximity of towns along the railway routes.

Transport facilities, energy, the existing infrastructure and the greater labour market caused the town to become a lo-

Table 6.6:   Steam-engines (HP)

		1849			1858		
		mining	metal-ind.	others [1]	mining	metal-ind.	others [1]
East	(towns)	–	121	333	–	89	944
	(rural)	–	–	88	–	–	760
Middle	(t)	542	515	4205.5	1050	669	13616
	(c)	1520	1338	2044	11766	6819	8241
West	(t)[2]	1722	1485.5	2483	4977	6925	10664
	(c)	9911	1839	1345.5	28127	12227	6081
Prussia	(t)	2264	2121.5	7011.5	6027	7683	25224
	(c)	11431	3177	3477.5	39893	19046	15082
total		13695	5298.5	10489	45920	26729	40306

[1] Excluding railways and ships [2], including Hohenzollern.
Sources: Tabellen und amtliche Nachrichten ... 1849, vol. VI, Berlin 1855, p. 925 ff.; Tabellen ... 1858, Berlin 1860, p. 347 ff.

cation factor (Standortfaktor) of particular significance in the subsequent years. Where the town had, even earlier under the putting-out-system ("Verlagssystem"), concentrated on disposition rather than production and certain specialized labour-processes, now it was becoming an important center of production in its own right. In the Lower Rhine textile town, Mönchengladbach, for example, where there were very few weaving-looms before the 40's, the Gladbacher Aktienspinnerei und -weberei was founded in 1853 by local entrepreneurs with capital accumulated earlier in the putting-out-system (Adelmann 1966), and in 1861 it already boasted a work force of 1,100. Weavers who had hitherto been resident in the country and were formally self-sufficient were forced, in this way, to move into the town.

In contrast to these tendencies, which were leading to a new urban-rural contrast and a concentration of functions on the town, stand the development of the heavy coal and steel industries. In the Ruhr and Saar areas these industries only partly managed to integrate themselves into the existing urban systems, and in Upper Silesia hardly at all. Thus industrial villages in the form of fast growing rural communities were already being created at this time, as was, simultaneously, a new form of city suburb. A new pattern of urban development, of primarily industrial nature, took shape during these three decades before the foundation of the Empire. During this period a differentiation of growth processes began to crystallize that was detrimental to the agricultural regions. No longer was agricultural surplus the basis of urban growth, but instead industrial production with its inherent conditions which became increasingly self-perpetuating. Thus during this phase factors became effective which previously had been in existence but which had only influenced development in the western areas of the country, whereas Prussia's development as a whole had been following a different pattern. The town was now, in an unprecedented manner, the focal point of finance, labor force, production and commerce. Conditions that were to be decisive for all further urban development took shape during this period.

6.4 Urban growth in the main industrialization period (1871-1914)

In the third phase, one of accelerated urbanization, tendencies that had already been evident during the second phase finally asserted themselves fully. This period was characterized not so much by new structures as by the intensity of the expansion of ones already in evidence.

The individual dimensions of urbanization (Table 6.7.) immediately reveal a distinct intensification of the West-East differential.

Table 6.7:   Dimensions of urbanization, 1871-1910

	Urbanization ratio		Average town size		Urban density		Population density		Growth-rates	
	1871	1910	1871	1910	1871	1910	1871	1910	total pop.	urban pop.
East	24.2	33.7	4337	7814	348	362	38	64	0.56	1.42
Middle	37.0	50.7	7607	16160	276	267	53	119	1.22	2.04
West *)	34.2	50.7	7594	23596	198	199	84	234	1.91	2.94
New Prov.	29.2	44.9	4644	11189	264	269	60	93	1.14	2.26
Prussia	32.5	47.2	6202	14862	269	273	71	115	1.26	2.24

*) including Hohenzollern
Sources: Preussische Statistik, 234 ^{I}, pp. 2 ff.

However, the new provinces, despite their relative westerliness, were ranked behind the middle provinces in all dimensions, but still well ahead of the eastern provinces. Seen as a whole, in the framework of further increasing population growth, there was an even higher rate of growth of the urban population, which increased to over twice its former size. Regional disparities became further pronounced. Population growth in the East remained well behind that in the West, but in the East also it was concentrated mainly in the towns so that, with regard to growth, a definite town-country polarity began to appear. This meant that the rural surplus population was pouring into the towns, and into the industrial centres of Middle Germany, predominantly Berlin/Brandenburg, and of West Germany, i.e. in particular the Ruhr-area (Köllmann 1974: 125). Despite considerable fluctuations between the individual administrative-districts the western provinces attained peak values in all dimensions. In the face of the breath-taking rapidity of growth in the western regions, it is hardly possible to call the limited continuation of urbanization tendencies in the eastern provinces anything but stagnation. The new provinces did at least manage to keep pace with the middle provinces.

The growth rates of the individual towns bring several remarkable features to light, if a regional comparison is made (Table 6.8a). Above average growth is shown only by towns of the western provinces, although the newly acquired provinces were in possession of a far more favourable growth-structure than

Table 6.8a: Regional urban growth, 1871-1910
(average annual growth-rates)

population decline	East		Middle		West		New prov.		Prussia	
	Towns	%	Towns	%	Towns	%	Towns	%	Towns	%
(below 0.0%)	54	21.7	121	24.4	10	4.3	44	16.9	229	18.5
moderate growth (0.0-0.6%) (0.6-1.2%)	79 45	31.7 18.1	139 106	28.1 21.4	32 63	13.9 27.4	74 65	28.4 24.9	324 279	26.2 22.6
strong growth (1.2-1.8%) (1.8-2.4%)	34 21	13.7 8.4	67 31	13.5 6.3	34 32	14.8 13.9	37 20	14.2 7.7	172 104	13.9 8.4
extreme growth (over 2.4%)	16	6.4	31	6.3	59	25.7	21	8.0	127	10.3
total	249	100.0	495	100.0	230	100.0	261	100.0	1235	100.0

the others. The middle provinces fared least favourable, their otherwise above average growth tendencies obviously having been, for the most part, due to the growth of Berlin.

More clearly here than in the previous phase, a positive connection between town size and growth was taking shape (cf. app. tab. E), though this did recede again after 1890.* This is probably partly due to the fact that a series of large towns had reached the limits of their growth possibilities on the basis of their existing surface areas, which gave rise to the necessity for incorporation ("Eingemeindungen") on a large scale (Matzerath 1978).

During this period, a further form of "town" comes to light: the "community" with over 2,000 inhabitants. It must also be taken into account that in the course of this phase

---

* The correlation-coefficient r between size and growth for the period 1871-90 worked out at 0.1883 (N = 1239, S = 0.001), for the period 1890-1900 r = 0.1131 (N = 1247, s = 0.001).

a large number of communities transcended this threshold, but that only those land-communities that already contained at least 2,000 inhabitants by 1871 are considered in this study.

Despite this limitation, it is possible to ascertain strong variations between the different parts of the country (Table 6.8b).

Table 6.8b: Regional growth of land-communities over 2,000 inhabitants, 1871-1910 (average annual growth-rates)

population decline (below 0.0%)	East		Middle		West		New prov.		Prussia	
	LC	%	LC	%	LC	%	LC	%	LC	%
	1	14.3	8	8.1	28	9.6	4	10.5	41	9.4
moderate growth (0.0-0.6%) (0.6-1.2%)	1 1	14.3 14.3	24 21	24.2 21.2	84 58	28.9 19.9	13 8	34.2 21.1	122 88	25.7 20.2
strong growth (1.2-1.8%) (1.8-2.4%)	0 1	0.0 14.3	10 11	10.1 11.1	31 28	10.7 9.6	3 3	7.9 7.9	44 43	10.1 9.9
extreme growth (over 2.4%)	3	42.9	25	25.3	62	21.3	7	18.4	97	22.3
total	7	100.0	99	100.0	291	100.0	38	100.0	435	100.0

These variations exist primarily in regional distribution: in the East they were practically non-existent and in the new provinces they were only thinly represented. Growth structures, nonetheless, displayed a noticeable conformity in all areas. Shrinking or weakly-growing land-communities as well as those with extreme growth, are both over-represented, which leads to the conclusion that the group as a whole was not at all homogeneous. Nevertheless, there was an even more distinct positive connection here between size and strength of growth* than in the towns, and this positive connection continued to increase in the last two decades.

As for the previous phase, the attempt shall be made here to discuss briefly the economic conditions of growth and stagnation with the help of the two extreme growth-groups. Among the shrinking towns was a series of places which had already registered losses of population in the previous phases. This suggests that the conditions for stagnation had perpetuated themselves in these cases in the same way that the conditions for growth had in others. One striking aspect, especially among extremely diminishing places, was the large number of small towns from the Brandenburg area. This must have been due to

---

* for 1871-90: $r = 0.1647$, $N = 487$, $s = 0.001$;
  for 1890-1910: $r = 0.3029$, $N = 669$, $s = 0.001$.

the negative impact of Berlin's power of attraction. Among the towns with extreme growth, too, there was a series of places familiar from the previous periods, for example Duisburg, Hagen, Bochum and Essen. These were now joined by new industrial places such as Wattenscheid, Recklinghausen, Kattowitz, Gleiwitz, and Saarbrücken as well as Leverkusen (Wiesdorf). On the whole, the spectrum had become more complex: in this group a series of large towns was appearing that had predominantly centralist functions, even if of differing character, towns such as Münster, Bonn, Frankfurt am Main, Allenstein, or port-towns like Kiel and Stettin. The new development towards the creation of large urban agglomerations (Schott 1912) was mirrored in the extraordinary growth of towns within their radius of influence, by this time not only in the regions around Berlin and Cologne, but also around Hannover (Linden), Hamburg (Harburg, Wilhelmsburg), and Frankfurt am Main (Hoechst, Wiesbaden). This becomes even more apparent in the case of land-communities with extreme growth almost all of which were around Berlin, in the Ruhr-area, or in Upper Silesia. The largest of these was Hamborn, with an average annual rate of growth in this period of 17.19%. With a population, in 1910, of over 100,000 inhabitants, it was the largest "village" in Prussia until it was raised, the following year, to the status of town.

A precise evaluation of the changes in the economic town-country relationship during the course of the nineteenth century is not possible on the basis of the availabe information, since the statistical categories and methods of collection as well as the different definition of town change so fundamentally. On the basis of the occupational census of 1907 (Table 6.9.) we can conclude, however, that for the beginning of the 20th century there was a considerable differential between town and country in all sectors. This town-country differential was strongest in the agrarian East which over the course of the whole period had become more and more resistant to industrialization (Schremmer 1978 : 217). In the West this occupational differential was smallest in the major sectors (Table 6.9 , categories A-D); even the percentage of town dwellers who worked in agriculture was higher in the western provinces than in the East. The middle and new provinces exhibited a similar profile. The distribution of the occupational structure according to town and country leads to the conclusion that the eastern urban system remained characterized above all by the function of towns as central places, the western system by industrial activity. Thus, the earlier town-country differential had been preserved also under industrial conditions; on the other hand the regional differences had been reinforced.

The phenomena discussed above are discernable in the maps (Figure 6.3). The relatively regular distribution of the town system, with only limited urban growth and a nearly complete lack of larger land-communities in East Prussia, reflect the traditional supply functions of towns in the frame-

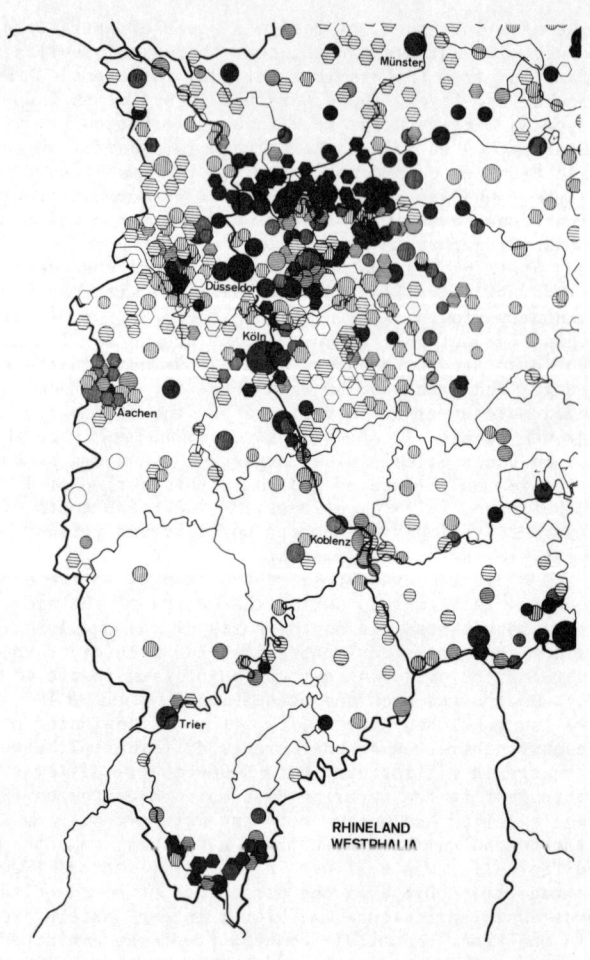

Figure 6.3:

URBAN GROWTH IN PRUSSIA
1871 - 1910

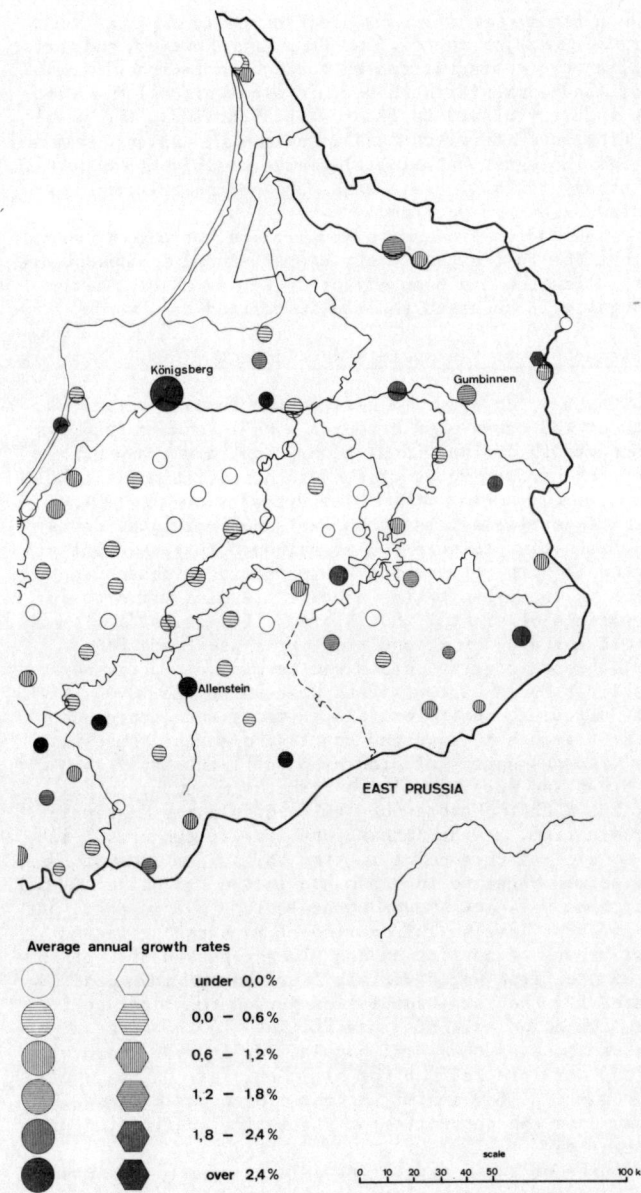

Average annual growth rates

- under 0,0 %
- 0,0 — 0,6 %
- 0,6 — 1,2 %
- 1,2 — 1,8 %
- 1,8 — 2,4 %
- over 2,4 %

work of an urban system which was hierarchically organized with Königsberg as the major center. The Rhineland, however, and parts of Wesphalia were characterized by the concentration of towns and larger land-communities in certain areas of agglomeration. The heavy industry districts (Ruhr area, Saarland), the metal industry districts (Bergisch Land), and the areas around several large cities (Cologne, Düsseldorf) emerge clearly as the actual zones of urban growth. In some cases the peripheral areas exhibited stagnation and decline.

The urbanization process in Prussia had not come to an end by 1914, but the full extent of structural changes in consequence of industrialization had been effected. By way of conclusion these changes will be discussed and summarized as a whole.

6.5. The structure of the overall development

Urban growth has been examined here on two levels: first, as the growth of the urban population as a whole and, second, as the average growth of individual towns. Contrary to the original assumption, the growth rates of the urban population as a whole (Figure 6.4) seem to be more helpful for an assessment of the overall course of development than those of the individual towns and land-communities (Figure 6.5), although the basic pattern is reflected in both curves. The above mentioned phases and differences in the urbanization process are also mirrored in the fluctuations of growth, though breaks ("caesurae") do occur which reveal certain deviations from our phase-formation.
Here, too, three differing phases can be made out in the period up to the First World War: a first phase up to the 1830's with relatively vigorous, short-term fluctuations and counter developments of growth in town and country; a second phase with similarly vigorous spurts of growth up until the early 1860's, in which urban and rural population-growths move in similar fashions, but with the urban-population displaying distinctly higher growth from, at the latest, the time of the crisis in the late 40's. From this point in time the schism between urban and rural growth began to increase and in the 3rd phase the two growth patterns were still running parallel to one another, but on very different levels. This period of unabated urban and weak rural growth of population had already passed its peak by the time of the First World War. It is evident from the positive growth-rates for the rural population during the total period that there can be no talk of "rural flight" in the sense of an effective decrease of the rural population. At most there was an occasional draining-off of the birth surplus. On the whole, town and country follow a similar course between 1871 and 1910 whether one uses the categories of statistical definition or legal categories.

The course of these growth-curves and, equally, the growth-rate of the Prussian national population evident in Figure 6.4 display a surprising similarity with the curve of the natural

Table 6.9: Regional distribution of the occupational structure in 1907 (%)

		Prussia		Eastern provinces		Middle Provinces		Western provinces [1]		New provinces	
		towns [2]	country [3]	towns	country	towns	country	towns	country	towns	country
A	Agriculture	7.8	65.2	8.9	76.0	5.8	63.4	10.1	58.6	7.8	62.2
B	Mining; manufacturing	50.4	19.5	35.5	10.0	49.7	20.6	57.6	27.4	44.9	21.6
C	Trade; transportation	16.9	4.1	17.5	2.6	18.2	4.1	13.8	4.9	20.1	5.0
D	Day-labourer; service workers	2.7	0.5	4.1	0.5	3.4	0.6	1.5	0.4	3.0	0.5
E	Civil service professions	8.5	1.9	16.2	1.7	8.6	1.8	5.7	2.4	10.5	2.1
F	Without profession; not stated	13.5	8.8	17.7	9.3	14.2	9.6	11.4	6.3	13.8	8.6
A – F		100.0	100.0	100.0	100.0	100.0	100.0	100.0	100.0	100.0	100.0

1) Including Hohenzollern
2) Towns = communities with more than 2000 inhabitants
3) Country = communities with fewer than 2000 inhabitants

Source: Statistik des Dt. Reichs, 211, pp. 60* ff., 20* ff.

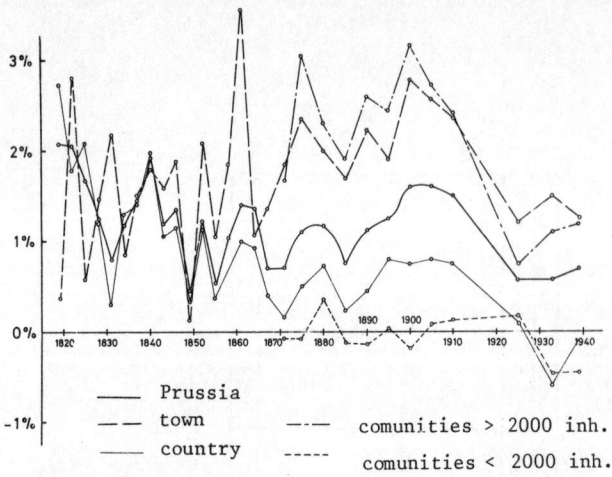

Figure 6.4: Urban and rural population growth (average annual growth-rates)

population-movement in Germany: strong and irregular fluctuations in the early years, constant, steady growth in the final third of the century, and regressive tendencies from the turn of the century. This points to the trivial, but fundamental fact that urbanization in Prussia was effected in the framework of strong and uninterrupted population growth, and that its course of growth was determined, from the 30's onwards, by the particular direction of this overall development.

This pattern must, however, not only be seen as the result of demographic conditions but equally as the expression of economic developments. The irregular criss-cross fluctuations of the first phase confirm the assertion made earlier that, at this time, proper conditions for urbanization did not yet exist. In view of the fact that these fluctuations took place exclusively in the positive sector, i.e. that they were accompanied by vigorous growth of population, it is, at least formally, possible to term this pattern "traditional", whereas in essence it was the outcome of a mobilization-process which took place primarily in the agricultural or rural protoindustrial sectors without being of significant consequence to the urbanization-process. In the 30's this phase was superceded by a new development which led, after the crisis in the late forties, to a new form of industrially conditioned urban growth that became stabilized on a high level during the period of sustained intensive industrialization and corresponding economic

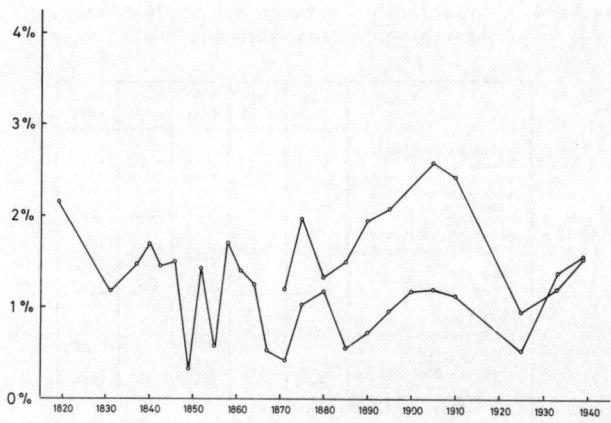

Figure 6.5: Population growth of towns, 1816-1940 and of land-communities over 2,000 inhabitants, 1871-1940 (average annual growth-rates)

growth.

The restructuralizations towards a new form of urban growth visible here are reflected in the relationship in which the above examined dimensions of urbanization stood variously to one another (Table 6.10). The direction of development of the correlation-coefficient shows an unmistakeable tendency: The individual dimensions were at the out-set, to a large extent still independent of one another, although a certain link between the factors was already starting to become apparent at the beginning of industrialization proper in 1849. This link became increasingly strengthened in the ensuing period, revealing as early as 1875 the basic connection between the individual dimensions. The strengthening of the correlation-coefficients indicates a new urbanization profile characterized by a concentration of large towns in heavily condensed areas with a high proportion of the total population; this, in turn, means major urban agglomeration. The significant correlation between the various dimensions reveals that a greater uniformity was coming about within the different administrative districts, but that the differential between the individual administrative districts was simultaneously being further intensified. Urbanization had obviously become a self-reenforcing process.

It remains, in conclusion, to be asked whether this new pattern of urbanization is at all compatible with the conventional town concept. Prussian policy concerning urbanization

Table 6.10: Relationship between the various modes of expression of urbanization

	1819 N=25	1849 N=25	1875 N=35	1900 N=35	1933 N=33
urbanization ratio - town size	0.43	0.49	0.66	0.69	0.77
urbanization ratio - town density	0.30	0.46	0.48	0.55	0.66
urbanization ratio - population density	-0.03	0.25	0.56	0.56	0.72
Town size - town density	-0.30	-0.15	-0.07	0.13	0.24
Town size - population density	0.24	0.39	0.53	0.66	0.83
Town density - population density	0.55	0.50	0.50	0.50	0.50

Correlation-coefficient r (Pearson's)
Levels of significance: -------- = 1%
——— = 0.27%
======== = 0.1%
N = Number of administrative districts

can only be described as conservative. Although the chief urban privileges were removed by the Prussian reform-policy at the start of the 19th century, there followed no redefinition of the town-concept. From the 1820's onwards the granting of town-status was, in view of the clear differentiation between town and country, a consciously political act: town-status meant admittance into the urban estate-corporation, and usually also the bestowal of the urban administrative statute (Städteordnung). Such bestowals were only made very unwillingly towards the end of the century in view of the rapidly growing city suburbs and the rapidly developing industrial centers with their high proportion of workers. But even then incorporations ("Eingemeindungen") were allowed by the state only in urgent cases.

The introduction of the statistical town-concept, in contrast, in particular by German Empire statisticians, meant that the numerous communities with more than 2,000 inhabitants that had not been recognized as towns were now taken into consideration. Thus, new phenomena could now also be taken into account, for example the suburbs in the areas around Berlin, Frankfurt and Hannover, or industrial places in industrial agglomeration-zones as in the Ruhr-area, in the industrial districts in Upper Silesia, in the Saarland and on the Lower Rhine. A decision as to which definition is more appropriate, the legal or the statistical, can only be reached by analyzing the qualitative differences between the critical elements of both definitions, i.e. between the towns with less than 2,000 inhabitants and the land-communities with more than 2,000 inhabitants, in other words between the dwarf-towns, on the one hand, and the large suburbs and industrial communities on the other. The simple development of the number and proportion of these cases makes certain inferences possible. Of the total Prussian population in 1817, 7.5% lived in a total of 665 towns with less than 2,000 inhabitants; in 1871 2.3% of the population lived in 417 such towns, and in 1910 only 1% of the population in 285 such towns. From this fact we can conclude that, with time, the problem of this fringe-group became increasingly insignificant for the legal town-concept. The number and proportion of population of rural communities with more than 2,000 inhabitants, however, grew in leaps: in 1871 (534 communities) with 7.1% to 1910 (1,180 communities) with 15.3% of the total population. Since the industrial places could hardly, in their early stages at least, be classified as "urban" and, moreover, communities in certain agricultural zones were breaking the 2,000 inhabitants-barrier in ever larger quantities, population figures alone proved to be increasingly unsuitable for the purpose of distinguishing between town and country.

The Prussian town system was remarkably stable because of the number of promotions to the status of town and a cautious policy of incorporation which, in some cases, also removed the autonomy of towns in the agglomeration-areas of industrial regions and large towns. This stability allowed the town-system to integrate the new manifestations of urban growth as they appeared.

Thus the traditional urban system proved itself capable of supporting a new revolutionary process of change. The speed and extent of the changes can also be assessed by the way the idea of what constitutes a "large" town (Grossstadt) altered: whereas a town with 10,000 inhabitants was considered "large" according to the Prussian Municipal Corporation Act of 1808, in the 1840's "large" towns had 30,000 inhabitants, and in the imperial statistics a community of upwards of 100,000 inhabitants was finally formally looked upon as a large town. It was this "large town" that governed conceptions of the town in the subsequent period. It was, however, in no way exclusively, and in some cases not even predominantly, styled by its industrial function, although it must be viewed, even in its non-industrial manifestations, as a product of the industrial age. At the turn of the century another new form of urbanization was already appearing that would finally supercede the idea of the town as a clearly-defined entity: the urbanized "agglomeration" ("massing", "region", "conurbation");

The question raised above concerning the relationship between urbanization and industrialization can only be answered to the extent that urban growth does indeed seem to be closely linked with the industrialization process from a certain point of time onwards. But industrialization did not so much cause

this growth of urban population as conduct it into the towns.
This concurs with the current interpretations of German social
history (Abel 1972; Conze 1966 : 132 ff.; Köllmann 1974 : 115)
that urbanization and industrialization created the prerequisites for relieving the rural problems and, in the long-term,
for overcoming old-established pauperism.

Appendix

Table A: Urbanization in Prussia (legal town concept)

	Towns (1)	Urban population [2] inh. (2)	urbanization ratio % (3)
1816	1,020	2,881,533	27.9
1819	1,027	3,023,292	27.5
1822	1,041	3,167,933	27.2
1825		3,223,173	26.3
1828		3,367,433	26.5
1831	983	3,592,355	27.6
1834		3,684,671	27.3
1837	972	3,854,495	27.3
1840	976	4,066,266	27.2
1843	979	4,246,173	27.4
1846	980	4,508,948	28.0
1849	980	4,582,198	28.1
1852	988	4,815,209	28.4
1855	993	4,968,156	28.9
1858	994	5,235,999	29.6
1861	1,000	5,625,852	30.4
1864	1,001	6,016,267	31.2
1867	1,272	7,443,362	31.1
1871	1,290	8,000,931	32.5
1875	1,288	8,791,834	34.2
1880	1,287	9,707,802	35.6
1885	1,287	10,554,596	37.3
1890	1,263	11,786,061	39.3
1895	1,266	12,954,591	40.7
1900	1,266	14,847,846	43.1
1905	1,279	16,866,963	45.2
1910	1,276	18,963,785	47.2
1925 [1]	1,099	20,854,855	54.7
1933 [1]	1,098	23,494,292	58.8
1939	1,152	25,627,948	61.5

1) Without Saarland
2) Whole population (including military population)

Sources: 1816, 1822, 1831, 1840, 1849, 1858: Das Anwachsen der Bevölkerung im Preussischen Staat seit 1816, in: Zeitschrift des Königl. Preussischen Statistischen Bureaus, vol. 1 (1861), pp.9 ff.;
1825, 1828, 1834: Preussische Statistik, 188, part B, p.2 f.;
1819: Beiträge zur Statistik des preussischen Staats, Berlin 1821, pp.51 ff.;
1837: J.G. Hoffmann, Die Bevölkerung des preussischen Staats, Berlin 1839, pp.225 ff.;
1843: W. Dieterici, Die Statistischen Tabellen des preussischen Staates nach der amtlichen Aufnahme des Jahres 1843, Berlin 1845, p.242;
1846, 1852, 1855: Archiv für Landeskunde der preussischen Monarchie, vol. 3 (1858), pp.212 ff.;
1861: Zeitschrift des Königlichen Preussischen Statistischen Bureaus, vol. 2 (1862), pp.25 ff.;
1864, 1867, 1875-1910: Preussische Statistik, 10, 16 [11], 39, 66, 96, 121, 148, 177 [1], 206, 234;
1871: R. Jannasch; Das Wachstum und die Konzentration der Bevölkerung des Preussischen Staates, in: Zeitschrift des Königlichen Preussischen Statistischen Bureaus, vol. 18 (1878). pp.263 ff.;
1925, 1933, 1939: Results of data base "Urbanisierung in Preussen".

Table B: Prussia; statistical town-concept

	Total population		Communities over 2000 inh.			Communities less than 2000 inh.		
	Comm.	Pop.	Number	Pop.	%	Number	Pop.	%
1867 [1]	53,493	23,971,337	1,400	8,585,954	35.8	52,093	15,385,383	64.2
1871	54,743	24,636,184	1,406	9,176,258	37.2	53,337	15,429,926	62.8
1875	54,907	25,742,404	1,517	10,359,771	40.2	53,390 [3]	15,382,633	59.8
1880	54,784	27,279,111	1,615	11,614,385	42.6	53,169 [3]	15,664,726	57.4
1885	55,286	28,318,470	1,648	12,754,674	45.0	53,638 [3]	15,563,796	55.0
1890	54,904	29,937,367	1,726	14,511,340	48.4	53,178 [3]	15,446,027	51.6
1895	53,784	31,835,123	1,842	16,383,266	51.4	51,942	15,471,857	48.6
1900	53,383	34,472,509	1,968	19,144,609	55.5	51,415	15,327,900	44.5
1905	53,021	37,293,324	2,090	21,908,499	58.8	50,932	15,384,825	41.3
1910	52,614	40,165,219	2,157	24,687,490	61.5	50,447	15,477,729	38.5
1925 [2]	42,746	38,120,173	1,917	25,253,710	66.2	40,829	12,866,463	33.8
1933	30,458	39,934,011	1,944	27,553,297	69.0	28,514	12,380,714	31.0
1939	29,243	41,655,252	2,113	29,594,754	71.0	27,130	12,060,498	29.0

Notes: 1) excluding Lauenburg (49,978) and troops abroad
2) taking into account the reorganisation, per decree of 1926, in the Rhineland-Westphalia industrial district and excluding the Saarland
3) mathematically calculated.

Sources: 1867 and 1871: F. Jannasch, Das Wachstum und die Concentration der Bevölkerung des Preussischen Staates, in: Zeitschrift des Kgl. Preuss. Stat. Bureaus, vol. 18 (1878), pp. 263 ff.;
1875: Statistik des Deutschen Reichs, vol. 25[1], 7, pp. 46 ff., pp. 56 f.;
1880: Stat. d. Dt. Reichs, vol. 57, pp. 18, pp. 26 f.;
1885: Stat. d. Dt. Reichs, vol. 32, pp. 18, pp. 25;
1890: Stat. d. Dt. Reichs, vol. 68, pp. 18, pp. 26;
1895: Vierteljahrshefte zur Stat. d. Dt. Reichs, vol. 7 (1898), 2, pp. 169;
1900-1925: Statistisches Jahrbuch für das Dt. Reich, vol. 24 (1903), pp. 4 f., vol. 29 (1908), pp. 6 f., vol. 35 (1914), pp. 4 f.; vol. 46 (1927), pp. 12 f.
1933: Stat. d. Dt. Reichs, pp. 451[1], pp. 176 f.;
1939: Stat. d. Dt. Reichs, vol. 552[1], pp. 1, pp. 144 ff.

Number of communities
1875-1895: Preuss. Statistik, 206[1], p. 1.

Table C: Growth in classes of size, 1816-40 (average annual growth-rates)

	small towns						medium towns				large towns		Prussia	
	less than 1000		1000-2000		2000-3500		3500-5000		5000-10000		over 10000			
	N	%	N	%	N	%	N	%	N	%	N	%	N	%
Population decline (below 0.0%)	5	2.5	4	1.1	6	3.0	2	3.2	2	3.3	0	0.0	19	2.1
moderate growth (0.0-0.6%)	10	5.5	28	7.7	25	12.4	6	9.5	11	18.3	2	6.7	82	8.9
(0.6-1.2%)	37	18.5	102	27.9	56	27.9	16	25.4	10	16.6	8	26.7	229	24.9
vigorous growth (1.2-1.8%)	69	34.5	129	35.3	66	32.8	20	31.7	24	40.0	10	33.3	318	34.6
(1.8-2.4%)	41	20.5	67	18.4	31	15.4	14	22.2	11	18.3	5	16.7	169	18.4
extreme growth (over 2.4%)	38	19.0	35	9.6	17	8.5	5	7.9	2	3.3	5	16.7	102	11.1
total	200	100.0	365	100.0	201	100.0	63	100.0	60	100.0	30	100.0	919	100.0

Table D: Growth in classes of size, 1840-71

	small towns						medium towns				large towns		Prussia	
	less than 1000		1000-2000		2000-5000		5000-10000		10000-30000		over 30000			
	N	%	N	%	N	%	N	%	N	%	N	%	N	%
Population decline (below 2.4%)	9	11.3	28	8.8	37	9.0	6	6.2	2	4.8	0	0.0	82	8.6
moderate growth (0.0-0.6%)	22	27.5	103	32.5	118	28.9	14	14.4	6	14.3	1	8.3	264	27.6
(0.6-1.2%)	28	35.0	107	33.8	127	31.1	33	34.0	12	28.6	1	8.3	308	32.2
vigorous growth (1.2-1.8%)	10	12.5	52	16.4	77	18.8	20	20.6	15	35.7	4	33.3	178	18.6
(1.8-2.4%)	4	5.0	11	3.5	24	5.9	12	12.4	4	9.5	2	16.7	57	6.0
extreme growth (over 2.4%)	7	8.8	16	5.5	26	6.4	12	12.4	3	7.1	4	33.3	68	7.1
total	80	100.0	317	100.0	409	100.0	97	100.0	42	100.0	12	100.0	957	100.0

Table E: Growth in classes of size, 1871-1910

	small towns						medium towns				large towns		Prussia	
	less than 2000		2000-5000		5000-20000		20000-50000		50000-100000		over 100000			
	N	%	N	%	N	%	N	%	N	%	N	%	N	%
population decline (below 0.0%)	114	30.2	104	19.0	11	4.2	0	0.0	0	0.0	0	0.0	229	18.5
moderate growth (0.0-0.6%)	123	32.5	164	30.0	37	14.1	0	0.0	0	0.0	0	0.0	324	26.2
(0.6-1.2%)	83	22.0	131	24.0	61	23.2	4	13.3	0	0.0	0	0.0	279	22.6
vigorous growth (1.2-1.8%)	26	6.9	71	13.0	68	25.9	6	20.0	1	8.3	0	0.0	172	13.9
(1.8-2.4%)	16	4.2	39	7.1	35	13.3	5	16.7	5	41.7	4	66.7	104	8.4
extreme growth (over 2.4%)	16	4.2	37	6.8	51	19.4	15	50.0	6	50.0	2	33.3	127	10.3
total	378	100.0	546	100.0	263	100.0	30	100.0	12	100.0	6	100.0	1235	100.0

REFERENCES

Abel, W. Massenarmut und Hungerkrisen im vorindustriellen Deutschland (Göttingen, 1972).
Adelmann, G. 'Strukturwandlungen der rheinischen Leinen- und Baumwollgewerbe zu Beginn der Industrialisierung' in VSWG, vol. 53 (1966) pp. 175 ff.
Beranys, M. Auslese und Anpassung der Arbeiterschaft der geschlossenen Grossindustrie. Dargestellt an den Verhältnissen der "Gladbacher Spinnerei und Weberei" AG. zu Mönchengladbach im Rheinland (Leipzig, 1910).
Borchardt, K. 'Regionale Wachstumsdifferenzen in Deutschland im 19. Jahrhundert unter besonderer Berücksichtigung des West-Ost-Gefälles' in Wirtschaft, Geschichte und Wirtschaftsgeschichte, Festschrift Lütge (Stuttgart, 1966) pp. 325-339.
Borchardt, K. Die industrielle Revolution (München, 1972).
Conze, W. 'Vom "Pöbel" zum "Proletariat" in H.U. Wehler (ed.) Moderne deutsche Sozialgeschichte (Berlin, Köln 1966) pp. 111-136.
Croon, H. 'Städtewandlung und Städtebildung im Ruhrgebiet im 19. Jahrhundert' in Aus Geschichte und Landeskunde, Festschrift f. Steinbach (Bonn, 1960) pp. 484-501.
Dewey, R. 'The rural-urban continuum: real but relatively unimportant' in American journal of sociology, vol. 66 (1960/61) pp. 60-66.
Dupeux, G. 'La croissance urbaine en France au XIXe siècle in Revue d'histoire économique et sociale 52 (1974) pp. 173-189.
Finck von Finkenstein, H.W. Die Entwicklung der Landwirtschaft in Preussen und Deutschland, 1800-1930 (Würzburg, 1960).
Fischer, W. 'Bergbau, Industrie und Handwerk' in H. Aubin and W. Zorn (eds.) Handbuch der deutschen Wirtschafts- und Sozialgeschichte, vol. 2 (Stuttgart, 1976) pp. 527-562.
Flora, P. Modernisierungsforschung. Zum empirischen Analyse gesellschaftlicher Entwicklung (Opladen, 1974).
Fremdling, R. and R.H. Tilly (eds.) Industrialisierung und Raum. Studien zur regionalen Differenzierung im Deutschland des 19. Jahrhunderts (Stuttgart, 1979).
Haufe, H. Die Bevölkerung Europas. Stadt und Land im 19. und 20. Jahrhundert (Berlin, 1936).
Hauser, Ph.M. 'The social, economic, and technological problems of rapid urbanization' in B.F. Hoselitz and W.E. Moore (eds.) Industrialization and society (Paris, 1968) pp. 199-217.
Henning, F.W. Die Industrialisierung in Deutschland 1800-1914 (Paderborn, 1973).
Higgs, R. 'Williamson and Swanson on city growth: A critique' in EEH, vol. 8 (1970/71) pp. 203-212.
Hoffmann, J.G. Die Bevölkerung des Preussischen Staats

(Berlin, 1839).
Hohorst, G. Wirtschaftswachstum und Bevölkerungsentwicklung in Preussen 1816 bis 1914 (New York, 1977).
Houtte, J.A. van, 'Stadt und Land in der Geschichte des flandrischen Gewerbes im Spätmittelalter und in der frühen Neuzeit' in Wirtschaft, Geschichte und Wirtschaftsgeschichte. Festschrift Lütge (Stuttgart 1966) pp. 88-98.
Hoselitz, B.F. 'The role of cities in underdeveloped countries' (1) in F. Hoselitz, sociological aspects of economic growth (Glencoe 1960) pp. 159-184.
Huber, E.R. Deutsche Verfassungsgeschichte seit 1789, vol 1 (Stuttgart, 1957).
Jäger, H. and eds. Probleme des Städtewesens im industriellen Zeitalter (Köln, Wien 1978).
Ipsen, G. 'Die Stadt' in HdSW, vol. 9 (Tübingen, Göttingen 1956) pp. 786 ff.
Jasper, K. Der Urbanisierungsprozess dargestellt am Beispiel der Stadt Köln (Köln, 1977).
Kaufhold, K.H. Das Metallgewerbe der Grafschaft Mark im 18. und frühen 19. Jahrhundert (Dortmund, 1975).
Kaufhold, K.H. 'Handwerk und Industrie 1800-1850' in H. Aubin and W. Zorn (eds.) Handbuch der deutschen Wirtschafts- und Sozialgeschichte, vol. 2 (Stuttgart, 1976) pp. 321-368.
Kellenbenz, H. 'Industries rurales en Occident de la fin du moyen âge au XVIII siècle' in Annales, XVIII (1963) pp. 833-882.
Köllmann, W. Bevölkerung in der industriellen Revolution (Göttingen, 1974).
Köllmann, W. 'Bevölkerung und Arbeitskräftepotential in Deutschland 1815-1865. Ein Beitrag zur Analyse des Pauperismus' in W. Köllmann, Bevölkerung in der industriellen Revolution (Göttingen, 1974) pp. 60-98.
Köllmann, W. 'Der Prozess der Verstädterung in Deutschland in der Hochindustrialisierungsperiode' in W. Köllmann, Bevölkerung in der industriellen Revolution, pp. 125 ff.
Koselleck, R. Preussen zwischen Reform und Revolution. Allgemeines Landrecht, Verwaltung und soziale Bewegung von 1791 bis 1848 (Stuttgart, 1967).
Kriedtke, P., H. Medick, and J. Schlumbohm, Industrialisierung vor der Industrialisierung. Gewerbliche Warenproduktion auf dem Land in der Formationsperiode des Kapitalismus (Göttingen, 1977).
Krug, L. and A.A. Mützell, Neues topographisch-statistisch-geographisches Wörterbuch des preussischen Staats, vol. 6 (Halle, 1825) pp. 384 ff.
Lampard, E.E. 'Historical aspects of urbanization' in Ph.M. Hauser, L.F. Schnore (eds.) The study of urbanization (New York, London, Sydney, 1965) pp. 541 ff.
Landes, D. Der entfesselte Prometheus (Köln, 1973).
Lee, R. 'Regionale Differenzierung im Bevölkerungswachstum

Deutschlands im frühen 19. Jahrhundert' in Fremdling/Tilly, pp. 192-229.
Matzerath, H. "Städtewachstum und Eingemeindungen im 19. Jahrhundert' in J. Reulecke (ed.) Die deutsche Stadt im Industriezeitalter (Wuppertal, 1978) pp. 67-89.
Moore, W.E. 'Industrialization and social change' in B.F. Hoselitz and W.E. Moore (eds.) Industrialization and society (Paris, 1967) pp. 299-370.
Mottek, H. Wirtschaftsgeschichte Deutschlands, vol. 2 (Berlin 1973, 2nd edition).
Obermann, K. 'Die Arbeitermigrationen in Deutschland im Prozess der Industrialisierung und der Entstehung der Arbeiterklasse in der Zeit von der Gründung bis zur Auflösung des Deutschen Bundes (1815-1867)' in Jahrbuch für Wirtschaftsgeschichte (1972) part 1, pp. 135-181.
Pfeil, E. Grossstadtforschung, 2nd edition (Hannover, 1972).
Pred, A. The spatial dynamics of U.S. urban-industrial growth, 1800-1914 (Cambridge Mass., 1966).
Quante, P. Die Abwanderung aus der Landwirtschaft (Kiel, 1958).
Reulecke, J. (ed.) Die deutsche Stadt im Industriezeitalter (Wuppertal, 1978).
Robson, B.T. Urban growth, an approach (London, 1973).
Rostow, W.W. Stadien wirtschaftlichen Wachstums (Göttingen, 1961).
Schott, S. Die grossstädtischen Agglomerationen des Deutschen Reichs 1871-1910 (Breslau, 1912).
Schremmer, E. 'Industrielle Rückständigkeit und strukturstabilisierender Fortschritt. Über den Einsatz von Produktionsfaktoren in der deutschen (Land-)Wirtschaft zwischen 1850 und 1913' in H. Kellenbenz (ed.) Wirtschaftliches Wachstum, Energie und Verkehr vom Mittelalter bis ins 19. Jahrhundert (New York, 1978) pp. 205-233.
Schremmer, E. 'Standortausweitung der Warenproduktion im langfristigen Wirtschaftswachstum' in VSWG, vol. 59 (1972) pp. 1-40.
Sombart, W. Der moderne Kapitalismus, vol. 3, 1st hf. vol. (1902) (Berlin, 1955) pp. 399 ff.
Sorokin, P.A. and C. Zimmermann, Principles of rural-urban sociology (New York, 1929).
Swanson, J. and J.G. Williamson, 'A model of urban capital formation and the growth of cities in history' Explorations in Entrepreneurial History vol. 8 (1970/71) pp. 213-222.
Thienel, I. Städtewachstum im Industrialisierungsprozess des 19. Jahrhunderts (Berlin, New York, 1973).
Thümmler, H. 'Zur regionalen Bevölkerungsentwicklung in Deutschland 1816-1871' in Jahrbuch für Wirtschaftsgeschichte (1977) part 1, pp. 55-72.
Weber, A.E. The growth of cities in the nineteenth century (New York, 1899).
Wehler, H.U. Modernisierungstheorie und Geschichte

(Göttingen, 1975).
Williamson, J.G. and J.A. Swanson, 'The growth of cities in the American Northeast, 1820-1870', <u>Explorations in Entrepreneurial History</u> 2nd Series, vol. 4 (1966) no.1, pp. 1-101.
Zapf, P. (ed.) <u>Theorien des sozialen Wandels</u> (Köln, 1969).

7. Urbanisation in Sweden, 1840–1920
B. Öhngren

7.1. Town and country – contrast or continuum?	183
7.2. The state of research	186
7.3. Urbanisation – an ambiguous process	188
7.4. Urban and rural population development	189
7.5. Economic driving forces towards urbanisation	198
7.6. Territorial patterns – a regulator of urbanisation	204
7.7. Town and hinterland	207
7.8. The economy and population development – town types and trends	208
7.9. Urban society 1840–1920	215
7.10. Conclusion	220
Appendix	223
References	224

7. Urbanisation in Sweden, 1840–1920
B. Öhngren

> "O tempora! O mores! To knock down houses!
> But build them? You can't be serious!"
> "Here they're knocked down for light and air
> Don't you think that that's sufficient?"

7.1. Town and country - contrast or continuum?

When August Strindberg published his famous poem, <u>Esplanadsystemet</u>, in 1883, Stockholm was going through a major phase of expansion with regard both to the growth of population and the erection of dwellings. What Strindberg saw was the effects of a greatly accelerated general development which was set in motion in the 1840s, when the urban rate of growth began to increase after a forty-year period of stagnation, at the same time as the urban share of the population also began to rise. The expansion of the urban population which occurred during the period 1840-1920 was the greatest hitherto experienced within such a short space of time in Sweden. As a result, pressure upon the towns' stock of dwellings, health welfare, sanitation, schools, the labour market and so on was greatly increased. Alterations in the administrative structure and practice became essential if the towns were to cope with these new developments and look after the well-being of their inhabitants. The growth in urban population and the problems thereby created thus marked the beginning of an expansion in the public sector.

Just as Strindberg's poem can be said to portray a physical change in society on the one hand and a change in the intellectual climate on the other, so the rapid growth of the towns can be said to reflect societal change as well as the creation of a new milieu of human activity. The urban milieu had of course existed in Sweden for a long time, but the urban societies which now began to take shape were influenced by industrialisation, either directly or indirectly, by rapid technological advances and by improvements in communications, which meant for example that the worker no longer necessarily needed to live close to his place of work. These changes led to mass production as well as mass consumption, and we find ourselves with a society characterised by strict economic specialisation and sharply defined categories of employment. These changes, together with the powerful and rapid increase of population, created a society which was far more complex than that of the pre-industrial era.

Irrespective of whether or not one accepts the view of a marked polarisation between rural and urban societies or the opposite view, which sees a gradual transition, a rural-urban continuum, the vigorous growth of the towns can be assumed to have influenced not only those who lived in them but also those who lived in their immediate vicinity: hence the concept of the urbanisation of the countryside. The continuous and at times intensive accumulation of people in the towns and other centres of population in the country meant for example a redistribution of the population from the countryside to densely populated areas, a transition from agrarian to urban forms of economic activity, from sparsely settled to densely populated patterns of habitation, from a natural to a money economy, from one cultural environment to another, from one pattern of social norms to another, and so on. Whether those who moved to the towns from the countryside really did move from one form of society to another has been the subject of lively debate in a number of different disciplines, and the debate is still going on. A hypothetical assumption can however be made that, if we take the above-mentioned societal changes as a background, some sections of the population at least must have been confronted with something new, even if it was sometimes only a difference of scale: that there were probably a number of modes of transition depending on regional differences in structure and on the rate of development is something of a truism.

Urbanisation should not however be seen simply as an independent variable. In a number of ways, it can be seen as a dependent variable. What for example were the implications of structural changes in the pattern of economic activity for the rate of development of the process of urbanisation? What were the consequences of the proletarianisation of the countryside? Was the development of a railway network simply designed to promote urban growth? These are some of the questions which must be asked.

The vigorous growth in urban population during the period 1800-1920 can be illustrated by a few simple relative figures. During the first sixty years of the nineteenth century, the population of the towns rose by 200,000, in other words an increase in the urban population from 10% to 12%. During the next sixty-year period, up to 1920, the number of people living in towns rose by 1,300,000, and the urban share of the national population reached around 29% in 1920. If we extend the notion of a town to include those who lived in communities which resembled towns in all but name, we find ourselves with a figure of almost 2,6 million, or 45% of the total population. The absolute increase in the population of the towns and other communities with urban features during the second half of the period under study was numerically somewhat greater than the total increase of population in Sweden for the same period. This indicates a significant stream of migration from the countryside to the towns, since the rural population continued to increase in absolute terms. During the first half of the 1880s for example, the net loss to the countryside as a result of internal migration was around 90,000, which corresponds to something like 80% of the increase in the number of inhabitants in the towns. If we then consider that this is only the net result, that migration to other centres of population is not included and that migration from the towns to densely-populated areas is reckoned to the benefit of the countryside, we can assume, on the evidence of earlier studies on migration, that total population movement was at least double.

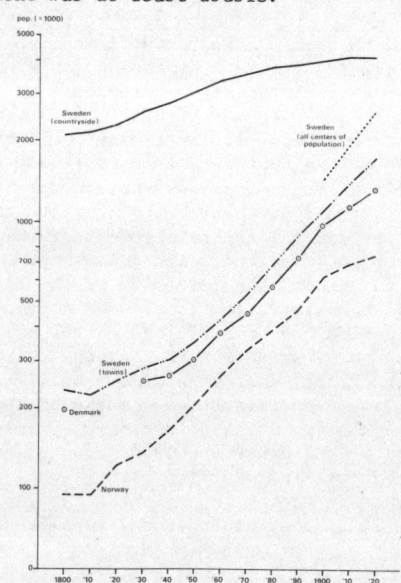

Figure 7.1: Population trends in Sweden, 1800-1920 (countryside, towns), Denmark (towns), Norway (towns) and for all centers of population in Sweden, 1900-1920.

Official statistics for the most part relate to conditions in towns and in the countryside, and very rarely provide information about other densely-populated areas. This is very much the case with urbanised suburbs, urban-type communities in the countryside which had grown up around a particular industry or a railway station or junction. There are no continuous series of statistics relating to densely-populated areas as is the case in Norway, which means that such areas can very seldom be brought into comparisons between town and country. Nevertheless, it is possible on the basis of certain evidence to make a hypothetical assumption that a certain pattern of development did occur in such areas. As a consequence of the fact that the official statistics are largely biased towards the towns and because of the lack of information on the 'urban type' communities in Sweden, this report will principally be concerned with developments in the towns and the difference between town and country. This in itself is an indication of the need for far more research into conditions in different types of densely-populated areas, all the more so since a significant part of the modern urbanisation process takes place in these communities and, with regard to the different theories which have been advanced in the urbanisation debate, this process may even be expected to have a somewhat different course to that of the towns and may also have different consequences.

Urbanised centres in the Swedish context before 1890 will be considered for the most part as administrative towns, mainly because other centres of population in any meaningful sense did not really exist before that date. From that time, especially as statistical information improves, the concept of centres of population can be expanded. In order to preserve continuity however, I shall be presenting the development of the administrative towns for the whole period, with an attempt to extrapolate information concerning the formation of the first administrative and non-administrative centres of population.

The choice of period can be explained in the Swedish context, for the 1840s can be said to have been the starting-point for an acceleration of the process of urbanisation in Sweden, and the 1920s can be said to have marked a new phase in that the rural population began to decline in absolute terms on the one hand, and on the other the 1920s saw the beginning of the automobile age, the introduction of universal suffrage, the beginnings of a new economic and financial policy, all in some way as the result of the international repercussions of the first world war.

7.2. The state of research

In Sweden, it were principally geographers who have looked at the process of urbanisation, whilst historians have tended to concentrate on town histories, and have only begun to turn their attentions to the urbanisation process in the 1970s. The reason why historians have only recently turned to the problems of urbanisation is partly because Swedish studies in urban history have mainly concentrated on administrative and political aspects.

Influenced largely by American studies in urban history,

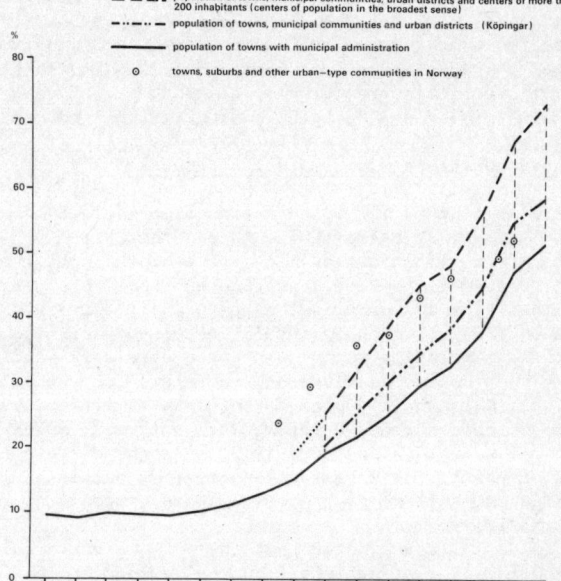

Figure 7.2: The 'urban' population of Sweden as percentage of the total population, 1800-1940.
Some intervals for Norway.
Sources: SOS series A, Statistisk Tidskrift, Micklebost 1960, p. 73

which are more interdisciplinary in approach, a new type of research has begun to take shape in the 1970s. Greater emphasis is now placed on the demographic, social and economic development of towns than before, and attempts are made to present a comparative perspective and relate the development to the social development in total.

In one respect, Swedish studies in urban history are in a more favourable position than elsewhere, in America and outside Northern Europe in general, as a consequence of Sweden's exceptional wealth of sources. Although Swedish studies tend to be more all-embracing, they are also thematic in the sense that they seek to investigate a small number of phenomena within the towns such as the state of the economy and geographical mobility, social structure and popular movements, demographic trends, social structure and trends in the economy, and so forth.

There is no overall study of the growth and structural changes of the Swedish towns for the period under review, nor is there a comprehensive overview of urbanisation as such. Such attempts as have been made to present a comprehensive picture of the towns or the relationship between town and country over a longer period of time have been undertaken in the fields of architectural history (Gregor Paulsson, ed., Svensk stad) and ethnology (Mats Hellspong & Orvar Löfgren, Land och stad).

7.3. Urbanisation - an ambiguous process

Before we look at the urbanisation process in Sweden in more detail, it might be worthwile to consider briefly the discussion of the term 'urbanisation'. In spite of the fact that towns have existed for a very long time and their populations have expanded over a similarly long period, it is very difficult to find an exhaustive and generally accepted definition of what urbanisation really means. As is the case with studies of other aspects of social development, there are many schools of thought, which have dominated research at different points in time and have stamped a particular analytical model with their ideas. I do not intend here to go into the different lines of thought concerning urbanisation studies, but I should like to examine some of the most common interpretations of the concept of urbanisation.

I have already noted that there is no universally accepted definition of what urbanisation really means. Likewise, there is no one definition of what a town is. It is to distinguish a town from other forms of settlement that the legal, economic and sociological elements have been added to the purely physical aspects of a town as a densely inhabited area. But even if distinct areas which are relatively compact and densely populated can be delineated, it is not certain that these units operate as a functional whole. Attempts have therefore been made to define the functional regions of towns, the field of influence (Dickinson 1947; Smailes 1947; Carter 1955). But since no town has a single field of influence, the result has been that no one definition gives a completely satisfactory description of a town and its functional area. To a large extent therefore, operational definitions have had to be applied as and when necessary.

The classic and most applicable definition of urbanisation has been advanced by Hope Tisdale, who argues that urbanisation is the process by which a growing section of the country's population comes to live in relatively densely populated, relatively large towns and urban-type communities. Parallel with this demographically quantitive definition has been advanced the concept of 'urban process', which implies that an increased proportion of the people, whether they live in towns as described above or not, are affected by way of life, ways of thinking and types of activity which in some way are 'urban' rather than 'rural'. This last definition goes back to the human ecology school, in paricular to Louis Wirth and his work, Urbanism as a way of life. Wirth also used the adjective 'heterogeneous' to show how size and population density accounted for the most obvious features of urban social life.

The basic difference between the concepts of urbanisation is whether one chooses to emphasize the quantitative or the qualitative aspects. In a historical perspective, there is more reason to follow a quantitative line of investigation and if possible to seek to complement it with available qualitative data. Tisdale's definition will therefore be used as a quantitative measure of urbanisation. When I come to look at the trends of development in the urbanisation process itself, I shall be using a number of different variable settings.

7.4. Urban and rural population development

In order to obtain an adequate measurement of the degree of urbanisation in Sweden, which can be compared to other countries, one must do more than calculate the proportion of the population living in the towns with municipal administration. In Sweden we have to reckon with a number of different kinds of population agglomerates or centres of population (tätorter). These can be divided into two main groups, administrative and non-administrative centres of population. To the former group belong towns, urban districts (köpingar) and municipal communities, whilst the latter comprises other independent localities and non-administrative suburbs. An interesting, albeit quantitatively speaking insignificant sub-group in the category of non-administrative localities is the so-called 'complementary communities' of the factories, which grew in response to the working population's need for different services: Borlänge near Domnarvet, Sandviken near Högbo, Timrå near Vivstavarv, and so on.

If we trace the process of urbanization back in time we encounter no difficulties if we limit ourselves to the towns with administrative functions. If we extend our research to take in municipal communities as well, there are no regular statistics before 1909, and if we take in the numerous non-administrative localities, we must wait until 1930 before the census gives us anything like reasonably precise figures to go on. Thanks to a reworking of the population statistics however there is a relatively reliable amount of material to go on for the period 1880-1920. From these reworkings it seems in all likelihood that the official statistics show a lower degree of centres of population.

At the beginning of the nineteenth century little more than 10% of the population of Sweden lived in towns. During the subsequent four decades there occured only minor fluctuations and it was not before the second half of the 1840s that this stagnant tendency was broken and the urban population rose above 10%. From that time the share of urban population continued to rise constantly, reaching about 29% at the end of the period under review in 1920. As Figure 7.2 shows, the difference between the town population and the total population for densely-populated areas begins to grow noticeable around the turn of the century. Not only did the population of the urban districts and the municipal communities begin to grow rapidly: the non-administrative localities also show a more rapid rate of growth than the towns. It can be assumed that this is related to the favourable state of the industrial market towards the latter part of the 1890s and the expansion of trading activities associated with this upsurge. Furthermore, there was a vigorous railway construction programme throughout the entire period under review, but there were also other improvements in communications which should have favoured the growth of other population centres at the expense of the suburbs. Here one can point to international parallels too, such as Sam Bass Warner's study of Boston, Ted Hershberg's study of Philadelphia, and others.

Whilst the towns increased their share of the total population by 8% during the period 1900-1920, that of all other centres of population increased by around 13%. Over a period of time the non-administrative centres of population came to share an ever increasing proportion of the population of urban-type communities. At certain periods, the share drops drastically, which usually means that a number of these localities had acquired incorporated status. Many were incorporated later than might be expected because of the lowly social status and unregulated pattern of settlement of these centres of population: this often meant increased expenditure for the welfare of the poor, and towards the construction of streets, water supplies and sewers. Economic reasons lay behind most decisions concerning incorporation, and not only negative prognoses, since it was also calculated that there would be an increased source of revenue to tap in many places. Because all communities outside the towns were reckoned to belong to the countryside, the depopulation of the countryside proper was significantly greater than that shown in the official statistics. But even if we simply confine ourselves to the development of the administrative towns, we find that there is a significant change in contrast to earlier periods. In order to obtain a framework of reference for Swedish developments, a number of limited comparisons have been made with developments in other countries.

Hence, Norway at the beginning of the period had a higher level of urbanisation than Sweden, but by the close of the period the opposite is the case. What makes this comparison interesting is that if we differentiate between administrative towns and all other centres of population, we find two different trends of development: the Swedish towns keep pace with the Norwegian up to the mid-1890s, when the Norwegian towns then begin to forge strongly ahead up to the 1910s. After that the growth of population in the Norwegian towns begins to fall off, whilst that of the Swedish towns continues to increase. In 1920 the share of the town population in both countries was around

29%. As regards all other centres of population the difference at the commencement of the period was significantly greater than that between the towns and this gap remained more or less constant to the turn of the century, after which time the share of the population in such areas in Sweden grew rapidly, overtaking the Norwegian equivalent proportion by the end of the period. If we apply the international definition of a centre of population, i.e. agglomerations of population of more than 2,000 inhabitants, Norway enjoys a higher degree of urbanisation than Sweden, but both countries are surpassed by Denmark, which had 46% of its population living in such centres of habitation in 1920. The corresponding figures for Norway are 38% and for Sweden 36%. In comparison, the urban population of Finland according to the 1897 census was 10%. Seen from a Scandinavian perspective, Sweden's degree of urbanisation was more or less average, but in an international perspective, Sweden occupied a relatively low position, especially in comparison with England, Wales and Scotland. One of the reasons why there was not the same high level of concentration of the population here in Sweden, in spite of a high degree of industrialisation, may be that even as late as 1920 more than half the industrial workforce was employed in the countryside.

In addition to the fact that the degree of urbanisation changed over the course of time, there were also significant regional differences. In 1840, the provinces' individual proportion of urban population varied from 1% in Jämtland to nearly 19% in Blekinge, whilst Göteborg and Bohus (county) and Malmöhus (county) also had relatively high proportions. Eighty years later the total population of the centres of population in Blekinge (county) reached about 42% but seven provinces had by now exceeded that share. The other five counties with the highest share of urban population in 1840 continued to occupy their positions at the top with a few slight alterations. A newcomer to the six top counties was Stockholm county which occupied third place in order (1840 = 16). With the exception of Gotland county which fell from its position of seventh to twenty-fourth, there were no other major changes in the order, which may indicate that Allan Pred's theories on the self-generating effect of urbanisation can also be applied to Sweden. If we limit the comparison simply to town population, only one of the six top counties in 1840 is not to be found amongst the seven top counties in 1920.

According to Tisdale's definition of urbanisation, it is fully possible to have an increasing urban population without the country becoming any more urbanised, i.e. if the rural population increases more rapidly. This is what happened during the decades 1820-1840 in Sweden. After that time the urban population has always grown faster than that of the countryside. Figure 7.3 shows how diametrically different developments have become in the countryside and the towns. It shows how the annual population increase per 1,000 inhabitants of the average population for the countryside reached zero growth during the 1880s and the last decade of the period of research. But in spite of the draining off of population, the number of people living in the countryside has grown in absolute terms.

This is possible as long as the number of people moving out of the countryside remains relatively small and at the same time makes up a greater part of the urban population into which they are absorbed. In the course of time it becomes more and more difficult to supply the centres of population with such large contingents of people and at the same time increase in absolute terms. During the 1920s the logical consequences became evident when the rural population began to decline in absolute terms as well, though of course this sort of situation had occurred before, but it is difficult to determine exactly the period because of a lack of statistical evidence on centres of population.

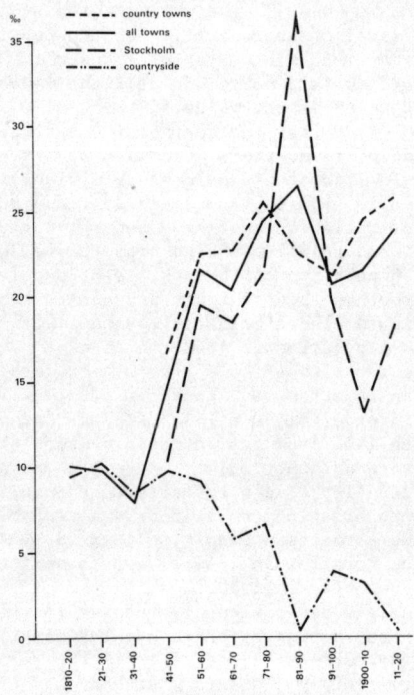

Figure 7.3: Annual population increase per decade, 1816-1920
Sources: SOS series A, Statistisk årsbok 1929

After the stagnant trend in urban growth disappeared in the
1840s, the average annual growth-rate became something above
the rate of 20 per 1,000 of mean population, reaching a peak
in the 1880s with a figure of around 26 per 1,000. With the
exception of the period before 1875 and the 1890s, the rate
of growth in Sweden was higher than that of Norway. Comparison
with developments in Denmark for the period 1850-1890 shows
that the Swedish growth-rate was at a relatively high level.

The trends described above relate to averages, so it is
quite natural that there will occur a number of individual
discrepancies, especially if we look at the changes from year
to year. Stockholm, with little more than a quarter of the
urban population as a whole, nevertheless exercised the greatest
influence over the average overall development. As Figure 7.3
shows, the rising rate of growth in the 1880s was wholly
caused by the great expansion of Stockholm, and the falling
rate of population increase in the capital after 1890 forced
down the mean rate of growth. The powerful influence of Stockholm
on the average figures is a permanent feature of the entire
study, and for this reason the development of Stockholm
will be dealt with separately as far as is possible. On the
whole it is difficult to utilise the mean figures on their own
before determining how representative they are for separate
groups of towns with regard to distribution on the one hand,
and importance on the other.

As an illustration, it may be noted that the three largest
towns comprised around 40% of the urban population during the
period under review.

Of the towns which had a population of over 10,000 in
1900, Borås and Söderhamn experienced the greatest mean rate
of growth during the period 1860-1900, whilst Västerås occupied
the same position between 1900 and 1920. It is noteworthy
that all three were industrial towns and for more than a decade
had an average annual rate of growth of more than 50 per 1,000
of mean population. In certain of the larger towns, the suburbs
were approaching a growth-rate of 70/1,000 during the
1890s, at a time when the average rate for all towns was about
22/1,000.

The growth in urban population described above for the
most part occurred within the boundaries of the towns already
existing in 1840. Although twenty-five new towns were created
during the period, eighteen of these were created after 1900,
and seventeen of these in or after 1910. These new towns at
the time of their acquisition of their new status added a
total of around 110,000 people or c. 7% of the growth in urban
population between 1840-1920. In addition, a further 200,000
people, or c. 13% of the total growth in urban population were
added through the incorporation of new areas into the old towns.
This means that 80% of the population growth in the towns between
1840-1920 and 55% of the total growth of population in
centres of habitation occurred within the towns which already

existed at the beginning of the period. The rest of the expansion
of population in centres of habitation (tätorter) was divided
between urban districts, municipal communities and 'other
urban-type or densely-settled areas' (non-administrative centres
of population).

Urban districts (köpinar) were the least numerous, no more
than forty in all. In terms of population too they formed the
smallest group under the heading centres of population. The
majority of new towns which were created during this period
were former urban districts. In terms of population, there were
wide differences: in 1910, the largest urban district, Limhamn,
had 9,126 inhabitants, whilst the smallest, Kristianopel, had
97. In 1920, the two largest urban districts had greater populations than half of the towns, and only two urban districts
had fewer inhabitants than the smallest town, which shows that
in terms of population there was not much difference between
the urban districts and the medium-sized and smaller towns.
Urban districts in most cases had their own municipal administration, and all were governed by legislation on urban planning
and by municipal regulations. But the urban districts did not
have the same sort of tight-knit economic and occupational
structure as the towns, and in consequence did not in most
cases have the same high degree of centralisation. This meant
that many urban districts were within the field of influence
of the towns.

A municipal community (municipalsamhället) was distinguished by the fact that there was no necessity to implement
all the municipal regulations. Furthermore, a municipal community did not have an independent administration. In order to
create a uniform pattern for the organisation of these communities, a new law was passed in the 1898 Riksdag, which was
intended to complement the 1862 ordinance on rural local
government. According to Edvard Söderberg, municipal communities
can be divided into three main categories: suburban communities,
station communities and fishing communities. Of the 114 municipal communities in existence in 1901, 20 were suburban communities, 58 station communities and 28 fishing communities.
The rest comprised docks and harbours, church settlements etc.,
and were mostly to be found in upper Noorland.

About half of the municipal communities in 1901 were inland and of these 58 were to be found centres on a railway
station, which shows the great importance of the railway network for this type of population development. The station communities had however a much lower rate of growth than the suburban communities, but surpassed the fishing communities by a
wide margin. In general it can be said that those rural
administrative districts which had municipal communities within their borders enjoyed a significantly higher rate of population increase than other districts. During the 1890s and the
first decade of the twentieth century the municipal communities
had a higher rate of growth than the towns and in certain rural

areas it was only the vigorous expansion of the municipal
communities which prevented an absolute decline in the rural
population. Of the municipal communities it was the suburban
group which increased its population most rapidly, and during
the period 1880-1900 the rate of growth was quadrupled in
comparison with that of the station communities. During the
1910s the increase of population in the municipal communities
and in urban districts slackened off as a result of incorporations and the creation of new towns in the case of the urban
districts. At the same time there was also an apparent shift
in the pattern of growth in the centres of population: an ever
increasing number of people settled in the non-administrative
districts, especially the suburbs, which during the second decade of this century saw an increase in population of 235%.
The other non-administrative centres of population experienced
a growth of 147% but in absolute terms this increase was about
two and a half times greater than in the suburbs. Together the
non-administrative centres of population made up around half
of the total increase in population growth in all centres of
population between 1910 and 1920. To put these figures in context, the non-administrative centres of population in 1910 accounted for c. 13% of the population of all centres of population.

As indicated earlier, there was no uniformity in the development of urban population. There were significant regional
differences, such as the differences at a county level. A
stratification of the towns according to their size also shows
periodic differences. The three largest towns in the kingdom
show a steadily increasing share of the urban population from
1840 to 1900, with a sharp increase during the period 1880-1900.
But it should be noted that Stockholm's share of the total population was in decline between 1840 and 1880. The first two
decades of the twentieth century saw a significant decline in
the major towns' share of the population, approaching the levels
of the early 1880s. One of the main reasons for this decline
was the channeling of new fiscal resources to the suburbs. In
1910, almost 40% of the suburban population was to be found on
the outskirts of Stockholm and 70% around the three largest
towns. In addition, the medium-sized (over 10,000 inhabitants)
inland towns underwent a major period of expansion: the industrial towns to a greater degree than the administrative centres.
In general, an increase in the share of the urban population on
the part of the inland towns can be seen, which in the first
instance may be attributed to the growth of the railways and
the localisation of branches of industry as a result of this.

With this brief outline of population development in the
centres of population as a background, we ought to be able to
summarise the development of population at different phases of
growth, which might hypothetically be as we would expect: when
the urban population of Sweden began to grow more rapidly than
that of the countryside during the 1840s, this was largely a

consequence of population pressures in the countryside which more or less drove certain sections of the rural population to the towns. In subsequent decades the rate of growth continued to increase, largely as a result of the first period of expansion of the railways and the abolition of restrictions on occupation and trade in the towns. Thereafter we can note the direct or indirect effects of industrialisation which further increased the rate of growth. Industrialisation brought with it an expansion of trade and in the service industries and occupations, and this tended to promote even more the process of specialisation in the labour market. The expansion of economic activity placed greater demands on the credit and capital markets which also developed during the period under review. To begin with the towns could take in the swollen stream of newcomers, but matters such as the availability of dwellings and building sites meant that the streams of migrants began more and more to settle in the nearest outskirts of the towns, and in the 1890s began the expansion of the suburbs. During the first decade of the twentieth century a number of new urban -type centres of population came into being, often with industrial expansion as a cause. As a result of technological advances, it was now possible to locate manufacturing industries on entirely different principles than had earlier been the case, and with the second period of railway expansion in the latter half of the 1880s one can see how more and more centres of population were created in the hinterland, often linked to the railways. The first two decades of the twentieth century can be characterised as the period of expansion for the non-administrative centres of population.

This trend in population which can be said to have been on the whole very dynamic should not be allowed to obscure the fact that many centres of population enjoyed a relatively tranquil existence with occasional losses of population, or else longish periods of stagnation.

Even before the first phase of nineteenth century urbanisation became perceptible in the 1840s, the towns had demographic features which differed from those of the countryside. When Gustav Sundbärg at the end of the 1880s considered the expansion of urban population he asked himself if a general overwhelming increase in 'the familiar characteristic drawbacks of towns: a high mortality rate, a low frequency of marriages, a high degree of illegitimate births etc.' was to be feared. But he also took up the question of whether an increase in the number of inhabitants in the towns altered the circumstances of their population.

That changes in the demographic characteristics of towns can be expected to occur as a result of an increased degree of urbanisation can be deduced from the results obtained by migration studies. Many studies have for example found that migrants make up a selection of the population in more than one way. From a demographic point of view, it is sex and age groupings

which above all stand out: in general, there is a predominance
of women amongst the migrants, and the most mobile age group is
generally between 15 and 35. By comparing the increase in population for the towns with that for the whole kingdom we find
that the growth of the towns and all other centres of population to a great extent must be based on the surplus created by
migration. This would mean that the centres of population over
a period of time would receive an influx of 15-35 year-olds,
and a significant proportion of women in the most fertile age-
group. The direction and intensity of the changes which occur
will depend on conditions in the receiving locality, in particular the already existing demographic structure, sanitary
conditions, standards of housing and other factors. Whereas a
heavy influx of migrants to Eskilstuna in the years 1870-1900
for example had relatively little impact on the age structure
of the town, there were very significant changes in Halmstad,
for instance. The lack of change in Eskilstuna can be attributed
to the fact that the younger population moved out to the suburbs at a faster rate than the older inhabitants, giving the
suburbs a completely different structure to the town with regard to age groups, civil status and nativity rates. Those who
moved to Halmstad could for the most part be accomodated within the town limits, and this led to significant changes. When
we come to interpret these changes over a period of time, we
must treat urbanisation both as a dependent and independent
variable. For example, can a reduced birthrate be attributed
to deliberate birth-control as a result of poor and inadequate
living accomodation (urbanisation independent variable): was
the reduced birthrate a cause of a diminution of the urbanisation process (a dependent variable)? Another very important
factor is the flow of people through the locality, i.e. how
long could the centres of population retain their cohorts of
immigrants. In this context, local economic conditions of
course played a major role.

A feature of the overall population development during the
nineteenth century and the beginning of the twentieth was the
trend towards a falling birthrate and mortality rate. A few
noteworthy interruptions in these overall trends did occur in
the 1820s and 1850s, when the birthrate temporarily rose, and
in the first decade of the nineteenth century, when the mortality rate likewise temporarily increased. The birthrate was
above 30 per thousand right up to the 1880s, thereafter declining rather rapidly; in 1920 the 20 per thousand mark was
exceeded for the last time. The mortality rate, which at the
beginning of the nineteenth century was just above 25 per
thousand declined more slowly but continuously, reaching 13 per
thousand in 1920. The balance between these two trends resulted in a surplus of births over deaths, which in itself was one
of the prerequisites for urbanisation.

Periodically the great excess of births over deaths was
markedly reduced, as in the peak years of mass emigration, but

in spite of this, the country's population continually increased, during this period from 3.1 million to 5.9 million, with the towns increasing from 300,000 to 1.7 million. It is within this framework that urbanisation in Sweden must be studied.

7.5. Economic driving forces towards urbanisation

7.5.1. The attraction of towns

In relative terms, urbanisation does not appear to be either dramatic or particularly far-reaching, but if we remember that for every hundred people who moved into the towns and centres of population, around eighty to ninety moved out, then the perspective becomes rather different. When we also bear in mind that movement into and away from centres of population did not follow a simultaneous pattern, we can see that the towns and other centres of population must have been able to accomodate for certain periods of the year a good many more people than the figures would have us believe. Studies of certain towns also show in fact that the effective net gain from migration is surprisingly low, often much less than ten percent. The accumulated gains from migration and a growing excess of births over deaths did however exercise considerable pressure on the centres of population from a number of different angles, since these were intended in the first instance for a much smaller permanent population and many of them had only a limited amount of surface area in which to expand, which necessarily led to an increased density of habitation.

The largest single component of growth in the process of urbanisation was the gains from migration, which corresponded to 50% of the increase in population of the towns between 1840 and 1920, and probably for even more in other centres of population during the period 1890-1920, though by how much is a subject for further research. To explain the phenomenon of population growth in the towns and centres of population therefore, we must also try to explain why people migrated and who migrated.

Most studies which deal with this question are more or less agreed that the great majority of migrants moved for economic reasons, related both to the place from which they moved and the place to which they came. The labour market, availability of work, the structure of the economy and its development are the factors which mainly determine population movements and also the process of urbanisation. Interwoven into these economic inducements are a great number of other factors, such as the need to provide for a family, education, living conditions and working conditions. The economic circumstances of the towns and centres of population are therefore the most important explanatory variable for the course followed by the process of urbanisation, but in no way provide a complete explanation, since we must also take into account political, legal and geographical factors as well, and more.

7.5.2. Industrialisation

Industrial take-off in Sweden occurred a good deal later, and the process of urbanisation was much slower than in the majority of European countries. The rate of urban growth was not as intensive as in many other countries either, which can partially be explained by the fact that even in the pre-capitalist era, industry was distinguished by being widely dispersed as a result amongst other things of the wide geographical distribution of raw materials and the sources of motive power. Moreover there was a heavy dependency on water-borne transport. Handicrafts and trade were restricted by the legislation relating to occupations to the towns, which were usually sited by a watercourse since this was necessary for the transport of goods. The harbour towns were at first favoured by their situation, their trading privileges, and even export and import industries were located for the most part in or near the larger harbour towns.

At the end of the eighteenth and the beginning of the nineteenth centuries the countryside experienced a great increase in population which in the long term led to a major proletarianisation of the rural population. Whilst the peasant class (i.e. the small farmers) increased by a third during the years 1770-1870, the number of tenant-farmers (torpare) doubled and the number of cottars (backstugusittare) and scrapholders (inhysesfolk) almost quintupled. This increase in population which largely took place in pre-industrial agrarian society created a future reserve of labour for the industrialisation which was to begin in the middle of the nineteenth century. When the rural surplus of population drove people into the towns, a significant pool of labour was thus concentrated in certain areas, which was one of the prerequisites for the growth of factory production. The chief characteristic of the early phase of factory production was above all the employment of large numbers of workers; mechanisation was relatively insignificant. At about the same time as this change in methods of production was taking place, the legislation regulating occupations was amended, which greatly stimulated economic activity, with the abolition of guild regulations in 1846 and the ending of the last restrictions on trade and industry in 1864.

At the same time as Sweden gradually urbanised, there occurred a transition from an agrarian to an industrial society on the economic front. Jörn Svensson has divided this transition schematically into three phases, which can also be used as a frame of reference in the study of the urbanisation process and in an analysis for the reasons behind this process.

The first phase, the commercial revolution, is marked by an upsurge of activity principally in certain sectors of foreign trade. The basis for this increased activity lay in the increased productivity of agriculture. In the second phase the successful big merchants take on the role of industrial pioneers with their capital gained from trade, one of the preconditions for the development of a capitalist industry. To begin with money was invested for the most part in those industries which could meet foreign demand for raw materials or semi-finished products, such as the sawmills of the coastal towns of Norrland. At the same time the first steps were also taken towards the creation of a consumer goods industry. Investment capital was placed in industries producing necessities for which there would be a demand in a rural society, for instance the textile industry, in Norrköping and Borås. The third phase involves the development of more and more processing and specialist industries within Sweden, which as a consequence of technological developments and the demand for labour no longer need to be sited in places where there is a supply of raw materials and cheap labour. Industry seeks out the centres of population such as the towns. Soon it reaches a stage where domestic industry becomes self-generating, which is perhaps the real sign of the breakthrough of industrialisation.

As late as the beginning of the 1870s Sweden found herself on the periphery of international progress and only marginally affected by economic changes. The factory system was still in its infancy, and characteristically the methods of production were still very much those of the era of handicraft production. Altogether some 50,000 workers were employed in the manufacturing industries in 1870, in other words about five percent of the population earned a living through industry.

A third of these industrial workers were engaged in the textile mills and one in three textile workers worked in Norrköping. Since something like 35% of all industrial workers were located in the countryside, this means that there must have been other major incentives than industrialisation during this period of urbanisation, prior to 1870. Thanks to its early specialisation in manufacturing, Norrköping was something of an exception. Bearing in mind our earlier plan of the phases of economic development, we may assume that the concentration of handicrafts and trade in the towns formed the basis for the early stages of expansion. The initial phase of urbanisation was greatly determined by geographic location, e.g. nearness to sought-after raw materials, and by fluctuations in international trade, although population growth and economic circumstances in the countryside also played a part. Handicrafts were more dependent upon the local market than was trade, which is why the major trading towns led the way before the phase of industrialisation. There were not enough people earning cash payments which might enable a consumer goods industry to develop, and an inadequate credit system also placed obstacles in the path of progress. Hence the development of a credit system and the fact that a greater number of people than before were brought within the cash wage system were two of the main elements behind industrial expansion and the concomitant socio-economic changes in society which were to take place.

Savings banks on the continental model were founded in Sweden from around 1820, starting in Gothenburg and Stockholm. The next four banks were established in Mariestad, Vänersborg, Karlstad and Filipstad, all within the area of influence of Gothenburg. Soon, savings banks had been established in most commercial and county towns, but there were also a few country savings banks, often connected with rural industries or the larger estates. Savings bank capital played little part however in the financing of enterprises and the expanding communications network. These were largely financed by Swedish merchants, either using their own capital or with the aid of foreign capital. The first commercial banks were mostly provincial banks, and their customers were mostly from the farming community. It was quite a long time before Sweden had a modern commercial banking system suitable for the investment of large sums of money. In the absence of such a system, the merchant houses and banking houses acted as the real banks in financial and industrial centres. Changes in the structure of the credit market occurred mainly because of technological advances and the new economic ideas, which demanded a far greater investment of capital than before, and this began to take effect from the middle of the nineteenth century. Industrial enterprises could draw upon debenture loans, for example, to obtain fixed long-term credit at relatively low interest rates. In this way larger manufacturing plants and mass production could be planned, with a concomitant growth of industrial concentration in the towns and centres of population.

A significant proportion of the payment made to those engaged in trade and handicrafts took the form of payment in kind, board and lodging, but a small amount was in the form of cash wages. This meant that the amount of money in circulation was relatively small. With the development of the factory system, the idea of cash wages become more widely accepted, although to a large extent the truck system was operative in the country areas. Wage levels were also very low to begin with and failed to provide the stimulus for business growth for trade and handicrafts, as the cases of Eskilstuna and Södertälje illustrate. In addition there were areas of urban employment where board and lodging for a long time made up a significant part of the employee's wages. Bakery employees for example were still fighting at the beginning of this century for the abolition of the board and lodging system. But the general spread of the cash wage system not only influenced patterns of consumption: it also meant that the worker was no longer obliged to live where his employer chose, an important loosening of the bonds of the patriarchal social order.
It might also be noted that another effect was the growth of mass movements such as trade unions, since social values are

usually related to new patterns of income distribution and consumption. In this way a new monetary system or new technology can promote social change. One of the consequences of a growing money economy is that goods and services acquire new values, which leads to dissatisfaction with the old socio-economic system (cf. Firth: <u>Money, Work and Social Change in Indo-Pacific Economic Systems</u>). It may also be assumed that a combination of the cash wage system and improved communications broadened the opportunities for people to move, both in terms of intensity and geographical distribution.

Industrialisation and the growth of commercial and manufacturing activities in the old-established crafts meant that there was a great increase in the sources of revenue at a local level, and this was reflected in the rapid rise in the amount of receipts of a large number of towns. In Södertälje for example, the amount received from local taxation rose from 10,000 kr. in 1895 to 64,000 kr. in 1914. It was this increase in revenue above all which laid the foundations for communal expansion.

During the 'factory phase' of industrialisation, decentralisation was a characteristic feature and for a long time industry was a long way from being an urban phenomenon. In 1896 for example, none of the counties of Sweden had fewer than 41% of its industrial workforce located in the countryside, which can hardly be described as a pronounced urban concentration, even if we bear in mind that the majority of pleople still lived in the countryside. Industrialisation in Sweden therefore deviates from the pattern outlined by L. Reissman, according to which 'industry requires the development of cities because it must be located near resources and have access to a constant labor supply'. Some 37% in total of the industrial workforce was located in towns in 1896 as against 48% in 1920. In comparison, about 20% of the industrial workforce of the USA in the latter half of the nineteenth century was located in the countryside. In England the concentration of industry in the towns was even greater.

Does this pattern of industrial location in Sweden mean that industrialisation played a subordinate role in urbanisation? If we consider the connection between migration and industrialisation at a countal level, we find firstly that the most industrialised counties had the highest gain in terms of internal migration, secondly that the net effects of internal migration are most pronounced in heavily industrialised regions, and thirdly that the degree and rate of progress of industrialisation have been the most important factors determining internal migration for all levels of administrative districts (<u>kommuner</u>). From these findings at a countal level it would seem reasonable to assume that industrialised towns made significant gains from migration and that the demands of industry for labour led to a growth of population. That there was a distinct connection between the demand for labour and the size of the net gain from migration can be seen in an intensive study dealing with Eskilstuna between 1871 and 1900. What is interesting is not that the absolute figures for the net migration of adult males and the number of industrial workers seem to be so close to one another, but that they follow such parallel lines of development.

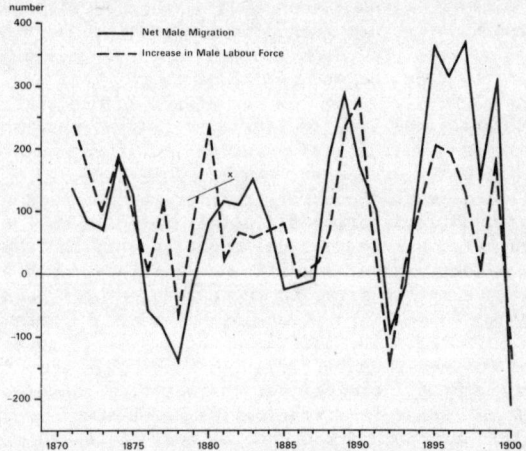

Figure 7.4: Net adult immigration and annual increase in the labour force in Eskilstuna, 1870-1900
Sources: BSOS series D, summary accounts of population and periods of migration for Eskilstuna

x = the likely net gain from migration acc. to calculations based on the difference between summary accounts of population and the periods of migration, as well as information contained in the 1880 census.

Further research is obviously desirable for these comparisons to be placed in perspective, studies of a number of places over a longer period of time, as well as attempts to relate the net gain from migration to the development of the labour force within several branches of industry. This type of research would complement the large-scale studies carried out by such people as Gunnar Myrdahl and his assistants. If we extend the concept of urbanisation to embrace other 'town-like' communities, then a rather larger proportion of industrial workers would be included within the urbanising sphere, whilst it is also very evident that many of these communities to a large extent grow as a result of net gains from migration.

What is of interest in the process of urbanisation is not whether or not industrialisation augmented the movement of

population in relative terms, but what were the consequences
of this augmentation in absolute terms. As long as the towns
had only a small number of inhabitants, industry or the general
housing market could cope reasonably well with increased in-
migration, even though in relative terms it might be as great
as future inflows of population. But as the population grew,
an unchanged relative net gain from inmigration meant a sifni-
ficant rise in absolute terms; and the greater the numbers re-
quiring accomodation the more problems there were.
Nevertheless, the situation was not always so drastic as in
Södertälje, where the local authorities' response to an acute
housing shortage was that the working population could be
lodged in big tents with extra canvas roofs.

There is however a contrary interpretation which main-
tains that industrialisation did not promote the sort of rate
of geographical mobility that one might expect, and therefore
did not have such a great significance for the growth of the
towns. This assumption rests on the evidence that the average
figures for migration into and out of the towns did not noticeably increase after 1860. This does not in itself invalidate
the conclusion that industrialisation to a large extent was
able to have a stimulating effect on migration and created
significant net gains in migration. As we have seen in the
preceding chapter, population developments in the towns and
centres of population were characterised by marked regional
and chronological variations; Norrköping with early industrialisation and rapid growth even before 1850, whilst
Västerås for example did not undergo a period of great expansion
until the turn of the century. Furthermore, it can be assumed
that the degree of industrialisation and the intensity of the
industrialisation process varied over a period of time for
individual towns, which is why the effects of industrialisation
may well be concealed behind these somewhat static series of
averages.

7.6. Territorial patterns - a regulator of urbanisation

Even if the economic factors for expansion can be defined it
is by no means certain that statistical returns reflect the
true course of events, since all statistics relate to administrative entities. To a great extent this effects the division
between town/centres of population and the countryside. In
this context, the age of the towns is of great importance.

An ancient town with tight boundaries had fewer opportunities to house a rapidly growing population within its
administrative limits than had a younger town with a large
territorial area in relation to its population. The age of
the towns also touches upon another range of issues, the morphology and ownership patterns of the towns, which Lennart
Améen has exhaustively investigated in his doctoral dissertation Town Settlement and Domain Structure. Urban Development

in Sweden in Relation to Patterns of Ownership and Administrative Boundaries. Améen demonstrates how towns founded at different periods had different opportunities to expand within their administrative boundaries as a result of the different attitudes of the city fathers towards the allotment of land. Medieval towns like Eskilstuna, which had town land outside the town limits, rapidly developed suburbs at an early stage when industrialisation took off, whilst for example the seventeenth century towns of Borås and Söderhamn, in spite of vigorous expansion, were able to provide accommodation for the majority of immigrants within the town limits.

A feature of many of the older towns was that they were in many cases artificial creations of the state which relied on state subsidies to continue their existence. There is also evidence to suggest that the whole apparatus of towns was over-inflated at the beginning of the nineteenth century. If we bear in mind the way in which these older towns came into being, it is hardly surprising that their organisation was strictly regulated. Most interesting from the urbanisation aspect is the disposition of rights of land ownership. The situation around about 1800 can be summarised as follows: the area under the town's ownership outside the central cluster of dense settlement consisted entirely of town land (stadsjord). In the towns created more recently, this consisted of donation lands (donationsjord) whilst in medieval towns, it comprised both donation and free lands. Free lands comprised the remainder of the land not 'donated' by the crown. These provisions were not fully conformed to, since there were also private domains which indicates that the pattern of ownership within the towns even before industrialisation had begun to shift towards greater private ownership. After 1810 all and sundry were given the right to own land within the towns' administrative boundaries, and towns could even sell off donation lands by dispensation, though such sales also took place without dispensation.

When Värnamo became a market town (köping) in 1860, the state for the first time departed from the principle that it should supply land when a town community was established. Since then town and market town status has been established in such a way as to regulate the state of affairs in already existing centres of population in an integrated manner, and it can be said that the crown since 1860 has not pursued an active land policy in connection with the creation of towns.

The spread of practices which transgressed the regulations relating to private ownership of donation land led to a decree of 1881 which stipulated that the towns must endeavour to regain this land within twenty years i.e. by 1901, after which time it would be declared to be private property. The land which many towns did manage to regain in this way by 1901 was subjected to partial town planning and sold off through dispensation to private individuals. A significant portion of building sites within and outside the towns thus was in private hands, even though the land in principle should have belonged to the town.

The state had attempted to regulate the settlement of towns by imposing restrictions in the local government laws of 1862 and the building regulations of 1874, but with mixed results. In some towns the planned town centre was virtually choked by the rampant and unhindered growth of working-class suburbs, which were built by private speculators and where the workers were merely tenants. In 1899 therefore a committee on home ownership was set up: two years later its report proposed state loans to workers wishing to build their own homes. When the proposal was debated in the Riksdag however, attention came to be focussed more on the problems of agriculture and the loan fund established in 1904 to aid those wishing to build their own homes was, contrary to the committee's intentions, a device for building homes for agricultural workers. The decision of the Riksdag can be said to reflect the imbalance which existed in the national parliament, which gave the rural interests a far greater influence than their share of the population justified.

Not only were rights of ownership in the towns and their immediate vicinity important for urbanisation: it can indeed be said that the system of land ownership and proprietal relationships with regard to land as a whole, and the land policies which were carried out were equally important. This theme is taken up by Ingemar Johansson's interesting thesis The Townless Big City, which deals with the suburbs around Stockholm between 1870 and 1970. It was the nature of land ownership amongst other things which led to the impoverishment and proletarianisation of the farm workers: the proletarianisation of the Norrland peasant farmers through the incursions of the big companies at the end of the 1800s: the pattern of large estates and manorial estates in Central Sweden, whilst the spread of the system of payments in kind to the agricultural labourers created a sizeable propertyless agricultural proletariat: the leasehold system in southern Sweden, which likewise created a propertyless agricultural proletariat. It was from these ill-fated groups that much of the unskilled workforce was recruited for industry. In an article written in 1907 Johan Hansson penned the following pithy sentiments concerning the proletarianisation of the farm workers and the subsequent flight to the towns:

> In our country too we find ourselves coming up against the same momentous fact, that the growth of the towns and the blossoming of big industry originated in the countryside, with its unjust system of private land ownership. Everywhere the same fact stares us in the face. As a result of short-sighted legislation and the power bestowed upon the big land-owners by the rights of land ownership, the rural population has been proletarianised. Any possibility the propertyless farm

worker has had to become independent of the landowner and the dreaded workhouse (fattiggård) has been taken away from him. Thus he has done all he can to find himself a better life either on the other side of the Atlantic or in the towns, and more often than not he has succeeded, although to the disadvantage of the established industrial workers, who have thereby been prevented from materially improving their living standards.

In his article Hansson mentions emigration as a means whereby the less fortunate from the country could improve their lot. One might also say that emigration, which in relative terms was greatest from the towns, also eased the town's situation with regard to their ability to take in migrants from the countryside. Emigration studies in fact consider a good deal of emigration as a prolonged search for work, which in turn tends to strengthen the view that it was not simply the attractive force of the town as such which caused people to leave the countryside, but rather it was the lack of work in the countryside and the hope of finding work in the towns or their immediate vicinity. For many, these hopes must have been cruelly dashed, as wages when they did find work often hardly sufficed to meet the basic necessities of life. The town's poor relief system thus came to be burdened by the unemployed and those with the lowest incomes. For many farm workers, 'urbanisation' simply meant becoming members of the industrial instead of the rural proletariat. But there were those who did experience great improvements in their condition, and in the course of time the situation of the industrial workers did improve, especially for those working in the engineering and other 'high wage' industries.

7.7. Town and hinterland

The development of the population and types of industry of a town/centre of population is thus influenced not only by factors to be traced to the town itself, but often by external factors, which may play a decisive role. If we consider the town, for example, as an economic entity, then we must also take into account the area over which it exercises dominant influence, its surroundings (hinterland). This factor becomes even more important the more communications and the sources of power for industry are developed. Geographers usually speak of the degree of centrality of a location, which is a way of measuring its surroundings. Taking the degrees of centrality as a starting point, we can also range localities into a hierarchy, although this poses problems of definition, since there is sometimes a conflict of functions between the surrounding environs of different localities. The functions of these surrounding areas may influence an analysis of urbanisation in a number of ways. For instance, the location of industry may in a number of cases be determined by the morphology or proprietal structure of a town, which may lead to industry being established outside the town limits. The labour force can either follow it or remain. In both instances problems are created when we try to explain the development of the town. In the first instance, the consequences may be industrial stagnation in the town, but a continued expansion of service industries where a town serves a surrounding area in which industrial growth is taking place. (Depending upon the rate of industrial growth, another phase can be postulated, in which a new centre of population is created which limits the area in which the town plays a dominant role, and which leads to stagnation in the town.) In the second instance, the town may expend in terms of population even though the primary reason for this is to be found outside the town limits. These contrasts come very much to the force in microanalyses.

Surrounding areas are therefore not static but change in the course of time. Allan Pred in his book <u>The External Relations of Cities during The Industrial Revolution</u> has shown that changes with regard to volume and surface expansion in a given function often leads to changes in other functions. Pred has tested his hypotheses in regard to Gothenburg during the breakthrough period of industrialisation (1889-1891), and has attempted to show how changes in the manner of production, the methods of financing in Gothenburg and the simultaneous improvements in communications affected relations between Gothenburg and its hinterland in a number of different ways, and how the economic activities of the surrounding area were adapted to these changes. In addition to the interaction between central location and hinterland, Pred has also demonstrated how the movement of population was affected by changing circumstances, especially the influence the mechanisation of industry had on the zones of migration and the social composition of the migrants.

There is a lot more that can be said about the relationship between town and hinterland; here I have been content to outline the general features and analystical guidelines. What is important is that the surrounding areas should not be regarded as an eternal constant, or simply as a passive entity receiving the surplus population of the towns or as an extension of the town's market. What pred has tried to show is the complexity of the relationships of the surrounding areas, and this complexity need not imply simultaneity, but may well involve chronological and functional discrepancies as between phases.

7.8. The economy and population development - town types and trends

The development of the towns may largely be seen as a reflection of local economic activity, and in certain instances of fluctuations in overseas trade. It would therefore seem appropriate to categorise the towns in a way which takes into account the economic structure, geographical situation and size. I intend to utilise a rather rough but for my purposes appropriate typology, as used by Maxwell Overton in his article 'Certain principal features in the development of economic activity, particularly industry, and population within different types of Swedish towns'. Overton is aware that the development of towns does not just occur according to severely regulated geographical patterns, but is also dependent upon political and other more irrational factors. But with regard to the localisation of economic activity, the geographical divisions fall into different stages of development, which can then be complemented with other data.

The basic distinction made in Overton's typology is between coastal and inland towns, with the inland ports as an intermediate group. In terms of size the towns are grouped into large towns of over 100,000 inhabitants, medium-sized towns of more than 10,000 and small towns of less than 10,000 inhabitants. The coastal towns are then grouped into west coast, east coast and north coast towns. Trelleborg falls into the first-named group and Ystad lies to the east of the dividing line, whilst Gävle belongs to the category of east coast towns, since it was not so dependent on the timber trade and industry as the towns further north.

The big inland towns have been divided into two main groups: the central inland towns - Uppsala, Linköping, Kristianstad, Lund and Örebro - and inland industrial towns - Eskilstuna, Jönköping and Borås. To the first group belong towns which have long been major centres of trade for the fertile agricultural plains and with the exception of Lund they have all been centres of administration and relatively important garrison towns. The medium-sized inland towns (10 - 20,000 inhabitants) - Växjö, Alingsås, Skövde, Falun and Östersund - make up a less homogeneous group than the aforementioned, but with the exception of the industrial town of Alingsås they are all important centres for areas of mixed timber and agriculture, are regimental towns and owe their expansion to improved railway communications.

Overton's principle of allowing the size of the towns in 1942 determine grouping according to size may be criticised, but since the development of the individual towns within the respective main groups was, with few exceptions, relatively similar, it may also be vindicated. Moreover the 10,000 inhabitants barrier is a natural demarcation line for the towns engaged in the wholesale trade regarding 'non-specialised goods'.

In 1870, such industry as existed was concentrated in the major coastal towns and inland industrial towns, which were the only ones with 50 industrial workers per 1,000 inhabitants. Industry was most concentrated on the east coast, where Norrköping played a very dominant role. The inland ports and some of the inland central towns had c. 20-40 industrial workers per 1,000 inhabitants, whilst the small towns and above all the coastal towns of Norrland had very little industry.

The industrial expansion which occurred in the first half of the 1870s was centred in the first instance on the major towns, which had earlier had a relatively low degree of industrialisation. The reason for the expansion of the big towns during the first half of the 1870s was principally because the construction of the first phase of the mainline railway network in the 1860s acted as a stimulus to trade and industry. The first major construction phase in the railway system also had a beneficial effect upon the central inland towns, but the other inland towns had to wait until the second phase of railway building in the 1870s. The result was that the inland towns' share of town-based industry increased by 50% during the period 1875-1890. The inland industrial towns of Borås (20.2%), Eskilstuna (19.4%) and Jönköping (13.3%) were amongst the five most industrialised towns in 1890, in terms of the number of industrial workers in relation to the number of inhabitants. The two others were the east coast town Norrköping (20.1%) and the west coast town Trelleborg (16.7%). With the exception of Jönköping, these towns all retained their positions ten years later. It can also be seen that the old inland industrial towns, in spite of earlier high figures, continue to increase their share of the urban industry of the country, against a background of stiff competition from the newly created towns, almost all of which were inland. The vigorous growth in the inland towns took place at the expense of the east coast towns' relative decline. The overall increased growth of the inland industry is attributable to the fact that larger industrial concerns could be set up inland as a result of improved communications. In general, the importance of communications for industrial development is clearly reflected in the development of the different urban groups. With each new phase of railway construction, we can see how the big towns, which first acquired new railway links, increase their share at the expense of other towns, only to fall back again when the other towns become linked up to the railway system. This connection is somewhat less evident in the 1890s if we look simply at the statistics for all kinds of occupation, because the 1896 figures include a significant number of sawmill workers in the coastal towns of Norrland.

The revision of the statistics in 1896 meant that a number of new occupational categories were now placed under the heading of industry - workers in sawmills, large bakeries, printing houses and mills, for example - and this meant a degree of levelling-out in the distribution of industry, since the smaller towns had a relatively large share of the new categories of industry. The small towns, which were characterised by their late industrial development, enjoyed an uninterrupted increase in their share of urban industry and as a result of the revision of 1896 this share was increased still further.

The sharp rise of the share of the west coast towns in relation to those of the east coast is connected with increased overseas trade westwards together with industrial expansion.

The share of the major towns in urban industry was relatively constant, though Stockholm's share shows a falling trend, which also reflects the capital's overall population development. The newly created towns' share, for obvious reasons, tended to grow over a period of time, but what is interesting is that their industrial share is greater than their share of the population, which suggests that urbanisation in this instance is a function of industrial development.

The primary function of the preindustrial town was to act as a trading post for the surrounding countryside. It is therefore quite surprising that in 1860, trade provided employment for only 12% of those engaged in some form of economic activity in the countal towns and 15% in Stockholm. Although trade formed the most rapidly expanding sector of urban economic activity, it never therefore employed anything like as large a share of the population as industry. At the end of the century Öraskölsvik, with 8% of the total population had the largest share of inhabitants engaged in some form of trade. The next four towns had between 6% and 8%. With the exception of Hälsingborg, none of these towns had more than 3,000 inhabitants. It is therefore doubtful if commercial occupations alone played any significant part in the growth of any town during the period 1860-1920. It is only when trade and transport are put together that we can regard individual towns as having expanded principally as a result of these occupational categories. If we then consider that the number of children per head of the working population was probably highest amongst industrial and craft workers, then industrial expansion must be taken as the most important single component on average in the process of urbanisation in Sweden during the period under study.

Handicrafts, as well as trade, were mostly geared towards the town itself and its trading periphery. It is therefore striking that the distribution of handicrafts and trade in the town groupings as early as 1860 were rather dissimilar. Bearing in mind the large surrounding areas of the inland towns, we may expect that their share of trade and handicrafts would be greater than their share of industry. Against this it seems that the large towns at first had an astonishingly high proportion, which meant that the inland towns' share of trade was less than their share of population. The large proportion of handicrafts attributed to the big cities before the turn of the century can partly be explained by the fact that the construction industry was included amongst handicrafts. The erection of stone buildings, which demanded a great deal of labour, was the main reason why the building industry occupied such a prominent position in the major towns. The declining share of the handicrafts of the big towns from the turn of the century up to 1920 can partly be attributed to the spread of building methods using stone to the other towns in Sweden, one of the reasons for this being the many destructive fires which ravaged their wooden houses.

With regard to trade, the dominance of the big cities was mainly due to the heavy concentration of the wholesale trade in these towns (c. 90% in 1860), but there was also a large amount of retail trade concentrated in these towns, where higher living standards probably counterbalanced the relatively larger trading areas of the other towns. The distribution of trade in 1860 shows that the countryside with its self-sufficient economy could have had little significance for the towns' trade, in spite of the fact that they enjoyed a monopoly over trade until 1864.

The big towns' dominant position in the trading sector lasted throughout the period under study, though with considerable fluctuations from a low of 47% to a peak of 59% of those engaged or employed in trade. This trend is reminiscent of the development of industry and is also linked to the development of communications. Improvements in the transport system may also lie behind the positive development of the larger inland towns, though here the gradual disappearance of the countryside's self-sufficient economy may also have played a role. The share of trade of the small towns and the medium-sized coastal towns shows a sharp decline throughout, which may largely be due to their inability to support a wholesale trade, but also because of the overwhelming competition of the larger towns, since the smaller and medium-sized towns in general tended to trade only in certain items. Oskarshamn can be said to exemplify the kind of smaller town which stagnated due to its high sensitivity to trade fluctuations, caused by drastic decline in its overseas trade and the stagnation of its chief employer of labour, the shipyards. Other forms of employment were unable to expand on their own resources.

Of the coastal towns, those on the west coast occupied a noticeably more favourable position than those on the east coast as a result of the expansion in overseas trade mentioned earlier combined with growing industrialisation: in particular, the engineering industry and shipbuilding, which was of a larger scale and more modern than for example was the case in Oskarshamn on the east coast.

The development of the towns can therefore be explained in terms of their occupational structure and geographical location, though their size is also important for the location of certain economic activities.

The development of the larger centres of population, unlike that of the smaller centres, cannot be attributed to one or another branch of production, although there are certain common features. They are principally central locations for specifically urban types of trading activity, political and administrative as well as cultural activities. Furthermore it is striking that the printing, metal and clothing industries were heavily concentrated in the big towns. The location of the printing industry in the big towns is because this type of industry is bound to the centres of economic, political and cultural activity. The case of the clothing industry is not so evident, though innovations in fashion often started first in the big towns and in this way may have contributed to its concentration in the big towns. Moreover it might have been easier to attract female labour in a larger town where this type of industry might also serve as a complementary industry to those with an overwhelmingly male labour force.

There is no direct connection with specifically urban types of activity in the location of the metal industry, which was largely determined by the need for reserves of labour, especially for firms which produced capital goods, which are extremely sensitive to market changes. Other typically big town industries are the foodstuffs and construction industries, the latter also being very sensitive to fluctuations in the economy, a subject dealt with by Uno Gustafson, for example, in his dissertation, The Big Industrial City.

The medium-sized and small centres of population were dependent for their development on one or a small number of areas of production. The many small, growing communities in the Småland uplands founded their success on the wood industry, especially carpentry and furniture manufacture, which declined in the environs of the big towns. The stonemason communities of Bohuslän found themselves in a backwater as a result of competition from new roadmaking and building materials; the fishing villages of Bohuslän waned whilst those around Gothenburg flourished, partly because rationalisation in the fishing industry cut the number of these employed in it and brought the trade nearer the market, and partly because the fishing villages near Gothenburg attracted many summer visitors from the town. Changes in the timber and pulp industries on the Norrland coast also led to some places expanding, others stagnating, as production was concentrated in larger units. The small localities were in a more exposed position than larger ones with their more varied pattern of trade and industry, but at the same time, small places could undergo an explosive development in the event of an intense upsurge in demand.

The above survey may serve to illustrate the fact that the larger towns had greater opportunities to expand by virtue of their own internal dynamism, as a consequence of a varied pattern of economic activity and because they provided a central point for a range of different activities. The smaller the town the more sensitive it was to trade fluctuations and the more dependent it was on larger towns. Moreover, communications - both the railways and sea transport - affected the location and development of towns. The importance of communications can perhaps be best seen with regard to the railways, which brought about

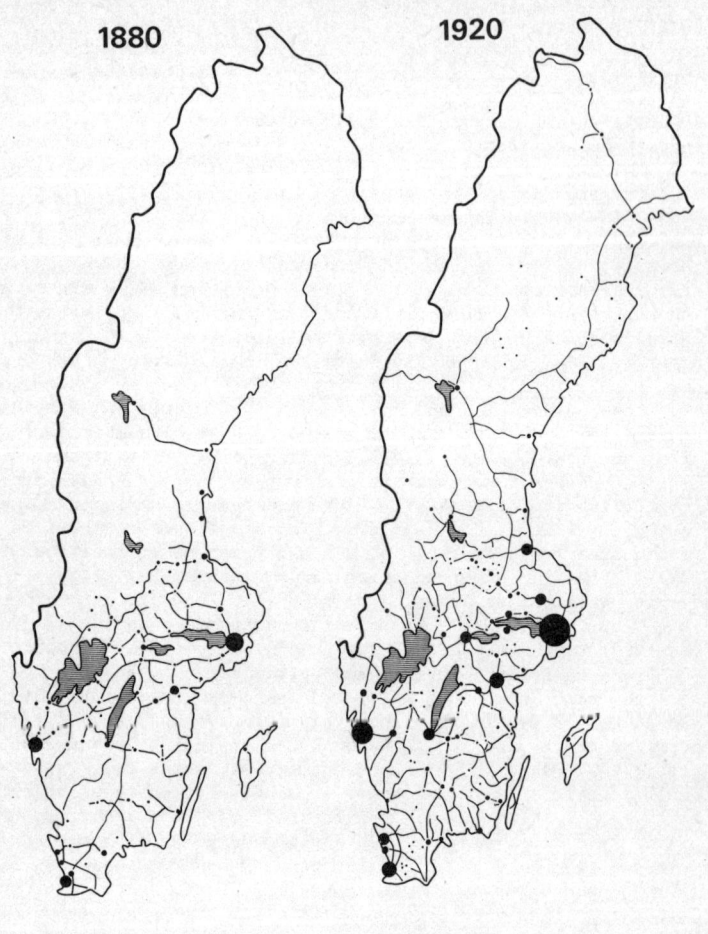

Figure 7.5: Centres of population in Sweden in 1880 and 1920

a shift away from the east coast towns to those of the interior. In total the Swedish railway network increased from 527 km. of track in 1860 to 15,160 km. in 1920. The greatest period of railway building was the 1870s, when the trackage rose from 1,727 to 5,876 km. The greater part of the railway network was in private hands, and as late as 1920, state-owned trackage was no more than 36%.

The extent and importance of the railways as a means of transport for the populace may be illustrated by the figures for the number of travellers to and from Norrköping during the period 1870-1913:

1870 - 75,000 passengers
1880 - 152,000
1890 - 262,000
1900 - 445,000
1913 - 976,000.

The great increase in the number of travellers after the turn of the century is largely due to the growth of the suburb of Åby. In 1913, no fewer than 425,000 journeys were made between Åby and Norrköping, including the intermediate halts. Monthly season tickets accounted for something like 90,000 of these journeys, which indicates a high level of commuting by the workforce between suburban areas and the centre. This type of commuting was not confined to Norrköping, but can also be seen taking place between for example Stockholm and Järva, Gothenburg and Partille, Malmö and Lund. In all the volume of passenger traffic on the railways in Sweden increased by 400% during the period 1880-1920.

The commercial benefits for the towns and larger centres of population as a result of the building of the railways was considerable, for it coincided with the gradual decline of the rural self-sufficient economy. The importance of railway communications for the spread of centres of population in Sweden can be seen from Figure 7.5. In addition, the building of railways and running of the railway system created many job opportunities e.g. in the engine works at Trollhättan and Motala and the carriage-works in Södertälje, though in terms of the numbers employed, the railway system was relatively insignificant. The same is true for shipping, whose real significance lay in the conveyancing of goods and the job-creating effects this had upon other areas of economic life. At the end of the period under review, motor transport also began to have an influence, which in the long run was to revolutionise rural transport both of people and of goods.

7.9. Urban society 1840-1920

The major technological, economic and demographic changes which Sweden underwent from around the middle of the nineteenth century were to exercise great influence upon the

physical and functional structure of the towns and upon the
population figures and social structure. Perhaps the most obvious changes were external, in the shape of building construction, which reflected changes in the town's function, from
being basically a country market town to a modern industrial
or commercial town. These changes in settlement patterns and
in town planning have been well documented in Gregor Paulsson's
Swedish Town and Lennart Améen's Town Settlement and Domain
Structure. These aspects will therefore only be summarised
briefly.

From country market town to industrial city

The inhabitants of the country market town, according to Gregor
Paulsson, may be divided into three main economic and social
categories: haute bourgeoisie, petite bourgeoisie and those
engaged in menial occupations (småfolk). The first stratum
consisted of three groups; persons of quality (ståndspersoner),
merchants, who at that time had their own trading housing,
manufacturers and 'factory bosses' (patroner). The petite
bourgeoisie consisted of craftsmen, lesser officials and others
belonging to this relatively homogeneous professional class.
The last layer, the menu peuple, consisted of clerks, shop-
assistants, journeymen and apprentices, labourers, farm-hands
and serving-girls as well as women supporting themselves.
The domestic economy of the different strata sought to create
its own environment in accordance with the manners and customs
of the appropriate social rank and its own economic limitations. The environment thus created can be consistently divided
into three regions, differing only in size, situation or
nuances of form, depending on the proportions of the different
major groupings. In all these regions, the large household
set its stamp on the character of the environment. The house
became the centre of work as well as domestic life, and as it
grew it acquired sharply differentiated functions. Améen has
attempted to construct a general model of what Paulsson in a
number of case-studies found to be common features, namely
that the haute bourgeoisie tended to concentrate at the heart
of the town, whilst the craftsmen were to be found in the
surrounding outer zones. Beyond these two zones was the area
of settlement of the lowest social stratum, often gathered
around the exit roads. Paulsson cites as examples Helsingborg
and Örebro, but one can find others: Uppsala, where the poorest sections of the community were to be found along the exit
road to Vaksala: Sundsvall, where they lived along the western
exit road towards Östersund, and so on. In this manner a
special sort of functional housing segregation came into
being at an early stage, and which later became a more purely
social and economic segregation of living styles. This latter
stage was the subject of research on the continent as early
as the 1840s, when the German cultural geographer J.C. Kohl

formulated more general propositions of the sort later applied by Arméen to Swedish conditions.

Another feature of the country market town was that the heads of households were also farmers and livestock owners. This varied from town to town, but for example Örebro had a strikingly agrarian stamp about it with almost thirty per cent of the haute bourgeoisie being owners of farms in 1840.

During the 1860s, the country market town was transformed into what may be described as the town of commercial capitalism. The old divisions of rank broke down and a more varied pattern of occupation emerged. There was also a transition from a natural to a money economy. Politically, these changes were to find expression in the introduction of freedom of occupation and the institution of town councillors. The new representative system of administration came to be dominated by the more affluent section of the populace, and thanks to the improved economic position of the bourgeoisie, there were opportunities to create a different environment to that of the country market town.

The residential environment of the big merchant in the new type of town was still tied to the place of work, as was that of the craftsman, but whereas trade was concentrated into larger units and together with the houses of the local authorities came to dominate the central precincts, the craftsmen's demands for space remained constant as a result of stagnation within their trades, mainly because of the beginnings of foreign competition in the form of cheaper mass-produced articles. The result was that the merchant area of the town stood up to the pressure of population as a result of increased immigration, whilst the areas occupied by the craftsmen were tightly squeezed and the old craftsmen's houses were the first to bear the brunt of the influx of rural proletariat and the rest of the labour force for nascent industry. It was mainly the smaller craftsmen who went under, since the bigger craftsmen could frequently continue as before or by utilising manufacturing processes go over to factory production. The handicraft zone therefore came to have a more heterogeneous social composition during the pre-industrial period than the mercantile zone, and also a more mobile population in a geographical sense, which may be associated with the system of learning within the crafts. Studies of geographical mobility in Eskilstuna during the 1850s and 1860s also show a very high rate of mobility amongst males, which was largely caused by itinerant journeymen.

It was a very common developmental tendency for industries in Swedish towns to be the final stage in a process which went from handicraft pure and simple to the introduction of machinery and on to factory production proper. This also goes a long way towards explaining why the factories in our towns were often located all over the place and not concentrated in one industrial area as on the continent. An extreme example of decentralised factory production is Eskilstuna, where even today there are factories scattered about in the midst of residential areas. Industry in Eskilstuna in fact emanated to a great extent from the old craft trades, whilst for example in Helsingborg, Norrköping and Södertälje there were whole industrial areas, where large concerns established themselves with no connection with an earlier craft-based set-up. Because of their very heavy demands on space for workshops, plant and warehouses, as well as large labour forces the engineering industry and other branches of machine manufacture occupied the most prominent areas of these new industrial zones. They also occupied a central position in economic terms thanks to their high output and relatively high wages which in turn gave their workers an important position politically.

There is no clearly defined line between the town characterised by commercial capitalism and that characterised by nascent industrialism either in respect of external appearances or functional features, and moreover it was largely the capital accumulated by commercial activity which financed a major part of this nascent industry.
In general, the beginning of the 1870s may be taken as the watershed between the two categories of town, in which we find a direct transition to an industrial town or an indirect transition to a town with distinct industrial features, where trade and handicraft are prevalent and where industrialisation in the form of factories has not established itself, but where the effects of industrialisation can be observed via communications or access to goods and in the different work routines of everyday life.

As I have already pointed out, industrialisation occurred gradually and at a different pace in different places, and with regard to different products. This meant that the industrial towns came to be affected in very different ways by the siting of industry.
In this context mention might be made of the many urban conflagrations during the nineteenth century, which was to influence the urban scene in a number of different ways. During reconstruction after these fires, a number of towns went in for a different type of town planning, which meant that these towns were years ahead of others in housing and building planning. A rather extreme example of this is Sundsvall, which was undergoing a boom period of growth at the time of the destructive fire of 1888. The town was also the centre of the country's greatest urbanised region, with its many sawmill communities and complementary communities. Sundsvall became a first haltingpoint, a sort of sluice for workers seeking employment in the sawmills. Because of the expansion of the surrounding industrial region, the wholesale trade of the town enjoyed a boom period, which also left its imprint on the building structure and social composition of the central quarters of the town.

What distinguished Sundsvall from the other countal

towns was the fact that the pattern of the old quarters and
building sites remained unaltered, but the whole of the central
area had to be rebuilt in stone to resist the danger of fire
in the narrow streets. In place of the more customary two-
storey terraces of wooden houses were erected four- or five-
storey palace-like stone buildings along the main thoroughfares.
What was for Sweden a real city rose up, with shops and offices
in the lower storeys and with large, elegant apartments higher
up. The high costs of these new buildings and the increased
site values brought in a new class of owners, dominated by the
big merchants and wholesalers and officials. The old property
owners were driven out to the city margins where they indulged
in speculation in the new working-class areas which sprang up
around the town. Sundsvall became a typical example of the sort
of settlement described by John Georg Kohl in 1841 in Verkehr
und Ansiedlung, with the higher social strata concentrated in
the centra of the city, with a lowering of the social strata
the further from the centra one travelled. The rapidly growing
working-class areas both within and outside Sundsvall's administrative boundaries meant that the town became, in Gregor
Paulsson's words: 'the clearest example to be found in our
country of the discrepancy between a town considered as a
functioning societal whole and a town which has grown much too
rapidly, consisting of two parts, one administratively regarded as a town, the other a chaotically formed urban 'penumbra''.

It was mainly due to the introduction of building regulations in 1874, with their stricter construction controls and
subsequent rising costs that the continually growing working-
class population in most towns were forced out into the outer
limits of the town and in many cases outside the town boundary.
The industrial town brought with it an increased degree of segregation in housing, though now this was for economic and
social, not functional reasons. With the development of communications, the better-off also began to settle outside the
town centre from the turn of the century onwards, and wealthy
suburbs of private residences began to make their appearance.
The wealthy had begun to settle outside the towns even earlier,
but mostly in smaller manor-houses and the like.

The growth of population and the spreading-out of settlement in the larger towns also created a demand for local public
transport and from the latter half of the 1870s horse-drawn
trams were introduced: around the turn of the century, there
were electric trams in some ten towns. Stockholm for obvious
reasons was first, but came after Copenhagen and Oslo for example. The introduction of local public transport also meant
a dispersal of people and settlements and created the basis
for the formation of smaller town centres in the larger cities.

At the beginning of the 1880s a new means of communication
made its appearance, the telephone. To begin with only businesses
and a few private individuals in the towns had a telephone and
it was not until after the turn of the century that the number

of subscribers began to rise significantly, although even then
they were usually members of the wealthier section of society.
The number of subscribers in the larger provincial towns in
1914 was around 60-70 per 1,000 inhabitants, whilst in Stockholm the figure was 250. In a heavily industrialised town like
Eskilstuna with a very large working-class population, the
number of subscribers was 9 per 1,000 inhabitants in 1884 and
17 in 1890.

7.10. Conclusion

Urbanisation in Sweden between 1840 and 1920 involved amongst
other things a vigorous increase in population both in absolute
and relative terms in all types of centres of population. Development was by no means even, however, and clearly distinguishable phases of growth can be observed for different
types of densely-populated areas. Up to the turn of the century
almost all growth was centred on the towns, but around the
turn of the century there occurred a shift which meant that
more and more of the increase in the population took place in
other centres of population. As well as chronological shifts
there were also significant regional variations. The different
shifting of phases reflects changing reasons for the process
of urbanisation if we take as our main criterion Tisdale's definition of urbanisation i.e. that an ever greater proportion
of the population settles in towns and town-type communities.

Around the middle of the nineteenth century, it was partly the excess of population in the countryside and the growing
proletarianisation of the rural population which drove people
to the towns, partly the expansion of trade and certain types
of handicraft which demanded a growing supply of labour. Somewhat later there began the first phase of railway construction.
Continuing industrialisation meant a continuous increase in the
demand for labour, especially as nascent industrialisation was
characterised by the fact that its methods of production demanded large resources of labour. Furthermore, work on the urban
environment, the construction of streets, water supplies and
sewers on the international model (Paris, London) also required
large numbers of workers.

During the 1890s, the formation of suburbs began to get
under way, large because of the high rents and scarcity of accommodation in the towns, at the same time as the development
of the railways and the location of industry which this helped
direct gave birth to a number of new centres of population,
above all inland. The 1910s came to be the great period of expansion for the non-administrative centres of population.

At the same time as changes in economic activity and economic development brought about a sizeable inflow of people to
different forms of urban settlement, there occurred major demographic changes in the centres of population. The towns show
a steadily falling mortality and birth rate, and since the mortal-

ity rate fell faster, this meant that there was a significant excess of births over deaths, although this was partly reduced by overall emigration. It may nevertheless be concluded that demographic development and the movement of population led to a notable shift of emphasis from the sparsely populated countryside to the centres of population, both as regards the distribution of settlements and occupation of the populace. The proportion of people living in Sweden's towns rose from 10% in 1840 to 29% at the end of the period, and the total population of centres of population to around 45%. Even if these changes show a significant movement of population between the countryside and the densely-populated centres, the net changes recorded are only a very small fraction of the total gross figure.

Sweden's urbanisation may therefore be explained partly in demographic and partly in economic and occupational terms, and these different explanatory factors varied over a period of time, which is why no one factor can be said to explain the general course of the process of urbanisation. Certain factors can be isolated and defined for certain periods. Here it may be noted that as far as demographic development is concerned, urbanisation should be used as an independent variable.

The economic, social, political and cultural consequences of urbanisation were in many respects important. But even in towns, where the process of urbanisation followed a leisurely course, the inflow of people from the countryside involved changes in the form of the distribution of work, patterns of housing, the wages system, consumption of goods, norms and values. It may be that the transition was easier in other types of population centres, but it is debateable whether even here one can speak of a 'rural-urban continuum'.

Industrialisation and urbanisation in the long run brought about social liberation within the working class above all, since one was no longer compelled to live with one's employer and one was also paid in cash. This, and the elementary education reforms were two major circumstances behind the growth of national and popular movements. The degree of activism and ability to mobilise support of these movements was clearly seen, especially during elections to the second chamber. Urbanisation and industrialisation also caused great changes in the distribution of income and indirectly thereby changes in the structure of political power. Despite a graded franchise, the popular movements and their allies succeeded in making great inroads into the established political patterns at a local government level.

The growth of urban population caused a sharp increase in the public sector at a local level and large investments were necessary to meet the most acute problems. On the whole there occurred a significant accumulation of capital in the towns during this time and it would be interesting to chart where different flows of capital did in fact emanate from.

In this present work only a few aspects of urbanisation and its consequences have been discussed. It should however be obvious that urbanisation is a very complex process, which necessitates a good deal of investigation in order that an overall picture can be presented. Our knowledge of the subject might best be served in the future by concentrating research on economic and population-related factors and linking these to the different phenomena which can be studied in the urban environment at different levels. There are of course great dangers of finding oneself engaged in the fruitless task of giving as broad and all-embracing definition as possible. It would be more useful to set in motion more comparative research both on a national and inter-Nordic basis, for example, preferably with more theoretical link-up than there is at present, which has relevance for the investigation of the urbanisation process.

Appendix: Population increase in the larger towns in Sweden per thousand of mean population, 1861-1910

Cities	Population 1860	1900	1910	Rate of total increase 1861-70	1871-80	1881-90	1891-00	1901-10	Nativity surplus 1861-70	1871-80	1881-90	1891-00	1901-10	Migration gains 1861-70	1871-80	1881-90	1891-00	1901-10
Stockholm	112391	300624	342323	18.3	21.1	36.7	19.8	12.9	2.3	1.5	9.8	7.2	8.4	16.0	19.6	26.9	12.6	4.5
Stockholm's environment	7222	30006	-	24.9	38.4	18.3	69.2	-	-	11.4	14.6	13.5	-	-	27.0	3.7	55.7	-
Uppsala	8459	22855	25960	29.3	32.5	30.0	6.1	12.7	6.8	3.8	8.3	4.7	4.1	18.1	28.7	21.7	1.4	8.6
Eskilstuna	4628	13663	28364	21.6	34.9	29.7	22.6	76.7	6.2	10.5	14.4	15.3	12.4	23.1	24.4	15.3	7.3	64.3
Eskilstuna's environment	2508	11062	-	14.2	8.9	58.2	66.3	-	12.4	11.7	18.2	23.5	-	-	2.8	40.0	42.8	-
Linköping	6138	14552	18149	16.6	18.2	35.7	14.8	22.2	2.1	6.8	8.9	6.5	8.4	14.5	11.4	26.8	7.8	13.8
Norrköping	19956	41008	46393	17.4	11.0	21.0	22.4	12.2	7.1	8.3	9.9	8.4	9.7	10.3	2.7	11.1	14.0	2.5
Norrköping's environment	4642	12415	-	13.4	30.8	29.0	25.4	-	9.6	10.4	17.2	15.5	-	-	3.8	11.8	9.9	-
Jönköping	7444	23143	26969	36.4	39.5	18.9	16.4	16.0	13.3	15.0	15.7	11.3	11.1	23.1	24.5	3.3	5.1	4.8
Kalmar	8061	12715	15535	13.6	17.0	6.9	7.7	20.1	6.3	4.5	4.6	5.8	8.8	7.3	12.5	2.3	1.9	12.6
Karlskrona	15300	23955	27434	7.6	10.1	11.9	14.9	13.3	7.6	7.3	10.3	9.0	10.1	0.0	2.8	1.6	5.9	3.2
Kristianstad[1]	5733	10318	11569	33.6	14.2	15.0	6.0	11.2	12.3	11.6	12.2	8.5	9.2	21.3	2.6	2.8	2.5	2.2
Malmö	18919	60857	83373	30.1	39.3	23.9	23.1	30.9	14.6	17.1	15.7	11.9	16.5	15.5	22.2	8.2	11.2	14.5
Malmö's environment	2639	15276	20139	16.2	43.2	50.1	68.1	19.0	13.4	20.1	23.6	25.7	-	-	21.5	26.5	42.4	-
Lund	8412	16621	16041	23.4	29.2	4.9	10.2	19.0	9.0	10.1	6.5	8.0	10.2	14.4	19.1	1.6	2.2	8.7
Landskrona	5703	14399	33347	31.2	21.8	22.4	16.2	10.7	14.9	14.8	15.5	15.1	14.1	14.3	7.0	6.9	1.1	3.4
Hälsingborg	5333	24670	18342	38.3	37.3	58.4	19.1	29.7	14.5	15.7	17.0	14.4	13.3	23.8	21.6	41.4	4.7	16.3
Halmstad	3945	15362	167809	37.7	39.3	34.3	26.1	17.5	11.3	17.1	17.3	16.9	15.3	26.4	22.2	17.0	9.2	2.2
Göteborg[2]	37043	130619	-	41.9	30.2	31.4	22.5	25.1	8.2	13.5	14.6	12.6	12.9	33.7	16.7	16.8	9.9	12.2
Göteborg's environment	3318	22989	21541	36.5	54.1	58.9	42.0	-	-	19.6	26.0	20.7	-	-	34.5	32.9	21.3	-
Borås	2988	15837	17192	8.3	37.6	54.0	69.6	30.7	9.3	9.3	16.3	10.4	19.1	27.2	28.3	50.5	12.0
Karlstad	4514	11869	30082	21.8	32.8	31.7	36.2	21.3	8.4	10.2	10.2	10.4	14.4	18.7	22.6	1.5	21.3	21.8
Örebro	7377	22013	19145	20.0	26.1	21.1	43.1	31.0	6.4	10.2	10.9	14.1	13.9	15.4	17.0	10.2	29.0	17.1
Västerås	4541	11999	35202	16.7	14.7	28.0	41.4	47.5	6.5	9.1	7.0	10.4	15.3	10.2	12.5	21.0	31.0	32.2
Gäfle	10975	29522	11412	23.1	29.0	22.9	23.3	18.3	0.0	2.2	12.4	12.9	16.7	15.9	16.6	8.8	10.4	5.9
Söderhamn	2786	11258	16854	52.0	52.2	23.4	11.1	1.3	7.2	18.7	22.4	16.1	11.6	38.2	33.5	1.0	5.0	10.2
Sundsvall	4432	14831	-	37.5	35.3	39.2	11.5	12.7	13.8	14.0	13.9	12.9	9.0	26.9	21.3	25.3	1.4	3.7
Sundsvall's environment	4338	24291	-	42.2	61.4	53.4	13.3	-	10.6	12.5	23.5	25.7	19.5	-	29.7	37.9	27.7	6.2	-

Source: SOS ser. A. 1890-1911

REFERENCES

Official Statistics

Bidrag till Sveriges officiella statistik

ser. A : Befolkningsstatistik
ser. D : Fabriker och manufakturer, efter 1895, Fabriker och hantverk.
ser. E : Inrikes sjöfart och handel, efter 1894.
ser. F : Handel.
ser. H : Kungl. Maj.:ts Befallningshafvandes femårsberättelser.
ser. R : Valstatistik.
ser. U : Kommunernas fattigvård och finanser.
ser. X : Løne- och pensionsstatistik.

Ahlberg, G.   Befolkningsutvecklingen och urbaniseringen i
    Sverige 1911-50 (Stockholm, 1953).
Ahlberg, G.   Stockholms befolkningsutveckling efter 1850
    (Uppsala, 1958).
Améen, L.   'Stadsbebyggelse och domänstruktur', Meddelande
    från Lunds Universitets Geografiska Institution,
    avhandlingar nr. 46 (Lund, 1964).
Anderson, N. (ed.) Urbanism and Urbanization (Leiden, 1964).
Andrae, C.G.   Från borgargård till hyreshus (no place, 1977).
Arosenius, E.   'Folkmängden i Sveriges köpingsliknande samhällen
    enligt folkräkningen år 1900', Statistisk Tidskrift (1903).
Arosenius, E.   'Folkmängden i Sveriges köpingsliknande samhällen
    enligt folkräkningen år 1910', Statistisk Tidskrift (1913).
Berry, B.   The Human Consequences of Urbanization (London,
    1973).
Blumin, S.   The Urban Treshold. Growth and Change in a Nine-
    teenth-Century American Community (Chicago, 1976).
Center for Population Research Monograph.   Rural-Urban Migration
    Research in the US (Washington D.C., 1975).
Edin, K.A.   Arbetarbefolkningens bostadsförhållanden i Uppsala
    (Uppsala, 1908).
Edin, K.A.   De mindre bemedlades bostadsförhållanden i Göteborg
    (Göteborg, 1912).
Firth, R.   Money, work and social change in Indo-Pacific eco-
    nomic systems (New York, no year).
Goldstein, S.   Patterns of Mobility 1910-1950. The Norristown
    Study (Chatham, 1958).
Guinchard, J.   Bostadsförhallåndena i Stockholm åren 1900 och
    1902 (Stockholm, 1903).
Gullberg, E. and L. Améen, Jönköpings stads historia, Del III
    (Värnamo, 1971).
Gustafson, U.   'Några förändringar i Stockholmsbornas dödlighet
    1861-1940', Från medeltid till dataålder. Festskrift till
    S.U. Palme (Uddevalla, 1972).
Gustafson, U.   Industrialismens storstad. Studier rörande
    Stockholms sociala, ekonomiska och demografiska struktur
    1860-1910 (Stockholm, 1976).
Hammarström, I.   Stockholm i svensk ekonomi 1850-1914
    (Stockholm, 1970).
Hammarström, I., R. Hagstedt, L. Nilsson, 'Projektet jämförande
    stadshistoria', HT (1975) p. 4.
Hedenskog, S.   Folkrörelserna i Nyköping 1880-1910 (Uppsala,
    1973).
Hauser, P.M. and L.F. Schnore, The Study of Urbanization (New
    York, 1965).
Hellspong, M. and O. Löfgren, Land och Stad (Lund, 1976).
Heckscher, E.   Till belysning av järnvägarnas betydelse för
    Sveriges ekonomiska utveckling (Stockholm, 1907).
Hägerstrand, T.   Urbaniseringen (Lund, 1970).

Johansson, B. Social differentiering och kommunalpolitik.
Enköping 1863-1919 (Uppsala, 1974).
Johansson, I. Den stadslösa storstaden. Förortsbildning och
bebyggelse-omvandling kring Stockholm 1870-1970.
Byggforskningen. Rapport R 26 : 1974 (Stockholm, 1974).
Kansky, K.J. Urbanization under Socialism (London, 1976).
Katz, M.B. The People of Hamilton, Canada West. Family and
Class in a Mid-Nineteenth-Century City (Cambridge, 1975).
Kronborg, B. and T. Nilsson, Stadsflyttare. Industrialisering-
migration och social mobilitet med utgångspunkt från
Halmstad (Uppsala, 1975).
Kuznets, S. Consumption, Industrialization and Urbanization,
in B. Hoselitz and W. Moore (eds.), Industrialization and
Social Change (Mouton, 1963).
Kohl, J.G. Der Verkehr und die Ansiedelungen der Menschen in
ihrer Abhängigkeit (Dresden, 1841).
Lampard, E.E. The History of Cities in the Economically Ad-
vanced Areas, Economic Development and Cultural Change,
vol. 3 (1955).
Larsson, Y. Inkorporeringsproblemet. Stadsområdets förändringar
med särskild hänsyn till svensk förvaltningspraxis, I och
II (Stockholm, 1912).
Leighly, J.B. The Towns of Mälardalen in Sweden. A study in
urban morphology: University of California Publications
in Geography, vol. 3 : 1 (Berkley, 1928).
Lewin, L., B. Jansson and D. Sörbom, The Swedish Electrorate
1887-1968 (Uppsala, 1972).
Lindman, C. Dödligheten i första lefnadsåret i Sveriges tjugo
större städer 1876-95 (Helsingborg, 1898).
Lindman, C. Sundhets och befolkningsförhållanden i Sveriges
städer (Helsingborg, 1911).
Lindroth, K. Dödsorsakerna och dödligheten i Stockholm 1871-
1890 (Stockholm, 1892).
Morris, R.N. Urban Sociology (London, 1968).
Myklebost, H. 'Norges tettbebygde steder 1875-1950', Ad Novas
4 (Trondheim, 1960).
Myrdahl, G., m.fl., 'Population Movements and Industrialization.
Swedish Counties 1895-1930', Stockholm Economic Studies
vol. II (1941).
Palander, T. Beiträge zur Standortstheorie (Uppsala, 1935).
Paulsson, G. Svensk stad, Del I och II (Lund, 1973).
Pred, A. The external Relations of Cities during 'Industrial
Revolution' (Chicago, 1962).
Reissman, L. The Urban Process (New York, 1964).
Robson, B.T. 'A view on the urban scene', Studies in Human
Geography (London, 1973).
Robson, B.T. Urban growth, an approach (London, 1973).
Rydberg, H. 'Stadsbygd och landsbygd. En studie inom Karls-
hamnsområdet', SGA (1936).
Smelser, N.J. Theory of Collective Behavior (New York, 1962).
Sundbärg, G. 'Bidrag till utvandringsfrågan, från befolknings-

statistisk synpunkt', Uppsala Universitets Årssskrift 1884, 1885 (Uppsala, 1885-86).
Sundbärg, G. 'Land och stad i Sverige från befolkningsstatistisk synpunkt', Statistisk Tidskrift (1887) p. 3.
Svensson, J.S. and K. Godlund, 'Norrköpings ekonomiska och sociala historia 1870-1914', (Stockholm, 1972).
Söderberg, E. 'Sveriges municipalsamhällen', Statistisk Tidskrift (1902).
Tilly, C. An Urban World (Boston, 1974).
Tisdale, H. 'The process of Urbanization', Social Forces 20, 1942 (no place, 1942).
Torstendahl, R. 'Dispersion of Engineers in a Transitional Society', Swedish Technicians 1860-1940 (Uppsala, 1975).
Warner, S.B.Jr. Problems in understanding the Social Events of Urban History (Stencil, 1969).
Warner, S.B. Jr. The Urban Wilderness (New York, 1972).
Warner, S.B.Jr. Streetcar Suburbs. The Process of Growth in Boston 1870-1900 (New York, 1970).
Weber, A.F. The growth of cities in the nineteenth century. A study in Statistics. (New York, 1899).
Westergaard, J. 'Scandinavian Urbanism. A Survey of Trends and Themes in Urban Social Research in Sweden, Norway and Denmark', New Social Science Monographs E 1 1966 (Köpenhamn, 1967).
William-Olsson, W. Huvuddragen av Stockholms geografiska utveckling 1850-1930 (Stockholm, 1937).
William-Olsson, W. Utvecklingen av tätorter och landsbygd i Sverige 1880-1935 (YMER, 1938).
William-Olsson, W. Ekonomisk-geografisk karta över Sverige (Stockholm, 1946).
Wirth, L. 'Urbanism as a Way of Life', The American journal of sociology (1938) pp. 1-24.
Åberg, I. Förening och politik. Folkrörelsernas politiska aktivitet i Gävle under 1880-talet (Uppsala, 1975).
Åkerman, S. 'Intern befolkningsomflyttning och emigration', Emigrationen fra Norden indtil I. Verdenskrig. Rapporter Til Det Nordiske Historikermode i Kobenhavn 1971 (Köpenhamn, 1971).
Åkerman, S. and B. Öhngren, 'Migration and Social Mobility. Dynamics and Stability in Mass Behavior', Opubl. uppsats presenterad vid konferensen, International Comparisons of Past Societies (Princeton, 1972).
Öhngren, B. 'Arbetare vid Oskarshamns mekaniska verkstad. En fallstudie', in: D. Papp, and B. Öhngren, Arbetarna vid Oskarshamns varv kring sekelskiftet (Stockholm, 1973).
Öhngren, B. Folk i rörelse. Samhällsutveckling, flyttningsmönster och folkrörelser i Eskilstuna 1870-1900 (Uppsala, 1974).

8. The rise of the 'Randstad', 1815–1930
R. van Engelsdorp Gastelaars and
M. Wagenaar

8.1.	Introduction	231
8.2.	'Randstad' - a ring of central cities	232
8.3.	Suburbanisation from "Randstad"-centers	240
8.4.	Some tentative conclusions	242
	References	246

8. The rise of the 'Randstad', 1815–1930
R. van Engelsdorp Gastelaars and
M. Wagenaar

8.1. Introduction

The Netherlands, it is sometimes said, is an urbanised nation without cities. That is to say that although population density for the nation as a whole is very high, big cities are conspicuously absent (Steigenga, 1968: 45-65; Steigenga, 1970).

Although exaggerated, there is some truth in this statement. To this day The Netherlands lacks a single, metropolitan center comparable to Paris, London, Brussels or Vienna which dominated the entire nation. Rather in Holland one finds a situation, both socially and ecologically, of more or less complementary cities and towns around a rural core (the 'green core'), viz., the 'Randstad' - literally 'rim' or 'ring', i.e. an urban conglomeration. Composed of three metropolitan centers of nearly the same size, this ring includes the cities of Amsterdam, Rotterdam, and The Hague (Hall, 1966; Steigenga, 1968: 55 ff; Ter Hart, 1975).

Table 8.1: Population of Amsterdam, Rotterdam and The Hague, 1795-1930

		Amsterdam	Rotterdam	The Hague
1795	population	211000	53212	38433
	population as a percentage of Amsterdam-total	100%	24%	17%
1815	population	180179	58552	42301
	population as a percentage of Amsterdam-total	100%	32%	23%
1840	population	211349	78098	63556
	population as a percentage of Amsterdam-total	100%	37%	30%
1869	population	264694	116232	90277
	popualtion as a percentage of Amsterdam-total	100%	44%	34%
1899	population	510853	318507	206022
	population as a percentage of Amsterdam-total	100%	62%	40%
1930	population	752003	581899	436568
	population as a percentage of Amsterdam-total	100%	77%	58%

Source: Ramaer, 1931 : 225-272.

This unique circumstance developed between 1800 and 1930. At the time of the French invasion in 1795, Amsterdam was both economically and culturally the only significant center of the old Republic. It was ecologically dominant both in virtue of the number of its inhabitants and the amount of enterprise, and was many times larger than its closest rival (De Vries, Jan, 1978 : 349-361).

By about 1930 this situation had changed radically. Although still the financial, commercial, and cultural center of the nation, Amsterdam had lost part of its central, social function. Political management and decision making was now concentrated in The Hague, and Rotterdam was busy becoming the world's largest seaport. As a consequence, Amsterdam was less impressive ecologically as well; proportionately it was only 1.3 times the size of Rotterdam, and 1.7 times the size of The Hague.

It is the purpose of this article to find some explanation for this radical change in urban structure. More specifically, we hope to show which factors contributed to the change from a monocentric urban system to a multicentered one which occurred between 1815 and 1930. That is, the shift from a situation where Amsterdam was the socially and ecologically dominant metropolis to one where Amsterdam, Rotterdam, and The Hague shared in an urban division of labour in the 'Randstad', i.e. a set of cities which are complementary in function and more or less equivalent in size constituting what might be termed a <u>metropolitan central region</u>.

8.2. 'Randstad' - a ring of central cities

The position of dominance which Paris, London, and Brussels enjoy in their respective countries is the result of a combination of social and inherently ecological processes which took place during the last centuries. The upshot of these processes was (a.) the national integration both in structural and spatial terms of a number of social institutions (policy, economy, culture, etc.), and (b.) an emergent contrast in these socially and economically integrated countries between the metropolitan center and capital, on one hand, and the remainder of the nation, on the other, whereby the latter became more and more 'peripheral' (Pred, 1977; Coates, 1977; Holland, 1976). By this we mean that ultimately the metropolitan centers and capitals became the nuclei of political, governmental, and economic decision making as well as the centers of cultural innovation, accumulation of wealth and capital, and concentrations of population (De Vries, Jan, 1976).

It is self-evident that today's multicentered structure in the Netherlands is the result of the divergent path these processes took in Holland. We must therefore consider how these processes of internal integration and structural contrast between core and periphery occurred in The Netherlands.

In the first place, The Netherlands became an industrialised nation only at the end of the 19th century; relatively late compared to Great Britain, France, Belgium and Germany. A discussion of the course of this late start is not within the scope of this paper (De Jonge, 1968; De Jonge, 1977 : 53-70), but suffice to say that when industrialisation finally began it was not an autonomous process as it was in the neighbouring countries, but was heavily dependent on resurgent trade and seaport activities. (De Jonge, 1978 : 249-281).

Two tendencies determined this resurgence. In the first place, port activities were stimulated by a rapid increase in transit trade to and from industrialising Germany, and in particular the Ruhr-Rhein-area. The second impuls came from the rapid growth of trade between the Dutch East Indies, producing mainly raw produce, and the European world exporting its industrial output (De Jonge, 1978 : 265; De Vries, Joh., 1961 : 33-62).

Flourishing trade and commerce in its turn stimulated manufacture, especially in those branches specialising in the processing of colonial produce, shipbuilding and textiles which found in the East Indies an important market. As a consequence prosperity rose, further stimulating a growing internal demand for a nascent industrial sector.

The net result of all this was that industry was finally taking off in The Netherlands. One can hardly say, however, that its pace was impressive.

Only in the course of the 20th century did industrialisation make a breakthrough.

This latter development was characterised by the increasing size of enterprise in both the manufacturing and transport sectors. A significant increase in the division of labour within enterprise accounted for part of this, and was coupled with a rising quota of machinery and raw material per employee. Finally, one notes a relative and absolute growth of financial and commercial services, i.e. banking, insurance, transport, and the communication and distribution services (De Jonge, 1968; Jansen and De Smidt, 1974).

In the second place, since the beginning of the 19th century, the Netherlands developed into a centrally organised state. A state, furthermore, to which various tasks in the socio-economic as well as cultural domain were assigned. There were several stages in this process. In the course of the 19th century the nation developed into a centrally governed parliamentry democracy, that is one with popular representation, a secular government and responsible departments (ministries). During this period the state apparatus remained relatively small. It was not until after the turn of the century that the number of public functions increased considerably. During the 20th century more and more forms of public welfare (for example those concerning education, social and medical care, public transport and housing) were seen as public affairs, as a result of which the public welfare system increased rapidly (Van Braam,

1957 : 36-62; De Swaan, 1976).

Table 8.2: Rise in the numbers of civil servants at state level

Date	Number	Relative (1930=100)	As % of total labour force
1849	20,000	9	1.6
1889	55,000	26	3.1
1899	69,000	33	3.4
1909	91,000	43	3.7
1920	204,000	96	6.9
1930	212,000	100	6.2

Source: Van Braam, 1957 : 22, 25.

From the outset, these developments meant a permanent *process of increase in structure*. Manufacture and commercial services were thus concentrated in fewer but larger enterprises with more and more complex organisations, while public administration and services were organised increasingly at the central state level. All sorts of private institutions, from political parties to trade unions and sports leagues were merged into nationally functioning units involving thousands of members. This increase in structure per association was manifest both in the growth of the number of participants as well as in a growing differentiation of internal organisation.

In addition, a *process of growing internal hierarchisation* was directly linked to it.

Increasing structures showed a tendency toward vertically organised internal relations, with a limited number of decision makers at the top. This tendency was manifest both in profit and non-profit organisations (Stein, 1965; Timms, 1971; Warren, 1978; Van Doorn, 1960:a).

There was more than one reason why these processes of increase in structure and growing internal hierarchisation took place. Within private enterprise the process found its origins in the constant attempt to increase profits, which entailed the need to increase production and for optimal organisational efficiency. In the public sector these processes were stimulated by the effort to offer a complete array of facilities to all those potential clients who could not possibly afford them if they were offered only on a private commercial basis.
This effort was reinforced by the emancipation of those citizens who, during the 19th century, were either excluded, or at best only marginally admitted to public affairs, but were entering the political arena in the past 75 years.

Both processes were made possible by the continuous growth in both quantity and quality of transport and communications in the past two centuries, during which we see the introduction of steam-powered locomotives and ships, of the automobile, telegraph and telephone (Groenman, 1959; Bos, 1976; Passchier and Knippenberg, 1978).

Increase in structures and growing internal hierarchy are both *social* processes but both had radical *ecological* implications.

In the first place a process of *spatial expansion in scale* took place: *The spatial range of operation of social institutions in Holland broadened.* This meant that the Kingdom of the Netherlands became the effective territory at the expense of the smaller regions. Ecologically, the Netherlands was integrated into a single region. This was manifest in an infrastructural system, which developed in the last hundred years into a road, rail and canal network of national reach (Van der Knaap, 1978).

In the second place, these processes resulted in a growing *polarisation* between the Western parts of the Netherlands, which developed into a *central* region, and the remaining parts, which assumed a more and more *peripheral* character. In the past 150 years these Western regions were pre-eminent in attracting (inter-)nationally functioning firms in the fields of trade, retail and wholesale; headquarters and research branches of large firms, both in the production and service sectors (banking, insurance, metallurgical and petrochemical industries); highly specialised social and cultural services like institutions for higher education, radio and television and the national orchestras, theater companies, musea and the national press. Nationally organised leagues, societies and clubs generally chose this area for their head offices. In short, the Western Netherlands in the last 150 years developed into the center of economic and political decisionmaking as well as the center of cultural innovation.

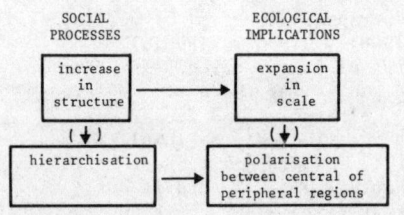

Figure 8.1:

Schematic relationship between social processes and ecological implications

There were obvious reasons for this concentration. The establishments mentioned above need each other's proximity. The need for frequent personal contacts in which information is exchanged, experts are consulted, and the top decision makers coordinate management is the main reason why these firms seek a common location. At the same time, this proximity was a necessary condition in prompting the appearance of innumerable highly specialised and skilled services. Finally, there were good reasons why this concentration took place in the Western Netherlands.

First of all, many of the activities mentioned above were already located in this area before 1800. The States General, the Court of the House of Orange, nearly all important trading firms and creditors, to name just a few of them, had already settled in the Western province. The only difference was that before 1800 this concentration was considerably smaller in size, and that its central function relative to the rest of the nation was less marked. Nevertheless, relocation of this concentration would have meant abandoning much already made local investment and attendant site benefits (mainly in terms of facilities). This explains the agglomeration of new establishments in the Western Netherlands (Lambooy, 1975).

Secondly, the presence of the Rhine estuar, the main link to industrialising Germany, reinforced locational quality strongly. The net result of all this was that the Western Netherlands built up an ever increasing amount and diversity of jobs and labour force which in turn attracted even more firms in the areas just mentioned. This process of self-propelling concentration resulted in a considerable rise of the costs of labor relative to the rest of the country. The same happened to real estate values.

The result was an accessibility constraint for the Western Netherlands. Labour intensive, financially weak firms and institutions either stayed in or were forced to move to the "peripheral" areas. And in due time, these areas would show a picture of self propelling decline.

Cultural and economic services lagged behind in terms of size and specialisation. It is true that well into the 20th century the number of manufacturing jobs was impressive in these areas, but they lacked the heavy capital investments of the Randstad. Finally there was an ever increasing gap between the Randstad population and that of the periphery in terms of wealth, skill and education (Steigenga, 1958; Van Doorn, 1960:b).

We have reached the crux of this section. Amsterdam at the end of the 18th century had by far the nation's largest concentration of population, enterprise and facilities. Why then did it not develop into the only metropolitan center in a socially and ecologically integrating Kingdom of the Netherlands? Or to put it another way, why did it not follow the example of London in Great Britain, or Paris in France? Why "Randstad", an urban belt with three large centers?

We think two factors were responsible for this development. First, The Hague became the political and administrative center of the Netherlands. Prior to the French occupation, the old Republic had been a federal admistrative system in which the primary protagonists of the political arena were on the one hand the House of Orange and their political clients and on the other hand the economic elite, the powerful merchants. In the 17th and 18th centuries, these factions were alternately in control. Ecologically, this meant that there were two centers of power; viz. The Hague, where the stadtholder resided and the (weak) Estates General assembled, and Amsterdam, the Republic's main center of international trade and finance. All this changed after 1815. Politically and administratively, the

Netherlands was transformed into a centrally organised kingdom with the House of Orange as rulers.

The choice of The Hague as residence seemed almost inevitable from a traditional point of view. During the 18th century, the princes of Orange had already built their mansions and palaces there, however modest they may seem in comparison to their British or French counterparts. Foreign embassies and diplomats were generally accredited to The Hague, close to the Estates General, which was at least formally ruling the country. Besides, there were negative considerations for the choice of The Hague as well. From the Republic's foundation onward Amsterdam's financial and commercial clique had displayed a more or less open animosity toward a powerful 'stadtholder'. i.e. the House of Orange, which culminated two times in their resignation from this function.

This animosity continued well into the 19th century and made it very unlikely that the Court would choose to settle in Amsterdam (Gerretson, 1971 : 164, Scheffer, 1976 : 25).

This decision had drastic long-term effects. The political and administrative organisation of the Netherlands would henceforth become more and more independant of the economical system. This had important ecological consequences for the formation of a center. The process of centralisation had several phases. Until 1830, royal court and national government resided alternately in The Hague and Brussels. Since 1830 till 1900, the central aspects of The Hague were mainly brought about by the presence of the Court, Members of Parliament, foreign diplomats and some leading officials. But after 1900 the state apparatus started growing in a rapid pace. From that date on The Hague became a city of civil servants. This had important effects upon the socio-economic composition of this city.

After 1830 The Hague attracted not only the members of the court and related social categories we mentioned above but also artisans oriented upon these wealthy clients, i.e. gold- and silversmiths, saddlers, cabinet-makers, pastry-cooks, carriage-makers etc. Next followed service firms catering to the wealthy. Theaters, fancy shops, clubs, art galleries and the like. A great number of domestic servants were assembled in The Hague, who served, among others, a large body of civil servants or servicemen, retired or on leave, from the East Indies.

Finally, there were lobbyists, and later on pressure groups, seeking to influence the government and its representatives. Together, they were responsible for the peculiar social composition of The Hague and for its considerable growth during the period under discussion.

Amsterdam lacked this stimulus for urban growth and consequently, it could never follow the line of Paris or London, although the city remained the largest national agglomeration (Ter Hart, 1975).

What is more, after 1815 the city lost its position as largest harbour of the country. Before French rule this position was unchallenged. During the 16th and 17th centuries, when it was still unusual for consumer-countries to buy directly from producer-countries, Amsterdam was able to establish itself as the main intermediary in the staple market for European grain (and other products as well). By the 18th century, however, this dominant position within the Atlantic trade system was already challenged. This was partly due to protectionist measures taken by other European states, who forced out foreign traders and shipowners, and created their own national staplemarkets. But even more important was the development of new trading tactics resulting in more and more direct contacts between trading partners, which gradually eliminated intermediates (De Vries, Joh., 1968 : 29 ff.). Undoubtedly, however, Amsterdam was still the Republic's largest trading port.

The French occupation ended all this. Until 1815 all commercial activity was brought to a halt. After its resumption in 1815, Amsterdam merchants tried in vain to restore the old staple market. In their absence, however, the world trade situation had altered decisively. The regulating, intermediate staple market's day had passed, and so was the time when Amsterdam merchants could confidently wait for foreign customers to come to the city.

At the same time, a different type of port rose to prominence, viz. the seaport handling the transit of goods between its own hinterland and the rest of the world. This development held an opportunity for the Netherlands as well. For industrialising Western Germany the Rhine was the only direct sea-link. This benefitted several ports in the Western Netherlands which succeeded in attracting a good deal of transit activity. But it was Rotterdam which profitted the most from Germany's industrialisation. No town could boast such optimal location on the Rhine estuary as Rotterdam did. The resulting urban growth took place in several stages, becoming impressive after 1870, when the German Unity was reached and after a new waterway linking the city directly to the sea, was completed. But even before that date Rotterdam was not doing badly. Nucleus of its wealth was the transit trade. Around this transit trade industrial activities flourished (refining of vegetable and mineral oils, shipbuilding etc.). It was not, however, a real center, and it would never become one. Rotterdam was a junction; the initiation of the flow of goods, its financing and management were done elsewhere (Van Dijk, 1976 : 49 ff., 290 ff.).

The net result for Amsterdam was, that in size of enterprise and population it lost ground relative to both Rotterdam and The Hague. That Amsterdam was still able to maintain its position as the nation's largest city was primarily due to a revival in colonial trade at the end of the 19th century. The city became a node between the Netherlands Indies as a producer of raw materials and consuming market of growing importance on the one hand, and the European Industrial nations on the other. The East Indies, it is true, formally were a colony from 1815 onward, but it took several decades, before a significant amount of this huge empire was "pacified", and, even more important, before its productive structure was sufficiently adapted to the needs of the home country (Stapel, 1940 : 143 ff.; De Waard, 1941).

As a consequence, the main colonial trading firms were concentrated in the city. They carried with them all sorts of related activities, viz. the highly specialised auctioning, storage and processing of colonial produce (Crone, no date, 45 ff.). Amsterdam became the main terminal for passenger steamers to and from the Eastern colony, and thus it is not amazing that docking, repair and construction of these steamers took place at Amsterdam shipyards.

A second impulse was given by the revival of financial and commercial services of which the city became the nation's main center. This revival was closely related to both colonial expansion and the industrialisation of the Netherlands (De Vries, Joh., 1961 : 33 ff.). This resulted in a clustering of skilled professions in the field of broking, insurance and stock exchange. The presence of these professions in combination with those related to colonial trade and finance mentioned above meant that the city had a public with substantial purchasing-power, attracting a considerable amount of 'luxury' manufacturing, in which the diamond industries took a prominent place (Van Tijn, 1965 : 270 ff.).

In spite of these specific stimuli for urban growth, the situation around 1920 was that Amsterdam, Rotterdam and The Hague did not differ greatly in size. Furthermore, in terms of the structure of enterprise and population the three cities had become more or less complementary. Table 8.3 shows this clearly.

Table 8.3: Share of some occupational categories in the total labour-force in Amsterdam, Rotterdam and The Hague, 1909

	Amsterdam %		Rotterdam %		The Hague %	
Manufacturing	42.6		38.0		39.4	
of which ship-building		1.4		2.3		0.2
other metal manufacturing		3.6		3.8		2.3
'luxury' manufacturing		13.8		7.4		10.5
Commercial services	33.9		43.0		24.3	
of which banking and assurance		3.2		1.3		1.9
wholesale and retail-trade		17.8		16.3		13.9
transport by sea- and inland shipping		4.3		15.5		0.5
other transport		8.7		9.8		8.0
Government	3.7		3.5		7.5	
of which civil servants at state level		1.2		0.9		4.8
Personal services	13.5		10.8		19.0	
Total labour force (in numbers)	226939		155033		102172	

Source: Occupational census, 1909

Finally, it is interesting to note that only Amsterdam and The Hague counted a financially powerful elite. Rotterdam, junction of transit goods produced and consumed elsewhere, was not a real moneymaking center. Fortunes at that time were made in trade, finance, colonial careers, and - since about 1870 - industry. It would take quite some time before transport and transit would yield such fortunes. Consequently, there were considerable differences between the three cities in size and quality of the firms and facilities catering to a wealthy clientele. These differences have not disappeared up until the present (Engelsdorp, 1980).

8.3. Suburbanisation from "Randstad"-centers

There was another reason why the differences in size of the three big cities became smaller in the period under discussion. Untill well into the 19th century, one could classify this country in *daily systems*, which were restricted to virtually the size of individual settlements. With *daily systems* we mean the classification of a territorial complex as *a network of relations between land using units and artefacts within this complex, manifest in a comprehensive, daily recurrent transfer pattern between these units and artefacts*. We define land using units as households, firms and facilities. The range of this pattern is determined by the limited time-space budget local inhabitants have, to cope with the daily time-space constraint. This implies that the majority of them have a regular, recurrent need to return to the place where they have dinner, bed and breakfast (Hägerstrand, 1970; Berry, 1973 : 38). We have the impression that in the late 19th century the size of Dutch daily urban systems started growing. They declined in number and grew to a supra-local scale. In nearly all of these growing daily systems a segregation took place between the central city and a zone of settlements surrounding it. This segregation was caused by *suburbanisation*, a process in which land using units no longer settled in the core area but in the zone surrounding it.

Suburbanisation first started around the three central cities. And it is in this area that we can see the first profound ecological results. It was at that time ($\pm$ 1920) in particular that the Amsterdam daily system, which had the largest and most densely populated built-up area, experienced a strong growth in suburbanisation and consequent changes in land use patterns. This retarded even further its growth as a central city relative to Rotterdam and The Hague (Steigenga, 1968 : 105 ff.). We think, again, that the explanation for this process has to be sought in the industrialisation of the country, in the transformation of the political and administrative system into a welfare state, and the inter-related rise in income which took place in the past 100 years. Typically these processes resulted in a growing demand for space per land using unit. There were at least two reasons for this.

(a) In the last 100 years there was a manifest tendency within these land using units *to split more and more functions in a process of internal specialisation*, and to house them in separate accomodations.

(b) Furthermore, there was a *growth in the number of material attributes per land using unit* (Van Paassen, 1955).

We shall try to specify the reasons for this.
Since the last quarter of the 19th century, the growing size and complexity of enterprise (both industrial and commercial) gave rise to increasingly specialised internal departments, all of which had their own specific spatial claims (e.g. offices, design and management departments). The fact that industry became more capital-intensive entailed a growing claim for space, i.e. space for machinery, raw materials and storage. The motive behind all this was of course the ever present drive to increase profits, i.e. to increase productivity and efficiency. It is remarkable that the same process took place at the household level. Here too there was a growing demand for space (separate bedrooms for parents and children, bathrooms, halls etc.). There was a tremendous per capita rise in household appliances ("capital") in which growing wealth was materialised. And again, this implies a claim on more space. Finally, both living and working space became matters of public concern. Especially after the introduction in 1901 of the Public Housing Law we notice a growing public involvement in housing (and later on working) conditions, resulting in an ever increasing demand for space. In addition to this, the growth of the public sector itself meant that the Administration made an autonomous claim for space. It too was confronted with a growing demand for space for her own offices, public utilities, transport, and military apparatus to name just a few branches of the State apparatus. Naturally the growth in scale of these daily systems could never have been possible without profound changes in the technology of transport and communications at the same time. These made possible the maintenance of the existing network of relations between land using units in spite of a rapidly growing spatial distance between them. But maintenance of this expanding network in its turn meant further spatial claims for linkage facilities such as roads and highways, airports, and terminals (Groenman, 1959).

The process we sketched above took place throughout the country, but it had the most marked ecological effect within the built-up area of the older towns. Here, the lack of space for extension was most sharply felt. The consequence of this congestion was that households, firms, and institutions needing each others daily contact no longer settled within the city but in its environs. Due to this movement the area contagious to the cities became more and more suburban. One of its characteristics was the rapid increase in land-use relative to the cities themselves. The cities and their surrounding (sub-)urban zones grew into one urban region. Firms, households and institutions were well under way toward the formation of one spatially indivisible labor and housing market, and were knit together through an intensive network of reciprocal interactions. This was evinced in a huge increase of traffic which visualised, so to say, the growing number and intensity of these relations. In other words, urban daily systems expanded.

Although it is certainly true that at the turn of the century the pace of suburbanisation was still modest, its forward movement had become irresistable (Rijksdienst, 1949 : 22 ff.; Hoekveld, 1964).

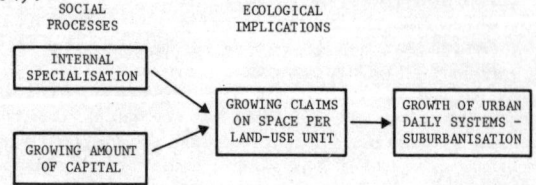

Figure 8.2: Schematic relation between internal specialisation and growing amount of capital within social units on the one hand, and suburbanisation on the other

Again, we have reached a crucial point in our argument. We said earlier that the expansion of daily systems was ecologically most marked in and around the older towns. Let us specify this hypothesis. Growing occupation of space per land use unit led to suburbanisation. Chronologically this occurred first in Amsterdam, with The Hague and Rotterdam following as second and third respectively.

There were good reasons for this sequence. At the end of the 19th century all of three central cities were distinct from other Dutch cities in that they formed the greatest concentration of land use, had the highest densities and suffered a severe lack of open space. Amsterdam was more congested than the others but all three were confronted with rising real estate values, rents, and residential densities (to hygienically unacceptable levels), and a forcing out of financially weak land users by stronger ones (Diederiks and Wagenaar, 1979).

As Amsterdam was the most congested city at that time, it is obvious that suburbanisation would begin here. The Hague and Rotterdam followed around 1900. The net result of this was that an important part of Amsterdams growth was no longer contributing to the size of the city itself but to its surrounding suburban zone. It caused further and earlier delay in the growth of a central city.

8.4. Some tentative conclusions

Until the end of the 18th century Amsterdam maintained a fully dominant position within the Dutch urban system. The city was

Table 8.4: Population growth of Amsterdam, Rotterdam and The Hague and their respective 'suburban' regions in 1869 and 1899

Source: Ramaer, 1931 : 225

	index-number of pop. growth 1869-1899 1869=100	index-number of pop. growth 1899-1930 1899=100
Amsterdam	193	147
Rotterdam	274	183
The Hague	228	212
Amsterdam-region (excl. Amsterdam) (= zone with a radius of about 25 km around A.)	157	175
Rotterdam-region (excl. Rotterdam and The Hague) (= zone with a radius of about 25 km around R.)	128	151
The Hague-region (excl. The Hague and Rotterdam) (= zone with a radius of about 25 km around The Hague)	129	169
Rural zone of Amsterdam-region (= A-region excl. municipalities 10,000 inh.)	146	173
Rural zone of Rotterdam-region (= R-region excl. municipalities 10,000 inh.)	122	149
Rural zone of The Hague (= T.H.-region excl. municipalities 10,000 inh.)	123	180
The Netherlands	143	155

highly influential in economic and political management, and ecologically it was by far the largest single urban land use unit. This changed in the course of the 19th and early 20th centuries. This period saw the rise of the "Randstad" i.e. an urban belt connecting the three centers Amsterdam, Rotterdam and The Hague, which became more or less complementary both in size and function.

This change within the Dutch urban system was primarily a result of growing internal integration, and a rising contrast between core and periphery. In most of the neighbouring countries such a process resulted in a monocentric urban system. But the Dutch development took a different path. The Hague, traditional seat of the States General and Court, now developed into the national center of politics and administration. Amsterdam lost its near-monopolistic grip upon national politics which until 1795 were very much its affairs. In addition, this period saw the rise of Rotterdam based on its optimal break of bulk location towards the German hinterland. During the 20th century, the Rotterdam seaport area attracted many important port-oriented firms.

Why then, if all this happened, wasn't Amsterdam reduced to a mere provincial town? There were two counterforces working to the city's benefit. First, at the end of the 19th century there was a revival of colonial trade, in which Amsterdam functioned as a junction between East Indian raw produce on the one hand, and finished European industrial export products on the other. Second, Amsterdam's traditional position as financial and commercial center was strengthened. The amount of services the city offered grew rapidly, both in size and quality, thanks to a concomitant and related growth in Dutch industrial and transport activities.

Amsterdam was thus able to maintain a central position within the Dutch and international economy. She remained therefore, the nation's largest concentration of population and enterprise.

The fact that it did remain the largest single city, however, was itself responsible for the catching up of Rotterdam and The Hague. As biggest and oldest city, Amsterdam was confronted rather early with congestion caused by its size and density. This resulted in lack of space for further expansion, high real estate values, and the forcing out of weak land users by powerful competitors. Amsterdam faced suburbanisation at an earlier date than the other two cities. This resulted in an extra slowdown of urban growth relative to Rotterdam and The Hague.

REFERENCES

Beroepstelling in het Koninkrijk der Nederlanden op 31 december 1909.
Bos, R.W.J.M. 'Van periferie naar centrum; enige kanttekeningen bij de Nederlandse industriële ontwikkeling in de 19e eeuw' in Maandschrift Economie (1976) pp. 181-205.
Braam, A. van, Ambtenaren en bureaucratie in Nederland ('s-Gravenhage, 1957).
Coates, B.E., et al., Geography and inequality (Oxford, 1977).
Crone, G.H. 'De ontwikkeling van de koloniale markten in Nederland' in De sociaal-economische invloed van Nederlandsch-Indië op Nederland (Wageningen, no date) pp. 45-62.
Diederiks, H., M. Wagenaar, 'Land-use in a pre-industrial and industrial trading town: Amsterdam 1810-1890', Paper "Problèmes d'histoire urbaine" (London, 1979).
Doorn, J.J.A. van, 'Schaalvergroting als een proces van sociale verandering', Sociologische Gids (1960 : a) pp. 2-20.
Doorn, J.A.A. van, De Nederlandse ontwikkelingsgebieden; schets van de sociale problematiek (no place, 1960 : b).
Dijk, H. van, Rotterdam 1810-1880 (Rotterdam, 1976).
Engelsdorp Gastelaars, R. van, Niet alle stadsbewoners zijn stedelingen. Constructie van een typologie van stadsbewoners mede aan de hand van gegevens uit een onderzoek onder Amsterdammers (1980, forthcoming).
Gerretson, C. Geschiedenis der "Koninklijke", 5 vols. (Bussum, 1971-1973).
Groenman, S. Ons deel in de ruimte (Assen, 1959).
Hägerstrand, T. 'What about people in regional science?', Regional Science Association, Papers, vol. XXIV (1970) pp. 7-21.
Hall, P.G. Zeven wereldsteden; problemen van groei en leefbaarheid (Zeist, 1966).
Hart, H.W. ter, and J.G. Lambooy, Amsterdam in de rij der Europese hoofdsteden (Amsterdam, 1975).
Hoekveld, G.A. Baarn, schets van de ontwikkeling van een villadorp (Baarn, 1964).
Holland, S. Capital versus the regions (New York, 1976).
Jansen, A.C.M. and M. de Smidt, Industrie en ruimte, De industriële ontwikkeling van Nederland in een veranderend sociaal-ruimtelijk bestel (Assen, 1974).
Jonge, J.A. de, De industrialisatie in Nederland tussen 1850 en 1914 (Amsterdam, 1968).
Jonge, J.A. de, 'Het economische leven in Nederland 1844-1873' Algemene Geschiedenis der Nederlanden, part 12 (Haarlem, 1977) pp. 53-70.
Jonge, J.A. de, 'Nijverheid, ontwikkeling en stimulans', Algemene Geschiedenis der Nederlanden, part 13 (Haarlem, 1978) pp. 262-272.
Jonge, J.A. de, 'The Role of the Outer Provinces in the Process of Dutch Economic Growth in the Nineteenth Century in J.S.

Bromley and E.H. Kossman (eds.) Britain and the Netherlands, Vol. IV (The Hague, 1971) pp. 208-225.
Knaap, G.A. van der, A spatial analysis of the evolution of an urban system: the case of the Netherlands (Utrecht, 1978).
Lambooy, J.G. Ekonomie en ruimte (Assen, 1975).
Paassen, C. van, 'Stedelijke overbevolking, een verwaarloosd aspect van de theorie der overbevolking', Tijdschrift voor Economische en Sociale Geografie (1955) pp. 265-276.
Passchier, N. and H. Knippenberg, 'Spoorwegen en industrialisatie in Nederland, Geografisch Tijdschrift, Nieuwe reeks XII (1978), 5, pp. 381-395.
Pred, A. City-systems in advanced economies (London, 1977).
Ramaer, J.C. Geschiedkundige atlas van Nederland. Het Koninkrijk der Nederlanden 1815-1931 ('s-Gravenhage, 1931).
Rijksdienst voor het nationale plan, De verspreiding van de bevolking in Nederland. Eerste rapport van de commissie ter bestudering van de bevolkingsspreiding (no place, 1949).
Stapel, F.W. Geschiedenis van Nederlandsch Indië, 5 vols. (Amsterdam, 1940).
Scheffer, H.J. Henry Tindal; een ongewoon heer met ongewone besognes (Bussum, 1976).
Steigenga, W. 'De decentralisatie van de Nederlandse industrie; een economisch-geografische en statistische analyse van de veranderingen in het spreidingspatroon der industriële werkgelegenheid in de periode 1930-1950', Tijdschrift voor Economische en Sociale Geografie (1958) pp. 129-148.
Steigenga, W. Moderne Planologie (Utrecht, 1968).
Steigenga, W. 'De verstedelijking van Nederland, een voorbeeld van een gedecentraliseerd urbanisatiepatroon' in A. Bours and J.G. Lambooy (eds.) Stad en stadsgewest in de ruimtelijke orde (Assen, 1970).
Stein, M. The eclipse of community. (New York, 1965).
Swaan, A. de, 'De mens is de mens een zorg; over verstatelijking van verzorgingsarrangementen', De Gids (1976) pp. 35-51.
Tijn, Th. van, Twintig jaren Amsterdam. De maatschappelijke ontwikkeling van de hoofdstad van de jaren '50 der vorige eeuw tot 1876 (Amsterdam, 1965).
Timms, D.W.G. The urban mosaic (Cambridge, 1971).
Vries, Jan de, The Economy of Europe in an age of crisis, 1600-1750 (London, 1976).
Vries, Jan de, 'Barges and Capitalism. Passenger transportation in the Dutch economy, 1632-1839', A.A.G. Bijdragen no. 21 (Wageningen, 1978) pp. 33-398.
Vries, Joh. de, De economische achteruitgang der Republiek in de achttiende eeuw (Leiden, 1968).
Vries, Joh. de, Met Amsterdam als brandpunt. Gedenkboek Kamer van Koophandel en Fabrieken, 1811-1961 (Amsterdam, 1961).
Waard, J. de, Nederlandsch-Indië als leverancier voor de wereldmarkt en als consument, in W.H.V. Helsdingen (ed.) Daar werd wat groots verricht ... (Amsterdam, 1941) pp. 497-507.
Warren, R.L. The community in America (Chicago, 1978).

9. The population growth of the urban municipalities in the Netherlands between 1849 and 1970, with particular reference to the period 1899–1930
M.C. Deurloo and G.A. Hoekveld

9.1. Introduction	249
9.2. Some urbanisation theories	250
9.3. Urbanisation in the Netherlands	251
9.4. Some temporal patterns of urban growth	255
9.5. A statistical analysis	258
9.6. The period 1899-1930	263
References	282

9. The population growth of the urban municipalities in the Netherlands between 1849 and 1970, with particular reference to the period 1899–1930

M.C. Deurloo and G.A. Hoekveld

9.1. Introduction

In this contribution we shall make use of research results which will be reported more extensively elsewhere. We shall concern ourselves with possible period distinctions in the course of urban population growth, as well as with the factors influencing this growth. After giving general consideration to the whole research period, we shall go on to look in greater detail at the period 1899-1930, which can be singled out as having a marked homogeneous character.

Before we consider the problems surrounding urbanisation in the Netherlands, some remarks should be made concerning the data used. The subjects of investigation were the 117 so-called C-municipalities, as distinguished by the Netherlands Central Bureau of Statistics in their publication 'Typologie van de Nederlandse gemeenten naar urbanisatie-graad 31 mei 1960' ('Typology of the Netherlands municipalities according to the degree of urbanisation, 31 May 1960'). The main categories distinguished are A-municipalities (rural municipalities), B-municipalities (urbanised rural municipalities, including suburban municipalities) and C-municipalities (urban municipalities, ranging from those with a few thousand inhabitants to the cities of Amsterdam and Rotterdam). The criteria applied for establishing the degree of urbanisation were the morphological structure of the municipality (continuous built-up areas, the percentage of dwellings to be found in multiple dwelling buildings), the economic and social structure of the resident economically active male population, and the presence of regional service functions.

For the purposes of this study we have measured urban growth according to the differences in the size of the population on 31 December of the years at the beginning and at the end of 10 year periods from 1849 to 1909 and from 1920 to 1970. This allows direct reference to most censuses. In this way an estimation could be made of annual growth in the relevant intercensus period.

9.2. Some urbanisation theories

The term urbanisation has several meanings. It may, for instance, refer to the growth of the number of towns, the rise in the proportion of the national population living in towns, the expansion of individual towns over the surrounding areas, or it may refer to the adoption of urban characteristics by non-urban population groups. In this study urbanisation will be taken to refer to the increase in urban population.

There has long been discussion as to how urbanisation can be explained, and there now exists a wealth of literature on the subject. Friedmann and Wulff (1976) inventarised this literature and concluded that there was still no real urbanisation theory. Berry has suggested that it is wrong to regard urbanisation as a universal process, but as 'several fundamentally different processes that have arisen out of differences in culture and time, but also that these processes are producing different world regions, transcending any superficial similarities' (1973 : XII). As far as urbanisation in the western world is concerned some degree of consensus seems to have emerged in recent years, at least among geographers in the English-speaking areas of the world. Johnston (1973 : 15) sees urbanisation as a series of modernisation processes which lead to the creation of, and also changes in, a 'national system of cities' by which he means 'a number of places performing both complementary and competitive roles in providing goods and services for the total population'. Like Vance (1970) en Pred (1977) he proposes various phases for the western world: the rise of a mercantile city system, which developed after the Middle Ages, the industrial city system phase, and a post-industrial city system phase. In Europe the latter has also been termed the welfare state phase.

This modern process of thought has been summarised by Simmons (1978 : 61). He points out that as a rule several different principles or forces combine to determine the spatial organisation of such a system. It may be that initially there was one dominant principle, but usually this was followed by others. The effect of such a sequence is that what originally was a sector-specific spatial system develops into a 'complex multi-purpose system'. As growth continues and the local resource basis loses significance, 'the urban system becomes more and more the dominant factor in the location and growth of any new economic or social activity - a principle of spatial organization in its own right' (62). The mercantile city system is seen by Simmons as being determined by accessibility with respect to goods (i.e. supply and distribution facilities), by information, technology and also by a great sensitivity to investment decisions and improvements in transport facilities. The urban system in an industrial society is probably determined by local characteristics such as the industrial structures present, the size of the population and accessibility with respect to raw materials and manufactured goods. These characteristics are connected with initial advantage and cumulative and circular growth. Finally, as far as post-industrial city systems are concerned, it is thought that above all social changes, related to rising incomes and education levels, living preferences and life styles, are determinants of rather than the results of other changes. Simmons states in this respect:

> Both the national economy and these cultural variables operate on and through the urban system, often through intermediaries that are themselves subject to change, such as the technology of communication, transportation and production processes, and the institutional infrastructure (political systems and legislation, educational and research procedures, service delivery systems and the like (62).

In each model described by Simmons other relations between towns (hierarchical, linked or diffuse) are presupposed, as well as further relations connected with these concerning the place in and the nature of the city system and the growth of individual towns. In the case of the initial growth of mercantile and industrial city systems it is mainly a matter of the developing of one or more sectors which subsequently stimulates other sectors.

These processes are described by the sector theory and the export-base theory, as well as by the modern literature concerning the concept of growth centres. As far as the post-industrial phase is concerned no theoretical models have been clearly worked out. As said above it is assumed that not only industrial or commercial sectors but also, and possibly above all, the authorities and the patterns of household expenditure supply the most important growth impulses. Since in a society and also in a spatial unit such as a country modernisation need not occur everywhere simultaneously, it may be that a series of more modern factors are at work in one part of a system and more traditional factors in another.

The literature discussed here implies that urbanisation is not caused by one factor or by a continually active complex of factors, but rather - depending on the stage of development of the society - by different factors or by complexes of factors which have different compositions. In the following section we shall see to what extent references can be found in the publications of a number of prominent Dutch social and economic historians to suggest that a similarly phased process of urbanisation may have taken place in the Netherlands in the period under investigation here.

9.3. Urbanisation in the Netherlands

There appears to be general agreement in the literature on Dutch urbanisation concerning the major aspects of the urbanisation process. Population growth in towns after 1860 was mainly determined, apart from a drop in the mortality rate and consequently a natural increase in population, by migration. According to Van Tijn (1978 : 82) this migration was fostered on the one hand by a movement away from agriculture, particularly after 1880, and also above all by the development of urban employment opportunities. Ter Heide (1965 : 209) has suggested that even for the periode 1948-60 employment opportunity factors are responsible for urbanisation, that is to say for migration to the cities. In his survey of the period 1870-1940, Keuning (1947 : 260) regards these employment opportunities as being primarily determined by industrialisation. Further, Van Stuyvenberg (1970 : 61) summarises the literature on the growth of the nineteenth century by concluding that this growth is seen in the literature as synonymous with the rising significance of industrialisation and the transition to an industrialised economic order. He goes on to say that all authors were of the opinion that after 1850-60 mechanised industry increased in importance and that the Netherlands progressed further on the road to industrialisation. Brugmans (1961) has gone further than others and has used the term industrial revolution. Pen and Bouman (1968 : 86) have claimed that one may apply Rostow's 5-phase theory to the Netherlands. They suggest that the take-off phase started between about 1860 and 1870 and the phase of maturity between about 1920 and 1930, and that the period of mass consumption started around 1960.

De Jonge has carried out an extensive investigation into Dutch industrialisation in which he denies the applicability of Rostow's theory to the Netherlands: 'Although already in the eighties, and sometimes even earlier, faint symptoms of incipient industrialisation could be noticed, the real phenomenon only started in the next decade rapidly and over a broad front of greatly diverging sectors and branches of industry. A remarkable feature of the process in this country is that it was not dominated by strongly marked "leading sectors" to use this term of Rostow's ... The process of industrialisation after 1880-90 took place as a process of balanced growth in which growth phenomena appear more or less simultaneously and independently of each other in whole series of sectors' (1971 : 217). In De Jonge's opinion the stimulus for this industialisation emanated from an autonomous rise in demand. The national prosperity was augmented by the flourishing of world trade and international shipping, in which the Netherlands played a significant role (1971 : 218). A study of the major transport flows in the Netherlands in the 19th and at the beginning of the 20th century as presented in Everwijn's Atlas gives the impression that transit flows and, with the exception of coal, transport flows to abroad were more significant than interregional transport flows. Such a course of industrialisation means that the growth of industrial employment opportunities did not represent the sole factor. Employment opportunities in transport, as well as commerce and general services, were of great importance right from the beginning of the economic development, irrespective of the inheritance from the period of mercantile urbanisation. De Jonge's late estimation of the flourishing of the industrialised system - between about 1891 and 1910 - is in accordance with that of Jansen and De Smidt (1974 : 33), who perceived a rapid industrialisation after about 1895. Even in 1950 - in other words before the emergence of a society dominated by the production of services - Steigenga (1970 : 11) was forced to affirm that a large majority of towns were to a great extent characterised by major employment opportunities in the industrial as well as the service sectors, and that real industrial towns formed a small minority.

One can only talk in terms of a city system if a communications-linked complex of towns has arisen. Waterway and rail transport were characterised for most of the 19th century by unconnected networks. Kuiler (1946 : 100) has pointed out that the differences in the regional waterway systems, with ships specially adapted to these systems, were not ironed out until shortly after the beginning of the 20th century. De Vries (1978 : 354) has also suggested that the dual-centred network which developed in the 18th century and was based on Amsterdam and Rotterdam continued to exist until the 20th century. Van der Knaap (1978 : 89) has pointed out the effective thinning out of the network of waterways in the 20th century (partly due to the use of larger types of ships), with the result that now only the larger towns are linked to each other. The basic structure of the rail network was completed between 1880 and 1890, with supply and distribution lines, often in the form of local railways, being added between 1900 and 1920 (Kuiler 1946 : 81). In the 1930s this local network was quickly broken up again when bus transport took over its functions. De Jonge (1971 : 215) considers the lack of economic integration in the first half of the 19th century to be partly due to defective transport networks. He points out that there were indeed enough major roads, but the secondary and tertiary road system was insufficient, particularly in the East and the South, which had less waterways than the rest of the Netherlands. Since mechanised industry required a good supply system for the coal it relied upon, it must be assumed that towns favourably located within transport networks enjoyed settlement advantages. De Jonge sees the emergence of industry in areas other than the West of the Netherlands as an indication that functional specialisation had become possible and that a regional system had started developing by at least no later than about 1910. This removed the split between the West and the North, which were orientated towards international trade and export and the semi-autarchic South and East. In this respect it must be said that industry in the first half of the 19th century was in general strongly deconcentrated, but as a result of mechanisation and modernisation a considerable degree of concentration had come about by the turn of the century (Everwijn, 1912). Although this concentration primarily concerned the towns, industrial areas of a rural nature had arisen in a number of districts, such as North Brabant, East Groningen, and along the River Zaan and the big rivers in South Holland and Twente. Keuning (1953, 1964) describes the formation of a mosaic of economic and geographical landscapes as an expression, first of a form of existence adapted within regional frameworks to the potentialities of the physical milieu, and later of an integration based on the needs of the towns of Holland situated at the top of an urban hierarchy (in the 17th and the 18th century). In the 20th century national integration gave a new dimension to these landscapes: the various areas developed a role-allocation, with some having a basic function and others a non-basic one. One consequence of this vision may be that the development of towns was related to that of the regions in which they were situated. Thus they may have functioned as the promoters of the city-concentrated development, or alternatively as the products of that development, for instance in the case of an expansion of agricultural activities or mining in the hinterland.

In the years after World War I there was a clear trend towards industrial decentralisation. The sandy areas in the South and East, and after 1945 also those in the North, were in particular able to profit from this. Residential decentralisation, which had arisen in the 19th century, was of little significance before 1930, at least in quantitative terms, and did not have any influence on urban growth (I.S.O.N.E.V.O., 1949 : 22). After World War II, however, this phenomenon assumed very large proportions, not only around the larger towns in the West but also around the smaller towns and elsewhere in the Netherlands. This postwar urbanisation differed from that in previous periods in as far as 'the compact city as a more or less complete functional entity has now evolved into a constellation of dependent agglomerations around a central one. Each of the agglomerations continues to be compact and sharply delineated, but the functional entity is no longer the city but the city region. The latter as a whole does not show contiguity of built-up areas' (Wissink, 1970 : 119). Steigenga (1970 : 45) has shown that there was also an increasing development in non-agrarian population growth after World War II outside these city regions as a result of industrial decentralisation and suburbanisation.*

---

* Since we have made use of the figures for individual municipalities, the results for the later periods of our investigation may be influenced. This is because our data could not take account of city region formation (which makes towns into components of a greater whole).

It has assumed by some Dutch demographers, e.g. Ter Heide, that the most recent migration to less urbanised areas is no longer an instance of suburbanisation, but of rurbanisation, although this mainly relates to very recent developments which fall outside the period of our investigation.

It is clear that urbanisation took place within different spatial frameworks, with regional growth preceding that of city region formation. Since we are concerned with all urban municipalities not only with the large ones and the rapidly expanding ones but also with small or stagnating municipalities, one may expect a great diversity of forms of growth. The total figures for urban growth are therefore made up of completely different components. In the following section we shall look more closely at the temporal patterns of urban growth.

9.4. Some temporal patterns of urban growth

The urbanisation of the 17th and 18th century had brought about major changes in the relations between the towns which had emerged in the previous centuries. The cities of Amsterdam, Rotterdam, and to a lesser extent Den Haag and Utrecht, all situated in the West of the country, had expanded strongly, whereas previously important towns in the South and East had become stagnated. Many places around the Zuiderzee, as well as in the heart and on the periphery of Holland, had greatly decreased in significance following a major period of growth in the 16th and 17th century (Faber et al., 1965 : 47 ff). There existed, therefore, a close network of historic towns each with an important phase of prosperity, be it in the Middle Ages or in the 16th and 17th century. The large towns mentioned above had also continued to grow in the 18th century. In this way a pattern had emerged of several large towns, a small number of mediumsized towns and many small ones. In 1849 more than 40% of the Dutch population lived in these towns (1,231,017 inhabitants out of 3,056,879). By 1930 this percentage had risen to 65.6%. After this the percentage gradually dropped to just under 53% in 1970.

Table 9.1: Average annual population growth of the individual C-municipalities, of the C-municipalities as a whole, and of the total Netherlands population per intercensus period from 1849 until 1970

Average annual growth (%)	1849/59	1859/69	1869/79	1879/89	1889/99	1899/1909	1909/20	1920/30	1930/40	1940/50	1950/60	1960/70
of indiv. C-municipalities	0,6	0,7	1,1	1,3	1,2	1,2	1,6	1,3	1,0	1,5	1,6	1,9
of C-municip. as a whole	0,8	0,9	1,4	2,0	2,1	1,6	2,1	1,7	1,2	1,3	1,2	1,2
of the total Neth. popul.	0,8	0,8	1,2	1,2	1,2	1,4	1,5	1,5	1,2	1,4	1,3	1,3

Until 1940 the average annual growth of the C-municipalities as a whole was greater than that of the individual C-municipalities. This was the result of a stronger growth of more large municipalities. Until 1889 there was an increase in the rate of growth of the latter, but after 1899 the difference in growth rate between larger and smaller municipalities diminished. After 1940 a new acceleration of growth made itself felt, but it was particularly the smaller towns where this took place.

There are different ways of classifying communities according to growth. Here we distinguish between declining municipalities (negative growth), stagnating municipalities (less than 1% growth per annum), municipalities with moderate growth (1% to 2% growth per annum) and rapidly growing municipalities (more than 2% growth per annum). This classification shows up great differences between the various periods. The periods from 1849 to 1869 and from 1920 to 1940 present a picture of much stagnation and even decline. Between 1869 and 1920 and between 1950 and 1970 the municipalities with moderate and rapid growth form the majority.

Table 9.2: Frequency distribution of the population growth of the C-municipalities per intercensus period

class	1849/59	1859/69	1869/79	1879/89	1889/99	1899/1909	1909/20	1920/30	1930/40	1940/50	1950/60	1960/70
declining	16	18	10	16	15	11	9	18	11	3	1	6
stagnating	76	63	45	40	41	46	42	47	54	13	30	26
moderate growing	21	25	51	37	39	40	41	28	39	79	53	42
rapidly growing	4	11	11	24	22	20	25	24	13	22	33	43

An analysis of declining municipalities after 1950 reveals that almost all the large cities belong to this group. The reversal in the growth of the largest cities has also been observed elsewhere and has been termed the 'retardation effect'.

Following Robson (1973 : 20) we have attempted to determine more closely the relation between population growth and population size. There are many theories which suggest that there is a strong link between these two characteristics. The theory of cumulative and circular causation, for instance, assumes that the largest cities have settlement advantages, can quickly acquire innovations, and therefore can generate new growth. However, just as Robson found in the case of England and Wales, we have noted that this relation cannot be clearly recognised in a great number of periods. For the Netherlands we only observed a

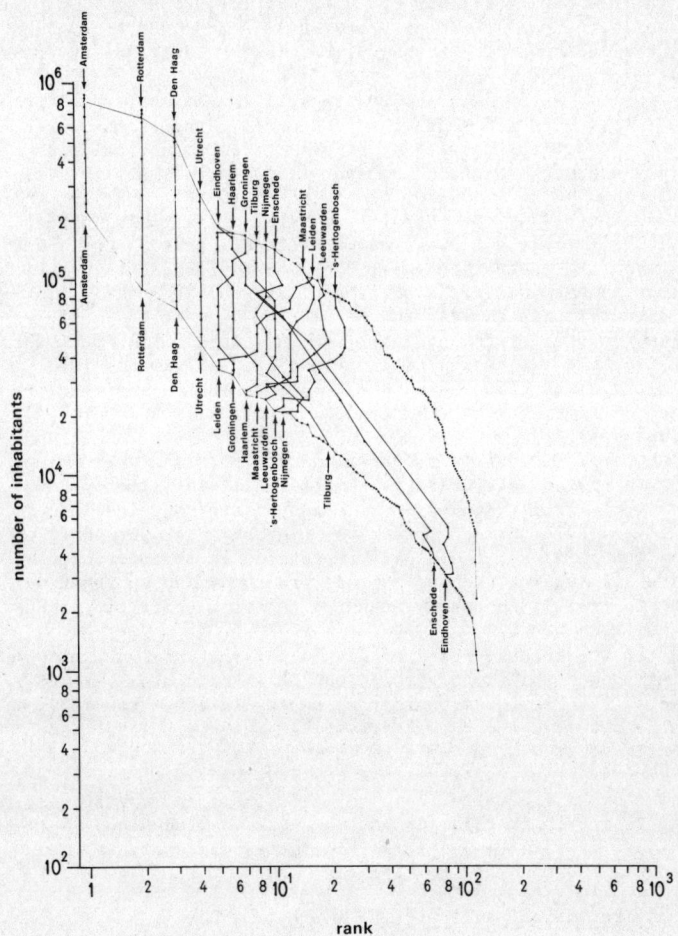

Figure 9.1: Rank-size distributions of the 117 municipalities in 1849 and 1970

reasonably strong positive correlation between 1889 and 1899, a strongly negative correlation after 1960 and a weak positive correlation in the periods 1879-89 and 1899-1909.
Before 1889 and after 1950 the greatest variation in growth occurred in the smaller towns. Between 1889 and 1930 it was the medium-sized towns which showed the greatest differences in growth.

To what extent was the growth in this period stable? To answer this question Kendall's rank-order correlations were calculated for the population of all the 117 municipalities between the beginning and the end of the period. All the values lay between +0.86 (1909-20) and +0.96 (1940-50). Over the whole period (1849-1970) the correlation between the ranks in 1849 and 1970 was only +0.53. We may therefore conclude that there was a certain instability over the whole period, but over short periods there was clear stability of growth. It must be pointed out here that the smaller the population size of the municipalities the greater the instability. This does not so much appear from the two rank-size distributions in 1849 and 1970 (Figure 9.1) as from the number of points that a municipality moved, on average over the decades, up or down the rank scale (Figure 9.2).

Attempts to discover spatial growth patterns which might indicate how to interpret the temporal patterns already found bore little fruit. Although the towns of the Randstad and Twente generally showed themselves over a longer period of time to be growth areas, the global impression is that during one or several linked intercensus periods growth regions sprung up which differed greatly in areal extension. After a short time these growth areas moved.

For the purposes of a rough classification of periods based on rate and stability of growth one may distinguish three periods. The first was an initial phase, lasting from 1849 until about 1879 and characterised by a highly volatile and short lived growth, as well as by much stagnation and decline. The second period ran from 1879 to 1940. Many municipalities, in particular the large ones, enjoyed stable and mostly moderate growth in this period. The third period began in 1940, and apart from the largest municipalities was characterised by a general and moderate to strong growth.

9.5. A statistical analysis

The descriptive summary of urban growth presented above reveals a great divergence between the municipalities in terms of time, place and size. In order to gain more insight into these differences a multiple regression analysis of growth per period was carried out. The problem which arose here was that some independent variables were indeed available for the whole period 1849-1970 but others were only available for a part of this period or for not all of the 117 municipalities. It was for this

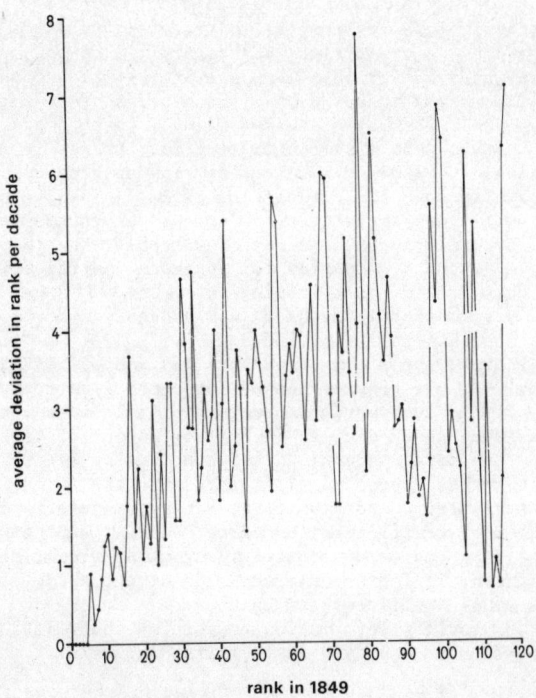

Figure 9.2: Rank in 1849 and average deviation in rank per decade between 1849 and 1970

reason that two types of analysis were carried out. In the first 10 independent variables were used. These include the logarithm of the population size at the beginning of the period (henceforth population size); the number of inhabitants in surrounding (within a range of 25 kilometers) C-municipalities as a percentage of the number of inhabitants of all C-municipalities at the beginning of a period (proximate cities), and the average yearly increase in population of all non-urban municipalities situated within 15 kilometers (the hinterland). The reason for employing the second and third variables was to try and identify possible regionally-based predictors for urban growth. The hinterland can, as a result of growth based, for instance, on the development of export-orientated agriculture, mining or industrialisation, bring about urban growth. If a town is situated in the middle of several urban municipalities then growth may also occur due to the presence of mutual stimulants and overspill effects. Further, six variables were employed to indicate the opening up of traffic routes. In the literature there are constant references to the great influence exerted by the position of municipalities with respect to transport networks as well as changes in this position. The centrality of a C-municipality in the waterway network, the railway network and the major road network was measured by 'the sum of shortest paths between the nodes', whereby a low sum meant a large degree of centrality. Indices were also constructed for changes in centrality as a result of new communication link-ups and extension of the networks through the building of railway lines, canals and roads. Finally, the growth in the immediately preceding period was also employed as a predictor variable. The theory of cumulative and circular causation for instance justifies the expectation that growth, once initiated, will be self-generating. Furthermore, developmental trends do not suddenly come to a stop at the end of an intercensus period.

Since, in the case of 76 towns for 1899 and all 117 towns for 1930 and 1960, all figures needed for comparison concerning the economically active population were available to us, these figures were added as predictors in another series of regression studies. The data concerning the economically active population were for these purposes classified into the following categories: Agriculture and Fisheries; Mining; Manufacturing; Construction; Public Utilities; Commerce; Banking and Insurance; Transport, Storage and Communications; General Services; Domestic Services; Unknown. No further use was made of the three categories Mining, Public Utilities and Unknown.

Table 9.3 provides information concerning the relation between the variables employed in the first analysis.

Table 9.3: Pearson's product-moment correlations between the population growth and the independant variables

| | | | | | | Predictor | | | | | |
| | | | | | | Decentrality in the | | | Changes in the | | |
Period	No. of C-municipalities used	Growth in preceding period	Hinterland growth	Proximate cities	Population size	railway network	waterway network	road network	railway network	waterway network	road network
1849-1859	117	-	+ 0,06	+ 0,00	+ 0,14	- 0,13	- 0,06	- 0,22	+ 0,05	+ 0,02	- 0,26
1859-1869	116	+ 0,30	+ 0,14	+ 0,09	+ 0,21	- 0,24	- 0,01	- 0,03	+ 0,19	+ 0,09	- 0,04
1869-1879	116	+ 0,40	+ 0,31	+ 0,24	+ 0,18	- 0,13	+ 0,02	- 0,03	+ 0,16	- 0,17	- 0,07
1879-1889	116	+ 0,34	+ 0,27	+ 0,18	+ 0,41	- 0,35	- 0,08	- 0,17	+ 0,09	+ 0,11	+ 0,02
1889-1899	117	+ 0,51	+ 0,33	+ 0,19	+ 0,40	- 0,36	+ 0,08	- 0,14	+ 0,16	+ 0,00	+ 0,22
1899-1909	114	+ 0,71	+ 0,36	+ 0,05	+ 0,23	- 0,29	+ 0,29	- 0,16	+ 0,06	- 0,05	+ 0,19
1909-1920	116	+ 0,69	+ 0,54	+ 0,10	+ 0,22	- 0,30	+ 0,48	- 0,27	- 0,09	+ 0,07	+ 0,25
1920-1930	116	+ 0,63	+ 0,54	- 0,05	+ 0,26	- 0,24	+ 0,43	- 0,07	- 0,15	+ 0,24	+ 0,16
1930-1940	115	+ 0,51	+ 0,39	+ 0,02	+ 0,37	- 0,42	+ 0,18	- 0,24	+ 0,06	+ 0,11	+ 0,12
1940-1950	116	+ 0,19	+ 0,34	- 0,08	- 0,05	- 0,14	+ 0,30	- 0,13	- 0,07	+ 0,10	- 0,09
1950-1960	117	+ 0,37	+ 0,24	+ 0,09	- 0,32	- 0,02	+ 0,05	- 0,18	- 0,12	- 0,01	+ 0,05
1960-1970	117	+ 0,37	+ 0,18	+ 0,22	- 0,46	+ 0,20	- 0,04	+ 0,02	- 0,06	+ 0,01	+ 0,01

In general the correlation with growth is small. The most favourable results come from growth in the preceding period, hinterland growth, and from population size, the last correlation being positive until 1940 and thereafter negative. The variables indicating accessibility seem to be of less importance. In many periods the places with a less central position with respect to the waterway network surprisingly exhibit more growth (the sign is negative since it was decentrality that was measured).

Table 9.4 : Overview of the selected regression models: variables employed for the description (marked by an ordinal number*), the multiple correlation coefficient resulting from the combination and the number of C-municipalities under observation

Period	predictor										Multiple correlation	No. of C-municipalities
	Growth in preceding period	Hinterland growth	Proximate cities	Population size	Decentrality in the railway network	Decentrality in the waterway network	Decentrality in the road network	Changes in the railway network	Changes in the waterway network	Changes in the road network		
1849-1859	-	-	-	-	3	-	2	-	-	1	0,37	117
1859-1869	1	4	-	-	3	6	7	2	5	-	0,51	116
1869-1879	1	2	-	5	-	6	-	4	3	-	0,56	116
1879-1889	3	7	-	1/2	1/2	6	-	4	5	-	0,59	116
1889-1899	1	2	-	4/5	3	-	7	6	-	4/5	0,67	117
1899-1909	1	3	-	-	-	2	5	4	-	-	0,77	117
1909/1920	1/2/3	1/2/3	-	-	-	1/2/3	4	-	-	-	0,83	114
1920-1930	1	2	5	-	4	3	-	-	-	-	0,76	116
1930-1940	1	3	-	-	2	-	5	-	-	4	0,66	115
1940-1950	-	1	5	4	3	2	-	-	-	-	0,53	116
1950-1960	1	3	-	2	-	-	4	5	-	-	0,53	117
1960-1970	2	4	3	1	-	5	-	-	-	-	0,67	117

At this stage a rough classification of periods becomes possible with the help of the regression analyses, some results of which are presented in Table 9.4. For some periods the municipalities with extreme growth (e.g. the mining towns) have been left out of consideration.

From 1849 until about 1879 there was a whole series of factors operating, but they were of short duration and in the main not powerful. This initial phase is characterised by developments of a strongly local nature. Study of the individual municipalities suggests that these developments in the first place involved the settling or founding of factories or shipyards, and in the second place the construction of large infrastructure such as canals, fishing and marine ports etc., while in some towns, for instance Den Haag and Arnhem, the latter even involved the expansion of the residential function for the welloff. What is striking is the considerable spatial and temporal variation in the population size of the municipalities.

A new tendency in growth occurred around 1879. Until about 1940 growth was influenced by a restricted number of factors, most of them being operative over a long period of time and sometimes very powerful. The period 1899-1930 was the most stable.

After 1930 the world crisis and the war exerted a disturbing influence. A transition period occurred until about 1950.

---

* These numbers are intended to indicate what in our opinion is the relative importance of the selected predictors in the regression model. This is a highly complicated statistical problem. Without going into detail we only wish to state here that, in addition to standardised partial regression coefficients, we also studied lots of partial and semi-partial correlation coefficients.

Finally, new urbanisation developments seem to have set in after
1950 which cannot be described with the help of the variables
which we employed:
factors of accessibility with respect to trade markets, supply
and distribution of raw material, or - as will be seen in a
while - the nature of employment opportunities. This conclusion
squares with Simmons' claim that different dominant factors
were at work in post-industrial urbanisation than in the preceding industrial phase. One might think here of indicators in
the domain of housing, recreation and schooling or of the provision of services.

The analyses further showed a strong relation, growing
stronger with time, between population size and centrality with
respect to the rail and road network, as well as between the
growth of the hinterland and the neighbourhood towns.

Over all the growth in the preceding period is the most
important predictor. The decreasing importance thereof may be
the result of an urbanisation process in the whole of society
caused by modernisation and the extending of activity ranges,
so that individual towns no longer needed to be seen as the
bearers of communications advantages and modernisation.

The second most significant predictor is the hinterland
growth. This factor can be interpreted in several ways, the
most obvious being a mutual exertion of influence on each other
by town and surrounding areas. Before about 1920 it will often
have been the case that the town grew under the influence of
developments in the surrounding area, for example due to the
growth of agricultural areas, land reclamation etc. After 1920
the influence of the town on the rural areas may have been
greater than vice versa, for example on account of suburbanisation and industrial decentralisation.

The third most important factor over all the periods was
the position with respect to the rail network. As mentioned
above, this factor indicates the size and accessibility of the
place. The negative relation with the waterway network is
probably due to the fact that the towns in the South and East
of the country which grew a lot in the periods when the waterway network was important were not centrally situated with respect to this network. The accessibility of the larger towns
continually found expression - given the noted relation between
the centrality with respect to the rail and road networks - in
the significance of the rail network. Many smaller places were
unfavourable situated with respect to the state road system,
which meant that this network assumed an insignificant role in
the analyses. This would seem to support De Jonge's remarks
concerning the significance of the system of state roads and
also of the secondary and tertiary road networks.

For the second series of regression analyses, which were
carried out for the periods 1899-1909, 1930-40 and 1960-70, the
list of predictors was supplemented by the composition of the
economically active population. The outcome of this series was

hardly different from that of the first. The addition of employment opportunity categories caused the value of the multiple correlation coefficient to rise to 0.83, 0.74 and 0.68 respectively. Had growth been measured solely on the basis of the composition of employment opportunities, then the multiple correlation coefficient would have had a value of 0.62 for the period 1899-1909, 0.43 for the period 1930-40 and 0.42 for 1960-70. Thus the importance of the composition of employment opportunities decreased considerably in time. This too gives an indication that a new development in the urbanisation process set in after 1940, although it may be that the selected operationalisation - the economically active population living in the town - influenced the results in a time of greater commuting and city region formation.

One may conclude at this stage that urbanisation in the Netherlands has been determined by temporally changing factors and that theories concerning this urbanisation must in turn be based on a discontinuity of causative factors. In keeping with the development in Canada observed by Simmons, as well as with many recent studies, it is clear that the Netherlands also experienced a pre-industrial phase, mainly based on local support sources and commerce (it is only in the case of the West of the Netherlands that one might be able to talk in terms of a mercantile phase), the pre-industrial phase being followed by an industrial phase most apparent between 1899 and 1930. It may further be assumed that a post-industrial form of urbanisation also began to emerge in the Netherlands after 1950. This would appear to demand a new theoretical approach. However, within the scope of the present study we should now like to go into more detail concerning the industrial phase.

9.6. The period 1899-1930

In the following we shall present a more detailed analysis of the development of employment opportunities and population size between 1899 and 1930 in the urban municipalities. The investigation relates to the in total 76 urban municipalities which in 1899 had at least 5,000 inhabitants (no systematic data concerning employment opportunities have been published for Dutch municipalities with less than 5,000 inhabitants). First of all the towns are divided up on the basis of their employment opportunities structure in 1899. Then we shall attempt to ascertain what general developments took place in the different employment opportunity categories between 1899 and 1930 and whether relationships exist with the characterisation in 1899. Finally, changes in the structure of employment opportunities will be related to the changes in the population of the towns.

An attempt has been made, using cluster analysis, to characterise each of the towns, based on the percentage of the occupational structure in 1899 made up by the eight previously mentioned categories. Using the methodology offered by this type

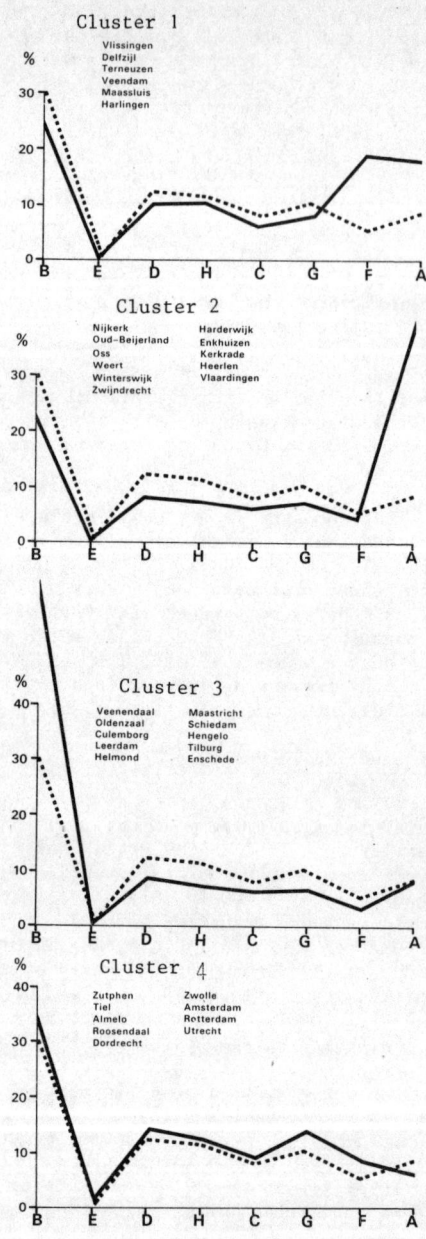

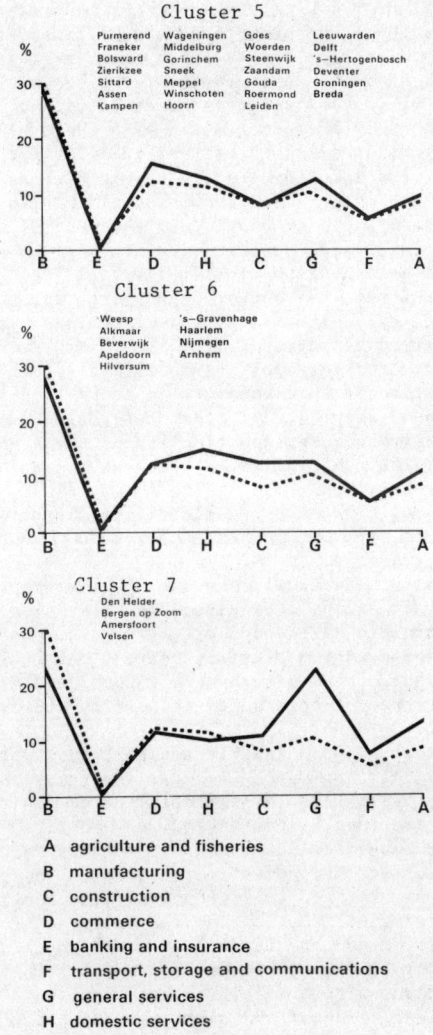

Figure 9.3: Composition and mean profile of the 7 clusters as distinguished by the structure of the 8 occupational categories in 1899
(Indicated by dotted line: median profile of all towns in the investigation.)

of analysis it is possible to trace internally homogeneous groups. Thus the elements of any group have a similar structure with regard to the economically active population. As a measure for homogeneity we used the determinant of the pooled - within groups matrix of sums of squares and cross products. The minimum of this can only be approximated with the available algorithms and for this reason the set of calculations was repeated several times. The solution finally chosen divides the towns into seven groups. Figure 9.3 shows the division and the average profile of each group. Clear and very diverse types have been distinguished.

The towns belonging to cluster 1 reveal a considerable overrepresentation in the sectors transport, storage and communications and agriculture and fisheries. They can all be clearly classified as ports.

Cluster 2 comprises small towns with a relatively large overrepresentation of the economically active population in agriculture and fisheries. All other categories are underrepresented. The group comprises old fishing towns and small country towns, the municipalities often having a large municipal territory.

The towns of cluster 3 can clearly be characterised as industrial centres par excellence and have a shortage of businesses in the tertiary sector.

Cluster 4 is made up of towns with an overrepresentation in all categories except agriculture and fisheries. These are towns with a broadly varied support structure, but above all strongly developed in the tertiary sector, particularly in banking and insurance, a branch weakly developed elsewhere. Often they have one or more superregional functions, according to their size.

The towns of group 5 exhibit a slight overrepresentation in the categories of commerce, general services and domestic services. They typically are regional service centres. Here too there is sometimes an instance of a superregional function.

Cluster 6 comprises towns notably overrepresented in the sectors of construction, domestic services and general services. They may be characterised as regional service centres with an important residential function for the elite and for the aged.

In the last group one finds four towns which are very heavily overrepresented in the service sector. They are primarily garrison towns with a major service function.

With the exception of the clusters comprising ports, fishing and country towns, and industrial towns, service functions for a smaller or greater area are present in all towns. These service functions are supplemented to a greater or lesser extent by other functions, such as manufacturing, fisheries or residential functions.

It is striking that the towns with approximately the same population size are not concentrated in a few clusters, but rather are spread over a large number of them.

Particularly as a result of the rapid fall in the death rate after 1870, the total Netherlands population rose from 5,104,137 inhabitants in 1899 to 7,935,565 in 1930. 59,5% of this increase was accounted for by the 76 towns under investigation here. One of the reasons for this was the rapid increase in the economically active population of these towns, as becomes clear from Table 9.5. The table includes the percentage increase with respect to total employment opportunities per town, averaged out over the 76 towns. Since the percentage in one category sometimes varies greatly from one town to the next, and since special cases do occur, both the variance and the median are given in each case.

Table 9.5 : Mean, median and variance of the growth in occupational categories between 1899 and 1930.

	average percentage of urban occupational structure in 1899	mean growth (%)	median growth (%)	variance
Agriculture and fisheries	14,0	0,35	- 0,57	53,13
Manufacturing	32,2	25,49	16,70	810,55
Construction	8,1	8,07	5,86	73,37
Commerce	12,6	15,40	12,42	111,73
Banking and insurance	0,5	1,90	1,53	2,09
Transport, storage and communications	6,7	7,50	5,40	55,48
General services	11,4	12,99	8,96	134,35
Domestic services	11,2	3,12	1,86	38,65

It can be seen from the table that in 1899 the manufacturing sector was already dominant in the towns and that this sector grew by far the strongest in the period under investigation - industrialisation was pressing on. The variance of the growth in this sector reveals that a number of towns experienced exceptionally high increases in this occupational sector. Such increases did not occur in the other sectors.

Agriculture and fisheries took second place in 1899 but no longer exhibited any growth. About 60% of the towns experienced a decline in this category. About 27% of the towns also felt a decline in the category of domestic services, although this was more than compensated for by the other towns. On the whole the other sectors grew considerably. In addition to manufacturing this was mainly true for commerce and general services, and to a somewhat lesser extent also for the construction and transport sectors. The sectors of agriculture and fisheries and domestic services excepted, one may apply a general rule of thumb that the growth in a sector had more or less the same level as the relative importance of the sector at the beginning of the period: the growth of a category was directly proportional to the size of that category in 1899.

Such a claim in respect of the whole of the group cannot be made for individual towns. This would only be possible had there been no clearly identifiable town types in 1899 and if the spread of the growth figures in each category were to be exceedingly small; Table 9.5, however, suggests that the contrary is the case.

Further tendencies which may be present can therefore only be traced if the changes in the composition of employment opportunities are analysed for each town. Here we rely on results from a second cluster analysis, using the same method as the first, but in this case carried out with respect to the growth in the sectors between 1899 and 1930. 9 urban types were distinguished, the characteristics of which are shown in Table 9.6.

Figure 9.4 graphically illustrates these profiles; in it every value has been standardised with respect to the corresponding sector average, thus permitting a better comparison of the profiles. The figure is optimal inasmuch as the chosen order of the categories gives a minimal number of profile intersections.

What is very striking in this illustration are the regular levels of most profiles over the sectors. Thus the clusters are above all characterised by a stable and even growth in practically all sectors. They differ from each other with respect to the level at which the general growth of employment opportunities takes place. These regular profiles comprise:

cluster 2, the towns which grew extremely strongly in practically all sectors. The towns in this group are the new industrial towns with metal and/or textile industry settlements: Almelo, Enschede, Beverwijk and Velsen. It is worthy of note that these are all situated in industrial zones.

cluster 4, with considerable growth in the secondary and tertiary sectors, although, relatively speaking, the general services category lagged behind somewhat. These towns are also clearly industrial towns: Rotterdam, Schiedam, Zwijndrecht, Zaandam, Helmond and Hengelo. Just as the towns in cluster 2 they are part of definite industrial areas, for example the Nieuwe Waterweg-Noord area, the Zaan area, South East Brabant and Twente.

clusters 5 and 6, the profiles of which have much in common. They show a moderate growth in almost all sectors. In the case of elements of cluster 5 there is a stress on the growth of general services, in the case of cluster 6 on the category of commerce.

Cluster 5 consists of: Weert, Wageningen, Goes, Gouda, Apeldoorn, Leiden, Maastricht, Dordrecht, Delft, Amersfoort, Tilburg, Nijmegen and Arnhem.

Cluster 6 comprises: Leerdam, Oss, Breda, Utrecht, Alkmaar, De-

Table 9.6: The growth in the occupational categories between 1899 and 1930; mean percentage per cluster

Cluster	no. of towns belonging to the type	Average growth percentage in the sector							
		Commerce	Domestic services	Transport, storage, & communications	Construction	General services	Banking & insurance	Manufacturing	Agriculture & fisheries
1	3	37,9	17,1	21,9	31,2	46,4	3,6	24,6	- 5,6
2	4	38,0	13,2	15,4	30,1	27,9	2,6	111,3	23,6
3	4	28,5	12,2	13,5	12,5	29,7	6,2	33,7	1,2
4	6	18,7	5,0	12,8	11,7	12,7	2,4	56,7	0,8
5	13	14,0	2,1	6,0	7,8	15,8	1,9	26,1	0,4
6	8	19,0	1,5	6,7	5,5	11,2	2,0	27,7	- 3,1
7	5	9,2	1,4	12,4	7,3	7,3	1,0	18,0	- 8,5
8	21	9,7	0,8	3,7	2,9	6,0	1,2	7,7	1,0
9	12	7,9	- 0,8	3,4	3,0	7,0	1,2	11,0	- 1,6

venter, Leeuwarden and Groningen.
Both groups include a surprisingly great number of medium-sized regional centres situated for the greater part outside industrial zones.

<u>clusters 8 and 9</u>, which in relation to the other towns lag behind in growth in practically all categories. The two profiles are very close to each other, so that the clusters could probably be viewed as one group. In cluster 8 there is a greater accent on the sectors of commerce, domestic services and agriculture and fisheries.

Cluster 8 comprises: Franeker, Bolsward, Oud-Beijerland, Zierikzee, Vlissingen, Assen, Kampen, Zutphen, Winterswijk, Sneek, Meppel, Winschoten, Terneuzen, Culemborg, Weesp, Steenwijk, Enkhuizen, Den Helder, Bergen op Zoom, Roermond and Zwolle.

Cluster 9 comprises: Nijkerk, Purmerend, Veenendaal, Middelburg, Gorinchem, Tiel, Harderwijk, Hoorn, Veendam, Woerden, Roosendaal and 's-Hertogenbosch.

Both clusters essentially contain towns which are service centres for rather small areas. *

These groups, containing 64 towns and spread over 4 levels, thus give an even picture of general growth almost across the whole board. It is a picture which is disturbed, however, by the profiles of clusters 1, 3 and 7, all of which have a marked growth in one or more sectors.

<u>Cluster 1</u> comprises the mining towns of Sittard, Kerkrade and Heerlen. In the period under observation these towns experienced an extremely powerful growth due to mining.

<u>Cluster 3</u> comprises the municipalities of Amsterdam, Den Haag, Haarlem and Hilversum, that is to say the economic and political capitals and two residential satellites of the former. They are characterised by a considerable growth in the tertiary sector particularly in banking and insurance.

<u>Cluster 7</u> is made up by the shipping towns of Delfzijl, Harlingen, Oldenzaal, Maassluis and Vlaardingen. Growth here is dominated by the sector of transport, storage and communications.

To summarise, the outcome of the clustering gives the impression that apart from the primary sector and a small number of towns which because of their particular location specialise in a number of tertiary sector functions, the vast majority of the towns present a picture of balanced growth in all sectors. This impression is confirmed by a principal component analysis of the growth figures for the 8 sectors.

The first principal component accounts for 65.9% of the variance, and can clearly be regarded, given the position of the variables in the space which spanned by the first two components (Figure

---

* Keuning's map of service areas in 1930 shows the differences between the size of the areas of clusters 5 and 6, and 8 and 9 (Keuning, 1948 : 571).

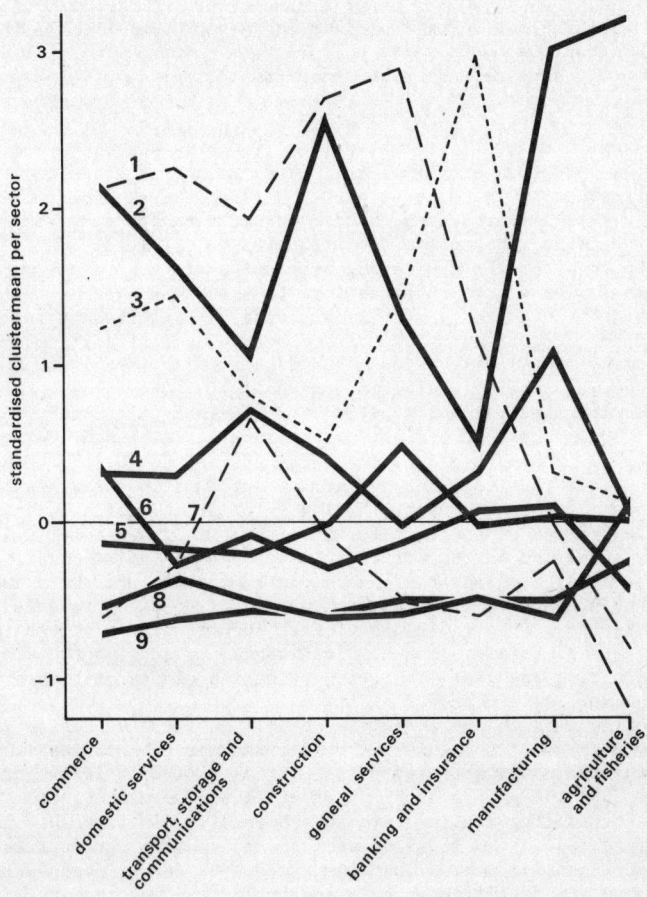

Figure 9.4: Mean profile of the 9 clusters, as distinguished by the growth in the 8 occupational categories between 1899 and 1930 (stadardised per sector)

9.5), as a general growth factor in the secondary and tertiary sectors. The second component accounts for 15.5% of the variance, bringing the total for the first and second components to 81.4%. The second component marks the contrast between the primary and secondary sectors on the one hand and the tertiary sector on the other.

The question may be asked to what extent the growth clusters which have been formed differ from each other and which sectors predominantly influenced the outcome of the clustering. The answers to these questions cannot be derived from the analysis thus far presented, but rather must be found by taking into account the sectors' contribution to the reduction in the variance after the clustering procedure. If the spread in a group is small for a particular sector, then the towns belonging to this group will be relatively homogeneous with respect to this feature. Sectors which in this respect play an important role discriminate clearly between the clusters. An impression of this may be gained from a discriminant analysis, the results of which are summarised in Table 9.7 and 9.8 and in Figure 9.6.

To what extent a discriminant function distinguishes the clusters is determined by the percentage of Sp $(W^{-1}B)$. Table 9.7 shows that the first three discriminant functions contain as much as 94% of the discriminating information, which is why in Table 9.8 the composition for these three functions only is given. This so-called factor structure comprises the relationship between the synthetically produced discriminators and the growth of the occupational groups, so that it is possible to gain an impression of the influence of each sector on the outcome of the clustering. This is of great importance for judging the discriminating power of each category in the classification of the clusters.

There is an overwhelming emphasis in this respect on the growth in construction. This sector assumes the heaviest weight in the two most important discriminant functions. It may be regarded as the indicator of the growth of employment opportunities in general. The clusters are thus primarily distinguished by differences in the total growth of employment opportunities, and not generally by a one-sided growth of one or more sectors. Because manufacturing experienced by far the most growth in this period and in 1899 was by far the largest occupational group, we are convinced that this was the promotor of the growth in the other occupational groups. To analyse this the period of investigation would have to be further subdivided and the secondary sector differentiated.

Figure 9.6 shows that the majority of the towns is already discriminated by the plain defined by the first two discriminant functions. Apart from some towns which with regard to the cluster analysis have an unexpected location in the plain only cluster 3 is in fact not clearly separate. This group, which is characterised by the growth of banking and insurance, is only definitely established and clearly distinguished from the rest

Table 9.7: The meaning of the various discriminating functions with respect to the clustering

discriminant function	Canonic correlation	Eigen value	Percentage of Sp $(W^{-1}B)$	Cumulative percentage of Sp $(W^{-1}B)$
1	0,98	19,6	63,6	63,6
2	0,93	6,2	20,3	83,9
3	0,87	3,1	10,1	94,0
4	0,70	1,0	3,1	97,1
5	0,56	0,5	1,5	98,6
6	0,55	0,4	1,4	100,0
7	0,09	0,0	0,0	100,0
8	0,04	0,0	0,0	100,0

Table 9.8: Factor structure of the discriminant functions (standardised discriminant function coefficients)

	Discriminant function		
	1	2	3
agriculture and fisheries	0,90	1,96	− 0,25
manufacturing	− 1,60	1,24	− 0,40
construction	− 6,47	− 2,81	− 0,81
commerce	2,47	2,24	0,90
banking and insurance	− 1,24	0,20	1,88
transport, storage and communications	0,13	− 0,25	− 1,56
general services	− 2,12	− 1,08	0,60
domestic services	3,84	0,37	0,11

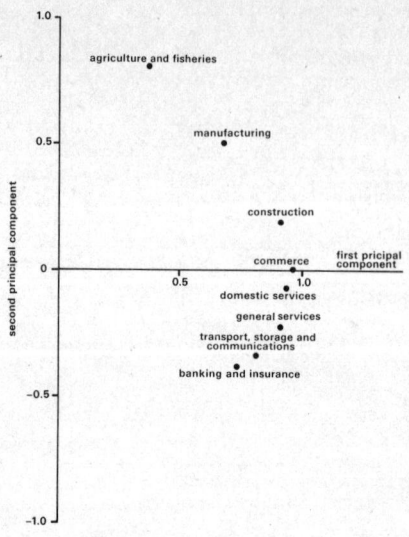

Figure 9.5: Pattern of 'growth in the 8 occupational groups' between 1899 and 1930. Their location in the two-dimensional vector space spanned by the first and second principal components.

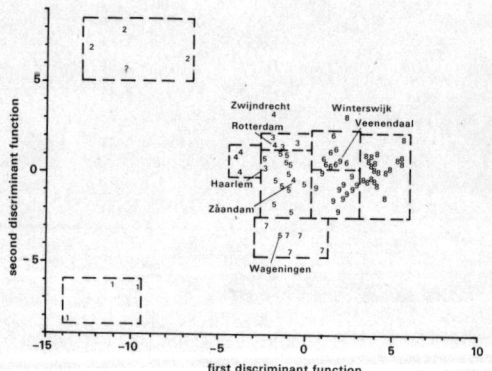

Figure 9.6: Scatter plot of the first two discriminant functions; the number indicates the growth cluster to which the municipality belongs

by the third discriminant function.

One may conclude from this discriminant analysis that the clusters form a number of clear types. Clusters 1 and 2 represent outliers with respect to the other clusters, but the latter can also be clearly distinguished from each other. The fact that the general growth in employment opportunities was the predominant feature of the period 1899-1930 accords with the above-mentioned findings of De Jonge concerning the beginning of the period (1972 : 218).

Figure 9.7 also illustrates this. It shows in scatter diagrams the increase between 1899 and 1930 in the most important occupational groups for the towns, as well as their average annual population growth. Apart from the sectors of banking and insurance, and transport, storage and communications, both of which also occupy a special place in the clustering, all scatter diagrams show strong correlations, the most pronounced being that for construction.

At this stage the typology of the employment opportunity structure which obtained in 1899 can be confronted with the various growth types. If the development of an urban system in a society undergoing industrialisation were in part to be determined by the existing employment structures, then the confrontation of the two cluster analyses would have to reflect something of this.

Table 9.9 gives the cross table. Allowing for the fact that the clusters vary in size, it will be noted that a number of cells occur which contain a disproportionately high number of municipalities. These cells are marked off. They can be regarded as the exponents of various more or less clearly observable tendencies:

1. A number of ports underwent a unidirectional development towards becoming typical exporters of agricultural and horticultural products and industrial processed products of agriculture coming from their hinterlands.
2. A number of typical industrial towns (parts of larger industrial zones) witnessed an intensified industrial development and a related growth of the transport sector in particular.
3. Towns which had an important residential function for the aged and the elite and which were also settlements for a large number of institutions and foundations in the area of social welfare, health and services and the like (a high percentage of the population was active in domestic services) exhibited a generally very powerful growth. There was a marked emphasis on general services, and also on banking and insurance in the case of the Randstad towns in the group.

The trends referred to here are in accordance with Simmons' findings concerning urbanisation in the industrial area that local features could play a role in the industrialisation process. However, Table 9.9 shows up another completely dif-

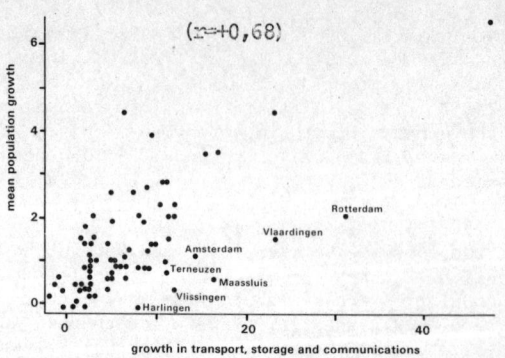
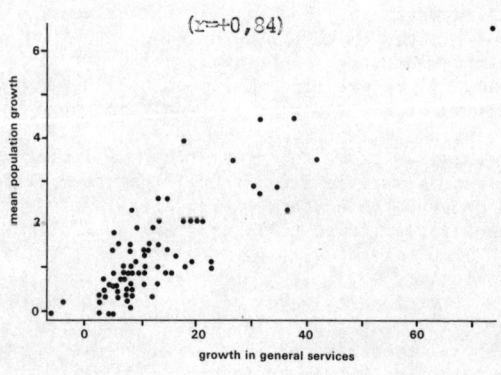
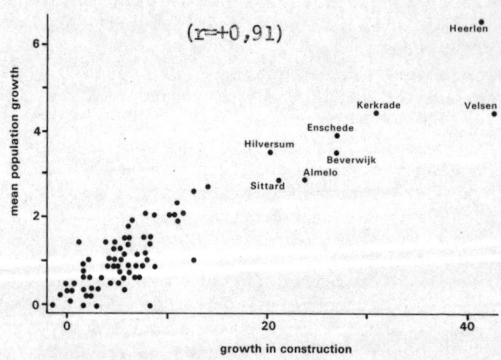

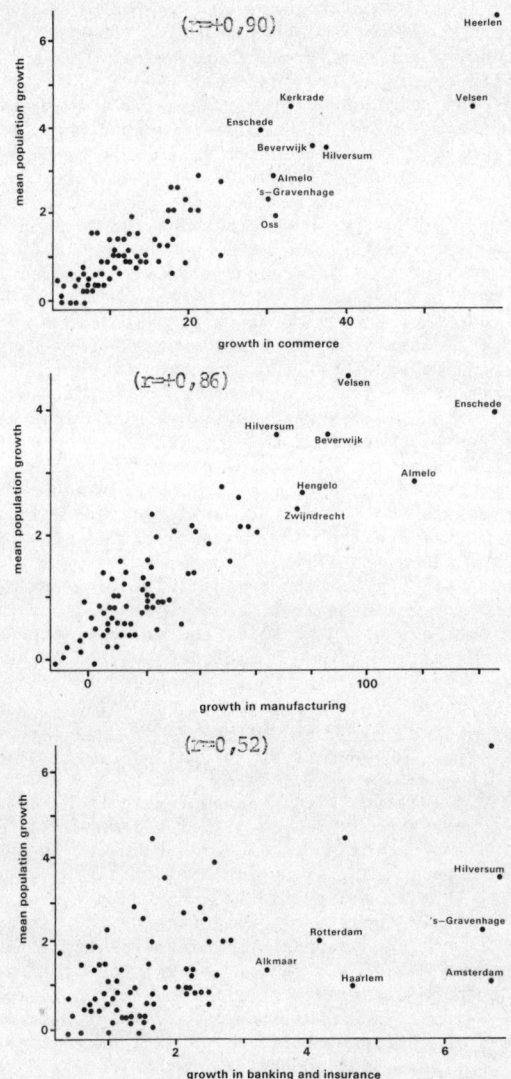

Figure 9.7: Scatter diagrams of the growth in 6 occupational categories and the mean population growth between 1899 and 1930 (from the plot concerning manufacturing the mining cities were excluded)

ferent and equally clear tendency: a disproportionately great number of the towns which lagged relatively behind with regard to all secondary and tertiary sectors belonged to the group of small service centres for rural areas. Industrialisation differentiated the relations between the service centres. In particular many towns whose growth lagged behind were to be found among the regional service centres which were strongly orientated towards a large agrarian hinterland and which in 1899 did not possess any superregional functions. We are indeed of the opinion that the interdependence between the towns and the countryside, as it existed in 1899, was by far the most important indicator for the difference between the growth clusters and could more or less serve as a substitute for the first discriminant function. Something of this, albeit in a very rough form, can be deduced from Table 9.10, which gives the average annual population growth of the non-urban hinterland of the towns comprising the growth clusters. However, it would be wise to approach these figures with caution, since the spread in some clusters is very great. What is clear is that the hinterland growth in the case of the towns of cluster 8 is the smallest and this is very definitely true for those towns in the cluster which with regard to the occupational structure in 1899 belonged to cluster 5; the average annual growth of the hinterland of this group of towns was no more than 4.3‰.

Another striking feature is the difference between clusters 5 and 6, both of which after all comprise mainly medium-sized towns. One interpretation of this, and of other characteristics of Table 9.10, can be gained by introducing the location of the towns as a new criterium for their grouping: in the Randstad, in the Green Heart and the peripheral expansion area of the Randstad (a zone about 30 kilometers wide), and in the rest of the Netherlands. The last group was further split into the sandy areas and other areas.

Such a reclassification is shown by Table 9.11 above, where the figures per category do not differ too much from each other. There is a strong accordance between the growth in the Green Heart and the peripheral expansion area of the Randstad on the one hand and that in the peripheral non-sandy areas on the other hand. The towns in these areas have considerably lower figures than those in the sandy areas, which experienced a powerful population growth during the period under investigation. In these sandy areas there occurred a natural population increase and changes in agrarian business management. The latter led to land reclamation, an intensification of production (increasingly concentrated on export and industrial processing), and to an attractive supply of cheap labour for industry. As a result this many industrial firms were attracted (Winsemius, 1949). Thus the rural surroundings play a major role for this group (category F), - irrespective of their own attractiveness for industrialisation - due to the expansion of service functions for growing populations in their hinterlands. In the case of the towns out-

Table 9.9: Cross table of the two clusterings; in the rows the clusters determined by the occupational categories in 1899, in the colums the clusters determined by the growth between 1899 and 1930

Classification of the growth in the economic categories between 1899 and 1930 / Classification of the employment structures in 1899	Cluster 4 (n=6) Strong growth leaded by manufacturing	Cluster 5 (n=13) Relative moderate growth	Cluster 6 (n=8) Relative moderate growth	Cluster 8 (n=21) Relative small growth	Cluster 9 (n=12) Relative small growth	Cluster 1 (n=3) Outliers Extreme growth leaded by mining	Cluster 2 (n=4) Extreme growth particularly in manufacturing	Cluster 3 (n=4) Profile dominated by the growth of one sector Characterised by banking and insurance	Cluster 7 (n=5) Characterised by transport
Cluster 1 (n=6) transportcities				Vlissingen Terneuzen	Veendam				Delfzijl Maassluis Harlingen
Cluster 2 (n=11) very small towns	Zwijndrecht	Weert	Oss	Oudtheyerland Wintersvijk Enkhuizen	Nijkerk Harderwijk	Kerkrade Heerlen			Vlaardingen
Cluster 3 (n=10) manufacturing centers	Velsevd Schiedam Hengelo	Maastricht Tilburg	Leerdam	Culenborg	Voenendaal		Enschede		Oldenzaal
Cluster 4 (n=9) cities with diversified employment structure	Rotterdam	Dordrecht	Utrecht	Zutphen Zwolle	Tiel Roosendaal		Almelo	Amsterdam	
Cluster 5 (n=27) towns with regional service functions	Zaandam	Wageningen Goes Gouda Leiden Delft	Leeuwarden Deventer Groningen Breda	Franeker Bolsward Zierikzee Assen Kampen Sneek Meppel Winschoten Steenwijk Roermond	Purmerend Middelburg Gorinchem Hoorn 's-Bosch Woerden	Sittard			
Cluster 6 (n=9) cities with regional service functions	Apeldoorn Nijmegen Arnhem		Alkmaar	Weesp			Beverwijk	Hilversum 's-Gravenhage Haarlem	
Cluster 7 (n=4) service towns		Amersfoort		Den Helder Bergen o.z.			Velsen		

279

Table 9.10: Average annual growth between 1899 and 1930 of the population of the non-urban municipalities up to a distance of 15 kilometers from the towns

Cluster	Description	Average annual population growth of hinterland (o/oo)
3	towns which are part of metropolitan areas within the Randstad	22,8
1	towns in the mining area	20,9
2	towns in an industrial zone	19,5
4	towns in an industrial zone	16,7
5	regional service centres	13,6
7	ports	11,4
9	regional service centres	9,7
6	regional service centres	9,5
8	regional service centres	7,2

Table 9.11: Average annual growth of the surrounding areas of the towns in the various growth clusters, partly regrouped according to location

Category	From cluster	Description		Average annual growth of the surroundings (o/oo)
A	3	Randstad	part of city region	22,8
B	2 + 4		part of industrial zone	15,8
C	5 + 6 + 8 + 9		other towns	17,0
D	5 + 6 + 8 + 9	Green Heart & peripheral expansion area		8,0
E	2 + 4	Part of industrial zone		16,8
F	5 + 6 + 8 + 9	Rest of the Netherlands	service towns in sandy areas	12,1
G	5 + 6		service towns not in sandy areas	8,8
H	8 + 9		service towns not in sandy areas	5,0
I	1	Mining towns		20,9
J	7	Ports		11,4

side the sandy areas, situated in areas with a different agrarian
production structure (category H), these stimuli from the surrounding areas are not present. Only the larger towns (category
G) were able, due to their own size, to maintain a certain
growth rate and even to bring about some growth in the surrounding areas.

The surroundings of those towns situated in the Randstad
which grew up within city regions or grew to become city regions
displayed the most growth. This was undoubtedly the result
rather than the cause of urban growth.

The surroundings of towns situated in industrial zones
likewise displayed considerable growth. Since suburbanisation
or decentralisation cannot fulfil a major role here, as is the
case with category A, the cause of growth must be sought here
mainly in industrialisation on a regional scale.
Finally, the ports and mining towns form special groups.

It has been seen that urbanisation in the period 1899-1930
was the result of a number of connected but different processes. Urbanisation manifested itself as modern city region formation. Some towns develop into financial and political control
centres and thus represent the top of a hierarchy. In addition,
urbanisation occurred as the result of a heavy concentration or
development of industrial activity (often on a large scale)
within zones characterised by certain spatial features (for
instance, position with respect to the whole transport system,
socio-economic structure). These zones probably have specific
internal and external linkage structures which also determine
the inter-urban relations and hierarchy. Furthermore, urbanisation also took place in the sense that service centres grew
in conjunction with the growth of rural population which stimulated such urbanisation by means of the development of urban
industrial and service functions. Finally, one must mention
the population growth of the larger service centres which are
not situated in rural growth areas but are part of the general
social and economic development inasmuch as they rise increasingly above the substratum of small service towns which are
dependent on surroundings with a stagnating population growth.

These various relations between urban growth on the one
hand and forms of industrialisation and development of the relation between town and countryside on the other hand suggest
that, despite the dominant role of industrialisation, there
existed in the Netherlands between 1899 and 1930 not one industrial urban system but several, only partially integrated
urban systems.

REFERENCES

Berry, B.J.L. The human consequences of urbanisation: divergent paths in the urban experience of the twentieth century (London, 1973).

Brugmans, I.J. Paardenkracht en mensenmacht. Sociaal-economische geschiedenis van Nederland 1795-1940 ('s-Gravenhage, 1961).

Delfgaauw, G.Th.J. 'De tendenzen tot decentralisatie in de vestiging der nijverheid', Nederlands Instituut voor Volkshuisvesting en Stedebouw VII (1932).

Everwijn, J.C.A. Beschrijving van handel en nijverheid in Nederland. Historisch-Economische Atlas (1912).

Faber, J.A., H.K. Roessingh, B.H. Slicher van Bath, A.M. van der Woude, H.J. van Xanten, 'Population changes and economic development in the Netherlands: a historical survey', A.A.G. Bijdragen no. 12 (Wageningen, 1965).

Friedmann, J. and R. Wulff, The urban transition, comparative studies of newly industrializing societies (London, 1976).

Heide, H. ter, Binnenlandse migratie in Nederland ('s-Gravenhage, 1965).

I.S.O.N.E.V.O. De verspreiding van de bevolking in Nederland (Den Haag, 1949).

Jansen, A.C.M. en M. de Smidt, Industrie en ruimte, de industriële ontwikkeling in Nederland in een veranderend sociaal-ruimtelijk bestel (Assen, 1974).

Johnston, R.J. Spatial structures (London, 1973).

Jonge, J.A. de, De industrialisatie in Nederland tussen 1850 en 1914 (Amsterdam, 1968).

Jonge, J.A. de, 'The role of the outer provinces in the process of Dutch economic growth in the nineteenth century' in J.S. Bromley and E.H. Kossmann (eds.) Britain and the Netherlands, vol. IV (The Hague, 1971) pp. 208-225.

Keuning, H.J. 'Proeve van een economische hiërarchie van de Nederlandse steden', Tijdschrift voor Economische en Sociale Geografie (1948) pp. 566-581.

Keuning, H.J. Het Nederlandse volk in zijn woongebied, 1e druk (Den Haag, 1947).

Keuning, H.J. Mozaiek der functies (Den Haag, 1955).

Knaap, G.A. van der, A spatial analysis of the evolution of an urban system: the case of the Netherlands (Utrecht, 1978).

Kuiler, H.C. Verkeer en Vervoer in Nederland, schets ener ontwikkeling sinds 1815 (Utrecht, 1946).

Pen, J. en P.J. Bouman, 'Een eeuw van toenemende welvaart', Drift en Koers, een halve eeuw sociale verandering in Nederland (Assen, 1968) pp. 85-104.

Pred, A. City-systems in advanced economies (London, 1977).

Robson, B.T. Urban growth, an approach (London, 1973).

Simmons, J.W. 'The organization of the urban system' in L.S. Bourne and J.W. Simmons (eds.) Systems of cities, readings on the structure, growth and policy (New York, 1978) pp. 61-69.

10. Epilogue: one subject, many views
H. Schmal

10.1. Introduction	287
10.2. Systems	288
10.3. City and systems	290
10.4. A more detailed look at some aspects	295
10.5. Urbanisation and industrialisation	305
10.6. Concluding remarks	307
References	308

10. Epilogue: one subject, many views *
H. Schmal

The International Conference on Urbanisation and Functional Differentiation resulted in a number of papers whose diversity was perhaps their most striking feature. In itself, this is not all that regrettable. It is what we have come to expect of a multidisciplinary event like this.
   At the 1966 International Round-table Conference of the Urban History Group at Leicester Dyos, whose death was so untimely, stated that there was very little point to overly restricting (topics in the framework of) urban history. So it is certainly not my intention to pursue the strictest borders and definitions of such terms as urbanisation and city.
   A great deal of research has already been conducted in the field of urban history. I shall not even attempt to give a chronological summary here of the developments in the field. Instead, I should like to refer interested readers to The Study of Urban History (1968), particularly the Agenda for Urban Historians, where Dyos summarised the developments up until 1966 and described the state of affairs at that moment. Suffice it to state that there has been no dearth of developments since then.
   Kooy's paper, which is also included in this book, does not fail to make this clear enough.

From the very first moment, numerous questions are raised at a multidisciplinary conference like this, where specialists in different fields of research conduct such different kinds of studies about different spatial entities, using different scales. In principle, the various researchers were all dealing with the same theme, but they each did so on the basis of their own academic background, each using their own conceptual framework, their own terminology, theories and techniques. Things that were significant to one researcher were not necessarily of any importance to another, and there were also essential differences in questions of interpretation. To a

---

* Translated by Sheila Gogol

certain extent the field has been plowed, as it were, but it is still impossible to detect exactly how and where. This is not a fact that calls for lamentation.

There may not be any generally accepted theory of urbanisation, but this does not alter the fact that a number of more general lines can be sketched on the basis of the papers and the discussions. During the first evaluation of the conference, Van Tijn was one of those to point out this fortunate fact. All of the papers contain something of a notion of urban systems. It must be noted, though, that the papers do differ widely in terms of their generalisation level and terminology pertaining to the urbanisation process etc.

Here and now, I shall try to construct something of a framework. In general, it is easy to apply the system approach to the study of a certain phenomenon (urbanisation) which is approached (here) from various angles. An attempt shall be made to fill in the lines of the concept of urbanisation, thus creating a framework within which as many of the papers as possible can be placed. In doing so, the urban system shall serve as the basis.

In the following sections, first I shall briefly go into the system approach in general (10.2). This seemed advisable, since a number of the features of systems furnish insight into the position of certain papers in the entirety, as well as into the possibilities and, more important, the difficulties involved in comparing the different studies.

Then I shall go into urban systems in a more general sense (10.3), which shall lead to a number of questions that will be dealt with in 10.4, whereby the various papers will be referred to. In 10.5, the relation between urbanisation and industrialisation will be discussed.

10.2. Systems

I should like to start with a few remarks about certain features of systems in the most general sense. A system can be defined as a limitable group of related elements. They form the units of the lowest order which the system is made of. They are determined by their properties and are thus studied on the basis of these properties.

Flexible as this might be, the problems involved when a subject meets with a multidisciplinary approach are manifold. One problem is that the same elements sometimes have different names, or that different elements are given the same name in the course of operationalising a study. In addition, it must be clear that in studying a system, it is of vital importance that the system be defined at the proper resolution level. Klir and Valach (1967 : 35) put it as follows:

> Every element is characterised by forming, from the point of view of the corresponding resolution level (at which

the system S is defined), an indivisible unit whose
structure we either cannot or do not want to resolve.
However, if we increase the resolution level in a
suitable manner .... the structure of the element
can be distinguished. In consequence, the original
element loses its meaning and becomes the source of
new elements of a relatively different system, i.e.
of a system defined at a higher resolution level.

Particularly in the case of inductive research, the chosen resolution level is often evident from the context. However, this is not always the case; certain properties are derived from features of the parts by means of an arithmetic process. They are properties which, in principle, can also be attributed to an element or individual. Dijkink (1979 : 17) summarised an inventory drawn up by Lazersfeld and Menzel (1972) listing the various angles from which a system can be viewed. Properties derived from features of the parts were referred to there as analytical properties.

In addition, this inventory distinguished structural properties which were solely characteristic of the resolution level of these particular properties. Properties of the system as a whole were also listed. There the totality of the relations between the elements of the system possessed an extra value which exceeded the sum of the individual relations. The properties which could thus be added to the whole were also referred to as global properties. Whereas the last two properties referred to above were characteristic of the functioning of a group of elements as a system, this did not necessarily hold true for the first category. As a further complication, Dijkink (1979 : 16) also noted that in some (non-inductive) studies, it was not clear whether the researcher devoted a sufficient amount of attention to the resolution level characteristic of the selected unit.

It generally holds true that the conduct of a system can be explained on the basis of the conduct of the sub-systems which it is made-up of, or on the basis of the higher (super) systems which it is part of. So the analysis either focuses on the internal structure of a system (whereby it must be clearly stated how "open" or how "closed" it is) or on the relation of the (open) system to the surroundings (the input and output are studied and the internal structure of the system is viewed as a "black box").

Urban systems can be collective terms for aggregations of individuals, groups, territorial units such as neighbourhoods, occupational groups, income categories, and socioeconomic, politico-legal or cultural-organisational units. In short, urban systems can consist of widely divergent elements or their properties. At the same time, it is also important here that in the course of time the different disciplines have set their own resolution levels in their paradigms, but in doing so often also standardised the selection and the naming of their "own" (properties of) elements.

This short digression into the concept of systems indicates that a multidisciplinary entrance is feasible. Once inside, however, a wide range of applications will prove possible.

The complexity of the problems touched upon above is particularly great when we try to formulate one problem which can be tranformed into sub-problems to be studied by the different disciplines, and will subsequently make it possible to integrate these disciplinary studies again. In the following sections, this problem will be dealt with.

10.3. City and system

10.3.1. Cities as sub-systems of urban systems

It is quite possible to occupy oneself with the historical development of individual cities by means of detailed descriptions, and for many reasons it is an extremely purposeful occupation. In this way, one can also gain insight into the changes which have taken place in the course of time in these cities. This provides a certain degree of knowledge about the growth and the present spatial structure of these cities. In order to discover the causes leading to the changes, the individual city can be viewed as a system. The numerous relations and processes within a system like this can then be presented as the explanation of these changes.

To a certain extent, the medieval city can be viewed as this kind of independent system. Most of the relations took place on a local level. The relations with the "outside area" were relatively insignificant.

Sometimes attention is focused on the individual city and the countryside immediately surrounding it. In its growth and change, the city is completely shaped by its function as a service centre. The city and the countryside bear a hierarchic relation to each other.

Of course starting points like these are important. They are partially linked to a certain period of time, and for anyone who wants to gain insight into the process of urbanisation which started to take place in the second half of the nineteenth century, it is difficult to make any useful more generalising statements on the basis of this kind of (spatially) rather limited conception.

In one of the papers, Matzerath noted that in Prussia, in what was referred to as the first growth stage (before 1840), many of the cities that were characterised as service centres for the surrounding countryside showed considerable growth. The agrarian revolution, also stressed by Bairoch, provided an important explanation for the growth of many cities at that particular time.

In the period after ± 1850 (but with great regional differences), however, a great number of relations extended past the borders of the city and its surrounding countryside. One would be doing an injustice to the very essence of the city if one were now to view these external relations, which played such a major role in shaping the cities, as an unchanging factor. It seems best to view cities as sub-systems of larger units.

So urbanisation will have to be studied on the basis of urban systems.

The formation of the urban systems can in turn be placed within the development of regional, national and continental systems. These, then, fit into an Atlantic or mondial development.

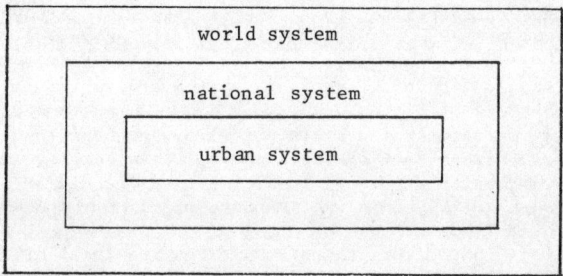

Not all the papers succeeded in distinguishing between the super-systems and the systems, in the descriptions as well as in the analyses (see 10.4.1.), probably because the super-systems exercised causal influences on the systems studied (input level).

10.3.2. Urban systems and urbanisation

The question as to the causes and nature of the growth of a city, or of the growth of cities in general, have been posed before. Some authors tried to describe the nature and the origins of systematic variations in the characteristic features of urban places. Names like Christaller and Lösch inevitably come to mind. I have little desire to elaborate upon all the authors and their ideas (an extensive assortment of handbooks is available), but I can hardly mention Christaller's name without also mentioning the terms hierarchy and Central Place Theory. It is worth nothing here that these studies were focused on the structure of the system. They were based on a centralistic order which functioned mainly one-sidedly.

In addition, there are studies which put more emphasis on the organic interaction between cities and their surroundings. They focused more on the analysis of socio-spatial relations. A number of important names in this respect include those of the classic sociologist Durkheim and the human ecologist Hawley, who stressed the principle of functional interdependence much more than the more structure-oriented authors. It was mainly Berry (1964) who conceptually developed the notions which were present under the surface in both of the schools of thought in system terms. This was expressed very clearly in the model pertaining to the urban system organisation developed by Berry for the more western society, which was summerised by Bourne (1975 : 12). It included at least three levels:

1 : a national system dominated by metropolitan centres and characterized by a step-like size hierarchy, with the number of centres in each level increasing with decreasing population size in a regular fashion.
2 : nested within the national system are regional subsystems of cities displaying a similar but less clearly differentiated hierarchical arrangement, usually organized about a single metropolitan centre, and in which city sizes are smaller over all and drop off more quickly than in (1) above as one moves down the hierarchy.
3 : contained within these subsystems are local or daily urban systems representing the life space of urban residents and which develop as the influence of each centre reaches out, absorbs and reorganizes the adjacent territory. In a small country level (2) and (3) may be difficult to differentiate whereas in larger countries both of these levels may show further subdivision.

The systems were hierarchic in terms of the size of the cities, the functions and the types of interaction. These defined the role of each urban centre within the larger area (see Figure 10.1).

The typology which Berry developed in this manner is mainly important because of the linkage it contained. These linkages could assume different forms at different scale levels. The interactions which defined the urban system on a national level were quite different from those that played a role on a regional level. And there was also the factor that these systems could be very dynamic in time.

Since the different scale levels were inter-related, it was no easy matter to differentiate between them within the system. So Berry created an urban system with a structural dimension, a spatial dimension and a temporal dimension.

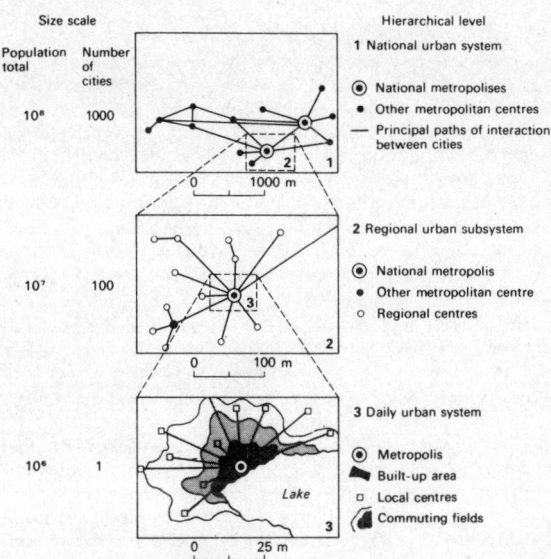

Figure 1.1: Schematic and highly generalised description of three (possible) levels of urban systems

Source: Bourne (1975:13)

Berry's conclusion, which was not surprising on the grounds of what has just been said, was that urbanisation could certainly not be viewed as a universal process, but should, instead, be viewed as a composite of numerous different processes based on cultural and time differences, with many regional variants.

The numerous elaborations on this theme in the general literature exhibit a wide range of urbanisation models; in his study, Kooy discussed a number of examples. In this connection it is interesting to note that it was Lampard (1968) who attempted to defy the torrent of economic and sociological models. According to him, it was impossible, in essence, to turn them into developmental models. He viewed the existing concepts as being inadequate in this sense, since they were all related to equilibrium models which could only allow for a restricted amount of change. The great changes of the last century and a half could not be classified as a process of adaptation, which could be described in models like these. For urban growth, a model was needed of an "open ended, information generating process" (p. 99). The fact that no one has been able to put Lampard's ideas into practice yet proves that the operationalising process here is no easy matter. Nevertheless, Lampard made it clear that reality was a great deal more complex than some people would have us believe.

Some authors specified a number of developmental stages in the urbanisation process (see e.g. Lampard, 1965; Pred, 1966; Vance, 1970; Simmons, 1978).

Simmons distinguished four models of urban system organisation for North America, basing the distinction mainly on the influence of external contacts, which changed so greatly in the course of time. He distinguished the Frontier-Mercantile Model, the Staple Export Model, the Industrial Model and the Social Change Model. The paper by Deurloo and Hoekveld briefly touched upon them. Simmons staged that in each of the models he described, different relations (hierarchical, linked or diffuse) between cities played a central role. Simmons made it clear (and it has been confirmed in the general literature as well as in most of the papers included here) that there was discontinuity in the developmental factors pertaining to urban systems. Although, as Simmons also stated (62), the urban system increasingly (as growth continued) became the dominant factor in the location and growth of each new economic or social activity and thus "a principle of spatial organisation in its own right", a group of new factors like these need not necessarily exactly cover the spatial borders of the existing system. If this is the case, anyone studying these new factors would have to focus on the developments within the urban network or the input from outside. So it could be a good idea to reestablish the borders of the urban system on the basis of the new factors. I shall get back to this spatial continuity aspect later in the article.

It is precisely this diversity of the forces that shape the spatial organisation of the urban system that makes the urban system such an extremely complex thing. Bourne (1975 : 16) was of the opinion that urban systems had a number of properties in common with social systems which were equally complex in nature. He mentioned the following:

1. adaptive rather than mechanistic systems. That is, a given stimulus A does not automatically call forth a predetermined response B.
2. learning systems, which are continually changing their centre of gravity, structure, and external linkages in a cumulative response to generative factors.
3. systems which are open to influences deriving from their external (or contextual) environment.
4. systems marked by extreme interrelatedness among the constituent parts - that is organized complexity.
5. systems in which there is considerable substitutability or interchange of parts and functions.

The first two properties were indicative of the varied manners in which urban systems developed: at any rate, the evolution of urban systems is not subject to simple predictability. The openness of the system makes it necessary to study it in partial conjunction with the surroundings. How and to what degree this is to be done is of course quite dependent on the specific aim of each analysis. In fact, this last characteristic shows why the detection of suddenly arising trends in the structure of the urban system is often so terribly difficult, and often so misinterpreted.

Trends like these are often concealed by large-scale substitution of the various elements of the system.

So as Simmons stated (1978), this is how a "complex multipurpose system" comes into being by means of the wide range of forces that shape the spatial organisation of urban systems.

The most important property that can be attributed to this kind of complex urban system as a totality is that the system is the dominant factor in the location and growth of every economic or social activity within it.

This, then, was a general description of urban systems. Their complexity gives rise to a great many questions. Some of these questions are: What exactly do we mean by systems? How are they analysed? What elements do they include? What terms do we use to refer to them? What properties are to be examined? In the study of the internal structure of systems, what role is played by the degree of closure of those systems? What about the continuity of the system? I shall discuss a number of these questions.

10.4. A more detailed look at some aspects

10.4.1. Systems and scale

Firstly, I shall briefly go into the various regions dealt with in this book which, to varying extents, include the elements studied.

These regions, which can be viewed as the systems dealt with, are: a large part of Europe (De Vries, Bairoch), England and Wales (Robson), the Netherlands (Deurloo and Hoekveld), Prussia (Matzerath), Sweden (Öhngren), Northern Italy (Caracciolo), and Randstad-Holland (Van Engelsdorp Gastelaars and Wagenaar). Upon further examination, it becomes evident that various studies can be more precisely specified as far as their system borders are concerned. In Northern Italy, Caracciolo distinguished three systems (the cities along the Via Emilia, the cities along the line from Florence to the coast, and the cities of the pre-Alpine Plain of Lombardy), which he dealt with separately as three very clearly distinct systems. De Vries did not view "Europe" as one system, but drew the distinction between Southern Europe and Northern Europe; nor did Bairoch view the "western world" as one system, but concerned himself much more with "countries".

Thus we get a clearer view of the systems chosen by the various authors, whereby the "cities" (the "elements" in all the studies) were the sub-systems. Although the elements were defined in different ways (see also 10.4.2.), we can nevertheless speak of a high degree of uniformity. But there were large differences in the spatial scale level within which these sub-systems were studied. This automatically affected the kind and the intensity of the (relevant) relations which (can) play a central role in the various studies. In the discussion, De Vries also made it clear that his region had a much less highly integrated system with network-like (trade) relations than for example the Randstad where there was a strong intertwining of different types of relations.

Without going into the relations among the system elements as such (see 10.4.2.), it would still be a good idea to make a few comments in this connection, mainly in a qualitative sense.

Caracciolo spoke of three lines of cities which each exhibited a strong coherence via the connecting lines dating back to Ancient times, and which later continued to develop in this sense. Deurloo and Hoekveld also spoke of a network of cities that was traditionally present in the Netherlands. After their analysis, they came to the conclusion that in the Netherlands between 1899 and 1930, it was not a case of one single industrial urban system, but of various only partially integrated systems. In this respect Matzerath similarly came to the conclusion that in the period after 1871, there were also a number of separate urban systems in Prussia which could be distinguished on the grounds of their specific functions.

Thus it seems as if a number of regional sub-systems could be sketched in between the systems (countries) and the sub-systems (cities).

An attempt to distinguish the super-systems between the lines of the various papers would give rise to manifold difficulties. Nobody used this term directly. In a number of cases, however, the influence of a super-system on the system in question could be detected. When De Vries spoke of the disintegrating influence of mercantilism on the urban system in Northern Europe, the influence of a property of a system functioning on a higher scale level could be detected.

Of course the same held true for Van Engelsdorp Gastelaars and Wagenaar when they explained the changes within their (Randstad) system by referring to developments in the national system. This made it clear that the super-systems that served as input-level for the systems exhibited enormous differences in their spatial scales.

What could be viewed by one author (De Vries) as a super-system might very well be viewed by others (Van Engelsdorp Gastelaars and Wagenaar) as a super-super-system. Since, as was previously stated pertaining to the confrontation between systems and sub-systems, the relations (that can be) studied are different for each spatial scale level, it will be clear that the spatial scale level itself shapes the specific system to a significant extent. Sub-systems and super-systems determine the system. Thus the differences in spatial scale levels of the systems and super-systems in question make it difficult to draw generalising conclusions on the grounds of comparisons. However, the spatial scale level is only one aspect.

10.4.2. Elements and relations

Of course it can not be denied that in the first place, the comparison of different studies is impeded by a certain degree of dissimilarity in the chosen research elements. During this conference, the "desirable" course of events, which was far beyond the actual possibilities, was extensively discussed.

In general, of course it can be stated that the research units consisted of "cities", but if we look at how this was put into effect, we see a wide range of differences. Sometimes, due to a dearth of source materials, it was even necessary to use different definitions of a city for different sub-periods.

De Vries, for instance, viewed places that had had a population of 10,000 at any point in the period 1500-1800 as cities. Robson considered the places with 2,500 inhabitants at any point between 1801 and 1911 to be cities. Matzerath focused on all the legally-recognized towns and, after 1867, all the communities with over 2,000 inhabitants. Deurloo and Hoekveld studied the C-municipalities, referred to by the Census Bureau as "urban municipalities". Their populations varied from a few thousand to more than half a million. The criteria that were used had to do with the "morphological structure of the municipality, the economic and social structure of the resident economically active male population and the presence of regional service functions".

At any rate, each study worked with its own basic units, and the only thing they all had in common was a certain minimum number of inhabitants.

The term urbanisation was viewed from so many different angles, especially during the discussion. It was interpreted as an increasing percentage of inhabitants of an area living in the cities, the process of migration to the cities, the expansion of a settlement into a city, the enlargement of the built-up areas to cover a certain expanse, suburbanisation and the alteration of the mentality of the inhabitants of an area in such a way that it became "urban". It is striking that the individual papers show an almost unanimous desire to interpret urbanisation in terms that can be made operational. Urbanisation was viewed as the increase in the urban population in a certain period of time, either in absolute growth or in relation to the national growth rate.

In the following section, I shall briefly discuss several methods (that can be) used to gain insight into urbanisation within the urban system concept.

Of course there is a wide range of possibilities. For

since we have seen that even in the various urban systems distinguished in this book, the elements defy any neat cubbyholing, it is clear (as a quick glance at the papers will show) that a high degree of diversity can be expected from the properties, whether or not sharply defined, in the papers themselves.

Classification

In order to gain insight into the structure and functioning of urban systems, in the past many authors have already devoted attention to the relations between certain properties of the elements shaping the system. By means of classification, a degree of order can be introduced to the undifferentiated mass of elements.

By far the most striking property is the size of the population. No other property of cities varies as much within the urban systems. Moreover, the size of the population can often be related to a wide range of other properties.

In the literature, size category is often related to rank. By means of the concept of the threshold value, a link is drawn between central-place studies and the size of the population in order to assess the total sum of services and industries in a city.

This relation between rank and size is known as Zipf's rank-size rule (see also Berry, 1961; Berry and Horton, 1970; Robson, 1973 and De Vries). The regularity of the rank-size rule has been put to the test on several occasions. However, not all the systems exhibit the regularity which it expresses. According to Berry (1964), deviations are mainly prevalent in small countries with a less highly developed economic structure where scale advantages lead to a large collection of activities and, consequently, of people in one large city. It is going too far, however, to equate a good rank-size distribution to an economically "advanced" system, and countries with a "primate city" to poor or possibly even economically under-developed systems.

At any rate, this line of reasoning does not hold true for numerous urban systems on a national level (Denmark, Austria, France). Here of course the objection can be raised that if the borders of the system were drawn differently, for example according to the national borders in the past (Austria) or according to what would often be a better way of drawing them in view of the degree of closure or the internal interdependence, the rank-size rule would be shown to much more advantage. Of course one can try to describe a given urban system in terms of the rank-size distribution, but then what? During the discussion, Robson stated that he viewed it as unfeasible to draw any kind of conclusion at all regarding growth from the rank-size distribution. De Vries, who made extensive use of rank-size distributions in his paper, responded to this point by stating that the graphic reproduction of rank-size distri

bution does have an elucidating effect. As an explanatory factor
(with respect to growth) he indeed did not view rank-size distribution as all that suitable. Pred wrote in 1977 that the
rank-size distribution was no more than an empirical regularity
without any theoretical foundation. He also viewed the rank-size rule as unsuitable for interpretative purposes. De Vries
could agree with this conclusion. He stated that cross-sectional
use almost automatically led to nonsensical conclusions, and
stressed the dynamic aspect by attributing a role to the time
dimension. If rank-size distributions for different periods in
time are compared, differences can be noted which, in themselves,
are interesting enough to merit further study. So according to
De Vries, a valuable degree of clarity can be attained by means
of rank-size distributions.

A classification of cities according to size category is also
often linked to a classification of cities according to their
basic activities. The basic activities of a city pertain to
those activities that serve a larger area than its own territory.
  In many studies, attempts were made to arrive at a classification of cities according to their economic base and the
degree of specialisation (see e.g. Bahl, Firestone and Phares,
1971; Smith and Morrison, 1975). An important study was conducted by Crowley (Bourne and Simmons, 1978), who applied a
shift-and-share analysis to changes in labour-force composition
in order to detect the sources of economic growth in the urban
system.
  The results suggested which cities grew (or declined) because of their particular economic structure or their share of
sectors that were growing (or declining) at the national level.
An important conclusion which Bourne and Simmons drew from the
significance of economic specialisation for growth was (Bourne
and Simmons, 1978 : 164):

> Growth and the economic role of one location are (only)
> partly determined by the characteristics of alternative
> locations. The potential productivity of a city is neither
> infinite nor entirely locally determined: it serves what
> is essentially a finite hinterland, which produces for a
> specialized market. At the same time, factors of production, such as labor, capital and fertilizers can and do
> move freely to other cities.
>
>   The growth of a city within an urban system, then,
> is jointly determined by its internal resources and productivity and by the resources and productivity of all
> alternative locations. That is the range of population
> sizes and growth rates for any given city is limited by
> the structural characteristics of the urban system as a
> whole and by its spatial organization. And for cities
> dependent on extensive space-using economic activities,

such as agriculture, forestry, or mining, the very limited potential density of production at any location is an important consideration in understanding how that urban system evolved. Urbanization, in effect, describes how the population living of a particular economic base is organized in space.

One of the papers in this book which linked "growth" most closely to "economic growth" is the one by Robson. His (cautious) conclusion was that places exhibiting the greatest growth variation in the course of time could be characterised as the most specialised places. They were highly dependent on a limited number of functions and activities, extremely highly differentiated as to their functions and therefore also the most dependent on "the circulation and shift of the social surplus within the economy".
In itself, this conclusion is significant enough and invites us to devote more attention within the system analysis to the concept of functional differentiation.
If all this might lead one to assume that a great deal of progress has already been made in this field, this assumption would be completely unfounded.
In most cases (no matter how noteworthy it might be in itself), the idea of economic base and the degree of economic specialisation have not led to much more than a (meek) attempt to classify cities. At most, a link has been drawn with size, but seldom with growth.

Some authors interpreted growth within urban systems as an individualisation of the general theory of innovation diffusion (Pederson, 1970; Berry, 1972 b; Pred, 1971, 1973 a, 1977; Brown, 1974).
The basic idea here was that in many cases the innovations were spread by means of the urban hierarchy. Spatial and hierarchic variability in urban growth rates were viewed as a function of two processes (Bourne, 1975 : 21):

> first the 'filtering' of growth-inducing innovations down the urban-size distribution from the centres of innovation to increasingly smaller centres. These smaller centres located in the nation's heartland receive the innovation first and then subsequently those in peripheral areas. The second process is the 'spreading' of these innovations outward from each centre into its tributary area, but primarily within what has been called above the daily urban system.

In his paper, Kooy briefly described the hierarchic aspect of innovation processes (applied to the spreading of power plants).
Bairoch was the only other author in this book to devote any attention (and then in general terms) to the relation be-

tween urban development and innovation in the nineteenth and twentieth centuries.

It is also possible, in a classification system, to take into account a complex of variables. By means of a factor analysis, one can look for differences or similarities between (groups of) cities within certain systems over an extremely wide range of properties. The first to attempt this kind of classification were Moser and Scott (1961). Many were to follow in their footsteps. Berry (1972) can be especially credited for his achievements in this field. Although no direct use was made of the method of relating growth to factor analytical classification, this method, in view of its very contents and the classification results, does seem to be a good way to gain better insight into the significance of functional differentiation to the growth of cities.

10.4.3. Openness/closure

As has been noted before, urban systems are by definition open systems. A number of elements interact with elements outside the system, and the system as a whole can be influenced by events taking place outside the system. Consequently, in the study of growth and developmental processes, insight into the degree of closure is of great importance.

Of course the careful attention that needs to be devoted to the degree of openness or closure is completely self-evident if we view the system as a black box and try to gain more insight into the functioning of the system as a whole by means of the study of the input and output.

This careful attention is less directly necessary, but no less important, if we examine the internal structure of the system.

As Robson noted in his article, this important aspect has been virtually neglected in many studies. Of course it is true that in the past, the degree of closure was greater than it is at the moment, and it has become increasingly difficult to isolate urban systems from their surroundings and examine them as independent units.

As I have said before, Simmons (1978) distinguished four stages of system organisation, mainly based on the influence of changing external contacts. Pred (1977) improvised very directly upon this theme by classifying urban systems according to their degree of internal interaction (low/high) and their degree of closure (low/high).

To an important extent, closure is a question of scale, and in the course of time there has been an enormous enlargement of the scale if we look at the scope of most systems. At any rate closure is stronger on a macro-scale. As the scale is reduced, closure becomes weaker and weaker. But an examination of the papers does indicate that the aspect of the degree of

closure has received less attention than it deserves on the
basis of the significance referred to above. In most cases,
the attention devoted to it went no further than noting that
(at certain moments) external forces were active in such a
way as to lead to alterations in the internal structure; the
research methods were usually qualitative. However, the
question remained: how should it be done?

All this need not arouse general consternation. As Robson
noted during the discussion, it is extremely difficult to justify any given manner of sub-division. If one attempts to demonstrate the borders between various (sub)systems, one meets
with conceptual and operational difficulties. It is usually
assumed that closure takes place on a national scale. However,
this is a very time-oriented perspective (see De Vries). Nevertheless, it can be stated that it is a relatively simple matter
to demonstrate breaks on precisely this level compared to most other
levels. According to Robson, it is impossible to show clear
breaks on a regional level.

It would require enormous quantities of data and a gigantic amount of input information. The measurement of flows, of
the origins and destinations of the various types of trans-
actions and the pursuit of meaningful breaks in them would
mean a tremendous burden. In spite of the analytical value of
this kind of work, it seems more realistic to see a system and
its boundaries in terms of well-founded assumptions about what
regularly goes on between (groups of) cities. In actual practice,
this seems to be the only way to develop sub-systems within a
national system. Robson illustrated this problem with his own
findings. During a study pertaining to British cities, he had
found it extremely frustrating that he was not able to find
"regional sets of cities" which behaved in accordance with his
expectations in terms of growth.

At any rate it is clear that the degree of closure of
systems represents an important preliminary problem in the
study of the growth and development of urban systems. The degree of closure is strongly dependent on the selected scale
level, and is strongly linked to a certain period or point in
time due to the developments in transport technology, the economy and the political organisation and administration, which
shape the interactive processes in the system.

10.4.4. The development of systems

In the literature, there is evidence that the growth and development of urban systems in the course of time can be explained on the basis of other (complexes of) factors (Lampard,
1965; Pred, 1966; Vance, 1970; Simmons, 1978). To what extent
do the papers in this book follow this line of reasoning?

If we look at the historical growth and development of urban
systems, one of the elements that strikes us is their high

degree of stability in their development. Madden (1956) and
Luckermann (1966) made this clear in the case of the United
States after 1970. Pred(1977) stated that if one divided the
United States into economic-geographic regions, it would become clear that the metropolitan units with the largest population at the moment were also the regionally most important
places in the past (when they only had a fraction of the population they have at the moment). In the case of Western Europe,
it also holds true that the ranking of cities according to
their population is strikingly stable. For example, Russell
(1972) seemed to show that the basic outlines of the present-day urban systems were already visible centuries ago. It is
possible that the basic patterns of accessibility, with certain exceptions, were largely determined by geographic conditions, and that the transport networks were responsible for
the fact that the locational advantages of a city continued
to exist for a long period of time, and that, consequently,
the size ranking of cities in a region remained stable.

A number of comments, however, are called for at this
point. The paper by Deurloo and Hoekveld, and the one by
Robson, for example, confirmed the idea that this stability
feature was relatively valid, at least for the largest metropolitan units; but for medium-sized and small units, in their
view, this was certainly not the case. On a more long-term
basis, upon further examination the picture also appears to
be less clear than at first glance. A wide range of external
influences (which thus can certainly not be viewed as constants)
are responsible for a changing evolution picture. But that is
not all. For the time being, the generalisation of explanatory
factors seems to be impossible.

De Vries made an essential contribution to the understanding of the developments on a more long-term basis (1500-
1800), and drew the distinction between three periods of urban
development on a macro-level.

Bairoch noted the discontinuity in the factors that
shaped the growth and development of urban systems in Europe
in the eighteenth and nineteenth centuries. He pointed out
that as soon as industrialisation takes place, a completely
new class of cities develops. The traditional urban system is
broken down and replaced or adjusted.

Most of the studies on a meso-level also mentioned some
measure of discontinuity, without this necessarily always
having affected the stability of the system to the same extent.

Caracciolo referred to three periods of growth, whereby
various political and economic factors played an important
explanatory role.

Matzerath commented on the phenomenon that on the one
hand, transport facilities, the existing infra-structure and
the larger labour market in the cities were responsible for
the city itself becoming an important location factor, where-

as on the other hand, there were various periods regarding the
intensity of urban growth which led in turn to a changing differentiation of urban growth. In the course of time, the agrarian surplus stopped functioning as the basis for urban growth,
and this function was taken over by the (industrial) cities
themselves. Thus the explanatory relation with the surrounding
countryside was largely eliminated.

In their analysis, Deurloo and Hoekveld also distinguished
various stages in the growth of C-municipalities in the Netherlands between 1849 and 1970. They concluded that urbanisation
in the Netherlands was determined by factors which changed in
the course of time, so that any theory on urbanisation would
have to take into account the discontinuity of causal factors.

An aspect which is directly related to this has to do
with the discontinuity of the system. It is advisable to regard a longer period, such as the one De Vries referred to
(1500-1800), as being one system and to keep the system as a
constant in spite of the changing relations within it (with
respect to their types as well as their intensity)? The same
question can be posed about Prussia (Matzerath) and Northern
Italy (Caracciolo).

De Vries noted that in Europe around the end of the fifteenth and the beginning of the sixteenth century, it was impossible to speak of one single urban system. By the beginning
of the seventeenth century, to a certain extent it was already
there. The trade relations between the cities in a large part
of Europe were intensive enough by that time.

It would undoubtedly be going too far to think here in
strictly hierarchic, intensive patterns. It would be better
to speak of a network pattern between the cities based on
inter-city circuits. Thus there was a network that was largely
complementary. At any rate, according to De Vries there was a
sufficient amount of relations by the beginning of the seventeenth century to merit a discussion of these cities. Later
this integration revival on a European scale slowly diminished.
Absolutism and mercantilism made the state into an important
spatial system-former. The desire to attain economic independence was responsible for the loss of many relations. In the
nineteenth century, in spite of the liberalism, this was made
even stronger by the national spatial organisation (railroads,
telegraphic communication etc.). Thus there were recurrent
shifts in the spatial framework within which urban systems
could be studied, and there was discontinuity not only with
respect to the factors but also with respect to the systems,
quantitatively as well as qualitatively.

This also becomes clear when we look at a number of
"meso" studies from this angle. Suffice it to mention the
papers by Matzerath (Prussia) and Caracciolo (Northern Italy)
about regions where there were different state administrations
within a relatively short period of time, the paper by Van
Engelsdorp Gastelaars and Wagenaar who noted extending frame-

works (daily urban systems), and the one by Öhngren, who noted several breaks in trends on the basis of his micro-data.

A cautious intermediate conclusion might be that in most countries, discontinuity does seem to be characteristic if one is looking for factors to explain the growth and development of urban systems in the course of time.

It is also clear that there is a certain degree of stability in the causal factors if we compare the various stages. The difference in dating need not be surprising if we look at the industrial stage as a whole (coinciding industrialisation and urbanisation).

The industrial stage was dated later for the Netherlands and Sweden (according to Deurloo/Hoekveld and Öhngren respectively, it took place around the beginning of the twentieth century) than for Prussia (according to Matzerath, it took place around 1840). There are differences in the dates when the industrial revolution or the industrial developments began in the different regions of Europe. This accounts for the fact that Robson chose such a vague periodisation in his analysis (1801-1911).

So urbanisation is always characterised by discontinuity. Completely new factors can simply turn up out of the blue. This makes it extremely difficult, if not completely impossible, to make any prediction about the evolution of the urban system. Describing it, however, makes its development clearer in retrospect. But it is not clear yet whether there is a convergence of developmental processes or that the time spans between the first (pioneer) development and the moment when the followers make up for the lag become shorter, and it is also unclear what the effects of the discrepancies between the forerunners and the laggers are for both of these groups.

10.5. Urbanisation and industrialisation

In the previous sections, it has been stated that, according to many authors, the growth of urban systems can be explained by completely different sets of factors in different periods of time. New elements can be identified, new patterns develop. According to some authors, the industrial revolution ushered in a new period in which new (complexes of) factors were responsible for urban growth. A number of authors focused their attention on precisely this period, and subsequently on the question as to whether, and to what degree, a relation existed between urbanisation and industrialisation in the nineteenth century.

In the general literature, this theme has been awarded its due share of attention. Simmons (1978) furnished an "industrial model" pertaining to the process of urbanisation, in which developments in the urban system were determined by the properties of the cities such as the industrial structure, the size of the population, and the availability of raw materials and finished products.

Pred (1966 : 12) was also of the opinion that industrialisation and urbanisation largely coincided in the nineteenth century. He proceeded on the assumption that the initial advantage of an already existing and expanded city was capable of catalysing a process of industrialisation and urbanisation. The growth repeatedly broke through the restricting threshold values (minimum population or minimum sales), and investments could ensue. A logical effect was that new or enlarged industries and their multiplier effects created the conditions that successfully attracted active and "passive" migrants to the cities, leading to an attendant industrial growth by directly or indirectly increasing the opportunities for inventions or innovations. The rise in the threshold values was not only brought about by the growth of the urban market itself, but also by the improvement of transport facilities. This reduced transport expenses and enlarged the markets.

In the end, the cities with a less favourable location suffered.

Which points in the papers fit in with this growth model and which ones don't?

In general it can be said that if and when the papers touched upon this issue, the existence of a relation between industrialisation and urbanisation was certainly not denied. Bairoch saw a new class of industrial cities develop; De Vries noted a completely different growth of cities in England and concluded that this was the result of the emerging industrial revolution there; Van Engelsdorp Gastelaars and Wagenaar stated (in the discussion) that the Dutch urbanisation pattern, as it had been visible ever since the seventeenth century, was not interrupted until the twentieth century when the industrial function joined the commercial function and the "new function of industrialisation" thus broke the continuity which had been present up until then. Starting at a certain point in time, Matzerath noted a close relation between the two. However, he did state "that urbanization didn't so much cause this growth of population as conduct it into the towns". On the basis of his behavioural approach, Caracciolo also stressed the importance of the already existing urban structure. In particular during the discussion, Caracciolo sited the significance of individual behaviour, manifested in Northern Italy in the role of the urban elite, in connection with (explaining) the urbanisation process. Once again, the urban system could be described as a dominant factor in the location and the growth of every economic or social activity.

Regarding the direction of the assumed relation, however, Caracciolo stated that the general presupposition underlying a question like "What is the influence of industrialisation on urbanisation?" should not merely be revised and perhaps should even be reversed.

Deurloo and Hoekveld confirmed the assumed relation, but

stated that in the Netherlands, the urbanisation between 1899 and 1930 resulted from a number of connected but different processes and

> .....occurred as a result of a heavy concentration of industrial activity within zones characterised by certain spatial features ..... Furthermore urbanisation also took place in the sense that service centres grew in conjunction with the growth of rural population which stimulated such urbanisation by means of the development of industrial and service functions. Finally, one must mention the population growth of the larger service centres which are not situated in rural growth areas but are part of the general social and economic development inasmuch as they rise increasingly above the substratum of small service towns which are dependent on surroundings with a stagnating population growth.

10.6. Concluding remarks

What kind of systems were all the papers actually talking about? Of course in principle they were all open systems, although it was often difficult to recognise them as such. There were the differences in scale (macro: Bairoch in his approach and De Vries; meso: the others). Some systems were hierarchic by definition (for example De Vries; demographic features of central significance), others were more complementary (Van Engelsdorp Gastelaars and Wagenaar). Robson focused more on inter-linkages.

To a certain extent, this could also be a question of scale. It is more important, however, to note that there are large differences between the various urban systems. If and when we want to compare our findings with those of our "neighbour", it will be obvious that this would and should only be possible after a systematic determination of the properties of the urban system.

We are all plowing the same field, and although the soil is coarse and our tools often date back to the Stone Age, it is still good for us to be able to try holding each other's plows every now and then. It helps us decide how and where to make our own furrows.

REFERENCES

Bahl, R.W., R. Firestone and D. Phares 'Industrial diversity in urban areas: alternative measures and intermetropolitan comparisons', Economic Geography, vol. 47 (1971) pp. 414-425.

Berry, B.J.L. 'City size distribution and economic development' Econ. dev. cult. change, 6 (1961) pp. 389-413.

Berry, B.J.L. 'Cities as systems within systems of cities', Papers and proceedings of the regional science association, 13 (1964) pp. 147-163.

Berry, B.J.L. 'Latent structure of the American urban systems' in B.J.L. Berry (ed.) City Classification Handbook (New York, 1972).

Berry, B.J.L. Growth centers in the American urban system, vol. 1, Community development and regional growth in the 60's and 70's (Cambridge Mass., 1973).

Berry, B.J.L. and F.E. Horton (eds.) Geographic perspectives on urban systems: text and integrated readings (Englewood Cliffs N.J., 1970).

Bourne, L.S. Urban systems: strategies for regulation (Oxford, 1975).

Bourne, L.S. and J.W. Simmons (eds.) Systems of cities, readings on the structure, growth and policy (New York, 1978).

Brown, L.A. (ed.) 'Studies in spatial diffusion processes', Economic Geography vol. 50 (1974).

Christaller, W. Die zentralen Orte in Süddeutschland (Jena, 1933).

Crowley, R.W. 'Labor force growth and specialization in Canadian cities' in L.S. Bourne and J.W. Simmons (eds.) Systems of cities, readings on the structure, growth and policy (New York, 1978) pp. 207-219.

Dijkink, G.J.W. Niveau's van analyse in de sociale geografie (Amsterdam, 1979).

Durkheim, E. De la division du travail social (Paris, 1893), translated by G. Simpson, 1947.

Dyos, H.J. (ed.) The study of urban history (London, 1968).

Harvey, D. Explanation in Geography (London, 1969).

Hawley, A. Human Ecology (New York, 1950).

Hauser, Ph.M. and L.F. Schnore (eds.) The study of urbanization (New York, 1965).

Klir, J. and M. Valach Cybernetic Modelling (London, 1967).

Lampard, E.E. 'Historical aspects of urbanization' in Ph.M. Hauser and L.F. Schnore (eds.) The study of urbanization (New York, 1965).

Lampard, E.E. 'The evolving system of cities in the United States: urbanization and economic development' in H.S. Perloff and L. Wingo (eds.) Issues in urban economics (Baltimore, 1968) pp. 81-139.

Lazersfeld, P.F. and H. Menzel 'On the relation between individual and collective properties' in A. Etzioni A sociological reader on complex organizations (New York,

1971).
Lösch, A. (1937) The economics of location Translated by W.H. Woglom and W.A. Stolper (New Haven, 1954).
Luckermann, F. 'Empirical expressions of nodality and hierarchy in a circulation manifold' East Lakes Geographer, vol. 2 (1966) pp. 17-44.
Madden, C.H. 'Some indications of stability in the growth of cities in the United States' Econ. dev. cult. change, 4 (1956) pp. 236-252.
Moser, C.A. and W. Scott British towns (London, 1961).
Pederson, P.O. 'Innovation diffusion within and between national urban systems' Geographical Analysis, 2 (1970) p. 223.
Pred, A.R. The spatial dynamics of U.S. urban industrial growth, 1800-1914: interpretive and theoretical essays (Cambridge Mass., 1966).
Pred, A.R. 'Large city interdependence and the pre-electronic diffusion of innovations in the U.S.' Geographical Analysis, 3 (1971) pp. 165-181.
Pred, A.R. Urban growth and the circulation of information, the United States system of cities, 1790-1840 (Cambridge Mass., 1973).
Pred, A.R. City systems in advanced economies (London, 1977).
Robson, B.T. Urban growth: an approach (London, 1973).
Russell, J.C. Medieval regions and their cities (Bloomington, 1972).
Simmons, J.W. 'The organization of the urban system' in L.S. Bourne and J.W. Simmons (eds.) Systems of cities, readings on the structure, growth and policy (New York, 1978) pp. 61-69.
Smith, P. and W.I. Morrison Stimulating the urban economy: experiments with input-output techniques (New York, 1975).
Vance, J.W. The merchant's world: the geography of wholesaling (Englewood Cliffs N.J., 1970).
Zipf, G.K. National unity and disunity (Bloomington, 1941).